Power up your prep with Official Practice Exams

Research shows that first-time GMAT test takers can **increase their scores by up to 75 points** after taking all Official Practice Exams!

Full-length, adaptive GMAT practice exams that simulate the real test-taking experience

Scaled section scores and a total score that aligns to the actual test

Detailed score performance report, including time management

Get started with GMAT™ Official Practice Exams at mba.com/gmatprep

GMAT™ Official Guide Data Insights Review 2024-2025

From the makers of the GMAT™ exam

- ✓ Only study guide that features **real exam questions**

- ✓ **250+ practice questions** with detailed answer explanations

- ✓ Digital flashcards, games, a **customizable question bank**, and more

- ✓ Exclusive **tips and tricks** for exam success from the exam creators

Book + Online + Mobile

GMAT™ Official **Prep**

GMAT™ Official Guide Data Insights Review 2024–2025

Table of Contents

Dear GMAT™ Test Taker,

Thank you for your interest in graduate management education. Today more than 7,700 graduate programs around the world use the GMAT exam to establish their MBA, business master's, and other graduate-level management degree programs as hallmarks of excellence. Seven out of ten candidates apply to business school with their GMAT exam score.*

By using the *GMAT™ Official Guide* to prepare for the GMAT exam, you're taking a very important step toward achieving your goals and pursuing admission to the MBA or business master's program that is the best fit for you.

The *GMAT™ Official Guide Data Insights Review 2024–2025* is designed to help you prepare for and build confidence to do your best on exam day. It's the only guide that features real GMAT questions published by the Graduate Management Admission Council (GMAC™), the makers of the GMAT exam. This guide and the other print and digital GMAT™ Official Prep products available at **www.mba.com** will give you the confidence to achieve your personal best on the GMAT exam and launch or reinvigorate a rewarding career.

For 70 years, the GMAT exam has helped candidates like you demonstrate their command of the skills needed for success in the classroom and showcase to schools their commitment to pursuing a graduate business degree. Schools use and trust the GMAT exam as part of their admissions process because it's a proven predictor of classroom success and your ability to excel in your chosen program.

The mission of GMAC is to ensure no talent goes undiscovered. We are driven to provide you with the tools and information you need to guide you through your journey in graduate management education, continuously improve the GMAT exam, and help you find and connect with the best-fit schools and programs for you.

We applaud your commitment to educational success and wish you the best on all your future educational and professional endeavors.

Sincerely,

Joy J. Jones

CEO, Graduate Management Admission Council

GMAT™ Official Guide
Data Insights Review 2024–2025

1.0 What Is the GMAT™ Exam?

1.1 What Is the GMAT™ Exam?

The Graduate Management Admission Test™ (GMAT™) is used in admissions decisions by more than 7,700 graduate management programs at over 2,400 business schools worldwide. Unlike undergraduate grades and courses, whose meanings vary across regions and institutions, your GMAT scores are a standardized, statistically valid, and reliable measure for both you and these schools to predict your future performance and success in core courses of graduate-level management programs.

Hundreds of studies across hundreds of schools have demonstrated the validity of GMAT scores as being an accurate indicator of business school success. Together, these studies have shown that performance on the GMAT predicts success in business school even better than undergraduate grades.

The exam tests you on skills expected by management faculty and admission professionals for incoming graduate students. These skills include problem-solving, data analysis, and critical thinking, which all require complex judgments and are tested in the three sections of the GMAT exam: Quantitative Reasoning, Data Insights, and Verbal Reasoning. These three sections feature content relevant to today's business challenges and opportunities, ensuring you are prepared for graduate business school and beyond.

Your GMAT Official Score is meant to be an objective, numeric measure of your ability and potential for success. Business schools will use it as part of their holistic admissions processes, which may also consider recommendation letters, essays, interviews, work experiences, and other signs of social and emotional intelligence, as well as leadership. Even if your program does not require a GMAT score, you can stand out from the crowd by doing well on the exam to show you are serious about business school and have the skills to succeed.

The exam is always delivered in English on a computer, either online (such as at home) or at a test center. The exam tests your ability to apply foundational knowledge in the following areas: algebra and arithmetic, analyzing and interpreting data, reading and comprehending written material, and reasoning and evaluating arguments.

Myth -vs- **FACT**

M – My GMAT score does not predict my success in business school.

F – The GMAT exam measures your critical thinking skills, which you will need in business school and your career.

1.2 Why Take the GMAT™ Exam?

Taking the exam helps you stand out as an applicant and shows you're ready for and committed to a graduate management education. Schools use GMAT scores in choosing the most qualified applicants. They know an applicant who has taken the exam is serious about earning a graduate business degree, and they know the exam scores reliably predict how well applicants can do in graduate business programs.

No matter how you do on the exam, you should contact schools that interest you to learn more about them, and to ask how they use GMAT scores and other criteria in admissions decisions. School admissions offices, websites, and publications are key sources of information when you are researching business schools. Note that schools' published GMAT scores are *averages* of the scores of their admitted students, not minimum scores needed for admission.

While you might aim to get a high or perfect score, such a score is not required to get into top business school programs around the world. You should try your best to achieve a competitive score that aligns with the ranges provided by the schools of your choice. Admissions officers will use GMAT scores as one factor in admissions decisions along with undergraduate records, application essays, interviews, letters of recommendation, and other information.

To learn more about the exam, test preparation materials, registration, and how to use your GMAT Official Score in applying to business schools, please visit **www.mba.com/gmat**.

Myth -vs- **FACT**

M – If I don't get a high GMAT score, I won't get into my top-choice schools.

F – Schools use your GMAT score as a part of their holistic evaluation process.

1.3 GMAT™ Exam Format

The GMAT exam has three separately timed sections (see the table on the following page). The Quantitative Reasoning section and the Verbal Reasoning section consist of only multiple-choice questions. The Data Insights section includes multiple-choice questions along with other kinds of graphical and data analysis questions. Before you start the exam, you can choose any order in which you will take the three sections. For example, you can choose to start with Verbal Reasoning, then do Quantitative Reasoning, and end with Data Insights. Or you can choose to do Data Insights first, followed by Verbal Reasoning, and then Quantitative Reasoning. You can take one optional ten-minute break after either the first or second section.

All three GMAT sections are computer adaptive. This means the test chooses from a large bank of questions to adjust itself to your ability level, so you will not get many questions that are too hard or too easy for you. The first question will be of medium difficulty. As you answer each question, the computer uses your answer, along with your responses to earlier questions, to choose the next question with the right level of difficulty. Because the computer uses your answers to choose your next question, you cannot skip questions.

Computer adaptive tests get harder as you answer more questions correctly. But getting a question that seems easier than the last one doesn't always mean your last answer was wrong. At the end of each section, you can review any question(s) and edit up to three answers within the allotted section time.

Though each test taker gets different questions, the mix of question types is always consistent. Your score depends on the difficulty and statistical traits of the questions you answer, as well as on which of your answers are correct. If you don't know how to answer a question, try to rule out as many wrong answer choices as possible. Then pick the answer choice you think is best. By adapting to each test taker, the exam can accurately and efficiently gauge a full range of skill levels, from very high to very low. Many factors may make the questions easier or harder, so don't waste time worrying if some questions seem easy.

To make sure every test taker gets equivalent content, the test gives specific numbers of questions of each type. While the test covers the same kinds of questions for everyone, some questions may seem harder or easier for you because you may be stronger in some questions than in others.

At the end of the exam, you will see your unofficial score displayed on the screen. A few days after your exam, you will receive your Official Score Report, which includes detailed performance insights. Once you receive your report, you can select to send your Official Score to schools of your choice.

Format of the GMAT™ Exam		
	Questions	Timing
Quantitative Reasoning Problem-Solving	21	45 min.
Data Insights Data Sufficiency Multi-Source Reasoning Table Analysis Graphics Interpretation Two-Part Analysis	20	45 min.
Verbal Reasoning Reading Comprehension Critical Reasoning	23	45 min.
	Total Time	135 min.

A ten-minute optional break can be taken after the first or the second section.

Each section of the GMAT exam contains the following features:

- **Bookmarking:** Mark any questions you are unsure about so you can easily get back to them after you complete the section. Bookmarking can make the Question Review & Edit process more efficient.

- **Question Review & Edit:** Review as many questions as you would like (whether or not they're bookmarked) and change or edit up to three answers per section, within the section's allotted time.

> ### *Myth* -vs- **FACT**
>
> **M** – Getting an easier question means I answered the previous one wrong.
>
> **F** – Many factors may make the questions easier or harder, so don't waste time worrying if some questions seem easy.

1.4 What Is the Testing Experience Like?

You can take the exam either online (such as at home) or at a test center—whichever you prefer. You may feel more comfortable at home with the online delivery format. Or you may prefer the uninterrupted, structured environment of a test center. It is your choice. Both options have the same content, structure, features, optional ten-minute break, scores, and score scales.

At the Test Center: Over 700 test centers worldwide administer the GMAT exam under standardized conditions. Each test center has proctored testing rooms with individual computer workstations that allow you to take the exam in a peaceful, quiet setting, with some privacy. To learn more about exam day, visit **www.mba.com/gmat**.

Online: In available regions, the GMAT exam is delivered online and is proctored remotely, so you can take it in the comfort of your home or office. You will need a quiet workspace with a desktop or laptop computer that meets minimum system requirements, a webcam, microphone, and a reliable internet connection. For more information about taking the exam online, visit **www.mba.com/gmat**.

Whether you're taking the GMAT exam online or at a test center, there are several accommodations available. To learn more about available accommodations for the exam, visit **www.mba.com/ accommodations**.

1.5 What Is the Exam Content Like?

The GMAT exam measures several types of analytical reasoning skills. The Quantitative Reasoning section gives you basic arithmetic and algebra problems. The questions present you with a mix of word or pure math problems. The Data Insights section asks you to use diverse reasoning skills to solve real-world problems involving data. It also asks you to interpret and combine data from different sources and in different formats to reach conclusions. The Verbal Reasoning section tests your ability to read and comprehend written material and to reason through and evaluate arguments.

The test questions are contextualized in various subject areas, but each question provides you everything you need to know to answer it correctly. In other words, you do not need detailed outside knowledge of the subject areas.

1.6 Data Insights Section

The GMAT Data Insights section tests the skills that today's business managers need to analyze intricate data sources and solve complex real-world problems. It tests how well you can assess multiple sources and types of information—graphic, numeric, and verbal—as they relate to one another. It also tests how well you can analyze a practical math and non-math problem to determine if enough data is given to solve it.

The Data Insights section has five types of questions:

- **Data Sufficiency:** Measures your ability to analyze a quantitative or logical problem, recognize which data is relevant, and determine at what point there is enough data to solve the problem. Questions can be presented in mathematical or non-mathematical real-world contexts.

- **Multi-Source Reasoning:** Measures your ability to examine data from several sources including text passages, tables, or graphics, and analyze each source of data carefully to answer multiple questions. Some questions will require you to recognize discrepancies among different sources of data, while others will ask you to draw inferences, or require you to determine whether data is relevant.

- **Table Analysis:** Measures your ability to sort and analyze a table of data, similar to a spreadsheet, in order to determine what information is relevant or meets certain conditions.

- **Graphics Interpretation:** Measures your ability to interpret the information presented in a graph or other graphical image (scatter plot, x/y graph, bar chart, pie chart, or statistical curve distribution) to discern relationships and make inferences.

- **Two-Part Analysis:** Measures your ability to solve complex problems. They could be quantitative, verbal, or a combination of both. The format is intentionally versatile to cover a wide range of content. These questions measure your ability to evaluate trade-offs, solve simultaneous equations, and discern relationships between two entities.

Data Insights questions may require math, data analysis, verbal reasoning, or all three. You will have to interpret graphs and sort data tables to answer some questions, but you won't need advanced statistics or spreadsheet skills. For both online and test center exam delivery, you will have access to an on-screen calculator with basic functions. It should be noted that this calculator is provided for the Data Insights section **only**, and **not** for the Quantitative Reasoning section.

Chapter 5 of this book, "Data Insights Review," reviews the basic data analysis skills you need to answer questions in the Data Insights section. Chapter 6, "Data Insights," explains the Data Insights question types, provides practice questions and answer explanations both in this book and in the Online Question Bank, and offers test-taking tips.

Because the Data Insights questions need to be rendered online, certain question types, such as Multi-Source Reasoning, Table Analysis, and Graphics Interpretation, are only available in the **Online Question Bank** that is included as a part of this guide.

You can access the **Online Question Bank** by going to **www.mba.com/my-account** and using your unique Access Code on the inside front cover of this book.

1.7 How Are Scores Calculated?

The Quantitative Reasoning, Data Insights, and Verbal Reasoning sections are each scored on a scale from 60 to 90, in 1-point increments. You will get four scores: a Section Score each for Quantitative Reasoning, Data Insights, and Verbal Reasoning, along with a Total Score based on your three section scores. The Total Score ranges from 205 to 805. Your scores depend on:

- Which questions you answered correctly.

- How many questions you answered.

- Each question's difficulty and other statistical characteristics.

There is a penalty for not completing each section of the exam. If you do not finish in the allotted time, your score will be penalized, reflecting the number of unanswered questions. Your GMAT exam score will be the best reflection of your performance when all questions are answered within the time limit.

Immediately after completing the exam, your unofficial scores and percentile for the Quantitative Reasoning, Data Insights, and Verbal Reasoning, as well as your Total Score, are displayed on-screen. You are **not** allowed to record, save, screenshot, or print your unofficial score. You will receive an email notification when your Official Score Report is available in your **www.mba.com** account.

The following table summarizes the different types of scores and their scale properties.

Score Type	Scale	Increment
Quantitative Reasoning	60–90	1
Data Insights	60–90	1
Verbal Reasoning	60–90	1
Total	205–805	10

Your GMAT Official Scores are valid for five years from your exam date. Your Total GMAT Score includes a percentile ranking, which shows the percentage of tests taken with scores lower than your score.

In addition to reviewing your Total and Section Scores, it's important to pay attention to your percentile ranking. Percentile rankings indicate what percentage of test takers you performed better than. For example, a percentile ranking of 75% means that you performed better than 75% of other test takers, and 25% of test takers performed better than you. Percentile ranks are calculated using scores from the most recent five years. Visit **www.mba.com/scores** to view the most recent predicted percentile rankings tables.

To better understand the exam experience and view score reports before exam day, we recommend taking at least one GMAT official practice exam to simulate the test-taking experience and gauge your potential score. The more practice exams you take, the better prepared you will be on your actual testing day. Visit **www.mba.com/examprep** to learn more about the practice exams offered by GMAC.

2.0   How to Prepare

2.1 How Should I Prepare for the GMAT™ Exam?

The GMAT™ exam has several unique question formats. We recommend that you familiarize yourself with the test format and the different question types before you take the test. The key to prepping for any exam is setting a pace that works for you and your lifestyle. That might be easier said than done, but the *GMAT™ Official 6-Week Study Planner* does the planning for you! Our step-by-step planner will help you stick to a schedule, inform your activities, and track your progress. Go to **www.mba.com/examprep** to download the planner.

Here are our recommended steps to starting your prep journey with your best foot forward.

1. **Study the structure.** Use the study plan in our **free GMAT™ Official Starter Kit** to become familiar with the exam format and structure. The study plan will guide you through each question type and give you sample questions. This will boost your confidence come test day when you know what to expect.

2. **Understand the question types.** Beyond knowing how to answer questions correctly, learn what each type of question is asking of you. GMAT questions rely on logic and analytical skills, not underlying subject matter mastery, as detailed in the *GMAT™ Official Guide 2024–2025* and **Online Question Bank**.

3. **Establish your baseline.** Take the **GMAT™ Official Practice Exam 1 (FREE)** to establish your baseline. It uses the same format and scoring algorithm as the real test, so you can use the Official Score Report to accurately assess your strengths and growth areas.

4. **Study the answer explanations.** Take advantage of each question you get wrong by studying the correct answers, so you know how to get it right the next time. **GMAT™ Official Practice Questions** provide detailed answer explanations for hundreds of real GMAT questions. This will help you understand why you got a question right or wrong.

5. **Simulate the test-taking experience.** Take the **GMAT™ Official Practice Exams**. All GMAT™ Official Practice Exams use the same algorithm, scoring, and timing as the real exam, so take them with test-day-like conditions (e.g., quiet space, use the tools allowed on test day) for the truest prep experience.

Remember, the exam is timed, so learning to pace yourself and understanding the question formats and the skills you need can be a stepping stone to achieving your desired score. The timed practice in the **Online Question Bank** can help you prepare for this. The time management performance chart provided in practice exam score reports can also help you practice your pacing.

Because the exam assesses reasoning rather than knowledge, memorizing facts probably won't help you. You don't need to study advanced math, but you should know basic arithmetic and algebra. Likewise, you don't need to study advanced vocabulary words, but you should know English well enough to understand writing at an undergraduate level.

2.2 Getting Ready for Exam Day

Whether you take the exam online or in a test center, knowing what to expect will help you feel confident and succeed. To understand which exam delivery is right for you, visit **www.mba.com/plan-for-exam-day**.

Our Top Exam Day Strategies:

1. Get a good night's sleep the night before.

2. Pacing is key. Consult your on-screen timer periodically to avoid having to rush through sections.

3. Read each question carefully to fully understand what is being asked.

4. Don't waste time trying to solve a problem you recognize as too difficult or time-consuming. Instead, eliminate answers you know are wrong and select the best from the remaining choices.

5. Leverage the bookmarking tool to make your question review and edit process more efficient.

> "Don't take a 'brute force' approach to GMAT questions—think strategically instead."
>
> — A test instructor from GMAT Genius

> "Compile summarized notes that can be reviewed on the morning of the test. Awareness of the key points and types of mistakes will boost your scores."
>
> — A test instructor from LEADERSMBA

2.3 How to Use the *GMAT™ Official Guide Data Insights Review 2024–2025*

The GMAT™ Official Guide series is the largest official source of actual GMAT questions. You can use this series of books and the included Online Question Bank to practice answering the different types of questions. The *GMAT™ Official Guide Data Insights Review* is designed for those who have completed the Data Insights questions in the *GMAT™ Official Guide 2024–2025* and are looking for additional practice questions, as well as those who are interested in practicing only Data Insights questions. Questions of each type are organized by difficulty level of easy, medium, and hard. Your rate of accuracy in each category might differ from what you expect. You might be able to answer the "hard" questions easily, while the "easy" ones are challenging. This is common and is not an indicator of exam performance. The questions in this book are not adaptive based on your performance but are meant to serve as exposure to the range of question types and formats you might encounter on the exam. Also, the proportions of questions about different content areas in this book don't reflect the proportions in the actual exam. To find questions of a specific type and difficulty level (for example, easy arithmetic questions), use the index of questions in Chapter 7.

We recommend the steps below for how to best use this book:

1. Start with the review chapters to gain an overview of the required concepts.

> "Building a strong foundation is crucial to achieve a high score. If you struggle with fundamental questions, your progress on more advanced questions will be hindered."
>
> — A test instructor from XY Education

2. Go through the practice questions in this book. Once you've familiarized yourself with the concepts and question types, use the Online Question Bank to further customize your practice by choosing your preferred level of difficulty, category of concepts, or question types.

> "The Official Guide offers in-depth answer explanations. After completing a question, reviewing it alongside the explanation helps you gain a deeper understanding of the question's key concepts and solution strategies. On the result interface of the online question bank, it serves a dual purpose: on one hand, it encourages us to review incorrect answers; on the other hand, it provides detailed insights into the time spent on each question, aiding in optimizing our pace during exercises."
>
> — A test instructor from JiangjiangGMAT

3. Use the **Online Question Bank** to continue practicing based on your progress. To better customize and enhance your practice, use the Online Question Bank to:

   a. Review and retry practice questions to improve performance by using the untimed or timed features along with a study mode or an exam mode.

   b. Analyze key performance metrics to help assess focus area and track improvement.

   c. Use flashcards to master key concepts.

> "The biggest mistake students make is completing too many new problems. Completing problems doesn't move your score! Learning from problems does. Keep a list of questions you want to go back to and redo. Redo at least three of these questions every time you study. This book is one of the most important resources you can use to create the future you want. Make sure you understand every question you complete extremely well. You should be able to explain every problem you complete to someone who is new to the exam. Don't focus on simply 'getting through' the book. That mindset will work against you and your dreams."
>
> — A test instructor from The GMAT Strategy

 TIP

Since the exam is given on a computer, we suggest you practice the questions in this book using the **Online Question Bank** accessed via **www.mba.com/my-account**. It includes all the questions in this book, and it lets you create practice sets—both timed and untimed—and track your progress more easily. The Online Question Bank is also available on your mobile device through the GMAT™ Official Practice mobile app. To access the Online Question Bank on your mobile device, first create an account at **www.mba.com**, and then sign into your account on the mobile app.

 TIP

Remember: Some of the Data Insights section questions are only available in the **Online Question Bank**.

2.4 How to Use Other GMAT™ Official Prep Products

We recommend using our other GMAT™ Official Prep products along with this guidebook.

- **For a realistic simulation of the exam:** GMAT™ Official Practice Exams 1–6 are the only practice exams that use real exam questions along with the scoring algorithm and user interface from the actual exam. The first two practice exams are free to all test takers at **www.mba.com/gmatprep**.

- **For more practice questions:** *GMAT™ Official Guide Verbal Review 2024–2025*, and *GMAT™ Official Guide Quantitative Review 2024–2025* offer over 200 additional practice questions not included in this book.

- **For focused practice:** GMAT™ Official Practice Questions for Quantitative, Data Insights, and Verbal products offer 100+ questions that are not included in the Official Guide series.

> **"Build teaching-level depth; don't just finish content mindlessly. Even if you solve thousands of questions on a shaky foundation, you will remain stuck on a really low accuracy."**
>
> — A test instructor from Top One Percent

2.5 Tips for Taking the Exam

Tips for answering questions of the different types are given later in this book. Here are some general tips to help you do your best on the test.

1. **Before the actual exam, decide in what order to take the sections.**
   The exam lets you choose in which order you'll take the sections. Use the GMAT™ Official Practice Exams to practice and find your preferred order. No order is "wrong." Some test takers prefer to complete the section that challenges them the most first, while others prefer to ease into the exam by starting with a section that they're stronger in. Practice each order and see which one works best for you.

2. **Try the practice questions and practice exams.**
   Timing yourself as you answer the practice questions and taking the practice exams can give you a sense of how long you will have for each question on the actual test, and whether you are answering them fast enough to finish in time.

 TIP

After you've learned about all the question types, use the practice questions in this book and practice them online at **www.mba.com/my-account** to prepare for the actual test. Reminder: Most types of Data Insights practice questions are only available online.

3. **Review all test directions ahead of time.**
   The directions explain exactly what you need to do to answer questions of each type. You can review the directions in the GMAT™ Official Practice Exams ahead of time so that you don't miss anything you need

to know to answer properly. To review directions during the test, you can click on the Help icon. But note that your time spent reviewing directions counts against your available time for that section of the test.

4. **Study each question carefully.**
Before you answer a question, understand exactly what it is asking, then pick the best answer choice. Never skim a question. Skimming may make you miss important details or nuances.

5. **Use your time wisely.**
Although the exam stresses accuracy over speed, you should use your time wisely. On average, you have just about 2 minutes and 9 seconds per Quantitative Reasoning question; 2 minutes and 15 seconds per Data Insights question; and under 2 minutes per Verbal Reasoning question. Once you start the test, an on-screen clock shows how much time you have left. You can hide this display if you want, but by checking the clock periodically, you can make sure to finish in time.

6. **Do not spend too much time on any one question.**
If finding the right answer is taking too long, try to rule out answer choices you know are wrong. Then pick the best of the remaining choices and move on to the next question.

Not finishing sections or randomly guessing answers can lower your score significantly. As long as you've worked on each section, you will get a score even if you didn't finish one or more sections in time. You don't earn points for questions you never get to see.

Pacing is important. If a question stumps you, pick the answer choice that seems best and move on. If you guess wrong, the computer will likely give you an easier question, which you're more likely to answer correctly. Soon the computer will return to giving you questions matched to your ability. You can bookmark questions you get stuck on, then return to change up to three of your answers if you still have time left at the end of the section. But if you don't finish the section, your score will be reduced.

7. **Confirm your answers ONLY when you are ready to move on.**
In the GMAT Quantitative Reasoning, Data Insights, and Verbal Reasoning sections, once you choose your answer to a question, you are asked to confirm it. As soon as you confirm your response, the next question appears. You can't skip questions. In the Data Insights and Verbal Reasoning sections, several questions based on the same prompt may appear at once. When more than one question is on a single screen, you can change your answers to any questions on that screen before moving on to the next screen. But until you've reached the end of the section, you can't navigate back to a previous screen to change any answers.

Myth -vs- **FACT**

M – Avoiding wrong answers is more important than finishing the test.

F – Not finishing can lower your score a lot.

Myth -vs- **FACT**

M – The first ten questions are critical, so you should spend the most time on them.

F – All questions impact your score.

2.6 Data Insights Section Strategies

Utilize the strategies below to better prepare for the exam. Creating a solid study plan and selecting the right prep materials are two key elements of getting accepted into your top business schools. But knowing how to strategically approach the exam is another crucial factor that can increase your confidence going into test day and help you perform your best.

> "Don't just read explanations. Review your notes and learn from your mistakes."
>
> — A test instructor from Admit Master

Data Sufficiency Questions

- Decide whether the problem allows only one value or a range of values. Remember: You are only determining whether you have enough data to solve the problem.

- Avoid making unwarranted assumptions based on figures. Figures are not necessarily drawn to scale.

Multi-Source Reasoning Questions

- Don't expect to be completely familiar with the material. All of the information you need to answer the questions is provided.

- Analyze each source of data carefully, as the questions require detailed understanding of the data presented. Text passages often build ideas in sequences, so be mindful of how each statement adds to the main idea of the passage. Graphic elements come in various forms, such as tables, graphs, diagrams, or charts.

- Make sure you understand what is being asked for each question. Some questions will require recognizing discrepancies among different sources of data. Others will ask you to draw inferences. Still others may require you to determine which one of the data sources is relevant.

- Select the answer choices that have the most support based on the data provided. Don't let your knowledge of the subject matter influence your answer choice. Answer the questions using only the data provided to you.

Table Analysis Questions

- Examine the table and accompanying text to determine the type of information provided.

- Read the question carefully to determine the data analysis required and know the choices you have to make by reviewing the answers.

- Judge each answer statement carefully based on the condition specified (i.e., yes or no, true or false). Focus your attention on whether the given condition has been met.

Graphics Interpretation Questions

- Familiarize yourself with the data presented in the graphic. Make note of the scales on the axis, marked values, and labels. Pay attention to any discrepancies between the units in the graph and the units discussed in the text.

- Read any accompanying text carefully. The text might present data that isn't contained in the graphic but that you need to answer the question.

- Make sure you understand what the problem is asking you to do. You will interpret and integrate data, discern relationships, and make inferences from a set of data.

- Read all the choices in the drop-down menu. By checking the menu options, you will get additional information about your assigned task.

- Choose the option that best completes the statement. More than one option in the drop-down menu may seem plausible. You will need to choose the one that makes the statement most accurate or logical.

Two-Part Analysis Questions

- Read the information carefully. It may cover a wide range of content, including quantitative, verbal, or some combination of both. All the material presented is designed to be challenging. Don't let any familiarity with the subject matter influence your response. Only use the data presented in the question.

- Determine exactly what the question is asking. Pay close attention to how the question describes the tasks. Sometimes the response column headings lack the details that could help you better understand what you are supposed to do.

- When making your answer choices, determine whether your tasks are dependent or independent. Some questions will pose two tasks that can be carried out individually. Others pose one task with two dependent parts.

- Keep in mind that the same answer choice might be the correct response for both columns. It is possible that one answer option satisfies the conditions of both response columns.

Important Note for Data Insights Practice

Multi-Source Reasoning, Table Analysis, and Graphics Interpretation questions are only available in the Online Question Bank. To access the Online Question Bank, go to **www.mba.com/my-account** and use your unique Access Code, which can be found on the inside front cover of this book.

To register for the GMAT™ exam, go to www.mba.com/register

3.0 Math Review

3.0 Math Review

This chapter reviews the math you need to answer GMAT™ Quantitative Reasoning questions and Data Insights questions. This is only a brief overview. If you find unfamiliar terms, consult other resources to learn more.

Unlike some math problems you may have solved in school, GMAT math questions ask you to *apply* your math knowledge. For example, rather than asking you to list a number's prime factors to show you understand prime factorization, a GMAT question may ask you to *use* prime factorization and exponents to simplify an algebraic expression with a radical.

To prepare for the GMAT Quantitative Reasoning section and the Data Insights section, first review basic math to make sure you know enough to answer the questions. Then practice with GMAT questions from past exams.

Section 3.1, "Value, Order, and Factors," includes:

1. Numbers and the Number Line
2. Factors, Multiples, Divisibility, and Remainders
3. Exponents
4. Decimals and Place Value
5. Properties of Operations

Section 3.2, "Algebra, Equalities, and Inequalities," includes:

1. Algebraic Expressions and Equations
2. Linear Equations
3. Factoring and Quadratic Equations
4. Inequalities
5. Functions
6. Graphing
7. Formulas and Measurement Conversion

Section 3.3, "Rates, Ratios, and Percents," includes:

1. Ratio and Proportion
2. Fractions
3. Percents
4. Converting Decimals, Fractions, and Percents
5. Working with Decimals, Fractions, and Percents
6. Rate, Work, and Mixture Problems

Section 3.4, "Statistics, Sets, Counting, Probability, Estimation, and Series," includes:

1. Statistics
2. Sets
3. Counting Methods
4. Probability
5. Estimation
6. Sequences and Series

Section 3.5, "Reference Sheets"

3.1 Value, Order, and Factors

1. Numbers and the Number Line

A. All *real numbers* match points on *the number line*, and all points on the number line represent real numbers.

The figure below shows the number line with labeled points standing for the real numbers $-\frac{3}{2}$, 0.2, and $\sqrt{2}$.

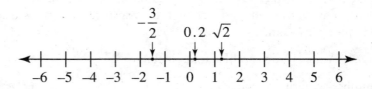

The Number Line

B. On a number line, points to the left of zero stand for *negative* numbers, and points to the right of zero stand for *positive* numbers. Every real number except zero is either positive or negative.

C. On the number line, each number is less than any number to its right. So, as the figure above shows, $-4 < -3 < -\frac{3}{2} < -1$, and $1 < \sqrt{2} < 2$.

D. If a number n is between 1 and 4 on the number line, then $n > 1$ and $n < 4$; that is, $1 < n < 4$. If n is "between 1 and 4, inclusive," then $1 \le n \le 4$.

E. The *absolute value* of a real number x, written as $|x|$, is x if $x \ge 0$ and $-x$ if $x < 0$. A number's absolute value is the distance between that number and zero on the number line. Thus, -3 and 3 have the same absolute value, since each is three units from zero on the number line. The absolute value of any nonzero number is positive.

Examples:

$|-5| = |5| = 5$, $|0| = 0$, and

$\left|-\frac{7}{2}\right| = \frac{7}{2}$.

For any real numbers x and y, $|x + y| \le |x| + |y|$.

Example:

If $x = 10$ and $y = 2$, then $|x + y| = |12| = 12 = |x| + |y|$.

If $x = 10$ and $y = -2$, then $|x + y| = |8| = 8 < 12 = |x| + |y|$.

2. Factors, Multiples, Divisibility, and Remainders

A. An *integer* is any number in the set $\{\dots -3, -2, -1, 0, 1, 2, 3, \dots\}$. For any integer n, the numbers in the set $\{n, n + 1, n + 2, n + 3, \dots\}$ are *consecutive integers*.

B. For integers x and y, if $x \neq 0$, x is a *divisor* or *factor* of y if $y = xn$ for some integer n. Then y is *divisible* by x and is a *multiple* of x.

> *Example:*
>
> Since $28 = (7)(4)$, both 4 and 7 are divisors or factors of 28.
>
> But 8 isn't a divisor or factor of 28, since n isn't an integer if $28 = 8n$.

C. Dividing a positive integer y by a positive integer x, and then rounding down to the nearest nonnegative integer, gives the *quotient* of the division.

To find the *remainder* of the division, multiply x by the quotient, then subtract the result from y. The quotient and the remainder are the unique positive integers q and r, respectively, such that $y = xq + r$ and $0 \leq r < x$.

> *Example:*
>
> When 28 is divided by 8, the quotient is 3 and the remainder is 4, because $28 = (8)(3) + 4$.

The remainder r is 0 if and only if y is *divisible* by x. Then x is a divisor of y, and y is a multiple of x.

> *Example:*
>
> Since 32 divided by 8 has a remainder of 0, 32 is divisible by 8. So, 8 is a divisor of 32, and 32 is a multiple of 8.

When a smaller integer is divided by a larger integer, the quotient is 0 and the remainder is the smaller integer.

> *Example:*
>
> When 5 is divided by 7, the quotient is 0 and the remainder is 5, since $5 = (7)(0) + 5$.

D. Any integer divisible by 2 is *even*; the set of even integers is $\{\dots -4, -2, 0, 2, 4, 6, 8, \dots\}$. Integers not divisible by 2 are *odd*, so $\{\dots -3, -1, 1, 3, 5, \dots\}$ is the set of odd integers. For any integer n, the numbers in the set $\{2n, 2n + 2, 2n + 4, \dots\}$ are *consecutive even integers*, and the numbers in $\{2n + 1, 2n + 3, 2n + 5, \dots\}$ are *consecutive odd integers*.

If a product of integers has at least one even factor, the product is even; otherwise, it's odd. If two integers are both even or both odd, their sum and their difference are even. Otherwise, their sum and their difference are odd.

E. A *prime* number is a positive integer with exactly two positive divisors, 1 and itself. That is, a prime number is divisible by no integer but itself and 1.

Example:

The first six prime numbers are 2, 3, 5, 7, 11, and 13.

But 15 is not a prime number, because it has four positive divisors: 1, 3, 5, and 15.

Nor is 1 a prime number, because it has only one positive divisor: itself.

Every integer greater than 1 is either prime or a product of a unique set of prime factors. A *composite number* is an integer greater than 1 that's not prime.

Example:

$14 = (2)(7)$, $81 = (3)(3)(3)(3)$, and

$484 = (2)(2)(11)(11)$ are composite numbers.

---

3. Exponents

A. An expression of the form k^n means the nth *power* of k, or k raised to the nth power, where n is the *exponent* and k is the *base*.

B. A positive integer exponent shows how many instances of the base are multiplied together. That is, when n is a positive integer, k^n is the product of n instances of k.

Examples:

x^5 is $(x)(x)(x)(x)(x)$; that is, the product in which x is a factor 5 times with no other factors. We can also say x^5 is the 5th power of x, or x raised to the 5th power.

The second power of 2, also called 2 *squared*, is $2^2 = 2 \times 2 = 4$. The third power of 2, also called 2 *cubed*, is $2^3 = 2 \times 2 \times 2 = 8$.

Squaring a number greater than 1, or raising it to any power greater than 1, gives a larger number.

Squaring a number between 0 and 1 gives a smaller number.

Examples:

$3^2 = 9$, and $9 > 3$.

$(0.1)^2 = 0.01$, and $0.01 < 0.1$.

C. A *square root* of a number n is a number x such that $x^2 = n$. Every positive number has two real square roots, one positive and the other negative. The positive square root of n is written as $\sqrt{n}$ or $n^{\frac{1}{2}}$.

> *Example:*
>
> The two square roots of 9 are $\sqrt{9} = 3$ and $-\sqrt{9} = -3$.

For any x, the nonnegative square root of x^2 equals the absolute value of x; that is, $\sqrt{x^2} = |x|$. The square root of a negative number is not a real number. It's called an *imaginary number*.

D. Every real number r has exactly one real *cube root*, the number s such that $s^3 = r$. The real cube root of r is written as $\sqrt[3]{r}$ or $r^{\frac{1}{3}}$.

> *Examples:*
>
> Since $2^3 = 8$, $\sqrt[3]{8} = 2$.
>
> Likewise, $\sqrt[3]{-8} = -2$ because $(-2)^3 = -8$.

4. Decimals and Place Value

A. A *decimal* is a real number written as a series of digits, often with a period called a *decimal point*. The decimal point's position sets the *place values* of the digits.

> *Example:*
>
> The digits in the decimal 7,654.321 have these place values:
>
> | Thousands | | Hundreds | Tens | Ones or units | | Tenths | Hundredths | Thousandths |
> |:---:|:---:|:---:|:---:|:---:|:---:|:---:|:---:|:---:|
> | 7 | , | 6 | 5 | 4 | . | 3 | 2 | 1 |

B. In *scientific notation*, a decimal is written with only one nonzero digit to the decimal point's left, multiplied by a power of 10. To convert a number from scientific notation to regular decimal notation, move the decimal point by the number of places equal to the absolute value of the exponent on the 10. Move the decimal point to the right if the exponent is positive or to the left if the exponent is negative.

Examples:

In scientific notation, 231 is written as 2.31×10^2, and 0.0231 is written as 2.31×10^{-2}.

To convert 2.013×10^4 to regular decimal notation, move the decimal point 4 places to the right, giving 20,130.

Likewise, to convert 1.91×10^{-4} to regular decimal notation, move the decimal point 4 places to the left, giving 0.000191.

C. To add or subtract decimals, line up their decimal points. If one decimal has fewer digits to the right of its decimal point than another, insert zeros to the right of its last digit.

Examples:

To add 17.6512 and 653.27, insert zeros to the right of the last digit in 653.27 to line up the decimal points when the numbers are in a column:

$$
\begin{array}{r}
17.6512 \\
+\,653.2700 \\
\hline
670.9212
\end{array}
$$

Likewise for 653.27 minus 17.6512:

$$
\begin{array}{r}
653.2700 \\
-\,17.6512 \\
\hline
635.6188
\end{array}
$$

D. Multiply decimals as if they were integers. Then insert the decimal point in the product so that the number of digits to the right of the decimal point is the sum of the numbers of digits to the right of the decimal points in the numbers being multiplied.

Example:

To multiply 2.09 by 1.3, first multiply the integers 209 and 13 to get 2,717. Since $2 + 1 = 3$ digits are to the right of the decimal points in 2.09 and 1.3, put 3 digits in 2,717 to the right of the decimal point to find the product:

$$
\begin{array}{r}
2.09 \quad \text{(2 digits to the right)} \\
\times\ 1.3 \quad \text{(1 digit to the right)} \\
\hline
627 \\
2090 \\
\hline
2.717 \quad (2+1 = 3 \text{ digits to the right})
\end{array}
$$

E. To divide a number (the ***dividend***) by a decimal (the ***divisor***), move the decimal points of the dividend and divisor the same number of digits to the right until the divisor is an integer. Then divide as you would integers. The decimal point in the quotient goes directly above the decimal point in the new dividend.

Example:

To divide 698.12 by 12.4, first move the decimal points in both the divisor 12.4 and the dividend 698.12 one place to the right to make the divisor an integer. That is, replace 698.12/12.4 with 6981.2/124. Then do the long division normally:

$$
\begin{array}{r}
56.3 \\
124\overline{)6981.2} \\
\underline{620} \\
781 \\
\underline{744} \\
372 \\
\underline{372} \\
0
\end{array}
$$

5. Properties of Operations

Here are some basic properties of arithmetical operations for any real numbers x, y, and z.

A. Addition and Subtraction

$x + 0 = x = x - 0$

$x - x = 0$

$x + y = y + x$

$x - y = -(y - x) = x + (-y)$

$(x + y) + z = x + (y + z)$

If x and y are both positive, then $x + y$ is also positive.

If x and y are both negative, then $x + y$ is negative.

B. Multiplication and Division

$x \times 1 = x = \dfrac{x}{1}$

$x \times 0 = 0$

If $x \neq 0$, then $\dfrac{x}{x} = 1$

$\dfrac{x}{0}$ is undefined.

$xy = yx$

If $x \neq 0$ and $y \neq 0$, then $\dfrac{x}{y} = \dfrac{1}{\left(\frac{y}{x}\right)}$.

$(xy)z = x(yz)$

$xy + xz = x(y + z)$

If $y \neq 0$, then $\left(\dfrac{x}{y}\right) + \left(\dfrac{z}{y}\right) = \dfrac{(x + z)}{y}$.

If x and y are both positive, then xy is also positive.

If x and y are both negative, then xy is positive.

If x is positive and y is negative, then xy is negative.

If $xy = 0$, then $x = 0$ or $y = 0$, or both.

C. Exponentiation

$x^1 = x$

$x^0 = 1$

If $x \neq 0$, then $x^{-1} = \frac{1}{x}$

$(x^y)^z = x^{yz} = (x^z)^y$

$x^{y+z} = x^y x^z$

If $x \neq 0$, then $x^{y-z} = \frac{x^y}{x^z}$.

$(xz)^y = x^y z^y$

If $z \neq 0$, then $\left(\frac{x}{z}\right)^y = \frac{x^y}{z^y}$.

If $z \neq 0$, then $x^{\frac{y}{z}} = (x^y)^{\frac{1}{z}} = \left(x^{\frac{1}{z}}\right)^y$.

3.2 Algebra, Equalities, and Inequalities

1. Algebraic Expressions and Equations

A. Algebra is based on arithmetic and on the concept of an ***unknown quantity***. Letters like ***x*** or ***n*** are ***variables*** that stand for unknown quantities. Other numerical expressions called ***constants*** stand for known quantities. A combination of variables, constants, and arithmetical operations is an ***algebraic expression***.

Solving word problems often requires translating words into algebraic expressions. The table below shows how some words and phrases can be translated as math operations in algebraic expressions:

3.2 Translating Words into Math Operations				
$x + y$	$x - y$	xy	$\frac{x}{y}$	x^y
x added to y *x increased by y* *x more than y* *x plus y* *the sum of x and y* *the total of x and y*	*x decreased by y* *difference of x and y* *y fewer than x* *y less than x* *x minus y* *x reduced by y* *y subtracted from x*	*x multiplied by y* *the product of x and y* *x times y*	*x divided by y* *x over y* *the quotient of x and y* *the ratio of x to y*	*x to the power of y* *x to the yth power*
		If $y = 2$: *double x* *twice x*	If $y = 2$: *half of x* *x halved*	If $y = 2$: *x squared*
		If $y = 3$: *triple x*		If $y = 3$: *x cubed*

B. In an algebraic expression, a **term** is a constant, a variable, or a product of terms that are each a constant or a variable. A variable in a term may be raised to an exponent. A term with no variables is a **constant term**. A constant in a term with one or more variables is a **coefficient**.

> *Example:*
>
> Suppose Pam has 5 more pencils than Fred has. If F is the number of pencils Fred has, then Pam has $F + 5$ pencils. The algebraic expression $F + 5$ has two terms: the variable F and the constant 5.

C. A **polynomial** is an algebraic expression that's a sum of terms and has exactly one variable. Each term in a polynomial is a variable raised to some power and multiplied by some coefficient. If the highest power a variable is raised to is 1, the expression is a **first degree** (or **linear**) **polynomial** in that variable. If the highest power a variable is raised to is 2, the expression is a **second degree** (or **quadratic**) **polynomial** in that variable.

> *Examples:*
>
> $F + 5$ is a linear polynomial in F, since the highest power of F is 1.
>
> $19x^2 - 6x + 3$ is a quadratic polynomial in x, since the highest power of x is 2.
>
> $\dfrac{3x^2}{(2x - 5)}$ is not a polynomial, because it's not a sum of powers of x multiplied by coefficients.

D. You can simplify many algebraic expressions by factoring or combining **like** terms.

> *Examples:*
>
> In the expression $6x + 5x$, x is a factor common to both terms. So, $6x + 5x$ is equivalent to $(6 + 5)x$, or $11x$.
>
> In the expression $9x - 3y$, 3 is a factor common to both terms: $9x - 3y = 3(3x - y)$.
>
> The expression $5x^2 + 6y$ has no like terms and no common factors.

E. In a fraction $\dfrac{n}{d}$, n is the **numerator** and d is the **denominator**. In a numerator and denominator, you can divide out any common factors not equal to zero.

> *Example:*
>
> If $x \neq 3$, then $\dfrac{(x - 3)}{(x - 3)} = 1$.
>
> So, $\dfrac{(3xy - 9y)}{(x - 3)} = \dfrac{3y(x - 3)}{(x - 3)} = 3y(1) = 3y$.

F. To multiply two algebraic expressions, multiply each term of one expression by each term of the other.

> *Example:*
>
> $$(3x - 4)(9y + x) = 3x(9y + x) - 4(9y + x)$$
> $$= 3x(9y) + 3x(x) - 4(9y) - 4(x)$$
> $$= 27xy + 3x^2 - 36y - 4x$$

G. To evaluate an algebraic expression, replace its variables with constants.

> *Example:*
>
> If $x = 3$ and $y = -2$, we can evaluate $3xy - x^2 + y$ as
>
> $3(3)(-2) - (3)^2 + (-2) = -18 - 9 - 2 = -29$.

H. An ***algebraic equation*** is an equation with at least one algebraic expression. An algebraic equation's ***solutions*** are the sets of assignments of constant values to its variables that make it true, or "satisfy the equation." An equation may have no solution, one solution, or more than one solution. For equations solved together, the solutions must satisfy all the equations at once. An equation's solutions are also called its ***roots***. To confirm the roots are correct, you can substitute them into the equation.

I. Two equations with the same solution or solutions are ***equivalent***.

> *Examples:*
>
> The equations $2 + x = 3$ and $4 + 2x = 6$ are equivalent, because each has the unique solution $x = 1$. Notice the second equation is the first equation multiplied by 2.
>
> Likewise, the equations $3x - y = 6$ and $6x - 2y = 12$ are equivalent, although each has infinitely many solutions. For any value of x, giving the value $3x - 6$ to y satisfies both these equations. For example, $x = 2$ with $y = 0$ is a solution to both equations, and so is $x = 5$ with $y = 9$.

2. Linear Equations

A. A ***linear equation*** has a linear polynomial on one side of the equals sign and either a linear polynomial or a constant on the other side—or can be converted to that form. A linear equation with only one variable is a ***linear equation with one unknown***. A linear equation with two variables is ***a linear equation with two unknowns***.

> *Examples:*
>
> $5x - 2 = 9 - x$ is a linear equation with one unknown.
>
> $3x + 1 = y - 2$ is a linear equation with two unknowns.

B. To solve a linear equation with one unknown (that is, to find what value of the unknown satisfies the equation), isolate the unknown on one side of the equation by doing the same operations on both sides. Adding or subtracting the same number on both sides of the equation doesn't change the equality. Likewise, multiplying or dividing both sides by the same nonzero number doesn't change the equality.

Example:

To solve the equation $\frac{5x - 6}{3} = 4$, isolate the variable x like this:

$$5x - 6 = 12 \quad \text{multiply both sides by 3}$$

$$5x = 18 \quad \text{add 6 to both sides}$$

$$x = \frac{18}{5} \quad \text{divide both sides by 5}$$

To check the answer $\frac{18}{5}$, substitute it for x in the original equation to confirm it satisfies that equation:

$$\frac{\left(5\left(\frac{18}{5}\right) - 6\right)}{3} = \frac{(18 - 6)}{3} = \frac{12}{3} = 4$$

So, $x = \frac{18}{5}$ is the solution.

C. Two equivalent linear equations with the same two unknowns have infinitely many solutions, as in the example of the equivalent equations $3x - y = 6$ and $6x - 2y = 12$ in Section 3.2.1.I above. But if two linear equations with the same two unknowns aren't equivalent, they have at most one solution.

When solving two linear equations with two unknowns, if you reach a trivial equation like $0 = 0$, the equations are equivalent and have infinitely many solutions. But if you reach a contradiction, the equations have no solution.

Example:

Consider the two equations $3x + 4y = 17$ and $6x + 8y = 35$. Note that $3x + 4y = 17$ implies $6x + 8y = 34$, contradicting the second equation. So, no values of x and y can satisfy both equations at once. The two equations have no solution.

If neither a trivial equation nor a contradiction is reached, a unique solution can be found.

D. To solve two linear equations with two unknowns, you can use one of the equations to express one unknown in terms of the other unknown. Then substitute this result into the second equation to make a new equation with only one unknown. Next, solve this new equation. Substitute the value of its unknown into either original equation to solve for the remaining unknown.

Example:

Let's solve these two equations for x and y:

$$(1) \quad 3x + 2y = 11$$
$$(2) \quad x - y = 2$$

In equation (2), $x = 2 + y$. So, in equation (1), substitute $2 + y$ for x:

$$3(2 + y) + 2y = 11$$
$$6 + 3y + 2y = 11$$
$$6 + 5y = 11$$
$$5y = 5$$
$$y = 1$$

Since $y = 1$, we find $x - 1 = 2$, so $x = 2 + 1 = 3$.

E. Another way to remove one unknown and solve for x and y is to make the coefficients of one unknown the same in both equations (ignoring the sign). Then either add the equations or subtract one from the other.

Example:

Let's solve the equations:

$$(1) \quad 6x + 5y = 29 \text{ and}$$
$$(2) \quad 4x - 3y = -6$$

Multiply equation (1) by 3 and equation (2) by 5 to get

$$18x + 15y = 87 \text{ and}$$
$$20x - 15y = -30$$

Add the two equations to remove y. This gives us $38x = 57$, or $x = \frac{3}{2}$.

Substituting $\frac{3}{2}$ for x in either original equation gives $y = 4$. To check these answers, substitute both values into both the original equations.

3. Factoring and Quadratic Equations

A. Some equations can be solved by *factoring*. To do this, first add or subtract to bring all the expressions to one side of the equation, with 0 on the other side. Then try to express the nonzero side as a product of factors that are algebraic expressions. When that's possible, setting any of these factors equal to 0 makes a simpler equation, because for any x and y, if $xy = 0$, then $x = 0$ or $y = 0$ or both. The solutions of the simpler equations made this way are also solutions of the factored equation.

Example:

Factor to find the solutions of the equation $x^3 - 2x^2 + x = -5(x - 1)^2$:

$$x^3 - 2x^2 + x + 5(x - 1)^2 = 0$$
$$x(x^2 - 2x + 1) + 5(x - 1)^2 = 0$$
$$x(x - 1)^2 + 5(x - 1)^2 = 0$$
$$(x + 5)(x - 1)^2 = 0$$
$$x + 5 = 0 \text{ or } x - 1 = 0$$
$$x = -5 \text{ or } x = 1$$

So, $x = -5$ or $x = 1$.

B. When factoring to solve equations with algebraic fractions, note that a fraction equals 0 if and only if its numerator equals 0 and its denominator doesn't.

Example:

Find the solutions of the equation $\dfrac{x(x - 3)(x^2 + 5)}{x - 4} = 0$.

The numerator must equal 0: $x(x - 3)(x^2 + 5) = 0$.

Thus, $x = 0$, or $x - 3 = 0$, or $x^2 + 5 = 0$. So, $x = 0$, or $x = 3$, or $x^2 + 5 = 0$.

But $x^2 + 5 = 0$ has no real solution, because $x^2 + 5 = 0$ for every real number x. So, the original equation's solutions are 0 and 3.

C. A *quadratic equation* has the standard form $ax^2 + bx + c = 0$, where a, b, and c are real numbers and $a \neq 0$.

Examples:

$$x^2 + 6x + 5 = 0$$
$$3x^2 - 2x = 0, \text{ and}$$
$$x^2 + 4 = 0$$

D. Some quadratic equations are easily solved by factoring.

Example (1):

$$x^2 + 6x + 5 = 0$$
$$(x + 5)(x + 1) = 0$$
$$x + 5 = 0 \text{ or } x + 1 = 0$$
$$x = -5 \text{ or } x = -1$$

Example (2):

$$3x^2 - 3 = 8x$$
$$3x^2 - 8x - 3 = 0$$
$$(3x + 1)(x - 3) = 0$$
$$3x + 1 = 0 \text{ or } x - 3 = 0$$
$$x = -\frac{1}{3} \text{ or } x = 3$$

E. A quadratic equation has at most two real roots but may have just one or even no root.

> *Examples:*
>
> The equation $x^2 - 6x + 9 = 0$ can be written as $(x - 3)^2 = 0$ or $(x - 3)(x - 3) = 0$. So, its only root is 3.
>
> The equation $x^2 + 4 = 0$ has no real root. Since any real number squared is greater than or equal to zero, $x^2 + 4$ must be greater than zero if x is a real number.

F. An expression of the form $a^2 - b^2$ can be factored as $(a - b)(a + b)$.

> *Example:*
>
> We can solve the quadratic equation $9x^2 - 25 = 0$ like this:
>
> $$(3x - 5)(3x + 5) = 0$$
> $$3x - 5 = 0 \text{ or } x + 5 = 0$$
> $$x = \frac{5}{3} \text{ or } x = -\frac{5}{3}$$

G. If a quadratic expression isn't easily factored, we can still find its roots with the **quadratic formula**: If $ax^2 + bx + c = 0$ and $a \neq 0$, the roots are

$$x = \frac{-b + \sqrt{b^2 - 4ac}}{2a} \text{ and } x = \frac{-b - \sqrt{b^2 - 4ac}}{2a}$$

These roots are two distinct real numbers unless $b^2 - 4ac \leq 0$.

If $b^2 - 4ac = 0$, the two root expressions both equal $-\frac{b}{2a}$, so the equation has only one root.

If $b^2 - 4ac < 0$, then $\sqrt{b^2 - 4ac}$ is not a real number, so the equation has no real root.

4. Inequalities

A. An *inequality* is a statement with one of these symbols:

$\neq$ is not equal to

$>$ is greater than

$\geq$ is greater than or equal to

$<$ is less than

$\leq$ is less than or equal to

> *Example:*
>
> $5x - 3 < 9$ and $6x \geq y$

B. Solve a linear inequality with one unknown the same way you solve a linear equation: isolate the unknown on one side. As in an equation, the same number can be added to or subtracted from both sides of the inequality. And you can multiply or divide both sides by a positive number without changing the order of the inequality. However, multiplying or dividing an inequality by a negative number reverses the order of the inequality. Thus, $6 > 2$, but $(-1)(6) < (-1)(2)$.

Example (1):

To solve the inequality $3x - 2 > 5$ for x, isolate x:

$3x - 2 > 5$

$3x > 7$ (add 2 to both sides)

$x > \dfrac{7}{3}$ (divide both sides by 3)

Example (2):

To solve the inequality $\dfrac{5x - 1}{-2} < 3$ for x, isolate x:

$\dfrac{5x - 1}{-2} < 3$

$5x - 1 > -6$ (multiply both sides by -2)

$5x > -5$ (add 1 to both sides)

$x > -1$ (divide both sides by 5)

---

5. Functions

A. An algebraic expression in one variable can define a ***function*** of that variable. A function is written as a letter like f or g along with the variable in the expression. Function notation is a short way to express that a value is being substituted for a variable.

Examples:

(i) The expression $x^3 - 5x^2 + 2$ can define a function f written as $f(x) = x^3 - 5x^2 + 2$.

(ii) The expression $\dfrac{2z + 7}{\sqrt{z + 1}}$ can define a function g written as $g(z) = \dfrac{2z + 7}{\sqrt{z + 1}}$.

In these examples, the symbols "$f(x)$" and "$g(z)$" don't stand for products. Each is just a symbol for a function, and is read "f of x" or "g of z."

The substitution of 1 for x in the first expression can be written as $f(1) = -2$. Then $f(1)$ is called the "value of f at $x = 1$."

Likewise, in the second expression the value of g at $z = 0$ is $g(0) = 7$.

B. Once a function $f(x)$ is defined, think of x as an input and $f(x)$ as the output. In any function, any one input gives at most one output. But different inputs can give the same output.

Example:

If $h(x) = |x + 3|$, then $h(-4) = 1 = h(-2)$.

C. The set of all allowed inputs for a function is the function's ***domain***. In the examples in Section 3.2.5.A above, the domain of f is the set of all real numbers, and the domain of g is the set of all numbers greater than -1.

Any function's definition can restrict the function's domain. For example, the definition "$a(x) = 9x - 5$ for $0 \leq x \leq 10$" restricts the domain of a to real numbers greater than or equal to 0 but less than or equal to 10. If the definition has no restrictions, the domain is the set of all values of x that each give a real output when input into the function.

D. The set of a function's outputs is the function's ***range***.

Examples:

(i) For the function $h(x) = |x + 3|$ in the example in Section 3.2.5.B above, the range is the set of all numbers greater than or equal to 0.

(ii) For the function $a(x) = 9x - 5$ for $0 \leq x \leq 10$ defined in Section 3.2.5.C above, the range is the set of all real numbers y such that $-5 \leq y \leq 85$.

---

6. Graphing

A. The figure below shows the rectangular ***coordinate plane***. The horizontal line is the ***x-axis*** and the vertical line is the ***y-axis***. These two axes intersect at the ***origin***, called O. The axes divide the plane into four quadrants, I, II, III, and IV, as shown.

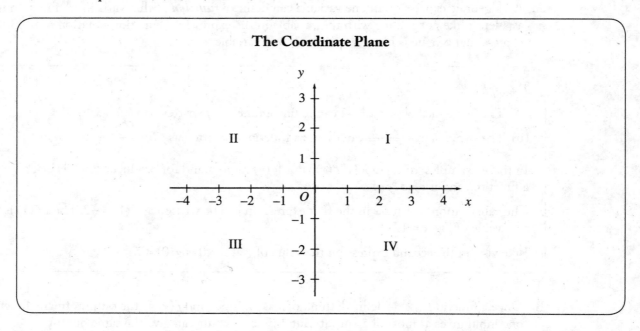

The Coordinate Plane

B. Any ordered pair (x, y) of real numbers defines a point in the coordinate plane. The point's ***x-coordinate*** is the first number in this pair. It shows how far the point is to the right or left of the y-axis. If the x-coordinate is positive, the point is to the right of the y-axis. If it's negative, the point is to the left of the y-axis. If it's 0, the point is on the axis. The point's ***y-coordinate*** is the second number in the ordered pair. It shows how far the point is above or below the x-axis. If the y-coordinate is positive, the point is above the x-axis. If it's negative, the point is below the x-axis. If it's 0, the point is on the axis.

Example:

In the graph below, the (x, y) coordinates of point P are $(2, 3)$. P is 2 units to the right of the y-axis, so $x = 2$. Since P is 3 units above the x-axis, $y = 3$.

Likewise, the (x, y) coordinates of point Q are $(-4, -3)$. The origin O has coordinates $(0, 0)$.

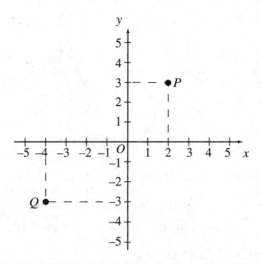

C. The coordinates of the points on a straight line in the coordinate plane satisfy a linear equation of the form $y = mx + b$ (or the form $x = a$ if the line is vertical).

In the equation $y = mx + b$, the coefficient m is the line's **slope**, and the constant b is the line's **y-intercept**.

The y-intercept is the y-coordinate of the point where the line intersects the y-axis. Likewise, the **x-intercept** is the x-coordinate of the point where the line intersects the x-axis.

For any two points on the line, the line's slope is the ratio of the difference in their y-coordinates to the difference in their x-coordinates. To find the slope, subtract one point's y-coordinate from the others. Then subtract the former point's x-coordinate from the latter's—not the other way around! Then divide the first difference by the second.

If a line's slope is negative, the line slants down from left to right.

If the slope is positive, the line slants up.

If the slope is 0, the line is horizontal. A horizontal line's equation has the form $y = b$, since $m = 0$.

A vertical line's slope is undefined.

Example:

In the graph below, each point on the line satisfies the equation $y = -\frac{1}{2}x + 1$. To check this for the points $(-2, 2)$, $(2, 0)$, and $(0, 1)$, substitute each point's coordinates for x and y in the equation.

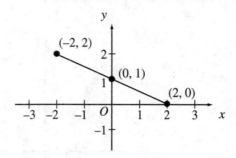

You can use the points $(-2, 2)$ and $(2, 0)$ to find the line's slope:

$$\frac{\text{the difference in the } y\text{-coordinates}}{\text{the difference in the } x\text{-coordinates}} = \frac{0 - 2}{2 - (-2)} = \frac{-2}{4} = -\frac{1}{2}.$$

The y-intercept is 1. That's y's value when x is 0 in $y = -\frac{1}{2}x + 1$.

To find the x-intercept, set y to 0 in the same equation:

$$-\frac{1}{2}x + 1 = 0$$
$$-\frac{1}{2}x = -1$$
$$x = 2$$

Thus, the x-intercept is 2.

D. You can use the definition of slope to find the equation of a line through two points (x_1, y_1) and (x_2, y_2) with $x_1 \neq x_2$. The slope is $m = \frac{y_2 - y_1}{x_2 - x_1}$. Given the known point (x_1, y_1) and the slope m, any other point (x, y) on the line satisfies the equation $m = \frac{(y - y_1)}{(x - x_1)}$, or equivalently $(y - y_1) = m(x - x_1)$. Using (x_2, y_2) instead of (x_1, y_1) as the known point gives an equivalent equation.

Example:

The graph below shows points (–2, 4) and (3, –3).

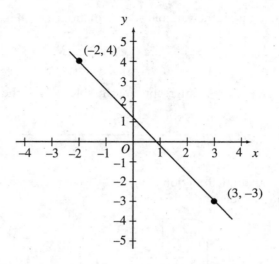

The line's slope is $\dfrac{(-3-4)}{(3-(-2))} = -\dfrac{7}{5}$. To find an equation of this line, let's use the point (3, –3):

$$y - (-3) = \left(-\frac{7}{5}\right)(x - 3)$$
$$y + 3 = \left(-\frac{7}{5}\right)x + \frac{21}{5}$$
$$y = \left(-\frac{7}{5}\right)x + \frac{6}{5}$$

So, the *y*-intercept is $\dfrac{6}{5}$.

Find the *x*-intercept like this:

$$0 = -\frac{7}{5}x + \frac{6}{5}$$
$$\frac{7}{5}x = \frac{6}{5}$$
$$x = \frac{6}{7}$$

The graph shows both these intercepts.

E. If two linear equations with unknowns *x* and *y* have a unique solution, their graphs are two lines intersecting at the point that is the solution.

If two linear equations are equivalent, they both stand for the same line and have infinitely many solutions.

Two linear equations with no solution stand for two parallel lines.

F. Graph any function $f(x)$ in the coordinate plane by equating *y* with the function's value: $y = f(x)$. For any *x* in the function's domain, the point $(x, f(x))$ is on the function's graph. For every point on the graph, the *y*-coordinate is the function's value at the *x*-coordinate.

Example:

Consider the function $f(x) = -\dfrac{7}{5}x + \dfrac{6}{5}$.

If $f(x)$ is equated with the variable y, the function's graph is the graph of $y = -\dfrac{7}{5}x + \dfrac{6}{5}$ in the example above.

G. For any function f, the x-intercepts are the solutions of the equation $f(x) = 0$. The y-intercept is the value $f(0)$.

Example:

To see how a quadratic function $f(x) = x^2 - 1$ relates to its graph, let's plot some points $(x, f(x))$ in the coordinate plane:

x	$f(x)$
-2	3
-1	0
0	-1
1	0
2	3

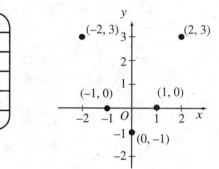

The graph below shows all the points for $-2 \le x \le 2$:

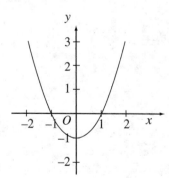

The roots of this equation $f(x) = x^2 - 1 = 0$ are $x = 1$ and $x = -1$. They match the x-intercepts, since x-intercepts are found by setting $y = 0$ and solving for x.

The y-intercept is $f(0) = -1$, because that's the value of y for $x = 0$.

7. Formulas and Measurement Conversion

A. A *formula* is an algebraic equation whose variables have specific meanings. To use a formula, assign quantities to its variables to match these meanings.

Example:

In the physics formula $F = ma$, the variable F stands for force, the variable m stands for mass, and the variable a stands for acceleration. The standard metric unit of force, the newton, is just enough force to accelerate a mass of 1 kilogram by 1 meter/second^2.

So, if we know a rock with a mass of 2 kilograms is accelerating at 5 meters/second^2, we can use the formula $F = ma$ by setting the variable m to 2 kilograms, and the variable a to 5 meters/second^2. Then we find that 10 newtons of force F are pushing the rock.

Note: You don't need to learn physics formulas or terms like this for the GMAT, but some specific GMAT questions may give you the formulas and terms you need to solve them.

B. Any quantitative relationship between units of measure can be written as a formula.

Examples:

(i) Since 1 kilometer is 1,000 meters, the formula $m = 1000k$ can stand for the relationship between kilometers (k) and meters (m).

(ii) The formula $C = \frac{5}{9}(F - 32)$ can stand for the relationship between temperature measurements in degrees Celsius (C) and degrees Fahrenheit (F).

C. Except for units of time, a GMAT question that requires converting one unit of measure to another will give the relationship between those units.

Example:

A train travels at a constant 25 meters per second. How many kilometers does it travel in 5 minutes? (1 kilometer = 1,000 meters)

Solution: In 1 minute the train travels $(25)(60) = 1,500$ meters, so in 5 minutes it travels 7,500 meters. Since 1 kilometer = 1,000 meters, we find 7,500 meters = 7.5 kilometers.

3.3 Rates, Ratios, and Percents

1. Ratio and Proportion

A. The *ratio* of a number x to a nonzero number y may be written as $x{:}y$, or $\frac{x}{y}$, or x to y. The order of a ratio's terms is important. Unless the absolute values of x and y are equal, $\frac{x}{y} \neq \frac{y}{x}$.

Examples:

The ratio of 2 to 3 may be written as 2:3, or $\frac{2}{3}$, or 2 to 3.

The ratio of the number of months with exactly 30 days to the number of months with exactly 31 days is 4:7, not 7:4.

B. A *proportion* is an equation between two ratios.

Example:

2:3 = 8:12 is a proportion.

C. One way to solve for an unknown in a proportion is to cross multiply, then solve the resulting equation.

Example:

To solve for n in the proportion $\frac{2}{3} = \frac{n}{12}$, cross multiply to get $3n = 24$, then divide both sides by 3 to find $n = 8$.

D. Some word problems can be solved using ratios.

Example:

If 5 shirts cost a total of $44, then what is the total cost of 8 shirts at the same cost per shirt?

Solution: If c is the cost of the 8 shirts, then $\frac{5}{44} = \frac{8}{c}$. Cross multiplying gives $5c = 8 \times 44 = 352$, so $c = \frac{352}{5} = 70.4$. Thus, the 8 shirts cost a total of $70.40.

2. Fractions

A. In a fraction $\frac{n}{d}$, n is the **numerator** and d is the **denominator**. A fraction's denominator can never be 0, because division by 0 is undefined.

B. *Equivalent* fractions stand for the same number. To check whether two fractions are equivalent, divide each fraction's numerator and denominator by the largest factor common to that numerator and that denominator, their **greatest common divisor** (GCD). This is called **reducing each fraction to its lowest terms**. Two fractions are equivalent if and only if reducing each to its lowest terms makes them identical.

Example:

To check whether $\frac{8}{36}$ and $\frac{14}{63}$ are equivalent, first reduce each to its lowest terms. In the first fraction, 4 is the GCD of the numerator 8 and the denominator 36. Dividing both the numerator and the denominator of $\frac{8}{36}$ by 4 gives $\frac{2}{9}$. In the second fraction, 7 is the GCD of the numerator 14 and the denominator 63. Dividing both the numerator and the denominator of $\frac{14}{63}$ by 7 also gives $\frac{2}{9}$. Since reducing $\frac{8}{36}$ and $\frac{14}{63}$ to their lowest terms makes them identical, they're equivalent.

C. To add or subtract two fractions with the same denominator, just add or subtract the numerators, leaving the denominators the same.

Examples:

$\frac{3}{5} + \frac{4}{5} = \frac{3+4}{5} = \frac{7}{5}$ and

$\frac{5}{7} - \frac{2}{7} = \frac{5-2}{7} = \frac{3}{7}$

D. To add or subtract two fractions with different denominators, first express them as fractions with the same denominator.

Example:

To add $\frac{3}{5}$ and $\frac{4}{7}$, multiply the numerator and denominator of $\frac{3}{5}$ by 7 to get $\frac{21}{35}$. Then multiply the numerator and denominator of $\frac{4}{7}$ by 5 to get $\frac{20}{35}$. Since both fractions now have the same denominator 35, you can easily add them: $\frac{3}{5} + \frac{4}{7} = \frac{21}{35} + \frac{20}{35} = \frac{41}{35}$

E. To multiply two fractions, multiply their numerators, and also multiply their denominators.

Example:

$\frac{2}{3} \times \frac{4}{7} = \frac{2 \times 4}{3 \times 7} = \frac{8}{21}$

F. The *reciprocal* of a fraction $\frac{n}{d}$ is $\frac{d}{n}$ if n and d are not 0.

Example:

The reciprocal of $\frac{4}{7}$ is $\frac{7}{4}$.

G. To divide by a fraction, multiply by its reciprocal.

> *Example:*
>
> $$\frac{2}{3} \div \frac{4}{7} = \frac{2}{3} \times \frac{7}{4} = \frac{14}{12} = \frac{7}{6}$$

H. A ***mixed number*** is written as an integer next to a fraction. It equals the integer plus the fraction.

> *Example:*
>
> The mixed number $7\frac{2}{3} = 7 + \frac{2}{3}$

I. To write a mixed number as a fraction, multiply the integer part of the mixed number by the denominator of the fractional part. Add this product to the numerator. Then put this sum over the denominator.

> *Example:*
>
> $$7\frac{2}{3} = \frac{(7 \times 3) + 2}{3} = \frac{23}{3}$$

3. Percents

A. The word ***percent*** means ***per hundred*** or ***number out of 100***.

> *Example:*
>
> Saying that 37 percent, or 37%, of the houses in a city are painted blue means that 37 houses per 100 in the city are painted blue.

B. A percent may be greater than 100.

> *Example:*
>
> Saying that the number of blue houses in a city is 150% of the number of red houses means the city has 150 blue houses for every 100 red houses. Since 150:100 = 3:2, this means the city has 3 blue houses for every 2 red houses.

C. A percent need not be an integer.

> *Example:*
>
> Saying that the number of pink houses in a city is 0.5% of the number of blue houses means the city has 0.5 of a pink house for every 100 blue houses. Since 0.5:100 = 1:200, this means the city has 1 pink house for every 200 blue houses.
>
> Likewise, saying that the number of orange houses is 12.5% of the number of blue houses means the ratio of orange houses to blue houses is 12.5:100 = 1:8. Therefore, there is 1 orange house for every 8 blue houses.

4. Converting Decimals, Fractions, and Percents

A. Decimals can be rewritten as fractions or sums of fractions.

> *Examples:*
>
> $$0.321 = \frac{3}{10} + \frac{2}{100} + \frac{1}{1,000} = \frac{321}{1,000}$$
>
> $$0.0321 = \frac{0}{10} + \frac{3}{100} + \frac{2}{1,000} + \frac{1}{10,000} = \frac{321}{10,000}$$
>
> $$1.56 = 1 + \frac{5}{10} + \frac{6}{100} = \frac{156}{100}$$

B. To rewrite a percent as a fraction, write the percent number as the numerator over a denominator of 100. To rewrite a percent as a decimal, move the decimal point in the percent two places to the left and drop the percent sign. To rewrite a decimal as a percent, move the decimal point two places to the right, then add a percent sign.

> *Examples:*
>
> $$37\% = \frac{37}{100} = 0.37$$
>
> $$300\% = \frac{300}{100} = 3$$
>
> $$0.5\% = \frac{0.5}{100} = 0.005$$

C. To find a percent of a number, multiply the number by the percent written as a fraction or decimal.

> *Examples:*
>
> 20% of $90 = 90\left(\dfrac{20}{100}\right) = 90\left(\dfrac{1}{5}\right) = \dfrac{90}{5} = 18$
>
> 20% of $90 = 90(0.2) = 18$
>
> 250% of $80 = 80\left(\dfrac{250}{100}\right) = 80(2.5) = 200$
>
> 0.5% of $12 = 12\left(\dfrac{0.5}{100}\right) = 12(0.005) = 0.06$

5. Working with Decimals, Fractions, and Percents

A. To find the percent increase or decrease from one quantity to another, first find the amount of increase or decrease. Then divide this amount by the original quantity. Write this quotient as a percent.

> *Examples:*
>
> Suppose a price increases from $24 to $30. To find the percent increase, first find the amount of increase: $30 − $24 = $6. Divide this $6 by the original price of $24 to find the percent increase: $\dfrac{6}{24} = 0.25 = 25\%$.
>
> Now suppose a price falls from $30 to $24. The amount of decrease is $30 − $24 = $6. So, the percent decrease is $\dfrac{6}{30} = 0.20 = 20\%$.
>
> Notice the percent **increase** from 24 to 30 (25%) doesn't equal the percent **decrease** from 30 to 24 (20%).

A percent increase or decrease may be greater than 100%.

> *Example:*
>
> Suppose a house's price in 2018 was 300% of its price in 2003. By what percent did the price increase?
>
> *Solution:* If n is the price in 2003, the percent increase is $\left|\dfrac{(3n - n)}{n}\right| = \left|\dfrac{2n}{n}\right| = 2$, or 200%.

B. A price discounted by n percent is $(100 - n)$ percent of the original price.

> *Example:*
>
> A customer paid \$24 for a dress. If the customer got a 25% discount off the original price of the dress, what was the original price before the discount?
>
> *Solution:* The discounted price is $(100 - 25 = 75)\%$ of the original price. So, if p is the original price, $0.75p = \$24$ is the discounted price. Thus, $p = (\$24/0.75) = \$32$, the original price before the discount.

Two discounts can be combined to make a larger discount.

> *Example:*
>
> A price is discounted 20%. Then this reduced price is discounted another 30%. These two discounts together make an overall discount of what percent?
>
> *Solution:* If p is the original price, then $0.8p$ is the price after the first discount. The price after the second discount is $(0.7)(0.8)p = 0.56p$. The overall discount is $100\% - 56\% = 44\%$.

C. *Gross profit* equals revenues minus expenses, or selling price minus cost.

> *Example:*
>
> A certain appliance costs a merchant \$30. At what price should the merchant sell the appliance to make a gross profit of 50% of the appliance's cost?
>
> *Solution:* The merchant should sell the appliance for a price s such that $s - 30 = (0.5)(30)$. So, $s = \$30 + \$15 = \$45$.

D. *Simple annual interest* on a loan or investment is based only on the original loan or investment amount (the ***principal***). It equals (principal) × (interest rate) × (time).

> *Example:*
>
> If \$8,000 is invested at 6% simple annual interest, how much interest is earned in 3 months?
>
> *Solution:* Since the annual interest rate is 6%, the interest for 1 year is $(0.06)(\$8,000) = \$480$. A year has 12 months, so the interest earned in 3 months is $\left(\frac{3}{12}\right)(\$480) = \$120$.

E. *Compound interest* is based on the principal plus any interest already earned.

Compound interest over n periods = (principal) × (1 + interest per period)^n – principal.

Example:

If $10,000 is invested at 10% annual interest, compounded every 6 months, what is the balance after 1 year?

Solution: Since the interest is compounded every 6 months, or twice a year, the interest rate for each 6-month period is 5%, half the 10% rate. So, the balance after the first 6 months is 10,000 + (10,000)(0.05) = $10,500.

For the second 6 months, the interest is based on the $10,500 balance after the first 6 months. So, the balance after 1 year is 10,500 + (10,500)(0.05) = $11,025.

The balance after 1 year can also be written as $10,000 \times \left(1 + \dfrac{0.10}{2}\right)^2$ dollars.

F. To solve some word problems with percents and fractions, you can organize the information in a table.

Example:

In a production lot, 40% of the toys are red, and the rest are green. Half of the toys are small, and half are large. If 10% of the toys are red and small, and 40 toys are green and large, how many of the toys are red and large?

Solution: First make a table to organize the information:

	Red	Green	Total
Small	10%		50%
Large			50%
Total	40%	60%	100%

Then fill in the missing percents so that the "Red" and "Green" percents in each row add up to that row's total, and the "Small" and "Large" percents in each column add up to that column's total:

	Red	Green	Total
Small	10%	40%	50%
Large	30%	20%	50%
Total	40%	60%	100%

The number of large green toys, 40, is 20% of the total number of toys (n), so $0.20n = 40$. Thus, the total number of toys $n = 200$. So, 30% of the 200 toys are red and large. Since (0.3)(200) = 60, we find that 60 of the toys are red and large.

---

6. Rate, Work, and Mixture Problems

A. The distance an object travels is its average speed multiplied by the time it takes to travel that distance. That is, ***distance = rate × time.***

> *Example:*
>
> How many kilometers did a car travel in 4 hours at an average speed of 70 kilometers per hour?
>
> *Solution:* Since distance = rate × time, multiply 70 km/hour × 4 hours to find that the car went 280 kilometers.

B. To find an object's average travel speed, divide the total travel distance by the total travel time.

> *Example:*
>
> On a 600-kilometer trip, a car went half the distance at an average speed of 60 kilometers per hour (kph), and the other half at an average speed of 100 kph. The car didn't stop between the two halves of the trip. What was the car's average speed over the whole trip?
>
> *Solution:* First find the total travel time. For the first 300 kilometers, the car went at 60 kph, taking $\frac{300}{60}$ = 5 hours. For the second 300 kilometers, the car went at 100 kph, taking $\frac{300}{100}$ = 3 hours. So, the total travel time was 5 + 3 = 8 hours. The car's average speed was $\frac{600 \text{ kilometers}}{8 \text{ hours}}$ = 75 kph. Notice the average speed was not $\frac{(60 + 100)}{2}$ = 80 kph.

C. A ***work problem*** usually says how fast certain individuals work alone, then asks you to find how fast they work together, or vice versa.

The basic formula for work problems is $\frac{1}{r} + \frac{1}{s} = \frac{1}{h}$, where r is how long an amount of work takes a certain individual, s is how long that much work takes a different individual, and h is how long that much work takes both individuals working at the same time.

> *Example:*
>
> Suppose one machine takes 4 hours to make 1,000 bolts, and a second machine takes 5 hours to make 1,000 bolts. How many hours do both machines working at the same time take to make 1,000 bolts?
>
> *Solution:*
>
> $$\frac{1}{4} + \frac{1}{5} = \frac{1}{h}$$
>
> $$\frac{5}{20} + \frac{4}{20} = \frac{1}{h}$$
>
> $$\frac{9}{20} = \frac{1}{h}$$
>
> $$9h = 20$$
>
> $$h = \frac{20}{9} = 2\frac{2}{9}$$
>
> Working together, the two machines can make 1,000 bolts in $2\frac{2}{9}$ hours.

If a work problem says how long it takes two individuals to do an amount of work together, and how long it takes one of them to do that much work alone, you can use the same formula to find how long it takes the other individual to do that much work alone.

Example:

Suppose Art and Rita both working at the same time take 4 hours to do an amount of work, and Art alone takes 6 hours to do that much work. Then how many hours does Rita alone take to do that much work?

Solution:

$$\frac{1}{6} + \frac{1}{R} = \frac{1}{4}$$

$$\frac{1}{R} = \frac{1}{4} - \frac{1}{6} = \frac{1}{12}$$

$$R = 12$$

Rita alone takes 12 hours to do that much work.

D. In ***mixture problems***, substances with different properties are mixed, and you must find the mixture's properties.

Example:

If 6 kilograms of nuts that cost $1.20 per kilogram are mixed with 2 kilograms of nuts that cost $1.60 per kilogram, how much does the mixture cost per kilogram?

Solution: The 8 kilograms of nuts cost a total of 6($1.20) + 2($1.60) = $10.40. So, the cost per kilogram of the mixture is $\frac{\$10.40}{8}$ = $1.30.

Some mixture problems use percents.

Example:

How many liters of a solution that is 15% salt must be added to 5 liters of a solution that is 8% salt to make a solution that is 10% salt?

Solution: Let n be the needed number of liters of the 15% solution. The amount of salt in n liters of 15% solution is $0.15n$. The amount of salt in the 5 liters of 8% solution is $(0.08)(5)$. These amounts add up to the amount of salt in the 10% mixture, which is $0.10(n + 5)$. So,

$$0.15n + 0.08(5) = 0.10(n + 5)$$

$$15n + 40 = 10n + 50$$

$$5n = 10$$

$$n = 2 \text{ liters}$$

So, 2 liters of the 15% salt solution must be added to the 8% solution to make the 10% solution.

3.4 Statistics, Sets, Counting, Probability, Estimation, and Series

1. Statistics

A. A common statistical measure is the ***average*** or ***(arithmetic) mean***, a type of center for a set of numbers. The average or mean of n numbers is the sum of the n numbers divided by n.

> *Example:*
>
> The average of the 5 numbers 6, 4, 7, 10, and 4 is $\dfrac{(6 + 4 + 7 + 10 + 4)}{5} = \dfrac{31}{5} = 6.2$.

B. The ***median*** is another type of center for a set of numbers. To find the median of n numbers, list the numbers from least to greatest. If n is odd, the median is the middle number in the list. But if n is even, the median is the average of the two middle numbers. The median may be less than, equal to, or greater than the mean.

> *Example:*
>
> To find the median of the 5 numbers 6, 4, 7, 10, and 4, list them from least to greatest: 4, 4, 6, 7, 10. The median is 6, the middle number in this list.
>
> The median of the 6 numbers 4, 6, 6, 8, 9, and 12 is $\dfrac{(6 + 8)}{2} = 7$. But the mean of these 6 numbers is $\dfrac{(4 + 6 + 6 + 8 + 9 + 12)}{6} = \dfrac{45}{6} = 7.5$.

Often about half the numbers in a set are less than the median, and about half are greater than the median. But not always.

> *Example:*
>
> For the 15 numbers 3, 5, 7, 7, 7, 7, 7, 7, 8, 9, 9, 9, 9, 10, and 10, the median is 7. Only $\dfrac{2}{15}$ of the numbers are less than the median.

C. The ***mode*** of a list of numbers is the number appearing most often in the list.

> *Example:*
>
> The mode of the list of numbers 1, 3, 6, 4, 3, and 5 is 3, since 3 is the only number appearing more than once in the list.

A list may have more than one mode.

> *Example:*
>
> The list 1, 2, 3, 3, 3, 5, 7, 10, 10, 10, and 20 has two modes, 3 and 10.

D. The dispersion of numerical data is how spread out the data is. The simplest measure of dispersion is the *range*, which is the greatest value in the data minus the least value.

> *Example:*
>
> The range of the numbers 11, 10, 5, 13, and 21 is 21 − 5 = 16. Notice the range depends on only 2 of the numbers.

E. Another common measure of dispersion is the ***standard deviation***. Generally, the farther the numbers are from the mean, the greater the standard deviation. To find the standard deviation of n numbers:

(1) Find their mean,

(2) Find the differences between the mean and each of the n numbers,

(3) Square each difference,

(4) Find the average of the squared differences, and

(5) Take the nonnegative square root of this average.

> *Examples:*
>
> Let's use the table below to find the standard deviation of the numbers 0, 7, 8, 10, and 10, which have the mean 7.
>
> | x | $x - 7$ | $(x - 7)^2$ |
> |-----|---------|-------------|
> | 0 | −7 | 49 |
> | 7 | 0 | 0 |
> | 8 | 1 | 1 |
> | 10 | 3 | 9 |
> | 10 | 3 | 9 |
> | | Total | 68 |
>
> The standard deviation is $\sqrt{\dfrac{68}{5}} \approx 3.7$

The standard deviation depends on every number in the set, but more on those farther from the mean. This is why the standard deviation is smaller for a set of data grouped closer around its mean.

As a second example, consider the numbers 6, 6, 6.5, 7.5, and 9, which also have the mean 7. These numbers are grouped closer around the mean 7 than the numbers in the first example. That makes the standard deviation in this second example only about 1.1, far below the standard deviation of 3.7 in the first example.

F. How many times a value occurs in a data set is its *frequency* in the set. When different values have different frequencies, a *frequency distribution* can help show how the values are distributed.

Example:

Consider this set of 20 numbers:

$$-4 \quad 0 \quad 0 \quad -3 \quad -2 \quad -1 \quad -1 \quad 0 \quad -1 \quad -4$$
$$-1 \quad -5 \quad 0 \quad -2 \quad 0 \quad -5 \quad -2 \quad 0 \quad 0 \quad -1$$

We can show its frequency distribution in a table listing each value x and x's frequency f:

Value x	Frequency f
−5	2
−4	2
−3	1
−2	3
−1	5
0	7
Total	20

This frequency distribution table makes finding statistical measures easier:

Mean: $= \dfrac{(-5)(2) + (-4)(2) + (-3)(1) + (-2)(3) + (-1)(5) + (0)(7)}{20} = -1.6$

Median: −1 (the average of the 10th and 11th numbers)

Mode: 0 (the number that occurs most often)

Range: $0 - (-5) = 5$

Standard deviation: $\sqrt{\dfrac{(-5 + 1.6)^2(2) + (-4 + 1.6)^2(2) + \ldots + (0 + 1.6)^2(7)}{20}} \approx 1.7$

---

2. Sets

A. In math, a *set* is a collection of numbers or other things. The things in the set are its *elements*. A list of a set's elements in a pair of braces stands for the set. The list's order doesn't matter.

Example:

$\{-5, 0, 1\}$ is the same set as $\{0, 1, -5\}$. That is, $\{-5, 0, 1\} = \{0, 1, -5\}$.

B. The number of elements in a finite set S is written as $|S|$.

> *Example:*
>
> $S = \{-5, 0, 1\}$ is a set with $|S| = 3$.

C. If all the elements in a set S are also in a set T, then S is a **subset** of T. This is written as $S \subseteq T$ or $T \supseteq S$.

> *Example:*
>
> $\{-5, 0, 1\}$ is a subset of $\{-5, 0, 1, 4, 10\}$. That is, $\{-5, 0, 1\} \subseteq \{-5, 0, 1, 4, 10\}$.

D. The **union** of two sets A and B is the set of all elements that are each in A or in B or both. The union is written as $A \cup B$.

> *Example:*
>
> $\{3, 4\} \cup \{4, 5, 6\} = \{3, 4, 5, 6\}$

E. The **intersection** of two sets A and B is the set of all elements that are each in **both** A and B. The intersection is written as $A \cap B$.

> *Example:*
>
> $\{3, 4\} \cap \{4, 5, 6\} = \{4\}$

F. Two sets sharing no elements are **disjoint** or **mutually exclusive**.

> *Example:*
>
> $\{-5, 0, 1\}$ and $\{4, 10\}$ are disjoint.

G. A **Venn diagram** shows how two or more sets are related. Suppose sets S and T aren't disjoint, and neither is a subset of the other. The Venn diagram below shows their intersection $S \cap T$ as a shaded area.

A Venn Diagram of Two Intersecting Sets

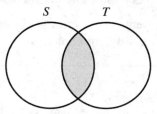

A Venn diagram of sets S and T, with their intersection $S \cap T$ shaded.

H. The number of elements in the union of two finite sets S and T is the number of elements in S, plus the number of elements in T, minus the number of elements in the intersection of S and T. That is, $|S \cup T| = |S| + |T| - |S \cap T|$. This is the ***general addition rule for two sets***.

Example:

$$|\{3, 4\} \cup \{4, 5, 6\}| = |\{3, 4\}| + |\{4, 5, 6\}| - |\{3, 4\} \cap \{4, 5, 6\}| =$$

$$|\{3, 4\}| + |\{4, 5, 6\}| - |\{4\}| = 2 + 3 - 1 = 4.$$

If S and T are disjoint, then $|S \cup T| = |S| + |T|$, since $|S \cap T| = 0$.

I. You can often solve word problems involving sets by using Venn diagrams and the general addition rule.

Example:

Each of 25 students is taking history, mathematics, or both. If 20 of them are taking history and 18 of them are taking mathematics, how many of them are taking both history and mathematics?

Solution: Separate the 25 students into three disjoint sets: the students taking history only, those taking mathematics only, and those taking both history and mathematics. This gives us the Venn diagram below, where n is the number of students taking both courses, $20 - n$ is the number taking history only, and $18 - n$ is the number taking mathematics only.

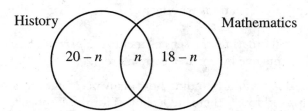

Since there are 25 students total, $(20 - n) + n + (18 - n) = 25$, so $n = 13$. So, 13 students are taking both history and mathematics. Notice that $20 + 18 - 13 = 25$ uses the general addition rule for two sets.

3. Counting Methods

A. To count elements in sets without listing them, you can sometimes use this ***multiplication principle***:

If an object will be chosen from a set of m objects, and another object will be chosen from a disjoint set of n objects, then mn different choices are possible.

> *Example:*
>
> Suppose a meal at a restaurant must include exactly 1 entree and 1 dessert. The entree can be any 1 of 5 options, and the dessert can be any 1 of 3 options. Then $5 \times 3 = 15$ different meals are available.

B. Here's a more general version of the multiplication principle: the number of possible choices of 1 object apiece out of any number of sets is the product of the numbers of objects in those sets. For example, when choosing 1 object apiece out of 3 sets with x, y, and z elements, respectively, xyz different choices are possible. The general multiplication principle also means that when choosing 1 object apiece out of n sets of exactly m objects apiece, m^n different choices are possible.

> *Example:*
>
> Each time a coin is flipped, the 2 possible results are heads and tails. In a set of 8 consecutive coin flips, think of each flip as a set of those 2 possible results. The 8 flips give us 8 of these 2-element sets. So, the set of 8 flips has 2^8 possible results.

C. A concept often used with the multiplication principle is the ***factorial***. For any integer $n > 1$, n factorial is written as $n!$ and is the product of all the integers from 1 through n. Also, by definition, $0! = 1! = 1$.

> *Examples:*
>
> $2! = 2 \times 1 = 2$
>
> $3! = 3 \times 2 \times 1 = 6$
>
> $4! = 4 \times 3 \times 2 \times 1 = 24$, etc.

Two other useful equations with factorials are $n! = (n-1)!(n)$ and $(n+1)! = (n!)(n+1)$.

D. Any sequential ordering of a set's elements is a ***permutation*** of the set. A permutation is a way to choose elements one by one in a certain order.

The factorial is useful for finding how many permutations a set has. If a set of n objects is being ordered from 1st to n^{th}, there are n choices for the 1st object, $n-1$ choices left for the 2nd object, $n-2$ choices left for the 3rd object, and so on, until only 1 choice is left for the nth object. So, by the multiplication principle, a set of n objects has $n(n-1)(n-2)\ldots(3)(2)(1) = n!$ permutations.

> *Example:*
>
> The set of letters A, B, and C has $3! = 6$ permutations: ABC, ACB, BAC, BCA, CAB, and CBA.

E. When $0 \leq k \leq n$, each possible choice of k objects out of n objects is a **combination** of n objects taken k at a time. The number of these combinations is written as $\binom{n}{k}$. This is also the number of k-element subsets of a set with n elements, since the combinations simply are these subsets. It can be calculated as $\binom{n}{k} = \frac{n!}{k!(n-k)!}$. Note that $\binom{n}{k} = \binom{n}{n-k}$.

Example:

The 2-element subsets of $S = \{A, B, C, D, E\}$ are the combinations of the 5 letters in S taken 2 at a time. There are $\binom{5}{2} = \frac{5!}{2!3!} = \frac{120}{(2)(6)} = 10$ of these subsets: $\{A, B\}, \{A, C\}, \{A, D\}, \{A, E\}, \{B, C\}$, $\{B, D\}, \{B, E\}, \{C, D\}, \{C, E\}$, and $\{D, E\}$.

For each of its 2-element subsets, a 5-element set also has exactly one 3-element subset containing the elements not in that 2-element subset. For example, in S the 3-element subset $\{C, D, E\}$ contains the elements not in the 2-element subset $\{A, B\}$, the 3-element subset $\{B, D, E\}$ contains the elements not in the 2-element subset $\{A, C\}$, and so on. This shows that a 5-element set like S has exactly as many 2-element subsets as 3-element subsets, so $\binom{5}{2} = 10 = \binom{5}{3}$.

---

4. Probability

A. Sets and counting methods are also important to **discrete probability**. Discrete probability involves **experiments** with finitely many possible **outcomes**. An **event** is a set of an experiment's possible outcomes.

Example:

Rolling a 6-sided die with faces numbered 1 to 6 is an experiment with six possible outcomes. Let's call these outcomes 1, 2, 3, 4, 5, and 6, each number being the one facing up after the roll. Notice that no two outcomes can occur together. One event in this experiment is that the outcome is 4. This event is written as $\{4\}$.

Another event in the experiment is that the outcome is an odd number. This event has the three outcomes 1, 3, and 5. It is written as $\{1, 3, 5\}$.

B. The probability of an event E is written as $P(E)$ and is a number between 0 and 1, inclusive. If E is an empty set of no possible outcomes, then E is **impossible**, and $P(E) = 0$. If E is the set of all possible outcomes of the experiment, then E is **certain**, and $P(E) = 1$. Otherwise, E is possible but uncertain, and $0 < P(E) < 1$. If F is a subset of E, then $P(F) \leq P(E)$.

C. If the probabilities of two or more outcomes of an experiment are equal, those outcomes are **equally likely**. For an experiment whose outcomes are all equally likely, the probability of an event E is

$$P(E) = \frac{\text{the number of outcomes in } E}{\text{the total number of possible outcomes}}.$$

Example:

In the earlier example of a 6-sided die rolled once, suppose all six outcomes are equally likely. Then each outcome's probability is $\frac{1}{6}$. The probability that the outcome is an odd number is

$$P(\{1, 3, 5\}) = \frac{|\{1, 3, 5\}|}{6} = \frac{3}{6} = \frac{1}{2}.$$

D. Given two events E and F, these further events are defined:

(i) "not E" is the set of outcomes not in E;

(ii) "E or F" is the set of outcomes in E or F or both, that is, $E \cup F$;

(iii) "E and F" is the set of outcomes in both E and F, that is, $E \cup F$.

The probability that E doesn't occur is $P(\text{not } E) = 1 - P(E)$.

The probability that "E or F" occurs is $P(E \text{ or } F) = P(E) + P(F) - P(E \text{ and } F)$. This is based on the general addition rule for two sets, given above in Section 3.4.2.H.

Example:

In the example above of a 6-sided die rolled once, let E be the event $\{1, 3, 5\}$ that the outcome is an odd number. Let F be the event $\{2, 3, 5\}$ that the outcome is a prime number. Then

$P(E \text{ and } F) = P(E \cap F) = P(\{3, 5\}) = \dfrac{|\{3, 5\}|}{6} = \dfrac{2}{6} = \dfrac{1}{3}$. So, $P(E \text{ or } F) = P(E) + P(F) -$
$P(E \text{ and } F) = \dfrac{3}{6} + \dfrac{3}{6} - \dfrac{2}{6} = \dfrac{4}{6} = \dfrac{2}{3}$.

The event "E or F" is $E \cup F = \{1, 2, 3, 5\}$, so $P(E \text{ or } F) = \dfrac{|\{1, 2, 3, 5\}|}{6} = \dfrac{4}{6} = \dfrac{2}{3}$.

Events E and F are **mutually exclusive** if no outcomes are in $E \cap F$. Then the event "E and F" is impossible: $P(E \text{ and } F) = 0$. The special addition rule for the probability of two mutually exclusive events is $P(E \text{ or } F) = P(E) + P(F)$.

E. Two events A and B are **independent** if neither changes the other's probability. The multiplication rule for independent events E and F is $P(E \text{ and } F) = P(E)P(F)$.

Example:

In the example above of the 6-sided die rolled once, let A be the event $\{2, 4, 6\}$ and B be the event $\{5, 6\}$. Then A's probability is $P(A) = \dfrac{|A|}{6} = \dfrac{3}{6} = \dfrac{1}{2}$. The probability of A occurring **if B occurs** is $\dfrac{|A \cap B|}{|B|} = \dfrac{|\{6\}|}{|\{5, 6\}|} = \dfrac{1}{2}$, the same as $P(A)$.

Likewise, B's probability is $P(B) = \dfrac{|B|}{6} = \dfrac{2}{6} = \dfrac{1}{3}$. The probability of B occurring **if A occurs** is $\dfrac{|B \cap A|}{|A|} = \dfrac{\{6\}}{|\{2, 4, 6\}|} = \dfrac{1}{3}$, the same as $P(B)$.

So, neither event changes the other's probability. Thus, A and B are independent. Therefore, by the multiplication rule for independent events, $P(A \text{ and } B) = P(A)P(B) = \left(\dfrac{1}{2}\right)\left(\dfrac{1}{3}\right) = \dfrac{1}{6}$.

Notice the event "A and B" is $A \cap B = \{6\}$, so $P(A \text{ and } B) = P(\{6\}) = \dfrac{1}{6}$.

The general addition rule and the multiplication rule discussed above imply that if E and F are independent, $P(E \text{ or } F) = P(E) + P(F) - P(E)P(F)$.

F. An event A is **dependent** on an event B if B changes the probability of A.

The probability of A occurring if B occurs is written as $P(A|B)$. So, the statement that A is dependent on B can be written as $P(A|B) \neq P(A)$.

A general multiplication rule for any dependent or independent events A and B is $P(A \text{ and } B) = P(A|B)P(B)$.

Example:

In the example of the 6-sided die rolled once, let A be the event $\{4, 6\}$ and B be the event $\{4, 5, 6\}$. Then the probability of A is $P(A) = \dfrac{|A|}{6} = \dfrac{2}{6} = \dfrac{1}{3}$. But the probability that A occurs **if B occurs** is $P(A|B) = \dfrac{|A \cap B|}{|B|} = \dfrac{|\{4, 6\}|}{|\{4, 5, 6\}|} = \dfrac{2}{3}$. Thus, $P(A|B) \neq P(A)$, so A is dependent on B.

Likewise, the probability that B occurs is $P(B) = \dfrac{|B|}{6} = \dfrac{3}{6} = \dfrac{1}{2}$. But the probability that B occurs **if A occurs** is $P(B|A) = \dfrac{|B \cap A|}{|A|} = \dfrac{|\{4, 6\}|}{|\{4, 6\}|} = 1$. Thus, $P(B|A) \neq P(B)$, so B is dependent on A.

In this example, by the general multiplication rule for events, $P(A \text{ and } B) = P(A|B)P(B) = \left(\dfrac{2}{3}\right)\left(\dfrac{1}{2}\right) = \dfrac{1}{3}$. Likewise, $P(A \text{ and } B) = P(B|A)P(A) = (1)\left(\dfrac{1}{3}\right) = \dfrac{1}{3}$.

Notice the event "A and B" is $A \cap B = \{4, 6\} = A$, so $P(A \text{ and } B) = P(\{4, 6\}) = \dfrac{1}{3} = P(A)$.

G. The rules above can be combined for more complex probability calculations.

Example:

In an experiment with events A, B, and C, suppose $P(A) = 0.23$, $P(B) = 0.40$, and $P(C) = 0.85$. Also suppose events A and B are mutually exclusive, and events B and C are independent. Since A and B are mutually exclusive, $P(A \text{ or } B) = P(A) + P(B) = 0.23 + 0.40 = 0.63$.

Since B and C are independent, $P(B \text{ or } C) = P(B) + P(C) - P(B)P(C) = 0.40 + 0.85 - (0.40)(0.85) = 0.91$.

$P(A \text{ or } C)$ and $P(A \text{ and } C)$ can't be found from the information given. But we can find that $P(A) + P(C) = 1.08 > 1$. So, $P(A) + P(C)$ can't equal $P(A \text{ or } C)$, which like any probability cannot be greater than 1. This means that A and C can't be mutually exclusive, and that $P(A \text{ and } C) \geq 0.08$.

Since $A \cap B$ is a subset of A, we can also find that $P(A \text{ and } C) \leq P(A) = 0.23$.

And C is a subset of $A \cup C$, so $P(A \text{ or } C) \geq P(C) = 0.85$.

Thus, we've found that $0.85 \leq P(A \text{ or } C) \leq 1$ and that $0.08 \leq P(A \text{ and } C) \leq 0.23$.

---

5. Estimation

A. Calculating exact answers to complex math questions is often too hard or slow. Estimating the answers by simplifying the questions may be easier and faster.

One way to estimate is to **round** the numbers in the original question: replace each number with a nearby number that has fewer digits.

For any integer n and real number m, you can **round m down** to a multiple of 10^n by deleting all of m's digits to the right of the digit that stands for multiples of 10^n.

To **round m up** to a multiple of 10^n, first add 10^n to m, then round the result down.

To **round m to the nearest** 10^n, first find the digit in m that stands for a multiple of 10^{n-1}. If this digit is 5 or higher, round m up to a multiple of 10^n. Otherwise, round m down to a multiple of 10^n.

Examples:

(i) To round 7651.4 to the nearest hundred (multiple of 10^2), first notice the digit standing for tens (multiples of 10^1) is 5.

Since this digit is 5 or higher, round up:

First add 100 to the original number: 7651.4 + 100 = 7751.4.

Then drop all the digits to the right of the one standing for multiples of 100 to get 7700.

Notice that 7700 is closer to 7651.4 than 7600 is, so 7700 is the nearest 100.

(ii) To round 0.43248 to the nearest thousandth (multiple of 10^{-3}), first notice the digit standing for ten-thousandths (multiples of 10^{-4}) is 4. Since 4 < 5, round down: just drop all the digits to the right of the digit standing for thousandths to get 0.432.

B. Rounding can simplify complex calculations and give rough answers. If you keep more digits of the original numbers, the answers are usually more exact, but the calculations take longer.

Example:

You can estimate the value of $\dfrac{(298.534 + 58.296)}{1.4822 + 0.937 + 0.014679}$ by rounding the numbers in the dividend to the nearest 10 and the numbers in the divisor to the nearest 0.1:

$$\frac{(298.534 + 58.296)}{1.4822 + 0.937 + 0.014679} \approx \frac{300 + 60}{1.5 + 0.9 + 0} = \frac{360}{2.4} = 150$$

C. Sometimes it's easier to estimate by rounding to a multiple of a number other than 10, like the nearest square or cube of an integer.

Examples:

(i) You can estimate the value of $\frac{2447.16}{11.9}$ by noting first that both the dividend and the divisor are near multiples of 12: 2448 and 12. So, $\frac{2447.16}{11.9} \approx \frac{2448}{12} = 204$.

(ii) You can estimate the value of $\sqrt{\frac{8.96}{24.82 \times 4.057}}$ by noting first that each decimal number in the expression is near the square of an integer: $8.96 \approx 9 = 3^2$, $24.82 \approx 25 = 5^2$, and $4.057 \approx 4 = 2^2$. So, $\sqrt{\frac{8.96}{24.82 \times 4.057}} \approx \sqrt{\frac{3^2}{5^2 \times 2^2}} = \sqrt{\frac{3^2}{10^2}} = \frac{3}{10}$.

D. Sometimes finding a *range* of possible values for an expression is more useful than finding a single estimated value. The range's *upper bound* is the smallest number found to be greater than (or no less than) the expression's value. The range's *lower bound* is the largest number found to be less than (or no greater than) the expression's value.

Example:

In the equation $x = \frac{2.32^2 - 2.536}{2.68^2 + 2.79}$, each decimal is greater than 2 and less than 3. So, $\frac{2^2 - 3}{3^2 + 3} < x < \frac{3^2 - 2}{2^2 + 2}$. Simplifying these fractions, we find that x is in the range $\frac{1}{12} < x < \frac{7}{6}$. The range's lower bound is $\frac{1}{12}$, and the upper bound is $\frac{7}{6}$.

6. Sequences and Series

A. A *sequence* is an algebraic function whose domain includes only positive integers. A function $a(n)$ that is a sequence can be written as a_n. Its value a_i for a specific positive integer i is its ith term. The domain of an *infinite sequence* is the set of all positive integers. For any positive integer n, the domain of a *finite sequence of length* n is the set of the first n positive integers. An *arithmetic sequence* has the form $a_n = b + c_n$, where b and c are constants. The first term of an arithmetic sequence is $a_1 = b + c$. For each term a_i, the next term $a_i + 1 = a_i + c$.

Example:

(i) The function $a(n) = n^2 + \left(\frac{n}{5}\right)$ whose domain is the set of all positive integers is an infinite sequence $a_n, \ldots$. Its third term is its value at $n = 3$, which is $a_3 = 3^2 + \frac{3}{5} = 9.6$.

(ii) The same function $a(n) = n^2 + \left(\frac{n}{5}\right)$ restricted to the domain $\{1, 2, 3\}$ is a finite sequence of length 3 whose range is $\{1.2, 4.4, 9.6\}$.

(iii) An infinite sequence like $b_n = (-1)^n(n!)$ can be written out by listing its values in the order $b_1, b_2, b_3, \ldots, b_n, \ldots$; that is, $-1, 2, -6, \ldots, (-1)^n(n!), \ldots$
The value $(-1)^n(n!)$ is the nth term of the sequence.

(iv) The function $a(n) = 2 + 3n$ whose domain is the positive integers is an arithmetic sequence a_n. Its first term is $a_1 = 5$. For any positive integer i, $a_i + 1 = a_i + 3$. Thus, $a_2 = a_1 + 3 = 8$.

B. A *series* is the sum of a sequence's terms.

For an infinite sequence $a(n)$, the ***infinite series*** $\sum\limits_{n=1}^{\infty} a(n)$ is the sum of the sequence's infinitely many terms, $a_1 + a_2 + a_3 + \ldots$

The sum of the first k terms of sequence a_n is called a ***partial sum***. It is written as $\sum\limits_{i=1}^{k} a_i$, or $a_1 + \ldots + a_k$.

Example:

The infinite series based on the function $a(n) = n^2 + \left(\dfrac{n}{5}\right)$ is $\sum\limits_{i=1}^{\infty} n^2 + \left(\dfrac{n}{5}\right)$. It's the sum of the infinitely many terms $\left(1^2 + \dfrac{1}{5}\right) + \left(2^2 + \dfrac{2}{5}\right) + \left(3^2 + \dfrac{3}{5}\right) + \ldots$

The partial sum of the first three terms of the same function $a(n) = n^2 + \left(\dfrac{n}{5}\right)$ is

$$\sum\limits_{i=1}^{3} a_i = \left(1^2 + \dfrac{1}{5}\right) + \left(2^2 + \dfrac{2}{5}\right) + \left(3^2 + \dfrac{3}{5}\right) = 1.2 + 4.4 + 9.6 = 15.2.$$

3.5   Reference Sheets

Arithmetic and Decimals

ABSOLUTE VALUE:

$|x|$ is x if $x \geq 0$ and $-x$ if $x < 0$.

For any x and y, $|x + y| \leq |x| + |y|$.

$\sqrt{x^2} = |x|$.

EVEN AND ODD NUMBERS:

Even × Even = Even	Even × Odd = Even
Odd × Odd = Odd	Even + Even = Even
Even + Odd = Odd	Odd + Odd = Even

ADDITION AND SUBTRACTION:

$x + 0 = x = x - 0$

$x - x = 0$

$x + y = y + x$

$x - y = -(y - x) = -y + x$

$(x + y) + z = x + (y + z)$

If x and y are both positive, then $x + y$ is also positive.

If x and y are both negative, then $x + y$ is negative.

DECIMALS:

Add or subtract decimals by lining up their decimal points:

17.6512	653.2700
+ 653.2700	−17.6512
670.9212	635.6188

To multiply decimal A by decimal B:

First, ignore the decimal points, and multiply A and B as if they were integers.

Next, if decimal A has n digits to the right of its decimal point, and decimal B has m digits to the right of its decimal point, place the decimal point in $A \times B$ so it has $m + n$ digits to its right.

To divide decimal A by decimal B, first move the decimal points of A and B equally many digits to the right until B is an integer, then divide as you would integers.

QUOTIENTS AND REMAINDERS:

The quotient q and the remainder r of dividing positive integer x by positive integer y are unique positive integers such that

$y = xq + r$ and $0 \leq r < x$.

The remainder r is 0 if and only if y is divisible by x. Then x is a factor of y.

MULTIPLICATION AND DIVISION:

$x \times 1 = x = \dfrac{x}{1}$

$x \times 0 = 0$

If $x \neq 0$, then $\dfrac{x}{x} = 1$.

$\dfrac{x}{0}$ is undefined.

$xy = yx$

If $x \neq 0$ and $y \neq 0$, then $\dfrac{x}{y} = \dfrac{1}{\left(\frac{y}{x}\right)}$.

$(xy)z = x(yz)$

$xy + xz = x(y + z)$

If $y \neq 0$, then $\left(\dfrac{x}{y}\right) + \left(\dfrac{z}{y}\right) = \dfrac{(x + z)}{y}$

If x and y are both positive, then xy is also positive.

If x and y are both negative, then xy is positive.

If x is positive and y is negative, then xy is negative.

If $xy = 0$, then $x = 0$ or $y = 0$, or both.

SCIENTIFIC NOTATION:

To convert a number in scientific notation $A \times 10^n$ into regular decimal notation, move A's decimal point n places to the right if n is positive, or $|n|$ places to the left if n is negative.

To convert a decimal to scientific notation, move the decimal point n spaces so that exactly one nonzero digit is to its left. Multiply the result by 10^n if you moved the decimal point to the left or by 10^{-n} if you moved it to the right.

Exponents

SQUARES, CUBES, AND SQUARE ROOTS:

Every positive number has two real square roots, one positive and the other negative. The table below shows the positive square roots rounded to the nearest hundredth.

n	n^2	n^3	$\sqrt{n}$
1	1	1	1
2	4	8	1.41
3	9	27	1.73
4	16	64	2
5	25	125	2.24
6	36	216	2.45
7	49	343	2.65
8	64	512	2.83
9	81	729	3
10	100	1,000	3.16

EXPONENTIATION:

Formula	Example
$x^1 = x$	$2^1 = 2$
$x^0 = 1$	$2^0 = 1$
If $x \neq 0$, then $x^{-1} = \frac{1}{x}$.	$2^{-1} = \frac{1}{2}$
If $x > 1$ and $y > 1$, then $x^y > x$.	$2^3 = 8 > 2$
If $0 < x < 1$ and $y > 1$, then $x^y < x$.	$0.2^3 = 0.008 < 0.2$
$(x^y)^z = x^{yz} = (x^z)^y$	$(2^3)^4 = 2^{12} = (2^4)^3$
$x^{y+z} = x^y x^z$	$2^7 = 2^3 2^4$
If $x \neq 0$, then $x^{y-z} = \frac{x^y}{x^z}$.	$2^{5-3} = \frac{2^5}{2^3}$
$(xz)^y = x^y z^y$	$6^4 = 2^4 3^4$
If $z \neq 0$, then $\left(\frac{x}{z}\right)^y = \frac{x^y}{z^y}$	$\left(\frac{3}{4}\right)^2 = \frac{3^2}{4^2} = \frac{9}{16}$
If $z \neq 0$, then $x^{\frac{y}{z}} = (x^y)^{\frac{1}{z}} = (x^{\frac{1}{z}})^y$.	$4^{\frac{2}{3}} = (4^2)^{\frac{1}{3}} = (4^{\frac{1}{3}})^2$

Algebraic Expressions and Linear Equations

TRANSLATING WORDS INTO MATH OPERATIONS:

$x + y$	$x - y$	xy	$\dfrac{x}{y}$	x^y
x added to y *x increased by y* *x more than y* *x plus y* *the sum of x and y* *the total of x and y*	*x decreased by y* *difference of x and y* *y fewer than x* *y less than x* *x minus y* *x reduced by y* *y subtracted from x*	*x multiplied by y* *the product of x and y* *x times y* If $y = 2$: *double x* *twice x* If $y = 3$: *triple x*	*x divided by y* *x over y* *the quotient of x and y* *the ratio of x to y* If $y = 2$: *half of x* *x halved*	*x to the power of y* *x to the yth power* If $y = 2$: *x squared* If $y = 3$: *x cubed*

MANIPULATING ALGEBRAIC EXPRESSIONS:

Technique	Example
Factor to combine like terms	$3xy - 9y = 3y(x - 3)$
Divide out common factors	$\dfrac{(3xy - 9y)}{(x - 3)} = \dfrac{3y(x - 3)}{(x - 3)} = 3y(1) = 3y$
Multiply two expressions by multiplying each term of one expression by each term of the other	$(3x - 4)(9y + x) = 3x(9y + x) - 4(9y + x)$ $= 3x(9y) + 3x(x) - 4(9y) - 4(x)$ $= 27xy + 3x^2 - 36y - 4x$
Substitute constants for variables	If $x = 3$ and $y = -2$, then $3xy - x^2 + y =$ $3(3)(-2) - (3)^2 + (-2) = -18 - 9 - 2 = -29.$

SOLVING LINEAR EQUATIONS:

Technique	Example
Isolate a variable on one side of an equation by doing the same operations on both sides of the equation.	Solve the equation $\frac{(5x-6)}{3} = 4$ like this: (1) Multiply both sides by 3 to get $5x - 6 = 12$. (2) Add 6 to both sides to get $5x = 18$. (3) Divide both sides by 5 to get $x = \frac{18}{5}$.
To solve two equations with two variables x and y: (1) Express x in terms of y using one of the equations. (2) Substitute that expression for x to make the second equation have only the variable y. (3) Solve the second equation for y. (4) Substitute the solution for y into the first equation to solve for x.	Solve the equations A: $x - y = 2$ and B: $3x + 2y = 11$: (1) From A, $x = 2 + y$. (2) In B, substitute $2 + y$ for x to get $3(2 + y) + 2y = 11$. (3) Solve B for y: $6 + 3y + 2y = 11$ $6 + 5y = 11$ $5y = 5$ $y = 1$ (4) Since $y = 1$, from A we find $x = 2 + 1 = 3$.
Alternative technique: (1) Multiply both sides of one equation or both equations so that the coefficients on y have the same absolute value in both equations. (2) Add or subtract the two equations to remove y and solve for x. (3) Substitute the solution for x into the first equation to find the value of y.	Solve the equations A: $x - y = 2$ and B: $3x + 2y = 11$: (1) Multiply both sides of A by 2 to get $2x - 2y = 4$. (2) Add the equation in (1) to equation B: $2x - 2y + 3x + 2y = 4 + 11$ $5x = 15$ $x = 3$ (3) Since $x = 3$, from A we find $3 - y = 2$, so $y = 1$.

Factoring, Quadratic Equations, and Inequalities

SOLVING EQUATIONS BY FACTORING:

Techniques	Example
(1) Start with a polynomial equation. (2) Add or subtract from both sides until 0 is on one side of the equation. (3) Write the nonzero side as a product of factors. (4) Set each factor to 0 to find simple equations giving the solution to the original equation.	$x^3 - 2x^2 + x = -5(x-1)^2$ $x^3 - 2x^2 + x + 5(x-1)^2 = 0$ (i) $x(x^2 - 2x + 1) + 5(x-1)^2 = 0$ (ii) $x(x-1)^2 + 5(x-1)^2 = 0$ (iii) $(x+5)(x-1)^2 = 0$ $x + 5 = 0$ or $x - 1 = 0$. So, $x = -5$ or $x = 1$.

FORMULAS FOR FACTORING:

$$a^2 - b^2 = (a-b)(a+b)$$
$$a^2 + 2ab + b^2 = (a+b)(a+b)$$
$$a^2 - 2ab + b^2 = (a-b)(a-b)$$

THE QUADRATIC FORMULA:

For any quadratic equation $ax^2 + bx + c = 0$ with $a \neq 0$, the roots are

$$x = \frac{-b + \sqrt{b^2 - 4ac}}{2a} \text{ and } x = \frac{-b - \sqrt{b^2 - 4ac}}{2a}$$

These roots are two distinct real numbers if $b^2 - 4ac \geq 0$.

If $b^2 - 4ac = 0$, the equation has only one root: $\frac{-b}{2a}$.

If $b^2 - 4ac < 0$, the equation has no real roots.

SOLVING INEQUALITIES:

Explanation	Example
As in solving an equation, the same number can be added to or subtracted from both sides of the inequality, or both sides can be multiplied or divided by a positive number, without changing the order of the inequality. But multiplying or dividing an inequality by a negative number reverses the order of the inequality. Thus, $6 > 2$, but $(-1)(6) < (-1)(2)$.	To solve the inequality $\frac{(5x-1)}{-2} < 3$ for x, isolate x: (1) $5x - 1 > -6$ (multiplying both sides by -2, reversing the order of the inequality) (2) $5x > -5$ (add 1 to both sides) (3) $x > -1$ (divide both sides by 5)

LINES IN THE COORDINATE PLANE:

An equation $y = mx + b$ defines a line with slope m whose y-intercept is b.

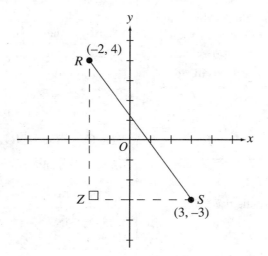

For a line through two points (x_1, y_1) and (x_2, y_2) with $x_1 \neq x_2$, the slope is $m = \dfrac{(y_2 - y_1)}{(x_2 - x_1)}$. Given the known

point (x_1, y_1) and the slope m, any other point (x, y) on the line satisfies the equation $m = \dfrac{(y - y_1)}{(x - x_1)}$.

Above, the line's slope is $\dfrac{(-3 - 4)}{(3 - (-2))} = -\dfrac{7}{5}$. To find an equation of the line, we can use the point $(3, -3)$:

$$y - (-3) = \left(-\frac{7}{5}\right)(x - 3)$$

$$y + 3 = \left(-\frac{7}{5}\right)x + \frac{21}{5}$$

$$y = \left(-\frac{7}{5}\right)x + \frac{6}{5}$$

So, the y-intercept is $\dfrac{6}{5}$.

Find the x-intercept like this:

$$0 = \left(-\frac{7}{5}\right)x + \frac{6}{5}$$

$$\left(\frac{7}{5}\right)x = \frac{6}{5}$$

$$x = \frac{6}{7}$$

The graph shows both these intercepts.

Rates, Ratios, and Percents

FRACTIONS:

Equivalent or Equal Fractions:

Two fractions stand for the same number if dividing each fraction's numerator and denominator by their greatest common divisor makes the fractions identical.

Adding, Subtracting, Multiplying, and Dividing Fractions:

$$\frac{a}{b} + \frac{c}{d} = \frac{ad}{bd} + \frac{bc}{bd}; \frac{a}{b} - \frac{c}{d} = \frac{ad}{bd} - \frac{bc}{bd}$$

$$\frac{a}{b} \times \frac{c}{d} = \frac{ac}{bd}; \frac{a}{b} \div \frac{c}{d} = \frac{ad}{bc}$$

MIXED NUMBERS:

A mixed number of the form $a\frac{b}{c}$ equals the fraction $\frac{ac + b}{c}$.

RATE:

distance = rate × time

PROFIT:

Gross profit = Revenues − Expenses, or

Gross profit = Selling price − Cost.

INTEREST:

Simple annual interest =

(principal) × (interest rate) × (time)

Compound interest over n periods =

(principal) × (1 + interest per period)^n − principal

PERCENTS:

$x\% = \frac{x}{100}$.

$x\%$ of y equals $\frac{xy}{100}$.

To convert a percent to a decimal, drop the percent sign, then move the decimal point two digits left.

To convert a decimal to a percent, add a percent sign, then move the decimal point two digits right.

PERCENT INCREASE OR DECREASE:

The percent increase from x to y is $100\left(\frac{y - x}{x}\right)\%$.

The percent decrease from x to y is $100\left(\frac{x - y}{x}\right)\%$.

DISCOUNTS:

A price discounted by n percent becomes $(100 - n)$ percent of the original price.

A price discounted by n percent and then by m percent becomes $(100 - n)(100 - m)$ percent of the original price.

WORK:

$\frac{1}{r} + \frac{1}{s} = \frac{1}{h}$, where r is how long one individual takes to do an amount of work, s is how long a second individual takes to do that much work, and h is how long they take to do that much work when both are working at the same time.

MIXTURES:

	Number of units of a substance or mixture	Amount of an ingredient per unit of the substance or mixture	Total amount of that ingredient in the substance or mixture
Substance A	X	M	X × M
Substance B	Y	N	Y × N
Mixture of A and B	X + Y	$\frac{(X \times M) + (Y \times N)}{X + Y}$	(X × M) + (Y × N)

Statistics, Sets, and Counting Methods

STATISTICS:

Concept	Definition for a set of n numbers ordered from least to greatest	Example with data set $\{4, 4, 5, 7, 10\}$
Mean	The sum of the n numbers, divided by n	$\frac{(4 + 4 + 5 + 7 + 10)}{5} = \frac{30}{5} = 6$
Median	The middle number if n is odd; The mean of the two middle numbers if n is even.	5 is the middle number in $\{4, 4, 5, 7, 10\}$.
Mode	The number that appears most often in the set	4 is the only number that appears more than once in $\{4, 4, 5, 7, 10\}$.
Range	The largest number in the set minus the smallest	$10 - 4 = 6$
Standard Deviation	Calculate like this: (1) Find the arithmetic mean, (2) Find the differences between each of the n numbers and the mean, (3) Square each of the differences, (4) Find the average of the squared differences, and (5) Take the nonnegative square root of this average.	(1) The mean is 6. (2) $-2, -2, -1, 1, 4$ (3) $4, 4, 1, 1, 16$ (4) $\frac{26}{5} = 5.2$ (5) $\sqrt{5.2}$

SETS:

Concept	Notation for finite sets S and T	Example
Number of elements	$|S|$	$S = \{-5, 0, 1\}$ is a set with $|S| = 3$.
Subset	$S \subseteq T$ (S is a subset of T); $S \supseteq T$ (T is a subset of S)	$\{-5, 0, 1\}$ is a subset of $\{-5, 0, 1, 4, 10\}$.
Union	$S \cup T$	$\{3, 4\} \cup \{4, 5, 6\} = \{3, 4, 5, 6\}$
Intersection	$S \cap T$	$\{3, 4\} \cap \{4, 5, 6\} = \{4\}$
The general addition rule for two sets	$|S \cup T| = |S| + |T| - |S \cap T|$	$|\{3, 4\} \cup \{4, 5, 6\}| =$ $|\{3, 4\}| + |\{4, 5, 6\}| - |\{3, 4\} \cap \{4, 5, 6\}| =$ $|\{3, 4\}| + |\{4, 5, 6\}| - |\{4\}| = 2 + 3 - 1 = 4$.

COUNTING METHODS:

Concept and Equations	Examples
Multiplication Principle: The number of possible choices of 1 element apiece from the sets $A_1, A_2, \ldots, A_n$ is $\lvert A_1 \rvert \times \lvert A_2 \rvert \times \ldots \times \lvert A_n \rvert$.	The number of possible choices of 1 element apiece from the sets $S = \{-5, 0, 1\}$, $T = \{3, 4\}$, and $U = \{3, 4, 5, 6\}$ is $\lvert S \rvert \times \lvert T \rvert \times \lvert U \rvert = 3 \times 2 \times 4 = 24$.
Factorial: $n! = n \times (n - 1) \times \ldots \times 1$ $0! = 1! = 1$ $n! = (n - 1)!(n)$	$4! = 4 \times 3 \times 2 \times 1 = 24$ $4! = 3! \times 4$
Permutations: A set of n objects has $n!$ permutations	The set of letters A, B, and C has $3! = 6$ permutations: ABC, ACB, BAC, BCA, CAB, and CBA.
Combinations: The number of possible choices of k objects from a set of n objects is $\binom{n}{k} = \dfrac{n!}{k!(n - k)!}$.	The number of 2-element subsets of set $\{A, B, C, D, E\}$ is $$\binom{5}{2} = \frac{5!}{2!3!} = \frac{120}{(2)(6)} = 10.$$ The 10 subsets are: $\{A, B\}, \{A, C\}, \{A, D\}, \{A, E\}, \{B, C\}, \{B, D\}, \{B, E\}, \{C, D\}, \{C, E\},$ and $\{D, E\}$.

Probability, Sequences, and Partial Sums

PROBABILITY:

Concept	Definition, Notation, and Equations	Example: Rolling a die with 6 numbered sides once
Event	A set of outcomes of an experiment	The event of the outcome being an odd number is the set $\{1, 3, 5\}$.
Probability	The probability $P(E)$ of an event E is a number between 0 and 1, inclusive. If each outcome is equally likely, $P(E) =$ $\dfrac{\text{(the number of possible outcomes in E)}}{\text{(the total number of possible outcomes)}}$.	If the 6 outcomes are equally likely, the probability of each outcome is $\frac{1}{6}$. The probability that the outcome is an odd number is $P(\{1, 3, 5\}) =$ $\dfrac{|\{1, 3, 5\}|}{6} = \dfrac{3}{6} = \dfrac{1}{2}$.
Conditional Probability	The probability that E occurs if F occurs is $P(E\|F) = \dfrac{|E \cap F|}{|F|}$.	$P(\{1, 3, 5\}\|\{1, 2\}) = \dfrac{|\{1\}|}{|\{1, 2\}|} = \dfrac{1}{2}$
Not E	The set of outcomes not in event E: $P(\text{not } E) = 1 - P(E)$.	$P(\text{not}\{3\}) = \dfrac{6 - 1}{6} = \dfrac{5}{6}$
E and F	The set of outcomes in both E and F, that is, $E \cap F$; $P(E \text{ and } F) = P(E \cap F) = P(E\|F)\,P(F)$.	For $E = \{1, 3, 5\}$ and $F = \{2, 3, 5\}$: $P(E \text{ and } F) = P(E \cap F) = P(\{3, 5\}) =$ $\dfrac{|\{3, 5\}|}{6} = \dfrac{2}{6} = \dfrac{1}{3}$
E or F	The set of outcomes in E or F or both, that is, $E \cup F$; $P(E \text{ or } F) = P(E) + P(F) - P(E \text{ and } F)$.	For $E = \{1, 3, 5\}$ and $F = \{2, 3, 5\}$: $P(E \text{ or } F) = P(E) + P(F) - P(E \text{ and } F)$ $= \dfrac{3}{6} + \dfrac{3}{6} - \dfrac{2}{6} = \dfrac{4}{6} = \dfrac{2}{3}$.
Dependent and Independent Events	E is dependent on F if $P(E\|F) \neq P(E)$. E and F are independent if neither is dependent on the other. If E and F are independent, $P(E \text{ and } F) = P(E)P(F)$.	For $E = \{2, 4, 6\}$ and $F = \{5, 6\}$: $P(E\|F) = P(E) = \dfrac{1}{2}$, and $P(F\|E) = P(F) = \dfrac{1}{3}$, so E and F are independent. Thus $P(E \text{ and } F) = P(E)P(F) = \left(\dfrac{1}{2}\right)\left(\dfrac{1}{3}\right) = \dfrac{1}{6}$.

SEQUENCE:

An algebraic function whose domain contains only positive integers.

Example: Function $a(n) = n^2 + \left(\dfrac{n}{5}\right)$ with the domain of all positive integers $n = 1, 2, 3, \ldots$ is an infinite sequence a_n.

PARTIAL SUM:

The sum $\displaystyle\sum_{i=1}^{k} a_i$ of the first k terms of series a_n is a partial sum of the series.

Example: For the function $a(n) = n^2 + \left(\dfrac{n}{5}\right)$, the partial sum of the first three terms is

$$\sum_{i=1}^{3} a_i = \left(1^2 + \dfrac{1}{5}\right) + \left(2^2 + \dfrac{2}{5}\right) + \left(3^2 + \dfrac{3}{5}\right).$$

To register for the GMAT™ exam, go to www.mba.com/register

4.0   Verbal Review

4.0 Verbal Review

To prepare for the GMAT™ exam's Verbal Reasoning section and Data Insights section, and to succeed in graduate business programs, you need basic skills in analyzing and evaluating texts and the ideas they express. This chapter explains concepts to help you develop these skills. This is only a brief overview. So, if you find unfamiliar terms or concepts, consult outside resources to learn more.

The sections below can help you develop skills you need for the Verbal Reasoning and Data Insights sections of the GMAT exam.

Section 4.1, "Analyzing Passages," includes:

1. Arguments
2. Explanations and Plans
3. Narratives and Descriptions

Section 4.2, "Inductive Reasoning," includes:

1. Inductive Arguments
2. Generalizations and Predictions
3. Causal Reasoning
4. Analogies

Section 4.3, "Deductive Reasoning," includes:

1. Deductive Arguments
2. Logical Operators
3. Reasoning with Logical Operators
4. Necessity, Probability, and Possibility
5. Quantifiers
6. Reasoning with Quantifiers

4.1 Analyzing Passages

1. Arguments

A. An *argument* gives one or more ideas as reasons to accept one or more other ideas. Often some of these ideas are implied but not stated.

> *Example:*
>
> The sidewalk is dry, so it must not have rained last night.
>
> This argument gives the observation that the sidewalk is dry as a reason to accept that it didn't rain last night. The argument implies but doesn't say that rain typically leaves sidewalks wet.

B. A *premise* is an idea that an argument gives as a reason to accept another idea. An argument can have any number of premises.

The words and phrases below often mark premises:

after all	*for one thing*	*moreover*
because	*furthermore*	*seeing that*
for	*given that*	*since*
for the reason that	*in light of the fact that*	*whereas*

Example:

Our mayor shouldn't support the proposal to expand the freeway **because** the expansion's benefits wouldn't justify the costs. **Furthermore**, most voters oppose the expansion.

This is an argument with two stated premises. The word *because* marks the first premise, that the expansion's benefits wouldn't justify the costs. The word *furthermore* marks the second premise, that most voters oppose the expansion. These premises are given as reasons the mayor shouldn't support the proposal.

C. A *conclusion* is an idea an argument supports with one or more premises. An *intermediate conclusion* is a conclusion the argument uses to support another conclusion. A *main conclusion* is a conclusion the argument doesn't use to support any other conclusion.

The words and phrases below often mark conclusions:

clearly	*it follows that*	*suggests that*
entails that	*proves*	*surely*
hence	*shows that*	*therefore*
implies that	*so*	*thus*

Example:

Julia just hiked fifteen kilometers, **so** she must have burned a lot of calories. **Surely**, she's hungry now.

This argument has a premise, an intermediate conclusion, and a main conclusion. The word *so* marks the intermediate conclusion: that Julia must have burned a lot of calories. The word *surely* marks the main conclusion: that Julia is hungry now. The premise that Julia just hiked fifteen kilometers supports the intermediate conclusion, which in turn supports the main conclusion.

Conclusions may be stated before, between, or after premises. Sometimes no marker words show which statements are premises and which are conclusions. To find premises and conclusions without marker words, consider which statements the author gives as reasons to accept which other statements. The reasons given are the premises. The ideas the author tries to persuade readers to accept are the conclusions.

Example:

For healthy eating, Healthful Brand Donuts are the best donuts you can buy. Unlike any other donuts on the market, Healthful Brand Donuts have plenty of fiber and natural ingredients.

In this argument, the author tries to persuade the reader that Healthful Brand Donuts are the best donuts to buy for healthy eating. So, the first sentence is the conclusion. The statement about Healthful Brand Donuts' ingredients is a premise because it's given as a reason to accept the conclusion. Since the author's intent is clear, no marker words are needed.

D. A *valid* argument is one whose conclusions follow from its premises. A valid argument can have false premises and conclusions. In a valid argument with false premises, the conclusion **would** follow if the premises **were** true.

A *sound* argument is a valid argument with true premises. Since a sound argument's premises are true, and its conclusions follow from those premises, its conclusions must also be true.

Examples:

(i) Everyone who tries fried eggplant is guaranteed to love the taste. So, if you try it, you'll love the taste too.

In example (i), the premise is false: not everyone who tries fried eggplant is guaranteed to love the taste. So, example (i) is not a sound argument. But it is a valid argument because if everyone who tried fried eggplant **were** guaranteed to love the taste, it would follow that you, too, would love the taste if **you** tried it.

(ii) Some people who try fried eggplant dislike the taste. So, if you try it, you'll probably dislike the taste too.

In example (ii), the premise is true: some people who try fried eggplant do dislike the taste. However, example (ii) is an invalid argument, so it's not sound. **Some** people dislike the taste of fried eggplant, but that does not mean **you personally** will **probably** dislike the taste.

E. An *assumption* is an idea taken for granted. An assumption may be a premise in an argument, a claim about a cause or effect in a causal explanation, a condition a plan relies on, or any other type of idea taken for granted. A conclusion is never an assumption—an argument doesn't take a conclusion for granted, but rather gives reasons to accept it.

A passage may also have *implicit assumptions* the author considers too obvious to state. These unstated ideas fill logical gaps between the passage's statements.

An argument, plan, or explanation with implausible assumptions is weak and vulnerable to criticism.

F. A *necessary assumption* of an argument is an idea that must be true for the argument's stated premises to be good enough reasons to accept its conclusions. That is, a necessary assumption is one the argument needs in order to work.

Example:

Mario has booked a flight scheduled to arrive at 5:00 p.m.—which should let him get here by around 6:30 p.m. So, by 7:00 p.m. we'll be going out to dinner with Mario.

In this argument, one necessary assumption is that the flight Mario booked will arrive not much later than scheduled. A second necessary assumption is that Mario caught his flight. Unless these and all the argument's other necessary assumptions are true, the argument's stated premises aren't good enough reasons to accept the conclusion.

G. A *sufficient assumption* of an argument is an idea whose truth would make the argument's main conclusion follow from the stated premises. That is, adding a sufficient assumption to an argument makes the argument valid.

> *Example:*
>
> The study of poetry is entirely without value since poetry has no practical use.
>
> In this argument, one sufficient assumption is that studying anything with no practical use is entirely without value. This assumption, together with the argument's stated premise, is enough to make the conclusion follow. If both the premise and the assumption are true, the conclusion must also be true. But this sufficient assumption is not a necessary assumption.

H. Arguments are often classified based on what kinds of conclusions they have.

> i. A *prescriptive* argument has a conclusion about what should or shouldn't be done. Prescriptive arguments may advocate for or against policies, procedures, strategies, goals, laws, or ethical norms.

> *Example:*
>
> Our company's staff is too small to handle our upcoming project. So, to make sure the project succeeds, the company **should** hire more employees.
>
> Another example of a prescriptive argument is shown above in Section 4.1.1.B. That argument is prescriptive because it concludes that the mayor ***should not*** support the proposed freeway expansion.

> ii. An *evaluative* argument concludes that something is good or bad, desirable or undesirable, without advocating any particular policy or actions.

> *Example:*
>
> This early novel is clearly one of the greatest of all time. Not only did it pioneer brilliantly innovative narrative techniques, but it did so with exceptional grace, subtlety, and sophistication.

> iii. An *interpretive* argument has a conclusion about something's underlying significance. An interpretive argument may be about the meaning, importance, or implications of observations, a theory, an artistic or literary work, or a historical event.

> *Example:*
>
> Many famous authors have commented emphatically on this early novel, either praising or condemning it. This suggests the novel has had an enormous influence on later fiction.

iv. A *causal* argument concludes that one or more factors did or did not contribute to one or more effects. A causal argument may be about the causes, reasons, or motivations for an event, condition, decision, or outcome. For example, a causal argument may support or oppose an account of the influences behind a literary or artistic style or movement.

> *Example:*
>
> Our houseplant started to thrive only when we moved it to a sunny window. So, probably the reason it was sickly before then was that it wasn't getting enough sunlight.
>
> Another causal argument can be found in the example in Section 4.1.1.C above, which concludes that Julia must be hungry now.

v. A basic *factual* argument has a factual conclusion that doesn't fit in any other category explained above.

> *Example:*
>
> All dogs are mammals. Rover is a dog. Therefore, Rover is a mammal.

2. Explanations and Plans

A. A *causal explanation* claims that one or more factors contribute to one or more effects. A causal explanation might not be an argument. It might have no premises or conclusions. But a causal explanation can be a premise or conclusion in an argument.

The words and phrases below often mark a causal explanation:

as a result	*due to*	*results in*
because	*leads to*	*that's why*
causes	*produces*	*thereby*
contributes to	*responsible for*	*thus*

Some of these words can also mark premises or conclusions in arguments. To tell what the words mark, you may have to judge whether the author is giving reasons to accept a conclusion or only saying what causes an effect. If the author is only saying what causes an effect, without trying to persuade the reader that the effect is real, then the passage is a causal explanation but not an argument.

Just as an argument may have premises, intermediate conclusions, and main conclusions, a causal explanation may claim that one or more factors cause one or more intermediate effects that, in turn, cause further effects.

Example:

Julia just hiked fifteen kilometers, **thereby** burning a lot of calories. **That's why** she's hungry now.

This is a causal explanation claiming that a factor (Julia's fifteen-kilometer hike) caused an intermediate effect (Julia burning a lot of calories) that, in turn, caused another effect (Julia being hungry now). The word *thereby* marks the intermediate effect, and the phrase *that's why* marks the final effect. This explanation doesn't try to convince the reader that Julia's hungry. It just explains what made her hungry. So, it's not an argument.

B. An *observation* is a claim that something was observed or is otherwise directly known. In the example of a causal explanation above, the claims that Julia just hiked fifteen kilometers and that she's hungry are observations. But if her burning of calories was not directly known or observed, the claim that she burned a lot of calories is not an observation.

C. A *hypothesis* is a tentative idea neither known nor assumed to be true. A hypothesis can be an argument's conclusion. Causal explanations are often hypotheses. A passage may discuss *alternative hypotheses*, such as competing explanations for the same observation. Sometimes a passage gives pros and cons of alternative hypotheses without arguing for any particular hypothesis as a conclusion.

Example:

A bush in our yard just died. The invasive insects we've seen around the yard lately might be the cause. Or the bush might not have gotten enough water. It's been a dry summer.

This example presents two alternative hypotheses. The first hypothesis gives the observation that invasive insects have been in the yard as a possible causal explanation for the bush's observed death. This hypothesis assumes the insects can hurt bushes like the one in the yard. The second hypothesis provides the observation that it's been a dry summer as an alternative causal explanation for the bush's observed death. This hypothesis assumes dry weather can result in bushes getting too little water. The passage presents observations to tentatively support each hypothesis. But it doesn't argue for either hypothesis as a conclusion.

D. A *plan* describes an imagined set of actions meant to work together to achieve one or more goals. A plan is not itself an argument. Its actions aren't proposed as reasons to accept a goal, but rather as ways to reach the goal. However, a prescriptive argument may recommend or oppose a plan. A plan may also be among an argument's premises.

Just as an argument may have premises, intermediate conclusions, and main conclusions, a plan may suggest actions to reach intermediate goals that, in turn, are meant to help achieve main goals. And like an argument, a plan may have assumptions, including necessary and sufficient assumptions. A necessary assumption of a plan is one that must be true for the plan to achieve its goals. And a sufficient assumption of a plan is one whose truth guarantees the plan would achieve its goals if followed.

A plan is not a causal explanation. The actions a plan suggests haven't been done yet, so they can't have caused anything. However, any plan does assume possible future causal links between its proposed actions and its goals.

> *Example:*
>
> To repaint our house, we'll need to buy gallons of paint. To do that, we could go to the hardware store.
>
> In this plan, going to the hardware store is an action imagined to help reach the intermediate goal of getting gallons of paint. The intermediate goal is imagined to help reach the main goal of repainting the house. This plan isn't itself an argument. But, combined with the premise that we **should** repaint the house, the plan could be part of a prescriptive argument that we **should** go to the hardware store.

3. Narratives and Descriptions

A. A *narrative* describes a sequence of related events. A narrative is not an argument, an explanation, or a plan. But it may contain one or more arguments, causal explanations, or plans—or be contained in them.

The words and phrases below often show narrative sequence:

after	*earlier*	*then*
afterwards	*later*	*thereafter*
before	*previously*	*until*
beforehand	*since*	*while*
during	*subsequently*	*when*

> *Example:*
>
> **While** Julia was hiking fifteen kilometers, she burned a lot of calories. **Afterwards**, she felt hungry.
>
> This narrative describes a sequence of three events. The word *while* shows that Julia's hike and her burning of calories happened at the same time. The word *afterwards* shows that her hunger arose soon after the first two events. Although you can reasonably assume these events were causally linked, the narrative doesn't say they were. So, it's not an explicit causal explanation. And since the narrative doesn't report the events as reasons to accept a particular conclusion, it's not an argument either.

B. Not all passages are arguments, causal explanations, plans, or narratives. Some passages report on views, findings, innovations, places, societies, artistic works, devices, organisms, etc., without arguing for a conclusion, explaining what caused what, suggesting actions to reach a goal, or narrating what happened.

C. Likewise, not all statements in passages are premises, conclusions, observations to be explained, hypotheses, or reports of events. Statements in passages can also:

- Give background information to help the reader understand the rest of the passage
- Describe details of something that the passage is discussing
- Express the author's attitude toward material in the passage
- Provide examples to illustrate general statements
- Summarize ideas that the passage is arguing against

4.2 Inductive Reasoning

1. Inductive Arguments

A. In an ***inductive argument***, the premises are meant to support a conclusion but not to fully prove it. For example, the premises may just be meant to give evidence that the conclusion is **probably** true, leaving a chance that the conclusion is false despite that evidence.

B. An inductive argument may be ***strengthened*** by adding reasons that directly support the conclusion or that help the argument's premises better support the conclusion. Conversely, an inductive argument may be ***weakened*** by adding reasons that directly cast doubt on the argument's conclusion, or that make the argument's premises less effective at supporting the conclusion. Below, we discuss how various types of inductive arguments are evaluated, strengthened, and weakened.

2. Generalizations and Predictions

A. An argument by ***generalization*** often uses premises about a sample of a population to support a conclusion about the whole population.

> *Example:*
>
> Six of the eight apartments available for lease in this building are studio apartments. So, probably about $\frac{3}{4}$ of all the apartments in the building are studio apartments.
>
> In this example, the whole set of apartments in the building is a population. The apartments available for lease are a ***sample*** of that population. Since six of the eight apartments available for lease are studio apartments, $\frac{3}{4}$ of the apartments in the sample are studio apartments. The argument generalizes from this by assuming the whole population is probably like the sample. It concludes that as in the sample, probably about $\frac{3}{4}$ of the apartments in the population are studio apartments.

B. A similar type of argument by generalization uses premises about a whole population to support a conclusion about part of that population.

> *Example:*
>
> About $\frac{3}{4}$ of all the apartments in the building are studio apartments. So, probably about $\frac{3}{4}$ of the apartments on the building's second floor are studio apartments.
>
> This example uses a premise about the proportion of studio apartments in the population of all the apartments in the building to support the conclusion that there's a similar proportion of studio apartments in just a part of the population—the apartments on the second floor.

C. A ***predictive*** argument by generalization uses a premise about the sample observed so far in a population to support a conclusion about another part of the population.

> *Example:*
>
> Of the eight apartments I've visited in this building so far, six have been studio apartments. So, probably about six out of the next eight apartments I visit in the building will also be studio apartments.
>
> In this example, the apartments the author has visited so far are a sample of the total population of apartments in the building. The observation about the proportion of studio apartments in the sample supports a prediction that roughly the same proportion of studio apartments will be found in another part of the population—the next eight apartments the author will visit in the building.

D. The strength of an argument by generalization partly depends on how similar the sample is to the overall population, or to the unobserved part of the population a prediction is about. A sample chosen in a way likely to make it relevantly different than the population is a ***biased sample***. An argument using a biased sample is flawed.

> *Example:*
>
> In a telephone survey of our city's residents, about four out of every five respondents said they usually answer the phone when it rings. So, about four out of every five residents of our city usually answer the phone when it rings.
>
> In this example, the sample is the respondents to the telephone survey. People who usually answer the phone when it rings are more likely than other people to respond to telephone surveys. Because the sample was selected through a telephone survey, probably a greater proportion of the sample than of all city residents usually answer the phone when it rings. So, the argument is flawed because the sample is biased.

E. The strength of an argument generalizing from a sample also partly depends on the sample's size. The smaller the sample, the weaker the argument. This is because a smaller sample is statistically likely to differ more from the population in its average traits. An argument by generalization that uses too small a sample to justify its conclusion is flawed by ***hasty generalization***.

> *Example:*
>
> A coin came up heads five of the eight times Beth flipped it. This suggests the coin she flipped is weighted to make it come up heads more often than tails.
>
> In this argument, the sample is the eight flips of the coin, and the population is all the potential flips of the same coin. The sample is probably not biased because Beth's flips of the coin are probably no more likely than anyone else's flips of the same coin to come up heads or tails. However, the sample is too small to justify the conclusion that the coin is weighted to favor heads. A fair, unweighted coin flipped eight times usually comes up heads more or fewer than exactly four times—just by chance. So, this argument is flawed by hasty generalization. If Beth and other people flipped the coin thousands or millions of times, and still saw it come up heads in five out of every eight flips, that would strengthen the argument. But no matter how many times the coin was flipped to confirm this pattern, a tiny chance would be left that the coin was not weighted to favor heads and that the results had been purely random.

F. An argument by generalization is weaker when its conclusion is more precise, and stronger when its conclusion is vaguer, given the same premises. That's because a sample usually doesn't precisely match the population it's extracted from. A less precise conclusion allows a larger range of potential mismatches between sample and population. So, it's more likely to be true, given the same evidence. An argument whose conclusion is too precise for its premises to justify is flawed by the ***fallacy of specificity***.

> *Example:*
>
> Biologists carefully caught, weighed, and released fifty frogs out of the hundreds in a local lake. These fifty frogs weighed an average of 32.86 grams apiece. So, the frogs in the lake must also weigh an average of 32.86 grams apiece.
>
> In this example, the sample might be biased because frogs of certain types might have been easier for the biologists to catch. But even if the biologists avoided any sampling bias, the average weight of the fifty sampled frogs probably wouldn't exactly match the average weight of the hundreds of frogs in the lake. The conclusion is too precise, so the argument suffers from the fallacy of specificity. A stronger argument might use the same evidence to conclude less precisely that the frogs in the lake weigh on average between 25 and 40 grams apiece. This less precise conclusion would still be true even if the average weight of the sampled frogs didn't exactly match the average weight of all the frogs in the lake. Since the less precise conclusion is more likely to be true given the same evidence, that evidence justifies it better. That means the argument for the less precise conclusion is stronger.

3. Causal Reasoning

A. Causal arguments use premises about correlations or causal links to support conclusions about causes and effects. Causal reasoning is hard because causal links can't be directly observed. And there's no scientific or philosophical consensus about what causality is. But saying that one type of situation causally contributes to another usually implies that after a situation of the first type, situations of the second type are more likely. It also implies that situations of the first type help to explain situations of the second type.

> *Example:*
>
> Bushes of the species in our yard tend to die after several weeks without water. So, they must need water at least every few weeks to survive.
>
> In this example, the premise is that after situations of one type (bushes of a certain species getting no water for several weeks), situations of another type become more likely (the bushes dying). The conclusion implies that the first type of situation causes the second: getting no water for several weeks causes bushes of that species to die.

B. A causal argument may use a general correlation to support the conclusion that a situation of one type caused a situation of another type.

> *Example:*
>
> A bush in our yard just died. There's been no rain this summer, and no one has been watering the yard. Bushes of the species in our yard tend to die after several weeks without water. So, probably, the bush died because it didn't get enough water.
>
> In this example, the first premises say that a *specific* situation of one type (a bush of a specific species dying) followed a specific situation of another type (the bush going without water for weeks). The final premise says that *in general*, situations of the first type (bushes of that species dying) follow situations of the second type (bushes of that species getting no water for weeks). These premises together support the conclusion that the lack of water caused the bush to die.

C. Causal arguments can be weakened by observations that suggest alternative causal explanations. A way to check which of two competing explanations is stronger is to look at situations with the possible cause from one explanation but not the possible cause from the other.

> *Example:*
>
> **Explanation 1:** Bushes of this species tend to die after several weeks without water. Maybe the lack of water kills the bushes.
>
> **Explanation 2:** Bushes of this species grow only in a region where long dry spells are always very hot. Maybe the heat alone kills these bushes during weeks without water.
>
> To check which of these two hypothetical explanations is stronger, we can run two experiments. Each experiment creates a situation with one of the two proposed causes but not the other.
>
> **Experiment 1:** Water some of the bushes often during weeks of extreme heat and see how well they survive.
>
> **Experiment 2:** Keep some of the bushes dry in cooler weather and see how well they survive.
>
> Finding that the bushes survive well in Experiment 1 but not in Experiment 2 would support Explanation 1 and cast doubt on Explanation 2.
>
> Finding that the bushes survive well in Experiment 2 but not in Experiment 1 would support Explanation 2 and cast doubt on Explanation 1.
>
> Finding that the bushes always die in both experiments would support both explanations, suggesting either heat or drought alone can kill the bushes.
>
> Finding that the bushes survive well in both experiments would cast doubt on both explanations. It would suggest that something other than drought or heat is killing the bushes—or that drought and heat must occur together to kill the bushes.

D. Experiments to test causal hypotheses shouldn't add or remove possible causal factors other than those tested for.

Examples:

(i) To run Experiment 1 above, a scientist planted some of the bushes in a tropical rainforest where very hot days are usually rainy.

(ii) To run Experiment 2 above, a scientist planted some of the bushes under an awning where rain couldn't reach them in cooler weather.

These versions of the two experiments are problematic because they add other possible causal factors. In example (i), the rainforest's soil type, insects, or humidity might make it harder or easier for the bushes to survive, regardless of the heat and rainfall. In example (ii), putting the bushes under an awning would likely help keep them shaded. That, too, might make it easier or harder for the bushes to survive, regardless of the heat and rainfall. These experimental design flaws cast doubt on any argument that cites these versions of the experiments as evidence to support Explanation 1 or Explanation 2.

Testing a hypothesis through experiments usually means reasoning by generalization: a conclusion about a whole population is reached by observing a sample in the experiment. Causal arguments based on experiments can have the flaws discussed above in Section 4.2.2, "Generalizations and Predictions." A causal argument is weak if it generalizes from a sample that's too small or chosen in a biased way. In small or biased samples, correlations between factors that aren't causally linked often appear just by chance or because of outside factors.

E. Even when two factors clearly are causally linked, it can be hard to tell which causes which, or whether a third, underlying factor causes them both.

Example:

One type of earthworm is far more often found in soil under healthy bushes of a certain species than in soil under sickly bushes of that same species.

Even if the earthworms' presence is causally linked to the bushes' health, the causal link could be that:

(i) the earthworms improve the bushes' health, or

(ii) healthier bushes attract the earthworms, or

(iii) certain soil conditions both improve the bushes' health and attract the earthworms.

More than one of these causal links, and others, may hold at once. A way to untangle the causal links is to find out:

(i) how healthy the bushes are in the same soil conditions without earthworms,

(ii) how attracted the earthworms are to those soil conditions without the bushes, and

(iii) whether the earthworms tend to appear around healthier bushes even in different soil conditions.

F. Even reliable correlations sometimes arise just by chance. One way to check whether a correlation between two types of situations is just a coincidence is to test whether stopping situations of the first type also stops situations of the other type. Even when no test is possible, you can consider whether there's any plausible way either type of situation could cause the other.

Example:

For years, Juan has arrived at work at a hair salon every weekday at exactly 8:00 a.m. Five hundred miles to the north, over the same years, Ashley has arrived at work at a car dealership every weekday at exactly 8:01 a.m. So, Juan's daily arrival at his work must make Ashley arrive at her work a minute later.

In this example, even though for years Ashley has always arrived at work a minute after Juan has, the argument is absurdly weak. That's because Juan's arrival at his work has no apparent way to affect when Ashley arrives at her work. But we could still test the hypothesis in the argument's conclusion. For example, we could persuade Juan to vary his arrival times, then see whether Ashley's arrival times change to match. With no plausible link between the two workers' arrival times, we'd need a lot of evidence like this to reasonably overcome the suspicion that the correlation is pure coincidence. However, finding out that Juan and Ashley know each other and have reasons to coordinate their work schedules could give us a plausible causal link between their arrival times. That would greatly strengthen the argument that their arrival times are indeed causally linked.

---

4. Analogies

A. An argument by *analogy* starts by saying two or more things are alike in certain ways. The argument then gives a claim about one of those two things as a reason to accept a similar claim about the other.

Example:

Laotian cuisine and Thai cuisine use many of the same ingredients and cooking techniques. Ahmed enjoys Thai cuisine. So, if he tried Laotian cuisine, he'd probably enjoy it.

This example starts by saying how Laotian cuisine and Thai cuisine are alike: they use similar ingredients and cooking techniques. The argument then makes a claim about Thai cuisine: that Ahmed enjoys it. By analogy, these premises support a similar claim about Laotian cuisine: Ahmed would enjoy it if he tried it.

B. For an argument by analogy to work well, the noted similarities must be *relevant* to whether the two things are also similar in the way the conclusion claims. The argument in the example above meets this standard. A cuisine's ingredients and cooking techniques usually affect how much a specific person would enjoy it. Noting that Laotian cuisine and Thai cuisine have similar ingredients and cooking techniques is relevant to whether Ahmed is likely to similarly enjoy the two cuisines.

An argument by analogy is weaker if its premises only note similarities that are less relevant to its conclusion.

> *Example:*
>
> Laotian cuisine and Latvian cuisine both come from nations whose English names start with the letter *L*. Ahmed enjoys Latvian cuisine. So, if he tried Laotian cuisine, he'd probably enjoy it too.
>
> This example notes that Laotian cuisine and Latvian cuisine are similar with respect to the English names of the nations they're from. Since the spelling of a nation's name almost never affects how much anyone enjoys that nation's cuisine, this similarity is irrelevant to whether Ahmed would similarly enjoy the two cuisines. The analogy is absurd, so the argument is flawed. To save the argument, we'd need a good reason why the noted similarity is relevant after all—for example, evidence that Ahmed is an unusual person whose enjoyment of different cuisines depends on English spellings.

C. A reasonable argument by analogy can be strengthened by noting other relevant similarities between the things compared, or weakened by noting relevant dissimilarities.

> *Example:*
>
> Beth and Alan are children living on the same block in the Hazelfern School District. Beth attends Tubman Primary School. Therefore, Alan probably does as well.
>
> Noting that Beth and Alan are both in the same grade would strengthen this moderately reasonable argument, because that similarity increases the odds that they attend the same school. However, noting that Beth is eight years older than Alan would weaken the argument, because that dissimilarity suggests Alan may be too young to attend the school Beth attends.

4.3 Deductive Reasoning

1. Deductive Arguments

A. The premises of a ***deductive argument*** are given to fully prove its conclusion. A valid deductive argument with only true premises **must** have a true conclusion. An argument presented as deductive is flawed if its premises can all be true while its conclusion is false. However, a flawed deductive argument might still work well as an inductive argument if the author doesn't wrongly present the premises as **proving** the conclusion. Deductive arguments often use ***logical operators*** or ***quantifiers*** or both, as explained below.

2. Logical Operators

A. A ***logical operator*** shows how the truth or falsehood of one or more statements affects the truth or falsehood of a larger statement made from those statements and the operator. The basic logical operators are ***negations***, ***logical conjunctions***, ***disjunctions***, and ***implications***.

B. A statement's ***negation*** is true just when the statement is false. Words and phrases like ***not***, ***it is false that***, and ***it is not the case that*** often mark negation.

Statements are often vague, ambiguous, context-sensitive, or subjective. They may be true in one sense and false in another, they may be only partly true, or their truth may be indefinite. If a statement is true only in one way or to a limited degree, its negation is false in the same way and to the same degree.

> *Example:*
>
> "The cat is on the mat" can have the negation "The cat is not on the mat." Either of these statements is true if the other is false—but only when both are about the same cat and the same mat, in the same sense and the same context. If you make the first statement while the cat is sleeping on the mat, but then the cat wakes up and leaves before you make the second statement, the context has changed. Then your second statement isn't the negation of your first. If the cat is only partly on the mat when both statements are made, then the second statement is *partly* false just as much as the first is partly true, and in just the same way.

C. A *logical conjunction* of two statements is true just when both are true. The words and phrases below can mark a logical conjunction of statements *A* and *B*:

A and B	*A even though B*	*not only A but also B*
Although A, B	*A. Furthermore, B.*	*A, whereas B*
A but B	*A, however, B*	

The conjunction markers *and, furthermore,* and *not only . . . but also* usually imply that *A* and *B* are relevant to each other or mentioned for similar reasons—for example, that both are premises supporting the same conclusion. On the other hand, the conjunction markers *although, but, even though, however,* and *whereas* suggest tension between *A* and *B*—for example, that it's surprising *A* and *B* are both true, or that *A* and *B* support conflicting conclusions, or that *A* and *B* differ in some other unexpected way.

> *Examples:*
>
> (i) Raul has worked for this company a long time, **and** he's searching for another job.
>
> (ii) **Although** Raul has worked for this company a long time, he's searching for another job.
>
> Both these examples say that Raul has worked for the company a long time, and that he's searching for another job. But in example (ii), *although* suggests Raul's search for another job is **surprising**, given that he's worked for the company a long time. In contrast, the *and* in example (i) suggests Raul's search for another job is **unsurprising** now that he's worked for the company a long time.

D. A *disjunction* of two statements is true only when one of them is true. The words and phrases *A or B*, *either A or B*, and *A unless B* often mark a disjunction of *A* and *B*.

There are two kinds of disjunction. An *inclusive disjunction* of two statements is true when **at least** one of them is true, and **also** when both are. An *exclusive disjunction* of two statements is true just when **exactly** one of them is true—**not** when both are. English disjunctions often aren't clearly inclusive or clearly exclusive. But *A or B or both* clearly means inclusive disjunction. And *A or B but not both* clearly means exclusive disjunction.

Examples:

(i) It will **either** rain **or** snow tomorrow.

(ii) It will rain tomorrow **unless** it snows.

These examples both say that at least one of the statements "It will rain tomorrow" and "It will snow tomorrow" is true. But neither example clearly says whether or not it might *both* rain *and* snow tomorrow. To clarify, we can say:

(iii) Tomorrow, it will rain or snow—or both. (*inclusive disjunction*)

or

(iv) Tomorrow, it will either rain or snow, but not both. (*exclusive disjunction*)

E. A *conditional* says that for one statement to be true, another must be true. In other words, a conditional means the first statement entails the second. The words and phrases below all mark the same conditional link between statements *A* and *B*:

A would mean that B	*B if A*	*A only if B*
If A, then B	*Not A unless B*	*B provided that A*

Conditionals of these forms do not mean that *A* is true, nor that *B* is. They do not give *A* as a reason to accept *B*. So, in a conditional, *A* isn't a premise and *B* isn't a conclusion. That is, a conditional is not an argument. However, the conditional *if A, then B* does mean that correctly assuming *A* as a premise lets you correctly reach *B* as a conclusion.

Examples:

(i) It will snow tonight **only if** the temperature falls below 5 degrees Celsius.

(ii) It **won't** snow tonight **unless** the temperature falls below 5 degrees Celsius.

(iii) **If** it snows tonight, it'll mean the temperature has fallen below 5 degrees Celsius.

These three conditionals all mean the same thing. Each says that snow tonight would require a temperature below 5 degrees Celsius. They do not say that it **will** snow tonight, nor that the temperature **will** be below 5 degrees Celsius. But they do suggest, for example, that seeing it snow tonight would tell you the temperature must be below 5 degrees Celsius.

Although conditionals often make or suggest causal claims, their meaning isn't always causal. The examples above do not mean that snow tonight would **cause** the temperature to fall below 5 degrees Celsius, nor vice versa.

None of these examples imply that it **must** snow if the temperature falls below 5 degrees Celsius tonight. A conditional *if A, then B* does not imply that *if B, then A*.

F. Two *logically equivalent* statements *A and B* are always both true or both false under the same conditions. Each implies the other. That is, *if A, then B*, and *if B, then A*. These two conditionals can be combined as *A if and only if B*.

3. Reasoning with Logical Operators

A. Here's a list of some types of logically equivalent statements made with logical operators. In this list, *not* means negation, *and* means logical conjunction, *or* means inclusive disjunction, and *if . . . then* means conditional implication.

Logical Equivalences with Logical Operators		
A and B	is logically equivalent to	*B and A*
not (A and B)	is logically equivalent to	*not-A or not-B*
A or B	is logically equivalent to	*B or A*
not (A or B)	is logically equivalent to	*not-A and not-B* (in other words, *neither A nor B*)
if A, then B	is logically equivalent to	*if not-B, then not-A*
if A, then (B and C)	is logically equivalent to	*(if A, then B) and (if A, then C)*
if A, then (B or C)	is logically equivalent to	*(if A, then B) or (if A, then C)*
if (A or B), then C	is logically equivalent to	*(if A, then C) and (if B, then C)*

B. Of any two logically equivalent statements, either can be a premise supporting the other as a conclusion in a valid deductive argument. For any line in the list above, a valid deductive argument has a premise of the form on one side and a logically equivalent conclusion of the form on the other side.

Examples:

The second line in the list above says that for any statements *A* and *B*, the statement *not (A and B)* is logically equivalent to *not-A or not-B*. This gives us two valid deductive arguments:

(i) *not (A and B), therefore not-A or not-B*

and

(ii) *not-A or not-B, therefore not (A and B)*

For example, the statement *Ashley and Tim don't both live in this neighborhood* is logically equivalent to *Either Ashley doesn't live in this neighborhood or Tim doesn't*. This lets us make two valid deductive arguments:

(iii) Ashley and Tim don't both live in this neighborhood. Therefore, either Ashley doesn't live in this neighborhood or Tim doesn't.

and

(iv) Either Ashley doesn't live in this neighborhood or Tim doesn't. Therefore, Ashley and Tim don't both live in this neighborhood.

C. Here's a list of some other valid deductive argument forms with logical operators, and of invalid forms often confused with them.

Valid and Invalid Inferences with Logical Operators

Valid: *A and B, therefore A*	**Invalid:** *A, therefore A and B*
Valid: *A, therefore A or B*	**Invalid:** *A or B, therefore A*
Valid: *not-A and not-B, therefore not (A and B)*	**Invalid:** *not (A and B), therefore not-A and not-B*
Valid: *not (A or B), therefore not-A or not-B*	**Invalid:** *not-A or not-B, therefore not (A or B)*
Valid: *if A, then B; and A; therefore B*	**Invalid:** *if A, then B; and B; therefore A*
Valid: *if A, then B; and not-B; therefore not-A*	**Invalid:** *if A, then B; and not-A; therefore not-B*

Examples:

The third line in the table above says that ***not-A and not-B, therefore not (A and B)*** is valid, but ***not (A and B), therefore not-A and not-B*** is invalid. A simple example of a **valid** argument is:

(i) Ashley doesn't live in this neighborhood, and Tim doesn't either. Therefore, Ashley and Tim don't both live in this neighborhood.

But swapping argument (i)'s premise with its conclusion makes this **invalid** argument:

(ii) Ashley and Tim don't both live in this neighborhood. Therefore, Ashley doesn't live in this neighborhood and Tim doesn't either.

As another example, the table's fifth line says that ***if A, then B; and A; therefore B*** is valid, but ***if A, then B; and B; therefore A*** is invalid. So, another **valid** argument is:

(iii) If Ashley lives in this neighborhood, so does Tim. Ashley does live in this neighborhood. Therefore, Tim also lives in this neighborhood.

However, swapping argument (iii)'s second premise with its conclusion makes this **invalid** argument:

(iv) If Ashley lives in this neighborhood, so does Tim. Tim does live in this neighborhood. Therefore, Ashley lives in this neighborhood.

4. Necessity, Probability, and Possibility

A. Some words and phrases mark how likely a statement is to be true. For example, they may mean that:

- The statement is ***necessarily*** true; that is, there's a 100 percent chance the statement is true; or

- The statement is ***probably*** true; that is, there's a good chance the statement is true;

- The statement is ***possibly*** true; that is, the odds are greater than 0 percent that the statement is true.

Saying a claim is possibly true or probably true usually implies it's not necessarily true.

B. The table below shows three categories of words and phrases that can stand for degrees of probability:

Words Standing for Necessity, Probability, and Possibility		
Necessity	**Probability**	**Possibility**
certainly	probably	can
clearly	likely	could
definitely	more likely than not	may
must		maybe
necessarily		might
surely		perhaps
		possibly

The words **probably** and **likely** sometimes mean high probability, like a 95 percent chance. Other times they mean a medium chance, even one below 50 percent. Don't give these terms any exact meanings when you find them on the GMAT exam.

C. The table below lists some valid deductive argument forms with necessity, probability, and possibility, as well as invalid forms often confused with them.

Valid and Invalid Inferences with Necessity, Probability, and Possibility	
Valid: Probably A, therefore possibly A	**Invalid:** Possibly A, therefore probably A
Valid: Possibly (A and B), therefore possibly A and possibly B	**Invalid:** Possibly A and possibly B, therefore possibly (A and B)
Valid: Probably (A and B), therefore probably A and probably B	**Invalid:** Probably A and probably B, therefore probably (A and B)
Valid: Probably A or probably B, therefore probably (A or B)	**Invalid:** Probably (A or B), therefore probably A or probably B
Valid: Necessarily A or necessarily B, therefore necessarily (A or B)	**Invalid:** Necessarily (A or B), therefore necessarily A or necessarily B

Examples:

The table's second line says that *possibly (A and B), therefore possibly A and possibly B* is valid, while *possibly A and possibly B, therefore possibly (A and B)* is invalid. A simple **valid** argument is:

(i) Possibly Tim and Ashley both live in this house. So, possibly Tim lives in this house, and possibly Ashley does.

Swapping argument (i)'s premise with its conclusion gives us this **invalid** argument:

(ii) Possibly Tim lives in this house, and possibly Ashley does. So, possibly both Tim and Ashley live in this house.

To see that argument (ii) is invalid, suppose you know only one person lives in the house, but you don't know whether that person is Tim, Ashley, or someone else. Then argument (ii)'s premise would be true, but its conclusion would be false.

5. Quantifiers

A. A *quantifier* is a word or phrase for a proportion, number, or amount. Some basic quantifiers are *all*, *most*, *some*, and *none*.

    i. A quantifier like *all* means 100 percent of the individuals in a category, or the whole of an amount.

    ii. A quantifier like *most* usually means more than half the individuals in a category, or more than half of a whole. *Most* usually implies *not all*, but not always. Writing *most but not all*, or else *most or all*, can clarify the meaning.

    iii. A quantifier like *some* often means one or more individuals in a category, or part of a whole. *Some* usually but not always implies *not all*. However, *only some* clearly does imply *not all*, while *at least some* clearly doesn't. *Some* with a plural usually means *more than one*. In contrast, *some* with a singular usually means *exactly one*. For example, "some dogs" usually means "more than one dog," while "some dog" usually means "exactly one dog." But "some dog or dogs" means "at least one dog."

    iv. A quantifier like *no* or *none of* means something is being denied about all the individuals in a category, or about all of some whole.

    v. Other common quantifiers have more nuanced meanings. For example, *a few* vaguely means a small number more than two. The upper limit of what counts as *a few* depends on context. For example, "a few Europeans" might mean thousands of people (still a tiny part of Europe's population). But "a few residents in our building" might mean only three or four people if the building has only fifteen residents.

B. The table below classifies some quantifier words by their meanings.

Basic Quantifier Words			
"All" and similar quantifier words	**"Most" and similar quantifier words**	**"Some" and similar quantifier words**	**"No" and similar quantifier words**
all	*generally*	*a number*	*never*
always	*a majority*	*a portion*	*no*
any	*most*	*any*	*none*
both	*more than half*	*at least one*	*not any*
each	*usually*	*occasionally*	*not one*
every		*one or more*	*nowhere*
everywhere		*some*	
whenever		*sometimes*	
wherever		*somewhere*	

Notice the table shows *any* both as a quantifier like *all* and as a quantifier like *some*. That's because *any* can have either meaning. For example, *Any of the students would prefer chocolate ice cream* means *Each of the students would prefer chocolate ice cream*. However, *I don't know if any of the students would prefer chocolate ice cream* means *I don't know if even one of the students would prefer chocolate ice cream*.

C. A quantifier used with a category usually implies the category isn't empty. But this doesn't always hold in hypothetical statements, in conditionals, or with the quantifier *any*.

Examples:

(i) **All** life forms native to planets other than Earth **are** carbon-based.

(ii) **Any** life forms native to planets other than Earth **would be** carbon-based.

In (i), the words *all* and *are* show the author is claiming there really are life forms native to planets other than Earth. But in (ii), the words *any* and *would be* show the author is carefully avoiding that claim.

D. Statements with two or more quantifiers sometimes look alike but differ in meaning because of word order and phrasing.

Example:

(i) Some beverage must be the favorite of every student in the class.

(ii) Each student in the class must have some favorite beverage.

Statement (i) suggests that every student in the class must have **the same** favorite beverage. In contrast, statement (ii) can be true even if each student has a **different** favorite beverage.

6. Reasoning with Quantifiers

A. Here's a list of some logically equivalent statement forms with quantifiers. In this list, *some* means **one or more**. The forms in the list use plurals, but similar equivalences can hold without plurals. For example, *No water is fire* is logically equivalent to *No fire is water*, even though those two statements don't have plurals like the forms in the list do.

Logical Equivalences with Quantifiers		
All As are Bs	is logically equivalent to	*No As are not Bs.*
Some As are Bs	is logically equivalent to	*Some Bs are As.*
No As are Bs	is logically equivalent to	*No Bs are As.*
Some As are not Bs	is logically equivalent to	*Not all As are Bs.*

However, *All As are Bs* is **not** equivalent to *All Bs are As*. And *Some As are not Bs* is **not** equivalent to *Some Bs are not As*.

Examples:

(i) The true statement *All ostriches are birds* is not equivalent to the false statement *All birds are ostriches*.

(ii) The true statement *Some birds are not ostriches* is not equivalent to the false statement *Some ostriches are not birds*.

B. As explained above, either of two logically equivalent statements can be a premise supporting the other as a conclusion in a valid deductive argument. This works for equivalences with quantifiers just like it does for equivalences with logical operators.

C. A *syllogism* is a type of simple deductive argument whose two premises have one quantifier apiece, and whose conclusion also has one quantifier.

Here's a list of some valid syllogism forms along with invalid forms sometimes confused with them. As above, in this list, *some* means *one or more*.

Valid and Invalid Syllogisms	
Valid: *All As are Bs. All Bs are Cs. So, all As are Cs.*	**Invalid:** *All As are Bs. All Bs are Cs. So, all Cs are As.* **Invalid:** *All As are Bs. All Cs are Bs. So, all As are Cs.* **Invalid:** *All Bs are As. All Bs are Cs. So, all As are Cs.*
Valid: *Some As are Bs. All Bs are Cs. So, some As are Cs.*	**Invalid:** *All As are Bs. Some Bs are Cs. So, some As are Cs.* **Invalid:** *Some As are Bs. Some Bs are Cs. So, some As are Cs.*
Valid: *All As are Bs. No Bs are Cs. So, no As are Cs.*	**Invalid:** *No As are Bs. All Bs are Cs. So, no As are Cs.* **Invalid:** *No As are Bs. No Bs are Cs. So, all As are Cs.* **Invalid:** *No As are Bs. All Bs are Cs. So, some As are not Cs.*

Examples:

The list's first line says that ***All As are Bs. All Bs are Cs. So, all As are Cs*** is valid. And here's a **valid** syllogism of that form:

(i) All the trees in the local park were planted by the town arborist. All the trees the arborist planted have been labeled by her. So, all the trees in the park must have been labeled by the arborist.

A similar-looking but **invalid** syllogism has the form ***All As are Bs. All Bs are Cs. So, all Cs are As*** from the list's second line:

(ii) All the trees in the local park were planted by the town arborist. All the trees the arborist planted have been labeled by her. So, all the trees the arborist has labeled must be in the park.

To see that argument (ii) is invalid, notice that even if both premises are true, the arborist might also have labeled trees outside the park—maybe even trees she didn't plant.

Another **invalid** syllogism has the form ***All As are Bs. All Cs are Bs. So, all As are Cs*** from the list's third line:

(iii) All the trees in the local park were planted by the town arborist. All the trees the arborist has labeled are trees she planted. So, all the trees in the park must have been labeled by the arborist.

To see that argument (iii) is invalid, notice that even if both premises are true, the arborist might not have labeled every tree she planted, nor even every tree she planted in the park.

The form in the list's fourth line (***All Bs are As. All Bs are Cs. So, all As are Cs***) gives us yet another **invalid** syllogism:

(iv) All the trees the town arborist has planted are in the local park. All the trees the arborist planted have been labeled by her. So, all the trees in the park must have been labeled by the arborist.

To see that argument (iv) is invalid, notice that even if both premises are true, the park might have many trees that the arborist neither planted nor labeled.

D. Some quantifier words in the table "Basic Quantifier Words" in Section 4.3.5.B above refer to time or place. For example, *whenever* means *every time*, *usually* means *most times*, and *never* means *at no time*. Understanding these meanings can help you rewrite deductive arguments using these words into standard syllogisms to check their validity.

Example:

Max never goes running when the sidewalks are icy. The sidewalks are usually icy on January mornings, so Max must not go running on most January mornings.

We can rewrite this argument in the valid syllogism form *No As are Bs. Most Cs are Bs. So, most Cs are not As*:

No occasions when Max goes running are occasions when the sidewalks are icy. Most January mornings are occasions when the sidewalks are icy. So, most January mornings are not occasions when Max goes running.

Since arguments in this syllogism form are valid, we can tell that the argument in this example is valid.

To register for the GMAT™ exam, go to www.mba.com/register

5.0 Data Insights Review

5.0 Data Insights Review

For the GMAT™ Data Insights section, and for graduate business programs, you need basic skills in analyzing data. This chapter is about the kinds of data in tables and charts. It's only a brief overview. If you find unfamiliar terms, consult outside resources to learn more. Before reading this chapter, read this book's Section 3.4.1, "Statistics," and Section 4.2.2, "Generalizations and Predictions," to review basic statistics and inductive generalization.

Section 5.1, "Data Sets and Types," includes:

1. Data Sets
2. Qualitative Data
3. Quantitative Data

Section 5.2, "Data Displays," includes:

1. Tables
2. Qualitative Charts
3. Quantitative Charts

Section 5.3, "Data Patterns" includes:

1. Distributions
2. Trends and Correlations

5.1 Data Sets and Types

1. Data Sets

A. A **data set** is an organized collection of data about a specific topic. A data set can be shown with one or more tables, charts, or both.

> *Example:*
>
> A data set might have data about all the employees in a company's human resources department, such as their first names, last names, home addresses, phone numbers, positions, salaries, hiring dates, and full-time or part-time statuses.

B. A **case** is an individual or thing that a data set holds data about. Often a data set has the same types of data about many cases together. Then a table or chart can show those types of data for all the cases.

> *Example:*
>
> In the example above, each employee in the human resources department is a case.

C. A **variable** is any specific type of data a data set holds about its cases. For each case, the variable has a **value**.

> *Example:*
>
> In the example above, each type of data held about the employees is a variable: *first name* is one variable, *home address* is another variable, *phone number* is a third variable, and so on. If Zara is an employee in the human resources department, one value of the variable *first name* is "Zara."

In a simple table, the top row often names the variables. Each column shows one variable's values for all the cases. In a chart, labels usually say which variables are shown.

D. The value of a ***dependent variable*** depends on the values of one or more other variables in the data set. An ***independent variable*** is not dependent.

> *Example:*
>
> In a data set of revenues, expenses, and profits, *revenue* and *expense* are independent variables. But *profit* is a dependent variable because profit is calculated as revenue minus expense. For each case, the value of the variable *profit* depends on the values of the variables *revenue* and *expense*.

E. A ***data point*** gives the value of one variable in one case. A cell in a table usually stands for a data point.

> *Example:*
>
> In the example above, one data point might be that Zara's position is assistant manager. That is, the data point gives the value "assistant manager" for the variable *position* in Zara's case.

F. A ***record*** is a set of the data points for one case. A row in a table usually shows one record. In a chart, a record might be shown as a point, a line, a bar, or a small shape with a specific position or length.

> *Example:*
>
> In the example above, one record might list Zara's first name, last name, home address, phone number, position, salary, hiring date, and full-time or part-time status.

2. Qualitative Data

A. ***Qualitative data*** is any type of data that doesn't use numbers to stand for a quantity. Statements, words, names, letters, symbols, algebraic expressions, colors, images, sounds, computer files, and web links can all be qualitative data. Even data that looks numeric is qualitative if the numbers don't stand for quantities.

> *Example:*
>
> Phone numbers are qualitative data. That's because they don't stand for quantities and aren't used in math—for example, they're generally not summed, multiplied, or averaged.

B. ***Nominal data*** is any type of qualitative data that's not ordered in any relevant way. The statistical measures of mean, median, and range don't apply to nominal data, because those measures need an ordering that nominal data lacks. But even in a set of nominal data, some values may appear more often than others. So, the statistical measure of mode does apply to nominal data, because the mode is simply the value that appears most often. To review these statistical terms, refer to Section 3.4.1, "Statistics."

Example:

In the example above, the first names of the human resources department's employees are nominal data if their alphabetical order doesn't matter in the data set. Suppose three of the employees share the first name "Amy," but no more than two of the employees share any other first name. Then "Amy" is the mode of the first names of the department's employees, because it's the first name that appears most often in the data set.

C. ***Ordinal data*** is qualitative data ordered in a way that matters in the data set. Because ordinal data is qualitative, its values can't be added, subtracted, multiplied, or divided. So, the statistical measures of mean and range don't apply to ordinal data, because they require those arithmetic operations. However, the statistical measure of median does apply to ordinal data, because finding a median only requires putting the values in an order. The statistical measure of mode also applies, just as it does for nominal data.

Example:

In a data set for a weekly schedule of appointments, the weekdays Monday, Tuesday, Wednesday, Thursday, and Friday are ordinal data. These days are in an order that matters to the schedule, but they're not numbers and don't measure quantities. Suppose the data set lists seven appointments: two on Monday, two on Tuesday, and three on Thursday. The fourth appointment is the median in the schedule, because three appointments are before it and three are after it. The fourth appointment is on Tuesday, so "Tuesday" is the median value of the variable *weekday* for these appointments. "Thursday" is the mode, because more of the appointments are on Thursday than on any other day.

D. ***Binary data*** takes only two values, like "true" and "false." Binary data is ordinal if the order of the two values matters, but nominal otherwise. Tables may show binary values with two words like "yes" and "no," or with two letters like "T" and "F," or with a check mark or "X" standing for one of the two values and a blank space standing for the other.

Example:

In the example above of the data set of employees in a human resources department, their employment status is a binary variable with two values: "full time" and "part time." A table might show the employment status data in a column simply titled "Full Time," with a check mark for each full-time employee and a blank for each part-time employee.

E. ***Partly ordered data*** has an order among some cases but not others. The statistical measure of median does not apply to a set of partly ordered values, though it might apply to a subset whose values are fully ordered.

Example:

Suppose a family tree shows how people over several generations are related as parents, children, and siblings, but doesn't show when each person was born. This tree lets us partly order the family members by the variable *age*. For example, suppose the family tree shows that Haruto's children are Honoka and Akari, and that Honoka's child is Minato. Since we know that all parents are older than their children, we can tell that Haruto is older than Honoka and Akari, and that Honoka is older than Minato. That also means Haruto is older than Minato. But we can't tell whether Akari is older or younger than her sister Honoka. We can't even tell whether Akari is older or younger than her nephew Minato. So, the family tree only partly orders the family members by age.

3. Quantitative Data

A. *Quantitative data* is data about quantities measured in numbers. Quantitative values can be added, multiplied, averaged, and so on. The statistical measures of mean, median, mode, range, and standard deviation all apply to quantitative data.

Example:

In the example above of the data set of the employees in the human resources department, the salaries are quantitative data. They're amounts of money shown as numbers.

B. Quantitative data is *continuous* if it measures something that can be infinitely divided.

Examples:

Temperatures are continuous data. That's because for any two temperatures, some third temperature is between them—warmer than one and cooler than the other. Likewise, altitudes are continuous data. For any two altitudes, some third altitude is higher than one and lower than the other.

A set of continuous quantitative values rarely has a mode. Because infinitely many of these values are possible, usually no two of them in a data set are exactly alike.

C. Quantitative data that isn't continuous is *discrete*.

Examples:

The numbers of students taking different university courses are discrete data, because they're whole numbers. A course normally can't have a fractional number of students.

As another example, prices in a currency are discrete data, because they can't be divided beyond the currency's smallest denomination. Suppose one price in euros is €3.00, and another is €3.01. No price in euros is larger than the first and smaller than the second, because the currency has no denomination below one euro cent (1/100 of a euro). That means you can't have a price of €3.005, for example. The prices in euros aren't continuous, so they're discrete.

Counted numbers of people, objects, or events are generally discrete data.

D. *Interval data* uses a measurement scale whose number zero doesn't stand for a complete absence of the factor measured. So, for interval data, a measurement above zero doesn't show how much greater than nothing the measured quantity is. Because of this, the ratio of two measurements in interval data isn't the ratio of the two measured quantities.

Examples:

Dates given in years are interval data. In different societies' calendars, the year 0 stands for different years. The year 0 in the Gregorian calendar was roughly the year 3760 in the Hebrew calendar, −641 in the Islamic calendar, and −78 in the Indian National calendar. In none of these calendars does 0 stand for the very first year ever. This means, for example, that the ratio of the numbers in the two years 500 CE and 1500 CE in the Gregorian calendar isn't the ratio of two amounts: the year 500 CE isn't 1/3 the amount of the year 1500 CE.

As another example, temperatures in Celsius or Fahrenheit are also interval data. The temperature 0 degrees Celsius is 32 degrees Fahrenheit. Neither temperature scale uses 0 degrees to mean absolute zero, the complete absence of heat. This means, for example, that the ratio of the numbers in the temperatures 30°F and 60°F isn't the ratio of two amounts of heat. Thus, 60°F isn't twice as hot as 30°F.

In a measurement scale for interval data, each unit stands for the same amount. That is, any two measurements that differ by the same number of units stand for two quantities that differ by the same amount.

Examples:

In the example above of dates given in years, the year 1500 CE was 1000 years after 500 CE, because 1500 − 500 = 1000. Likewise, the year 1600 CE was 1000 years after 600 CE, because 1600 − 600 = 1000. Although you can't divide one year by another to find a real ratio, you can subtract one year from another to find a real length of time—in this case, 1000 years.

Likewise, 60°F is the same amount warmer than 40°F as it is cooler than 80°F. A 20°F difference in two temperatures always stands for the same real difference in heat between those temperatures.

E. *Ratio data* uses a measurement scale whose number zero stands for the absence of the measured factor. In ratio data, as in interval data, the difference between two measurements stands for the actual difference between the measured amounts. However, in ratio data, unlike interval data, the ratio of two measurements also stands for the actual ratio of the measured amounts.

Examples:

Measured weights are ratio data, whether they're in kilograms or pounds. That's because 0 kilograms stands for a complete absence of weight, as does 0 pounds. So, the ratio of 10 kilograms to 5 kilograms is a ratio of two real weights. Because the ratio of 10 to 5 is 2 to 1, 10 kilograms is twice as heavy as 5 kilograms, and 10 pounds is twice as heavy as 5 pounds.

As another example, temperatures in Kelvin are ratio data. That's because 0 K stands for absolute zero, the complete absence of heat. Thus, 200 K is really twice as hot as 100 K. As explained above, this isn't true for temperatures in Celsius or Fahrenheit, which are interval data.

F. *Logarithmic data* use a measurement scale whose higher units stand for amounts exponentially farther apart. For logarithmic data, as for ratio data, the number zero stands for a complete absence. But in logarithmic data, when two measurements a certain number of units apart are higher, the real difference between the measured amounts is greater.

Example:

Noise measured in decibels is logarithmic data. Although 0 decibels means complete silence, 30 decibels is 10 times as loud as 20 decibels, not just 1.5 times as loud. And the real difference in loudness between 40 decibels and 30 decibels is 10 times the real difference in loudness between 30 decibels and 20 decibels, even though the two differences are each 10 decibels.

Because higher units on a logarithmic scale stand for greater amounts of difference, you can't just sum and divide logarithmic data to find a statistical mean. Nor can you subtract one logarithmic measurement from another to find a statistical range. Finding the mean and range requires more complex calculations, which you won't have to do on the GMAT.

5.2 Data Displays

1. Tables

A. A *table* shows data in rows and columns. In a simple table, the top row shows the names of the variables and is called the *header*. Below the header, usually each row shows one record, each column shows one variable, and each cell shows one data point. Sometimes another row above the header has the table's title or description. Sometimes a column or a few rows within the table are used only to group the records by category. Likewise, a row or a few columns within the table are sometimes used only to group the variables by category. Sometimes a row or column shows totals, averages, or other operations on the values in other rows or columns.

Example:

The table below shows revenues, expenses, and profits for two branches of Village Shoppe for one year. The top row is the header listing the independent variables *revenue* and *expense* and the dependent variable *profit*. In each row, the profit is just the revenue minus the expense.

The table has only four rows of records. These are the third row showing the Mapleton branch's January–June finances, the fourth row showing the Mapleton branch's July–December finances, the sixth row showing the Elmville branch's January–June finances, and the seventh row showing the Elmville branch's July–December finances. The second row, "Mapleton branch" serves to group the third and fourth rows together. Likewise, the fifth row, "Elmville branch" serves to group the sixth and seventh rows together. The bottom row, "Annual grand totals" doesn't show a record but rather sums the values in the four records for each of the three variables.

Village Shoppe	Revenue	Expense	Profit
Mapleton branch			
January–June	125000	40000	85000
July–December	90000	35000	55000
Elmville branch			
January–June	85000	30000	55000
July–December	115000	25000	90000
Annual grand totals	**415000**	**130000**	**285000**

B. Sometimes a table's title or description explains the data shown. To understand the data, always study any title or description.

Example:

In the table below, the title says the populations are in **thousands**. So, to find the total population aged 44 and under, add 63,376 thousand and 86,738 thousand. This gives 150,114 thousand, which is 150,114,000. If you only read the numbers without noticing the title, you'll get the wrong result for the total population aged 44 and under.

Population by Age Group (in thousands)	
Age	Population
17 years and under	63,376
18–44 years	86,738
45–64 years	43,845
65 years and over	24,051

2. Qualitative Charts

A. Many different types of charts show qualitative data. This book's Section 3.4.2, "Sets," discusses one type of qualitative chart, the ***Venn diagram***. Here we describe a few other common types. But the GMAT may also challenge you with unfamiliar types of charts this book doesn't discuss. To understand any type of chart, study its labels. The labels will tell you how to read the chart's various points, lines, shapes, symbols, and colors. Several labels may be together, sometimes inside a rectangle on the chart, to make a ***legend***.

B. A *network diagram* has lines connecting small circles or other shapes. Each small shape is a *node* standing for an individual, and each line stands for a relationship between two individuals. In some network diagrams, the lines are one-way or two-way arrows standing for one-way or two-way relationships.

Example:

In the network diagram below, the lettered nodes stand for six pen pals: Alice, Ben, Cathy, Dave, Ellen, and Frank. The arrows show who got a letter from whom in the past month. Each arrow points from the pen pal who sent the letter to the one who got it. A two-way arrow means both the pen pals got letters from each other. This diagram tells us many facts about the pen pals and their relationships over the past month. For example, it shows who got the most letters (Cathy received three) and who got the fewest (Frank received none).

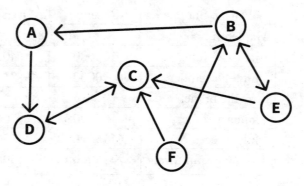

C. A *tree diagram* is a type of network diagram that shows partly ordered data like organizational structures, ancestral relationships, or conditional probabilities. In a tree diagram, each relationship is one way.

Example:

Expanding on the example in Section 5.1.2.E above, the tree diagram below shows how Haruto and his descendants are related. Each line connects a parent above to his or her child below. The diagram shows that Haruto has two children, four grandchildren, and one great-grandchild. From the diagram we can tell that Akari is older than her grandchild Mei, and that Himari and Minato are cousins. But we can't tell whether Akari, Mei, or Himari is older than Minato.

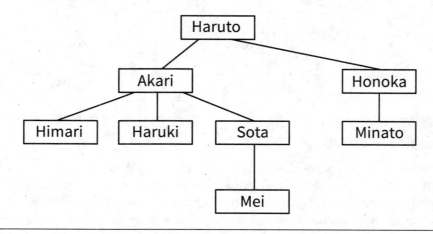

D. In a *flowchart*, each node stands for a step in a process. Arrows direct you from each step to the next. An arrow pointing back to an earlier step tells you to repeat that step. A flowchart usually has at least three types of nodes. *Process nodes* stand for actions to take and are usually rectangles. *Decision nodes* show questions to answer and are usually diamond shaped. At least two labeled arrows lead from each decision node to show how choosing the next step depends on how you answer the question. *Terminal nodes* show the start or end of the process and are usually oval.

Example:

The flowchart below shows a simple process for getting cereal from a store. The top oval shows the first step, going to the store. The arrow below it then takes us to a process node saying to look for a cereal we like. For the third step, we reach a decision node asking whether we've found the cereal we want. If we have, we follow the decision node's "Yes" arrow to another process node telling us to buy the cereal we found, and then we move on to the bottom terminal node telling us to go home. On the other hand, if we haven't found the cereal we want, we follow the decision node's "No" arrow to a second decision node asking whether the store offers other good cereal choices. If it doesn't, we follow another "No" arrow telling us to give up and go home. But if the store does offer other good cereal choices, we follow a "Yes" arrow back to the "Look for a cereal you like" step to peruse the choices again. We repeat the loop until we either find a cereal we want to buy or else decide the store has no more good cereal choices. Since the store won't have infinitely many cereals, we eventually end at the bottom terminal node and go home.

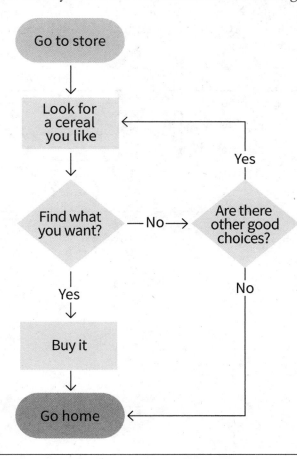

E. A ***Gantt chart*** is used to plan and schedule projects. The horizontal axis has a time scale showing the period planned for a project. The time units usually are qualitative ordinal units, such as months or calendar dates. The vertical axis is divided into labeled rows, each typically standing for one task in the project. In each row, a bar stretches from the planned start time to the planned end time for that row's task. Sometimes a second bar stretches out past the first to show how a task might take longer than expected. An arrow pointing from the end of one task's bar to the beginning of another's bar means the second task can't begin until the first is finished.

Example:

The Gantt chart below shows a schedule for writing a children's book. The top bar shows that Task A, writing the first draft, should be done over about five weeks in May and early June. Task B, the editor's review, and Task C, adding illustrations, start when Task A ends. The lines pointing from the end of Task A to the beginnings of Tasks B and C mean that Tasks B and C can't start until Task A is finished. So, if Task A isn't finished on time, Tasks B and C will both have to be delayed. Tasks B and C are both scheduled to be finished by mid-August. But the thinner gray bar at the end of Task B's main bar means the plan allows the editor's review to take until the beginning of September if necessary—perhaps in case the editor needs extra time to review the illustrations. The arrows from Tasks B and C to Task D, the final revisions, mean that the final revisions can't start until Tasks B and C are finished. Although Task D is supposed to be done by mid-October, a final thinner gray bar at the end of Task D's main bar shows that the plan allows Task D to take until mid-November in case of delays. Notice that although this chart uses qualitative data, it can still support quantitative estimates of how long different parts of the project may take under various conditions.

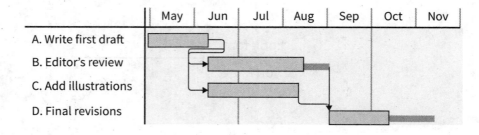

3. Quantitative Charts

A. Here we discuss a few common types of charts that normally show quantitative data. The GMAT may also use rarer types this book doesn't discuss. To understand any type of quantitative chart, study the description and any labels to find out what cases and variables are shown, and how. Also notice any axes. These show the measurement scales. Some quantitative charts have no axes. Others have one, two, or, rarely, three or more. For each axis, notice whether it starts below, at, or above 0. Note the numbers on the axes, as well as the units the numbers stand for. You must read the axes correctly to understand the data.

Example:

In the chart below, labels say that the scale on the left is for temperature data and the scale on the right is for precipitation data. The bottom axis shows four months of the year, spaced three months apart. The chart's title tells us each data point gives the **average** temperature or precipitation in City X during a given month. This implies that the temperatures and precipitations shown are averages over many years. Suppose we're asked to find the average temperature and precipitation in City X in April. To do this, we don't have to calculate averages of any of the values shown. Those values are **already** averages. So, to find the average temperature for April, we simply read the April temperature data point by noting it's slightly lower than the 15 on the temperature scale at the left. Likewise, to find the average precipitation for April, we read the April precipitation data point by noticing it's about as high as the 8 on the precipitation scale on the right. This means the chart says that in April, the average temperature is around 14° Celsius and the average precipitation around 8 centimeters. Since the question is only about April, the data shown for January, July, and October are irrelevant.

AVERAGE TEMPERATURE AND PRECIPITATION IN CITY X

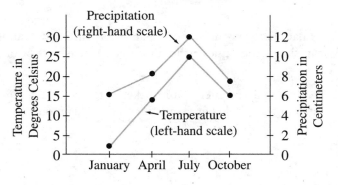

B. A *pie chart* has a circle divided into sections like pie slices. The sections make up the whole circle without overlapping. They stand for parts that together make up some whole amount. Usually, each section is sized in proportion to the part it stands for and labeled with that part's fraction, or percent, of the whole amount. You can use these fractions or percents in calculations. Refer to Section 3.3, "Rates, Ratios, and Percents," to review how.

Example:

In the pie chart below, the sections are sized in proportion to their percent amounts. These percents add up to 100%. Suppose we're told that Al's weekly net salary is $350 and asked how many of the categories shown each individually took at least $80 of that $350. To answer, first we find that $\frac{\$80}{\$350}$ is about 23%. This means each category that took at least $80 of Al's salary took at least 23% of his salary. So, the graph shows exactly two categories that each took at least $80 of Al's salary: **Savings** took 25% of his salary, and **Rent and Utilities** took 30%.

DISTRIBUTION OF AL'S WEEKLY NET SALARY

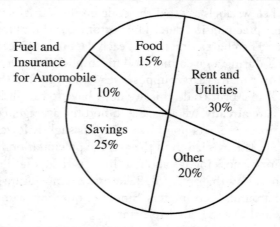

C. A **bar chart** has vertical or horizontal bars standing for cases. A simple bar chart has only one quantitative variable. The bars' different heights or lengths show this variable's values for different cases.

A **grouped** bar chart may have more than one quantitative variable. Its bars are grouped together. Each group shows the values either of different variables for one case or of related cases for one variable.

In a **stacked** bar chart, segments are stacked into bars. Each segment inside a bar stands for part of an amount, and the whole bar stands for the whole amount.

Example:

The bar chart below is both grouped and stacked. Each pair of grouped bars shows population figures for one of three towns. In each pair, the bar on the left shows the town's population in 2010, and the bar on the right shows the town's population in 2020. Inside each bar, the lower segment shows how many people in the town were under age 30, and the upper segment shows how many were age 30 or older. For example, the chart's fifth bar shows that in 2010, Ceburg's population was around 2,000, including about 1,100 people under 30 and 900 people 30 or older. And the chart's sixth bar shows that by 2020, Ceburg's population had grown to around 2,400, including about 1,200 people under 30 and 1,200 people 30 or older. By reading the amounts shown, we can also estimate various other amounts, like the three towns' combined number of residents 30 or older in 2020.

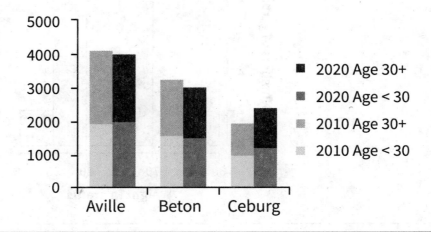

D. A ***histogram*** looks like a bar chart but works differently. In a histogram, each bar stands for a range of values that the same variable can take. These ranges don't overlap. Together they usually include every value the variable can take, or at least every value it does take in some population. The bars are in order from the one farthest left, which stands for the lowest range of values, to the one farthest right, which stands for the highest range. Each bar's height shows the number or proportion of times the variable's value is in the range the bar stands for. A bar chart shows clearly how the values are distributed.

Example:

The histogram below shows the weights of 31 gerbils. Each bar's height shows how many gerbils were in a specific weight range. For example, the bar farthest left says 3 gerbils each weighed from 60 to 65 grams. The histogram doesn't show any individual gerbil's weight. However, it does give us some statistical information. For example, by adding the numbers of gerbils in the different weight ranges, we can tell that the 16th-heaviest of the 31 gerbils weighed between 75 and 80 grams. This means the gerbils' median weight was in that range. The histogram also shows that the gerbils mainly weighed between 70 and 85 grams apiece, though several weighed less or more.

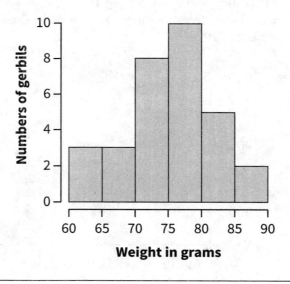

E. A *line chart* often shows how the values of one or more quantitative variables change over time. Typically, the horizontal axis has the time scale, and the vertical axis has one or more scales for the variable or variables. One or more lines connect the data points. Different lines may stand either for different variables or for a single variable applied to different cases. Line charts make it easy to see trends and correlations.

Some line charts show probability distributions instead of changes over time, as we'll see in Section 5.3.1 below.

Examples:

In Section 5.2.3.A above, the chart of average monthly temperatures and precipitations is a line chart whose two variables have two separate scales, one on the left and one on the right.

The line chart below shows how many toasters of three different brands were sold each year from 2017 to 2022. Each sloping line shows how sales changed for one of the brands during those years. The legend on the bottom says which line stands for which brand. All three lines use the scale on the left, whose numbers stand for thousands of units sold annually. The chart shows that over the six years, annual sales of Crispo toasters increased dramatically, annual sales of Brownita toasters declined to almost zero, and annual sales of Toastador toasters fluctuated.

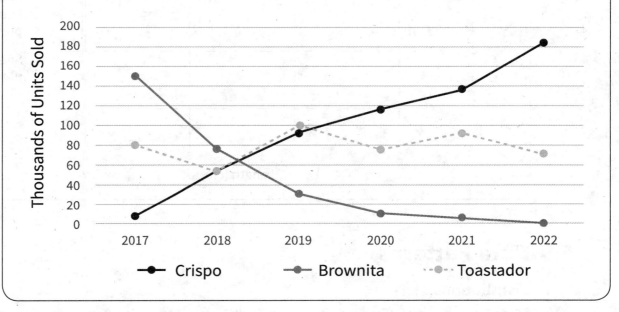

F. A *scatterplot* has at least two quantitative variables, one on each axis. For each case in the data, a dot's position shows the variables' values. No lines connect the scattered dots, but a line through the scatterplot may show an overall trend in the data. Sometimes the dots have a few different shapes or colors to show they stand for cases in different categories. And in scatterplots called *bubble charts*, the dots have different sizes standing for values of a third variable.

Scatterplots are useful for showing correlations. They also show how much individual cases fit an overall correlation or deviate from it.

Example:

The scatterplot below shows measured widths and lengths of leaves on two plants. Each dot stands for one leaf. The dot's position stands for the leaf's width and length in centimeters, as the scatterplot's two axes show. The legend says how one set of dots stands for leaves on the first plant, and another set for leaves on the second. The scatterplot shows that, in general, the longer leaves tend to be wider, and vice versa. It also shows how leaves on the second plant tend to be somewhat longer and wider than those on the first, with some exceptions.

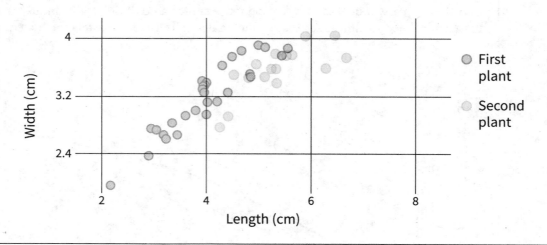

5.3 Data Patterns

1. Distributions

A. A data *distribution* is a pattern in how often different values appear in data. How data in a sample is distributed can tell you how likely different values are to appear in the same population outside the sample. In this book, Section 4.2.2, "Generalizations and Predictions," discusses generalizations and predictions based on samples.

B. A distribution is *uniform* if the values each occur about equally often. It's less uniform when the values differ more in how often each occurs. The more uniform a distribution is for a sample, the better it supports the conclusion that the distribution for other cases in the population is likewise uniform.

Example:

Suppose the six faces on a die are numbered 1 to 6. And suppose that when rolled sixty times, the die comes up 1 eleven times, 2 nine times, 3 ten times, 4 eleven times, 5 ten times, and 6 nine times. This isn't a **perfectly** uniform distribution, because the six values 1 to 6 didn't occur exactly ten times apiece. But because each value did occur between nine and eleven times, the distribution is **fairly** uniform. This suggests that each of the six values is about equally likely to occur whenever the die is rolled, and that their distribution for future rolls will stay fairly uniform.

C. A variable's values are often distributed unevenly. Sometimes one central value occurs most often, with other values occurring less often the farther they are from the central value. When this type of distribution is *normal*, each value below the central value occurs just as often as the value equally far above the central value. For a perfectly normal distribution, the central value is the mean, the median, and the mode. When plotted on a chart, a normal distribution is bell shaped, with a central hump tapering off equally into tails on both sides. But a distribution with a larger tail on one side of the hump than the other is not normal but *skewed*. For a skewed distribution, the mean is often farther out on the larger tail than the median is.

Example:

The two charts below show distributions of lengths for two beetle species. The chart on the left shows that Species A beetles have roughly a normal distribution of lengths. The central hump is symmetrical, with equal tails on both sides. From the chart on the left, we can tell that the mode, the median, and the mean of the lengths for Species A are all around 5 millimeters. In contrast, the chart on the right shows that Species B beetles have a skewed distribution of lengths. The tail on the right side of the hump is larger than the tail on the left side. This means more beetles of Species B have lengths above the mode than below it. As a result, the median length for Species B is above the mode, and the mean is above the median.

Normal Distribution   **Skewed Distribution**

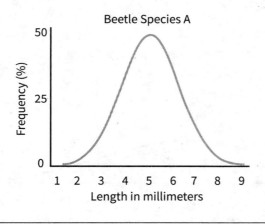
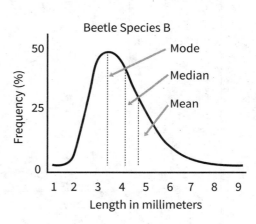

D. The more tightly clustered a distribution is around a central value, the higher and narrower the hump is, and the smaller the tails are. A more tightly clustered distribution also has a smaller standard deviation, as discussed in Section 3.4.1, "Statistics." The more tightly clustered a distribution is for an observed sample, the more likely a new case from the population outside that sample is to have a value near the distribution's central value.

Example:

For each of three tasks, the chart below shows how frequently it takes workers different lengths of time in minutes to complete that task. Even though the bottom axis shows times from 1 to 5 minutes, it doesn't stand for a single period starting at 1 minute and ending at 5 minutes. Instead, it stands for a range of lengths of task completion times.

Notice how the chart uses smooth curves to show the frequencies of different completion times. That suggests it shows trends idealized from the observed data points, which could be shown more precisely as separate dots or bars.

For each task, the distribution of completion times is uniform, with a mode, median, and mean of 3 minutes. But the completion times are most tightly clustered around 3 minutes for Task A, and least tightly clustered for Task C. That means the standard deviation of the completion times is lowest for Task A and highest for Task C. It also means the probability is higher that an individual worker will take close to 3 minutes to complete Task A than to complete Task C. A worker's completion time for Task C is less predictable and likely to be farther from 3 minutes. So, the chart gives **stronger evidence** for the conclusion that finishing Task A will take a worker between 2 and 4 minutes than for the conclusion that finishing Task C will take that worker between 2 and 4 minutes.

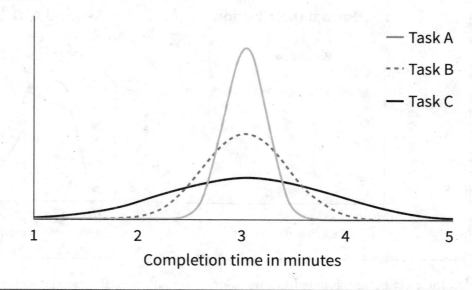

E. Data distributions take many other shapes too. Some have two or more humps, and others have random variations in frequency among adjacent values. In general, the less the values in a sample cluster around one central hump, the larger the standard deviation is, and the less predictable the values are for cases in the population outside the observed sample.

2. Trends and Correlations

A. Charts often show trends over time. They may show that a variable's values increase, decrease, fluctuate, or change in cycles. They may also show values of different plotted variables changing in the same ways or opposite ways.

Usually, an observed trend over a period is evidence that the same trend extends at least slightly before and after that period. This evidence is stronger the longer the observed trend has lasted and the more varied the conditions it's lasted through. Generalizing from a longer observed period with more varied conditions is like generalizing from a larger sample, as discussed in Section 4.2.2, "Generalizations and Predictions." But the odds increase of other factors disrupting the observed trend at times farther from the observed period, and in conditions that differ more from those observed.

> *Example:*
>
> The line chart in Section 5.2.3.E above shows that annual sales of Crispo toasters rose from fewer than 10,000 in 2017 to over 180,000 in 2022. If this trend continues another year, even more than 180,000 Crispo toasters will be sold in 2023. But many factors might disrupt Crispo's surging popularity. For example, another company might start making better or less expensive toasters, drawing consumers away from Crispo toasters. Or broader social, economic, or technological changes might reduce demand for toasters altogether. The more years that pass outside the observed period of 2017 through 2022, the more likely such disruptions become. So, the observed trend gives stronger evidence that annual Crispo toaster sales will be over 180,000 in 2023 than it gives that they'll still be over 180,000 in 2050.

B. Two quantitative or ordinal variables are ***positively correlated*** if they both tend to be higher in the same cases. They're ***negatively correlated*** if one tends to be higher in cases where the other is lower.

> *Examples:*
>
> If warmer days tend to be rainier in a certain region, then temperature and precipitation are positively correlated there.
>
> But if warmer days tend to be drier in a different region, then temperature and precipitation are negatively correlated there.

C. On a line chart, the lines standing for positively correlated variables tend to slope up or down together. The more consistently the slopes match, the stronger the positive correlation. But when two variables are negatively correlated, the line standing for one tends to slope up where the other slopes down, and vice versa. The more consistently the lines slope in opposite directions, the stronger the negative correlation.

> *Examples:*
>
> The chart in Section 5.2.3.A shows a positive correlation between average monthly temperature and precipitation in City X. The temperature and precipitation lines both slope up together from January through July, and then slope down together.
>
> The chart in Section 5.2.3.E shows a negative correlation between annual sales of Crispo toasters and annual sales of Brownita toasters. Throughout this chart, the line standing for Crispo toaster sales slopes up and the line standing for Brownita toaster sales slopes down. But the chart shows no clear positive or negative correlation of Crispo or Brownita toaster sales with Toastador toaster sales. The line standing for Toastador toaster sales fluctuates, sometimes sloping up and sometimes down. It shows no consistent trend relative to the other two lines. So, the chart doesn't clearly support a prediction that in future years Toastador sales will increase or decrease as Crispo or Brownita sales do the same or the opposite.

D. When a scatterplot shows a positive correlation, the dots tend to cluster around a line that slopes up. When it shows a negative correlation, they tend to cluster around a line that slopes down. The stronger the correlation, the more tightly the dots cluster around the sloped line. If the dots spread farther away from the sloped line, or cluster around a line with a less consistent slope, the correlation is weaker or nonexistent.

Example:

The scatterplot in Section 5.2.3.F shows leaf width as positively correlated with leaf length for both plants. The dots mostly cluster around a line sloping up, which means wider leaves tend to be longer and vice versa. Thus, the scatterplot supports a prediction that if another leaf on one of the plants is measured, it too will probably be wider if it's longer. But the correlation in the scatterplot isn't perfect. For example, the dot farthest to the right is lower than each of about a dozen dots to its left. That dot farthest to the right stands for a leaf that's both longer and thinner than any of the leaves those other dozen dots stand for. This inconsistency in the correlation somewhat weakens the scatterplot's support for the prediction that another leaf measured on one of the plants will be wider if it's longer.

E. Values of a nominal variable may also be associated with higher or lower values of an ordinal or quantitative variable. Different values of two nominal variables can also be associated with each other.

Examples:

Species is a nominal variable. Individuals of some species tend to weigh more than individuals of other species, so different values of the nominal variable *species* are associated with higher or lower values of the quantitative variable *weight*.

As another example, university students majoring in certain subjects like physics are more likely to take certain courses like statistics than university students majoring in other subjects like theater are, even though a student's *major* and *course enrollment* are both nominal variables.

An association involving a nominal variable like *species* isn't a positive or negative correlation, because nominal variables aren't ordered; one species isn't greater or less than another. Still, these nominal associations can be shown in qualitative charts and tables, and they can support predictions. Knowing an animal's species gives you some evidence about roughly how much it likely weighs. And knowing a student's major gives you some evidence about what courses that student is more likely to take.

6.0   Data Insights

6.0 Data Insights

This chapter describes the Data Insights section of the GMAT™ exam, explains what it measures, discusses the five types of Data Insights questions, and offers strategies for answering them.

Because most Data Insights questions are interactive, you need a computer to access them fully. Among Data Insights questions, only the Data Sufficiency questions and Two-Part Analysis questions can be shown on paper as they are on the test. So, those are the only Data Insights practice questions in this book.

> For practice with other Data Insights practice questions, go to www.mba.com/my-account and access the Online Question Bank using the Access Code inside the front cover of this book.

Overview of the Data Insights Section

The Data Insights section measures your skill at analyzing data shown in formats often used in real business situations. You'll need this skill to make informed decisions as a future business leader. Data Insights questions ask you to assess multiple sources and types of information—graphic, numeric, and verbal—as they relate to one another.

This section asks you to:

- Use math, verbal reasoning, and data analysis,

- Solve connected problems together, and

- Give answers in different formats, not just traditional multiple choice.

Many Data Insights questions ask you to study graphs and sort tables to find information. These questions don't require advanced statistics or spreadsheet expertise. Other Data Insights questions ask you to tell whether given information is enough to answer a question but don't ask you to actually answer it. You have 45 minutes to respond to the 20 questions in the Data Insights section, an average of 2 minutes and 15 seconds per question. Throughout the section are questions of five types. Some need multiple responses. A question may use math, data analysis, verbal reasoning, or all three. Questions with math require knowing the topics reviewed in Chapter 3, "Math Review": Value, Order, Factors; Algebra, Equalities, Inequalities; Rates, Ratios, Percents; and Statistics, Sets, Counting, Probability, Estimation, and Series. Questions with verbal aspects require reasoning, understanding texts, evaluating arguments, and using other skills reviewed in Chapter 4, "Verbal Review." Questions involving data analysis require understanding different types of data in tables or graphs, finding patterns in that data, and using other skills reviewed in Chapter 5, "Data Insights Review."

To prepare for the Data Insights section, first review basic math, data analysis, and verbal reasoning skills to make sure you know enough to answer the questions. Then practice on GMAT questions from past exams.

Special Features:

- Unlike other sections of the GMAT exam, the Data Insights section sometimes shows two or more questions on one screen. When it does, you can change your answers before clicking "Next" to go on to the next screen. But once you're on a new screen, you can't return to the previous screen.

- The Data Insights section uses some math, but it doesn't ask you to calculate by hand. An on-screen calculator with basic functions is available for this section. For more information, please go to **www.mba.com/exampolicies.**

6.1 What Is Measured

The Data Insights section measures how well you use data to solve problems. Specifically, it tests the skills described below:

Skill Category	Details	Examples
Apply	Understand principles, rules, or other concepts Use them in a new context or say what would follow if new information were added	• Tell if new examples follow or break given rules • Tell how new situations affect a trend • Draw conclusions about new data from given principles
Evaluate	Judge information as evidence	• Tell if information in one source supports or weakens a claim in another source • Tell if information justifies a course of action • Judge how well evidence supports an argument or plan • Find errors or gaps in information
Infer	Draw unstated conclusions from information	• Find an outcome's probability using data • Tell if statements follow logically from given information • Say what a term means in a context • Find a rate of change in data gathered over time
Recognize	Identify information given explicitly, including details or relationships between pieces of information	• Find agreements and disagreements between information sources • Find how strongly two variables are correlated • Give a ranking based on combined factors from a table (for example, saying which product maximizes revenue and minimizes costs) • Tell which data an argument uses as evidence
Strategize	Find ways to work toward a goal given constraints	• Choose a plan that minimizes risks and maximizes value • Identify trade-offs among ways to reach a goal • Tell which math formula gives a desired result • Decide which ways of doing a task meet given needs

6.2 Question Types and Test-Taking Strategies

The Data Insights section has five types of questions: Multi-Source Reasoning, Table Analysis, Graphics Interpretation, Two-Part Analysis, and Data Sufficiency. We describe each below.

1. Multi-Source Reasoning

What you see:

- Two or three tabs on the left side of your screen. Each tab shows a written passage, a table, a graph, or another information source. The different tabs may show information in different forms. Click on the tabs to see what's on them and find what you need to answer the questions.

Example of information sources on multiple tabs:

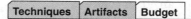

| Techniques | Artifacts | Budget |

For outside laboratory tests, the museum's first-year budget for the Kaxna collection allows unlimited IRMS testing, and a total of $7,000—equal to the cost of 4 TL tests plus 15 radiocarbon tests, or the cost of 40 ICP-MS tests—for all other tests. For each technique applied by an outside lab, the museum is charged a fixed price per artifact.

- A question with answer choices on the right side of your screen. With each set of tabs, three questions appear one at a time.

The response type:

- Some questions are traditional multiple choice, with five answer choices.

- Others are "conditional statement" questions. Each question gives a condition. Below the condition are three rows with content such as sentences, phrases, words, numbers, or formulas. For each row, mark "yes" or "true" if the row's contents meet the given condition, or mark "no" or "false" if not.

- Mark one answer PER ROW.

- You must mark all three rows correctly to get credit for the question.

Example of a conditional statement question:

For each of the following artifacts in the museum's Kaxna collection, select *Yes* if, based on the museum's assumptions, a range of dates for the object's creation can be obtained using one of the techniques in the manner described. Otherwise, select *No*.

Yes	No	
○	○	Bronze statue of a deer
○	○	Fired-clay pot
○	○	Wooden statue of a warrior

Tips for Answering Multi-Source Reasoning Questions

- **Answer using only the information given.**

  The tabs show all the information you need to answer correctly. If you already know about the topic, don't use that knowledge to answer. Use only the information in the tabs.

- **Analyze each information source.**

  As you read a passage, note each statement's role. Section 4.1, "Analyzing Passages," explains how.

Read labels and scales to understand the data in tables and graphs. Chapter 5, "Data Insights Review," explains how.

- **Read the whole question.**

  You need to understand what each question is asking you to do. For example, some questions ask you to spot conflicts between information sources. Others ask you to draw conclusions by combining information from different sources. And some questions ask you to judge which information sources are relevant to an issue.

  While answering the questions, you can always click on the tabs to review any of the information.

2. Table Analysis

What you see:

- A data table. You can sort it by any data column.

  Example of data table with sorting drop-down menu:

  The table displays data on Brazilian agricultural products in 2009.

  Sort By: Production, world share (%) ▼

Commodity	Production, world share (%)	Production, world rank	Exports, world share (%)	Exports, world rank
Pork	4	4	12	4
Cotton	5	5	10	4
Corn	8	4	10	2
Chickens	15	3	38	1
Beef	16	2	22	1
Sugar	21	1	44	1
Soybeans	27	2	40	2
Coffee	40	1	32	1
Orange juice	56	1	82	1

The response type:

- The questions are in "conditional statement" form. Each question gives a condition. Below the condition are three rows with contents such as sentences, phrases, words, numbers, or formulas. For each row, mark "yes" or "true" if the row's contents meet the condition, or mark "no" or "false" if not.

- Mark one answer PER ROW.

- You must mark all three rows correctly to get credit for the question.

  Example of a conditional statement question:

  For each of the following statements, select *Yes* if the statement can be shown to be true based on the information in the table. Otherwise select *No*.

Yes	No	
○	○	No individual country produces more than one-fourth of the world's sugar.
○	○	If Brazil produces less than 20% of the world's supply of any commodity listed in the table, Brazil is not the world's top exporter of that commodity.
○	○	Of the commodities in the table for which Brazil ranks first in world exports, Brazil produces more than 20% of the world's supply.

Tips for Answering Table Analysis Questions

- **Study the table and any text around it to learn what kind of data it shows.**

  Knowing what kind of data is in the table helps you find the information you need.

- **Study the condition in the question.**

  The question gives a condition like *"is consistent with the information provided"* or *"can be inferred from the information provided."* Understanding that condition helps you understand how to mark each row.

- **Read each answer row to decide how to sort the table.**

  Often an answer row's contents hint at how to sort the table by one or more columns to make the data you need easier to find.

- **Judge whether each answer row's contents meet the given condition.**

  In each row, you can only mark one of the two answer choices, and only one is right. Decide whether the row's contents meet the condition in the question.

3. Graphics Interpretation

What you see:

- A graphic. Section 5.2, "Data Displays," explains some kinds of graphics you might see.

- One or more statements with blanks in missing parts. Each blank part has a drop-down menu you use to fill it in.

Example of graphics:

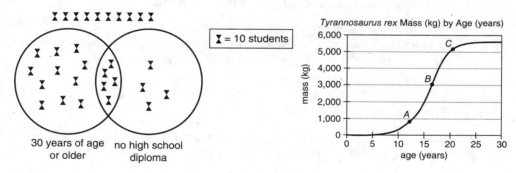

Example of a statement with a drop-down menu to fill in a blank:

Use the drop-down menu to complete the statement according to the information presented in the diagram.

If one student is selected at random from the 300 surveyed, the chance that the student will be under 30 or a high school graduate or both is Select... ▼

1 out of 6

1 out of 3

2 out of 3

5 out of 6

If one student is selected at random from the 300 surveyed, the chance that the student will be both under 30 and a high school graduate is 1 out of 3 ▼

The response type:

- Each drop-down menu shows a list of choices, such as words, phrases, or numbers. Pick the best choice in the drop-down menu to fill in the blank in the statement.

- If the question has two or more drop-down menus, you must pick the best choices in all of them to get credit for the question.

Tips for Answering Graphics Interpretation Questions

- **Study the graphic.**

  Find the information in the graphic. Notice any marked values on the axes. Also notice any differences between units in the graphic and units the text discusses. Don't assume the graphic is drawn to scale.

- **Read any text around the graphic.**

  Text near the graphic may clarify what the graphic means. The text may also give information that's not in the graphic but is needed to answer the question.

- **Study the statements with drop-down menus.**

  Studying these statements helps you understand what the question is asking you to do. Graphics Interpretation questions may ask you to interpret and connect data, to find how different pieces of data are related, or to draw conclusions from a data set. You may have to do some math, for example to find or compare rates of change.

- **Read all the choices in each drop-down menu.**

  The menu choices may have clues about how to answer the question.

- **Pick the choice that best completes the statement.**

  More than one choice in the drop-down menu may seem plausible. Pick the one that makes the statement most accurate or logical. If the drop-down menu comes after a phrase like *nearest to* or *closest to*, pick the choice closest to your calculated answer. Reading the statement again with your answer choice in place may help.

4. Two-Part Analysis

Two-Part Analysis questions challenge you to use varied skills, such as judging trade-offs, solving simultaneous equations, or noticing relationships.

What you see:

- A passage.

- Instructions saying to use the passage to make two choices that together or separately meet one or more conditions.

- A response table with three columns.

Example of a passage:

A literature department at a small university in an English-speaking country is organizing a two-day festival in which it will highlight the works of ten writers who have been the subjects of recent scholarly work by the faculty. Five writers will be featured each day. To reflect the department's strengths, the majority of writers scheduled for one of the days will be writers whose primary writing language is not English. On the other day of the festival, at least four of the writers will be women. Neither day should have more than two writers from the same country. Departmental members have already agreed on a schedule for eight of the writers. That schedule showing names, along with each writer's primary writing language and country of origin, is shown.

- Day 1:

    Achebe (male, English, Nigeria)

    Weil (female, French, France)

    Gavalda (female, French, France)

    Barrett Browning (female, English, UK)

- Day 2:

    Rowling (female, English, UK)

    Austen (female, English, UK)

    Ocantos (male, Spanish, Argentina)

    Lu Xun (male, Chinese, China)

Example of a response based on passage information:

Select a writer who could be added to the schedule for either day. Then select a writer who could be added to the schedule for neither day. Make only two selections, one in each column.

Either day	Neither day	Writer
○	○	LeGuin (female, English, USA)
○	○	Longfellow (male, English, USA)
○	○	Murasaki (female, Japanese, Japan)
○	○	Colette (female, French, France)
○	○	Vargas Llosa (male, Spanish, Peru)
○	○	Zola (male, French, France)

The response type:

- The response table's top row names the columns. Below that, the first two columns have buttons you click to choose from a list in the third column.

- Pick one answer PER COLUMN, not per row.

- To get credit for the question, you must pick one correct answer in the first column, and one in the second column.

- You can pick the same answer in both columns.

Tips for Answering Two-Part Analysis Questions

- **Answer using only the information given.**

    The question tells you everything you need to know to pick the right answers. If you already know about the topic, don't use that knowledge to answer the question. Rely on the given information to answer the question.

- **Read the instructions below the passage.**

    The table's top row may not fully explain the tasks in the first two columns. Notice how the instructions describe the tasks.

- **Make two choices.**

    Pick one answer in the first column and one answer in the second column.

- **Read all the answer choices before picking any.**

  Before you pick answers in the first two columns, read all the answer choices in the third column.

- **Notice if the instructions say the two answers depend on each other.**

  Some Two-Part Analysis questions ask you to make two independent choices. Others ask you to pick two answers that combine into one correct response. Follow the instructions to make sure your two answer choices combine the right way.

- **Pick the same answer in both columns if it is the best choice for both.**

  Sometimes the same answer is the best choice for both columns.

5. Data Sufficiency

A Data Sufficiency problem asks you to analyze a question. Usually, the question is about an information source, such as a written passage, a table, a graph, or an equation. You must then decide whether either or both of two new statements give enough new information to answer the question. But you don't have to give the answer. Instead, you pick one of five response choices to classify how the two statements relate to the question. These five choices are the same for each Data Sufficiency question.

What you see:

- A question, usually with background information.

- Two statements labeled (1) and (2).

Example of a Data Sufficiency Problem and Statements

Kim has a deck of forty colored cards. The deck is comprised of cards of four different colors. Kim shuffles the cards and keeps drawing cards from the deck, one after the other, to count the number of cards of each color. Is there a chance that Kim might draw thirty-one cards without drawing a blue card—and then draw a blue card?

(1) The four colors are red, blue, green, and yellow.

(2) The deck contains the same number of cards of each of the four colors.

The response type:

- Each question is multiple choice, always with these five answer choices:

  (A) Statement (1) ALONE is sufficient, but statement (2) alone is not sufficient.

  (B) Statement (2) ALONE is sufficient, but statement (1) alone is not sufficient.

  (C) BOTH statements TOGETHER are sufficient, but NEITHER statement ALONE is sufficient.

  (D) EACH statement ALONE is sufficient.

  (E) Statements (1) and (2) TOGETHER are NOT sufficient.

Pick exactly one of these answer choices. To answer correctly, you must judge whether statement (1) alone gives enough information to solve the math problem, and whether statement (2) alone does. If neither statement alone gives enough information to solve the problem, you must judge whether both do.

Tips for Answering Data Sufficiency Questions

- **Analyze the question and the two statements step by step.**

  First study the question and any information shown. Then read statement (1). Decide whether it gives enough new information to answer the question. Next go on to statement (2). Ignore statement (1) while you decide whether statement (2) alone gives enough new information to answer the question. If you find that either statement alone gives enough information to answer the question, you now know enough to pick the right answer choice from among answer choice (A), answer choice (B), and answer choice (D).

  If you find that neither statement alone gives enough information to answer the question, decide whether both give enough information together. If so, the right answer choice is answer choice (C). Otherwise, it's answer choice (E).

  Here's a flowchart showing how to find the right answer choice step by step.

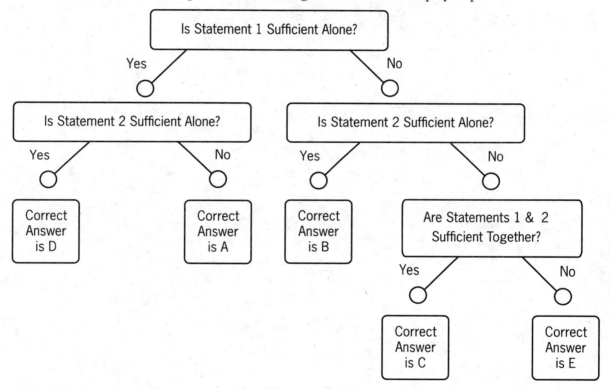

- **Don't waste time finding the answer to the question.**

  You only have to decide whether the two statements give enough information to answer it.

- **Check whether there's enough information to answer the exact question asked.**

  For example, suppose the question is what unique value a variable y must take. Then you have to decide whether either statement alone or both together give enough information to find **one and only one** value for y. Here, the question is not whether the statements give enough information to find an equation like $y = x + 2$. Nor is it whether they give enough information to find a range of values rather than y's unique value. So, ignore those irrelevant questions.

- **Don't assume any images are drawn to scale.**

  They may not be. For example, if a figure described as a rectangle looks like a square, that doesn't mean it is a square.

6.3 Online Question Bank Instructions

Accessing the Data Insights Practice Questions

Below are Data Sufficiency and Two-Part Analysis Data Insights practice questions. Because the Data Insights questions need to be rendered online, certain question types, such as Multi-Source Reasoning, Table Analysis, and Graphics Interpretation, are only available in the **Online Question Bank** that is included as a part of this book.

Use your unique Access Code from the inside front cover of this book to access additional practice questions with answer explanations at **www.mba.com/my-account.** You can buy more Data Insights practice questions on **www.mba.com/gmatprep.**

6.4 Practice Questions: Data Sufficiency

Each Data Sufficiency question has a math problem and two statements, labeled (1) and (2), which present data. Using this data with your knowledge of math and everyday facts (such as the number of days in July or what *counterclockwise* means), decide whether the data in the statements are enough to solve the problem. Then pick one of these answer choices:

A   Statement (1) ALONE is sufficient, but statement (2) alone is not sufficient.
B   Statement (2) ALONE is sufficient, but statement (1) alone is not sufficient.
C   BOTH statements TOGETHER are sufficient, but NEITHER statement ALONE is sufficient.
D   EACH statement ALONE is sufficient.
E   Statements (1) and (2) TOGETHER are NOT sufficient.

Note: In Data Sufficiency questions that ask for a quantity's value, the data given in the statements are sufficient only when they make it possible to find exactly one numerical value for the quantity.

Questions 1 to 38 — Difficulty: Easy

1. Each car at a certain dealership is either blue or white. What is the average (arithmetic mean) sticker price of all the cars at the dealership?

    (1)   Of all the cars at the dealership, $\frac{1}{3}$ are blue and have an average sticker price of $21,000.

    (2)   Of all the cars at the dealership, $\frac{2}{3}$ are white and have an average sticker price of $24,000.

2. A box contains only white balls and black balls. What is the probability that a ball selected at random from the box is white?

    (1)   There are 100 balls in the box.
    (2)   There are 40 black balls in the box.

3. Rita's monthly salary is $\frac{2}{3}$ Juanita's monthly salary. What is their combined monthly salary?

    (1)   Rita's monthly salary is $4,000.
    (2)   Either Rita's monthly salary or Juanita's monthly salary is $6,000.

4. Each of the 120 students in a certain dormitory is either a junior or a senior. How many of the juniors have credit cards?

    (1) $\frac{2}{3}$ of the 120 juniors and seniors have credit cards.

    (2)   The number of seniors who have credit cards is 20 more than the number of juniors who have credit cards.

5. If the average (arithmetic mean) cost per sweater for 3 pullover sweaters and 1 cardigan sweater was $65, what was the cost of the cardigan sweater?

    (1)   The average cost per sweater for the 3 pullover sweaters was $55.

    (2)   The most expensive of the 3 pullover sweaters cost $30 more than the least expensive.

6. In each quarter of 1998, Company M earned more money than in the previous quarter. What was the range of Company M's quarterly earnings in 1998?

    (1)   In the 2nd and 3rd quarters of 1998, Company M earned $4.0 million and $4.6 million, respectively.

    (2)   In the 1st and 4th quarters of 1998, Company M earned $3.8 million and $4.9 million, respectively.

7.   The range of the heights of a group of high school juniors and seniors is 20 centimeters. What is the average (arithmetic mean) of the height of the tallest senior in the group and the height of the shortest junior in the group?

   (1)   The average of the heights of the juniors in the group is 165 centimeters.
   (2)   The average of the heights of the seniors in the group is 179 centimeters.

8.   In a certain factory, hours worked by each employee in excess of 40 hours per week are overtime hours and are paid for at $1\frac{1}{2}$ times the employee's regular hourly pay rate. If an employee worked a total of 42 hours last week, how much was the employee's gross pay for the hours worked last week?

   (1)   The employee's gross pay for overtime hours worked last week was $30.
   (2)   The employee's gross pay for all hours worked last week was $30 more than for the previous week.

9.   Did Insurance Company K have more than $300 million in total net profits last year?

   (1)   Last year Company K paid out $0.95 in claims for every dollar of premiums collected.
   (2)   Last year Company K earned a total of $150 million in profits from the investment of accumulated surplus premiums from previous years.

10.   How many hours would it take Pump A and Pump B working together, each at its own constant rate, to empty a tank that was initially full?

   (1)   Working alone at its constant rate, Pump A would empty the full tank in 4 hours 20 minutes.
   (2)   Working alone, Pump B would empty the full tank at its constant rate of 72 liters per minute.

11.   Maria left home $\frac{1}{4}$ hour after her husband and drove over the same route as he had in order to overtake him. From the time she left, how many hours did it take Maria to overtake her husband?

   (1)   Maria drove 60 miles before overtaking her husband.
   (2)   While overtaking her husband, Maria drove at an average rate of 60 miles per hour, which was 12 miles per hour faster than her husband's average rate.

12.   In a school that had a total of 600 students enrolled in the junior and senior classes, the students contributed to a certain fund. If all of the juniors but only half of the seniors contributed, was the total amount contributed more than $740?

   (1)   Each junior contributed $1 and each senior who contributed gave $3.
   (2)   There were more juniors than seniors enrolled in the school.

13.   How much did credit-card fraud cost United States banks in year X to the nearest $10 million?

   (1)   In year X, counterfeit cards and telephone and mail-order fraud accounted for 39 percent of the total amount that card fraud cost the banks.
   (2)   In year X, stolen cards accounted for $158.4 million, or 16 percent, of the total amount that credit-card fraud cost the banks.

14.   Company X's profits this year increased by 25% over last year's profits. Was the dollar amount of Company X's profits this year greater than the dollar amount of Company Y's?

   (1)   Last year, the ratio of Company Y's profits to Company X's profits was 5:2.
   (2)   Company Y experienced a 40% drop in profits from last year to this year.

15.   A certain company consists of three divisions, A, B, and C. Of the employees in the three divisions, the employees in Division C have the greatest average (arithmetic mean) annual salary. Is the average annual salary of the employees in the three divisions combined less than $55,000?

   (1)   The average annual salary of the employees in Divisions A and B combined is $45,000.
   (2)   The average annual salary of the employees in Division C is $55,000.

16.   A candle company determines that, for a certain specialty candle, the supply function is $p = m_1x + b_1$ and the demand function is $p = m_2x + b_2$, where p is the price of each candle, x is the number of candles supplied or demanded, and m_1, m_2, b_1, and b_2 are constants. At what value of x do the graphs of the supply function and demand function intersect?

   (1) $m_1 = -m_2 = 0.005$
   (2) $b_2 - b_1 = 6$

17. A certain ski shop sold 125 pairs of skis and 100 pairs of ski boots for a total of $75,000. What was the average (arithmetic mean) selling price of a pair of the ski boots?

    (1) The average selling price of a pair of skis was $300.
    (2) The selling price of a pair of ski boots varied from $150 to $900.

18. Last year Publisher X published 1,100 books, consisting of first editions, revised editions, and reprints. How many first editions did Publisher X publish last year?

    (1) The number of first editions published was 50 more than twice the number of reprints published.
    (2) The number of revised editions published was half the number of reprints published.

19. How old is Jane?

    (1) Ten years ago she was one-third as old as she is now.
    (2) In 15 years, she will be twice as old as she is now.

20. What was the population of City X in 2002?

    (1) X's population in 2002 increased by 2 percent, or 20,000 people, over 2001.
    (2) In 2001, X's population was 1,000,000.

21. Yesterday Bookstore B sold twice as many softcover books as hardcover books. Was Bookstore B's revenue from the sale of softcover books yesterday greater than its revenue from the sale of hardcover books yesterday?

    (1) The average (arithmetic mean) price of the hardcover books sold at the store yesterday was $10 more than the average price of the softcover books sold at the store yesterday.
    (2) The average price of the softcover and hardcover books sold at the store yesterday was greater than $14.

22. A customer purchased 6 shirts priced at $10.99 each, excluding sales tax. How much sales tax did he pay on this purchase?

    (1) The customer paid a 5 percent sales tax on the total price of the shirts.
    (2) The customer paid a total of $11.54 for each shirt, including sales tax.

23. The sum of the lengths of two pieces of rope is 65 feet. How long is the shorter piece?

    (1) The lengths of the pieces of rope are in the ratio 8:5.
    (2) One piece of rope is 15 feet longer than the other piece.

24. An initial investment of $10,000 was deposited in a bank account one year ago, and additional deposits were made during the year. If no withdrawals were made, what was the total amount of interest earned on this account during the year?

    (1) The additional deposits during the year totaled $5,000.
    (2) The account earned interest at the annual rate of 6 percent compounded quarterly.

25. A poplar tree was 3 feet high when it was planted on January 1, 1970. During what year did it pass the height of 20 feet?

    (1) On January 1, 1973, it was 24 feet high.
    (2) It doubled its height during each year.

26. Which weighs more, a cubic unit of water or a cubic unit of liquid X?

    (1) A cubic unit of water weighs more than $\frac{1}{3}$ cubic unit of liquid X.
    (2) A cubic unit of liquid X weighs less than 3 cubic units of water.

27. What were the individual prices of the vases that an antique dealer bought at store *X*?

    (1) The antique dealer bought exactly 3 vases at store *X*.
    (2) The antique dealer's total bill at store *X* was $225.

28. Was the average (arithmetic mean) sale price of a new home in region *R* last month at least $100,000?

    (1) Last month the median sale price of a new home in region *R* was at least $100,000.
    (2) Last month the sale prices of new homes in region *R* ranged from $75,000 to $150,000.

29. If the capacity of tank X is less than the capacity of tank Y and both tanks begin to fill at the same time, which tank will be filled first?

    (1) Tank X is filled at a constant rate of 1.5 liters per minute.
    (2) Tank Y is filled at a constant rate of 120 liters per hour.

30. At a certain company, 30 percent of the employees live in City R. If 25 percent of the company's employees live in apartments in City R, what is the number of the employees who live in apartments in City R?

    (1) Of the employees who live in City R, 6 do not live in apartments.
    (2) Of the employees, 84 do not live in City R.

31. What was Mary's average (arithmetic mean) score on 4 tests?

    (1) Her average (arithmetic mean) score on 3 of the tests was 97.
    (2) Her score on one of the tests was 96.

32. Is there a causal relationship between smoking and lung cancer?

    (1) Research consistently shows a strong correlation between smoking and the development of lung cancer.
    (2) Some medical researchers support a proposed mechanism by which smoking could cause lung cancer.

33. A research project has a successful outcome if its research is reported in a blind peer-reviewed academic publication. Can interdisciplinary collaborations on research projects at least sometimes produce a successful outcome?

    (1) Some interdisciplinary research groups experience conflict and rivalry.
    (2) A peer-reviewed and well-regarded interdisciplinary review of published papers on urban greening trends found that there was little if any evidence that planting more trees in an urban area significantly improved air quality there.

34. It has been proposed that teenagers aged 10 to 15 years be restricted to less than 2 hours per day engaging with social media. Would a significant number of teens aged 10 to 15 years get an overall developmental or health benefit from such a restriction?

    (1) A peer-reviewed study indicates a 23% increase in the incidence of chronic anxiety or depression among teenagers aged 10 to 15 years who average 2 or more hours per day engaging with social media.
    (2) Certain kinds of engagement with social media averaging 2 or more hours per day by teenagers aged 10 to 15 years lead, in about 28% of cases, to meaningful friendships and social and emotional learning, both of which are valuable for development at those ages.

35. A milk vendor mixes water with milk and sells the mixture at the same price per liter as if it were undiluted milk. The selling price per liter of the mixture is the vendor's cost per liter of the milk plus a markup of *x*%. The water costs the vendor nothing. If the vendor gets a 50% profit on the sale of the mixture, what is the value of *x*?

    (1) If the vendor mixes half the intended quantity of water and sells every liter of the mixture at the cost price per liter of the undiluted milk, the vendor will get a 10% profit.
    (2) The concentration of milk in the mixture after adding water is 5/6.

36. Does it benefit a company overall to invest in employee training?

    (1) Companies that invest in comprehensive employee training programs often observe improved job performance among their workforce.

    (2) Well-trained employees are likely to excel in their roles and take the company forward.

37. Can regular exercise reduce the risk of chronic diseases?

    (1) Regular exercise is often associated with better physical health.

    (2) Engaging in regular physical activity contributes to overall well-being.

38. Does effective advertising require a higher budget expense than ineffective advertising?

    (1) Companies that allocate higher budgets to advertising tend to experience increased sales revenue.

    (2) Effective advertising can drive higher consumer demand.

Questions 39 to 74 — Difficulty: **Medium**

	Yes	No	Don't Know
Program X	400	200	400
Program Y	300	350	350

39. The table shows the number of people who responded "yes" or "no" or "don't know" when asked whether their city council should implement environmental programs X and Y. If a total of 1,000 people responded to the question about both programs, what was the number of people who did not respond "yes" to implementing either of the two programs?

    (1) The number of people who responded "yes" to implementing only Program X was 300.

    (2) The number of people who responded "no" to implementing Program X and "no" to implementing Program Y was 100.

40. An estimate of an actual data value has an error of p percent if $p = \dfrac{100|e - a|}{a}$, where e is the estimated value and a is the actual value. Emma's estimate for her total income last year had an error of less than 20 percent. Emma's estimate of her income from tutoring last year also had an error of less than 20 percent. Was Emma's actual income from tutoring last year at most 45 percent of her actual total income last year?

    (1) Emma's estimated income last year from tutoring was 30 percent of her estimated total income last year.

    (2) Emma's estimated total income last year was $40,000.

41. Was Store K's profit last month at least 10 percent greater than its profit the previous month?

    (1) Store K's expenses last month were 5 percent greater than its expenses the previous month.

    (2) Store K's revenues last month were 10 percent greater than its revenues the previous month.

42. Gross profit is equal to selling price minus cost. A car dealer's gross profit on the sale of a certain car was what percent of the cost of the car?

    (1) The selling price of the car was $\dfrac{11}{10}$ of the cost of the car.

    (2) The cost of the car was $14,500.

43. When the wind speed is 9 miles per hour, the wind-chill factor w is given by

    $$w = -17.366 + 1.19t,$$

    where t is the temperature in degrees Fahrenheit. If at noon yesterday the wind speed was 9 miles per hour, was the wind-chill factor greater than 0?

    (1) The temperature at noon yesterday was greater than 10 degrees Fahrenheit.

    (2) The temperature at noon yesterday was less than 20 degrees Fahrenheit.

44. How many members of a certain legislature voted against the measure to raise their salaries?

    (1) $\frac{1}{4}$ of the members of the legislature did not vote on the measure.

    (2) If 5 additional members of the legislature had voted against the measure, then the fraction of members of the legislature voting against the measure would have been $\frac{1}{3}$.

45. During a certain bicycle ride, was Sherry's average speed faster than 24 kilometers per hour?
    (1 kilometer = 1,000 meters)

    (1) Sherry's average speed during the bicycle ride was faster than 7 meters per second.

    (2) Sherry's average speed during the bicycle ride was slower than 8 meters per second.

46. Working together, Rafael and Salvador can tabulate a certain set of data in 2 hours. In how many hours can Rafael tabulate the data working alone?

    (1) Working alone, Rafael can tabulate the data in 3 hours less time than Salvador, working alone, can tabulate the data.

    (2) Working alone, Rafael can tabulate the data in $\frac{1}{2}$ the time that Salvador, working alone, can tabulate the data.

47. Yesterday between 9:00 a.m. and 6:00 p.m. at Airport X, all flights to Atlanta departed at equally spaced times and all flights to New York City departed at equally spaced times. A flight to Atlanta and a flight to New York City both departed from Airport X at 1:00 p.m. yesterday. Between 1:00 p.m. and 3:00 p.m. yesterday, did another pair of flights to these 2 cities depart from Airport X at the same time?

    (1) Yesterday at Airport X, a flight to Atlanta and a flight to New York City both departed at 10:00 a.m.

    (2) Yesterday at Airport X, flights to New York City departed every 15 minutes between 9:00 a.m. and 6:00 p.m.

48. Of the total number of copies of Magazine X sold last week, 40 percent were sold at full price. What was the total number of copies of the magazine sold last week?

    (1) Last week, full price for a copy of Magazine X was $1.50 and the total revenue from full-price sales was $112,500.

    (2) The total number of copies of Magazine X sold last week at full price was 75,000.

49. What is the average (arithmetic mean) annual salary of the 6 employees of a toy company?

    (1) If the 6 annual salaries were ordered from least to greatest, each annual salary would be $6,300 greater than the preceding annual salary.

    (2) The range of the 6 annual salaries is $31,500.

50. In a certain order, the pretax price of each regular pencil was $0.03, the pretax price of each deluxe pencil was $0.05, and there were 50% more deluxe pencils than regular pencils. All taxes on the order are a fixed percent of the pretax prices. The sum of the total pretax price of the order and the tax on the order was $44.10. What was the amount, in dollars, of the tax on the order?

    (1) The tax on the order was 5% of the total pretax price of the order.

    (2) The order contained exactly 400 regular pencils.

51. A total of 20 amounts are entered on a spreadsheet that has 5 rows and 4 columns; each of the 20 positions in the spreadsheet contains one amount. The average (arithmetic mean) of the amounts in row i is R_i ($1 \leq i \leq 5$). The average of the amounts in column j is C_j ($1 \leq j \leq 4$). What is the average of all 20 amounts on the spreadsheet?

    (1) $R_1 + R_2 + R_3 + R_4 + R_5 = 550$
    (2) $C_1 + C_2 + C_3 + C_4 = 440$

52. Was the range of the amounts of money that Company Y budgeted for its projects last year equal to the range of the amounts of money that it budgeted for its projects this year?

    (1) Both last year and this year, Company Y budgeted money for 12 projects and the least amount of money that it budgeted for a project was $400.

    (2) Both last year and this year, the average (arithmetic mean) amount of money that Company Y budgeted per project was $2,000.

53. What is the probability that Lee will make exactly 5 errors on a certain typing test?

    (1) The probability that Lee will make 5 or more errors on the test is 0.27.

    (2) The probability that Lee will make 5 or fewer errors on the test is 0.85.

54. A small factory that produces only upholstered chairs and sofas uses 1 cushion for each chair and 4 cushions for each sofa. If the factory used a total of 300 cushions on the furniture it produced last week, how many sofas did it produce last week?

    (1) Last week the factory produced more chairs than sofas.

    (2) Last week the factory produced a total of 150 chairs and sofas.

DISTRIBUTION OF SALESPERSONS
BY GENDER IN THREE SECTORS, YEAR X

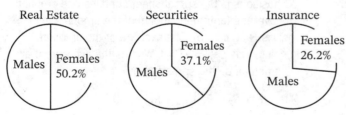

55. In year X, were there more female salespersons in the securities sector than in the insurance sector?

    (1) There were more male salespersons in the insurance sector than in the securities sector.

    (2) The total number of salespersons was greater in the securities sector than in the insurance sector.

56. If a club made a gross profit of $0.25 for each candy bar it sold, how many candy bars did the club sell?

    (1) The total revenue from the sale of the candy bars was $300.

    (2) If the club had sold 80 more candy bars, its gross profits would have increased by 20 percent.

57. In one year 2,100 malpractice claims were filed with insurance company X, and of these $\frac{1}{4}$ resulted in a financial settlement. Of those resulting in a financial settlement of less than $400,000, what was the average payment per claim?

    (1) Company X paid a total of 24.5 million dollars to the claimants.

    (2) Only 5 claims resulted in payments of $400,000 or more.

58. If there are 13 boys in club X, what is the average age of these boys?

    (1) The oldest boy is 13 years old and the youngest boy is 9 years old.

    (2) Eleven of the boys are either 10 years old or 11 years old.

59. If all the employees of a company fall into one and only one of 3 groups, X, Y, or Z, with 250, 100, and 20 members in each group, respectively, what is the average (arithmetic mean) weekly salary of all the employees of this company, if all employees are paid every week of the year?

    (1) The average (arithmetic mean) annual salary of the employees in Group X is $10,000, in Group Y $15,000 and in Group Z $20,000.

    (2) The total annual payroll is $4,400,000.

DISTRIBUTION OF SALES INCOME
FOR STORE *S* LAST WEEK

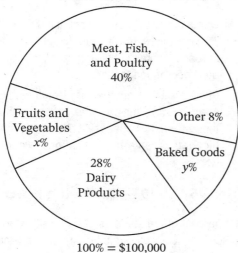

100% = $100,000

60. According to the graph above, the sale of fruits and vegetables in Store *S* last week accounted for what percent of the total sales income for the week?

   (1) Last week the total income from the sale of fruits and vegetables in Store *S* was $16,000.

   (2) *x* = 2*y*

61. Larry saves *x* dollars per month. Will Larry's total savings one year from now exceed his present savings by at least $500? (Assume that there is no interest.)

   (1) In 6 months Larry's total savings will be $900.

   (2) In 3 months Larry's total savings will exceed his present savings by $150.

62. If Randy has twice as many coins as Alice, and if Maria has 7 times as many coins as Alice, what is the combined number of coins that all three of them have?

   (1) Alice has 4 fewer coins than Randy.

   (2) Maria has 20 more coins than Randy.

63. A line of people waiting to enter a theater consists of seven separate and successive groups. The first person in each group purchases one ticket for each person in the group and for no one else. If *n* is the total number of tickets sold for the first six groups, is *n* an even number?

   (1) There are no more than 4 people in each group.

   (2) The 19th person in line purchases the tickets for the seventh group.

64. If John has exactly 10 coins each of which was minted in 1910 or 1920 or 1930, how many of his coins were minted in 1920?

   (1) Exactly 6 of his coins were minted in 1910 or 1920.

   (2) Exactly 7 of his coins were minted in 1920 or 1930.

65. The total profit of corporation K was $3,400,000 in year X. What was the total profit in year Y?

   (1) Income in year Y was 30 percent more than in year X.

   (2) Costs in year Y were 40 percent more than in year X.

66. Zelma scored 90, 88, and 92 on 3 of the 6 mathematics tests that she took. What was her average (arithmetic mean) score on the 6 tests?

   (1) Her average (arithmetic mean) score on 5 of the tests was 90.

   (2) Her score on one of the tests was 91.

67. Will a company lose sales if its strategy focuses on consumer well-being rather than exploiting consumer fears?

   (1) The company's current marketing strategy exploits its consumers' fears to drive sales, resulting in increased profits.

   (2) From an ethical standpoint, the company should prioritize consumer well-being over short-term profits and refrain from exploiting their fears.

68. Should a holistic approach be used to measure academic success?

   (1) Traditional education policies focus on standardized testing as the primary measure of academic success.

   (2) To foster holistic learning, education policies should prioritize a well-rounded curriculum that includes critical thinking, creativity, and practical skills.

69. Can financial budgeting help individuals avoid debt?

(1) Many individuals struggle with mounting debt due to excessive spending resulting from a lack of financial planning.

(2) To avoid taking out loans, individuals should practice responsible budgeting, enabling them to save for emergencies and achieve financial stability.

70. What kind of behavior is usually displayed by conflicting factions?

(1) In conflicts, some factions resort to aggression and hostility, which escalates the situation.

(2) To promote peaceful resolutions, factions should engage in open communication, empathy, and compromise to find mutually beneficial solutions.

71. What is the probability of landing on tails at least once in a sequence of 100 tosses of a specific coin?

(1) When tossing the coin, there are only two possible outcomes, heads or tails, and both have an equal chance of occurring.

(2) In a series of 100 tosses of the coin, we can expect almost 50 heads.

72. What are some possible signs of impending rainfall in Exville today?

(1) The weather forecast correctly predicts a 90% chance of rain in Exville today based on heavy cloud cover and low-pressure systems moving into the region.

(2) Given the darkening sky, the sudden drop in temperature, and strong winds, it is highly likely that a rainstorm is imminent in Exville today.

73. A patient experiencing cold-like symptoms goes to a doctor. Is the patient suffering from a viral infection?

(1) Based on their symptoms and medical history, the patient thinks they are suffering from a viral infection.

(2) Due to their knowledge of common illnesses in the local area, the doctor thinks it is more likely that seasonal allergies are the cause of the patient's symptoms.

74. What should generally be expected if you venture into areas surrounding a road closure?

(1) With a major G20 event happening at the Jawahar Lal Nehru Stadium tonight and reports of road closures in the area, there's a strong likelihood of congestion.

(2) Given the large number of attendees expected at an event at the Jawahar Lal Nehru Stadium tonight, shuttle buses will be provided between the stadium and the International Media Centre.

Questions 75 to 110 — Difficulty: **Hard**

75. What percent of the students at University X are enrolled in a science course but are not enrolled in a biology course?

(1) 28 percent of the students at University X are enrolled in a biology course.

(2) 70 percent of the students at University X who are enrolled in a science course are enrolled in a biology course.

76. Each Type A machine fills 400 cans per minute, each Type B machine fills 600 cans per minute, and each Type C machine installs 2,400 lids per minute. A lid is installed on each can that is filled and on no can that is not filled. For a particular minute, what is the total number of machines working?

(1) A total of 4,800 cans are filled that minute.

(2) For that minute, there are 2 Type B machines working for every Type C machine working.

77. In a two-month survey of shoppers, each shopper bought one of two brands of detergent, X or Y, in the first month and again bought one of these brands in the second month. In the survey, 90 percent of the shoppers who bought Brand X in the first month bought Brand X again in the second month, while 60 percent of the shoppers who bought Brand Y in the first month bought Brand Y again in the second month. What percent of the shoppers bought Brand Y in the second month?

(1) In the first month, 50 percent of the shoppers bought Brand X.

(2) The total number of shoppers surveyed was 5,000.

78. If the total price of *n* equally priced shares of a certain stock was $12,000, what was the price per share of the stock?

    (1) If the price per share of the stock had been $1 more, the total price of the *n* shares would have been $300 more.

    (2) If the price per share of the stock had been $2 less, the total price of the *n* shares would have been 5 percent less.

79. In Year X, 8.7 percent of the men in the labor force were unemployed in June compared with 8.4 percent in May. If the number of men in the labor force was the same for both months, how many men were unemployed in June of that year?

    (1) In May of Year X, the number of unemployed men in the labor force was 3.36 million.

    (2) In Year X, 120,000 more men in the labor force were unemployed in June than in May.

80. On Monday morning a certain machine ran continuously at a uniform rate to fill a production order. At what time did it completely fill the order that morning?

    (1) The machine began filling the order at 9:30 a.m.

    (2) The machine had filled $\frac{1}{2}$ of the order by 10:30 a.m. and $\frac{5}{6}$ of the order by 11:10 a.m.

81. After winning 50 percent of the first 20 games it played, Team A won all of the remaining games it played. What was the total number of games that Team A won?

    (1) Team A played 25 games altogether.

    (2) Team A won 60 percent of all the games it played.

82. Michael arranged all his books in a bookcase with 10 books on each shelf and no books left over. After Michael acquired 10 additional books, he arranged all his books in a new bookcase with 12 books on each shelf and no books left over. How many books did Michael have before he acquired the 10 additional books?

    (1) Before Michael acquired the 10 additional books, he had fewer than 96 books.

    (2) Before Michael acquired the 10 additional books, he had more than 24 books.

83. Last year in a group of 30 businesses, 21 reported a net profit and 15 had investments in foreign markets. How many of the businesses did not report a net profit nor invest in foreign markets last year?

    (1) Last year 12 of the 30 businesses reported a net profit and had investments in foreign markets.

    (2) Last year 24 of the 30 businesses reported a net profit or invested in foreign markets, or both.

84. For each landscaping job that takes more than 4 hours, a certain contractor charges a total of *r* dollars for the first 4 hours plus 0.2*r* dollars for each additional hour or fraction of an hour, where *r* > 100. Did a particular landscaping job take more than 10 hours?

    (1) The contractor charged a total of $288 for the job.

    (2) The contractor charged a total of 2.4*r* dollars for the job.

85. If 75 percent of the guests at a certain banquet ordered dessert, what percent of the guests ordered coffee?

    (1) 60 percent of the guests who ordered dessert also ordered coffee.

    (2) 90 percent of the guests who ordered coffee also ordered dessert.

86. A tank containing water started to leak. Did the tank contain more than 30 gallons of water when it started to leak? (Note: 1 gallon = 128 ounces)

    (1) The water leaked from the tank at a constant rate of 6.4 ounces per minute.

    (2) The tank became empty less than 12 hours after it started to leak.

87. Each of the 45 books on a shelf is written either in English or in Spanish, and each of the books is either a hardcover book or a paperback. If a book is to be selected at random from the books on the shelf, is the probability less than $\frac{1}{2}$ that the book selected will be a paperback written in Spanish?

    (1) Of the books on the shelf, 30 are paperbacks.

    (2) Of the books on the shelf, 15 are written in Spanish.

88. A small school has three foreign language classes, one in French, one in Spanish, and one in German. How many of the 34 students enrolled in the Spanish class are also enrolled in the French class?

    (1) There are 27 students enrolled in the French class, and 49 students enrolled in either the French class, the Spanish class, or both of these classes.

    (2) One-half of the students enrolled in the Spanish class are enrolled in more than one foreign language class.

89. Last year $\frac{3}{5}$ of the members of a certain club were males. This year the members of the club include all the members from last year plus some new members. Is the fraction of the members of the club who are males greater this year than last year?

    (1) More than half of the new members are male.

    (2) The number of members of the club this year is $\frac{6}{5}$ the number of members last year.

90. Machines K, M, and N, each working alone at its constant rate, produce 1 widget in x, y, and 2 minutes, respectively. If Machines K, M, and N work simultaneously at their respective constant rates, does it take them less than 1 hour to produce a total of 50 widgets?

    (1) $x < 1.5$

    (2) $y < 1.2$

91. Stations X and Y are connected by two separate, straight, parallel rail lines that are 250 miles long. Train P and train Q simultaneously left Station X and Station Y, respectively, and each train traveled to the other's point of departure. The two trains passed each other after traveling for 2 hours. When the two trains passed, which train was nearer to its destination?

    (1) At the time when the two trains passed, train P had averaged a speed of 70 miles per hour.

    (2) Train Q averaged a speed of 55 miles per hour for the entire trip.

92. In a two-story apartment complex, each apartment on the upper floor rents for 75 percent as much as each apartment on the lower floor. If the total monthly rent is $15,300 when rent is collected on all of the apartments, what is the monthly rent on each apartment on the lower floor?

    (1) An apartment on the lower floor rents for $150 more per month than an apartment on the upper floor.

    (2) There are 6 more apartments on the upper floor than on the lower floor.

93. A motorboat, which is set to travel at k kilometers per hour in still water, travels directly up and down the center of a straight river so that the change in the boat's speed relative to the shore depends only on the speed and direction of the current. What is the value of k?

    (1) It takes the same amount of time for the boat to travel 4 kilometers directly downstream as it takes for it to travel 3 kilometers directly upstream.

    (2) The current flows directly downstream at a constant rate of 2.5 kilometers per hour.

94. If the book value of a certain piece of equipment was $5,000 exactly 5 years ago, what is its present book value?

    (1) From the time the piece of equipment was purchased, its book value decreased by 10 percent of its purchase price each year of its life.

    (2) The present book value of another piece of equipment is $2,000.

95. The total cost to charter a bus was shared equally by the people who went on a certain trip. If the total cost to charter the bus was $360, how many people went on the trip?

    (1) Each person who went on the trip paid $9 to charter the bus.

    (2) If 4 fewer people had gone on the trip, each person's share of the total cost to charter the bus would have increased by $1.

96. If each of the stamps Carla bought cost 20, 25, or 30 cents and she bought at least one of each denomination, what is the number of 25-cent stamps that she bought?

    (1) She spent a total of $1.45 for stamps.
    (2) She bought exactly 6 stamps.

97. A car traveled a distance of d miles in t minutes at an average rate of r miles per minute. What is the ratio of d to r?

    (1) $t = 30$
    (2) $d = 25$

98. Pat is reading a book that has a total of 15 chapters. Has Pat read at least $\frac{1}{3}$ of the pages in the book?

    (1) Pat has just finished reading the first 5 chapters.
    (2) Each of the first 3 chapters has more pages than each of the other 12 chapters in the book.

99. Should the choices made by 100 participants in a survey about Product X be said to proportionately represent the preferences of the entire population?

    (1) In the survey of 100 participants, 70% said they preferred Product X.
    (2) While the survey provided valuable insights into Product X, the small sample may not be representative of the entire population's preferences.

100. What is a limiting factor when it comes to us using the most effective solution?

    (1) We have identified several potential solutions, but a lack of funding hinders their implementation.
    (2) As the most effective solution requires extensive resources, we must opt for a more affordable option given our budget.

101. What are all the important considerations for making accurate projections?

    (1) Based on the available data, we believe that the market demand for our product will increase by 20% in the next quarter.
    (2) Without comprehensive market research, our projection may not account for external factors that could influence fluctuations in demand.

102. Does Company X strive to maintain a low defect rate in order to ensure product quality?

    (1) Company X's manufacturing process has a defect rate of 2% according to quality control data.
    (2) Monitoring the defect rate in a manufacturing process is essential to ensure product quality, and a low percentage indicates a well-maintained production process.

103. How might career advancement be described as potentially linked to both growth and decline?

    (1) Working long hours and overtime may lead to higher productivity and career advancement but is likely to cause a decline in physical and mental well-being.
    (2) Maintaining a work-life balance is important to reduce the negative effect that working too much has on a person's quality of life.

104. What is an example of how investment in healthcare resources might sometimes create a challenge?

    (1) Investment in both advanced medical technology and specialized treatments can improve patient outcomes for certain conditions. Nevertheless, it may put a strain on healthcare budgets.
    (2) When it comes to allocating resources in the healthcare sector, directing money toward the purchase of advanced medical equipment could potentially limit access to other essential services and treatments.

105. A person bought x number of apples, y number of oranges, and z number of mangoes from a shop. What is the total price of this transaction if each apple costs $2, each orange costs $2.50, and each mango costs $3?

    (1) The number of apples bought is 12 more than the number of oranges bought. The number of mangoes bought is half the number of apples bought.
    (2) The average number of fruits purchased from the three varieties is greater than 29 and less than 33.

106. Adam received a certain monetary amount in bills having only three denominations: $1, $5, and $10. What is the total monetary amount in bills that he received?

    (1) The numbers of $1, $5, and $10 bills Adam received, respectively, are in the ratio 3:5:8.

    (2) The ratio of the monetary amount Adam received in $1 bills to the monetary amount he received in $10 bills is 3:80.

107. Exactly 3 investors—A, B, and C—invested in a certain business, each for a certain number of months. For these investments, what is the ratio of the profit earned by A to the profit earned by B to the profit earned by C? (Note: Profit earned is proportional to the product of investment amount and investment duration.)

    (1) A invested twice as much as B, and C invested half as much as A and B together.

    (2) All 3 investments were for the same number of months.

108. The ratio of A's current age to B's current age is 5:8. What will be the sum of their ages 10 years from now? (Note: Assume that neither A nor B dies in the next 10 years.)

    (1) If A had been born 2 years later and B had been born 2 years earlier, then the ratio of A's current age to B's current age would be 14:25.

    (2) A's age 5 years ago was half the age that B will be 2 years from now.

109. A's father is 6 years older than her mother. The ratio of A's age to her mother's age is 1:4. What is the age of A's father?

    (1) A's father is 30 years older than A.

    (2) The ratio of A's age to her father's age is 4:19.

110. The salary of A is what percentage of the combined salaries of B and C?

    (1) Twice the salary of A is equal to three times the salary of B.

    (2) 150% of B's salary is $160 more than 120% of C's salary.

6.5 Answer Key: Data Sufficiency

1.	C	23.	D	45.	A	67.	E	89.	E
2.	C	24.	E	46.	D	68.	E	90.	D
3.	A	25.	B	47.	E	69.	D	91.	A
4.	C	26.	E	48.	D	70.	E	92.	A
5.	A	27.	E	49.	E	71.	A	93.	C
6.	B	28.	E	50.	D	72.	D	94.	E
7.	E	29.	E	51.	D	73.	E	95.	D
8.	A	30.	D	52.	E	74.	E	96.	E
9.	E	31.	E	53.	C	75.	C	97.	A
10.	E	32.	E	54.	B	76.	C	98.	E
11.	B	33.	B	55.	B	77.	A	99.	E
12.	E	34.	B	56.	B	78.	D	100.	B
13.	B	35.	D	57.	E	79.	D	101.	E
14.	C	36.	E	58.	E	80.	B	102.	E
15.	B	37.	E	59.	D	81.	D	103.	A
16.	C	38.	E	60.	D	82.	A	104.	D
17.	A	39.	A	61.	B	83.	D	105.	E
18.	C	40.	A	62.	D	84.	B	106.	E
19.	D	41.	C	63.	B	85.	C	107.	C
20.	A	42.	A	64.	C	86.	E	108.	D
21.	C	43.	E	65.	E	87.	B	109.	D
22.	D	44.	E	66.	E	88.	A	110.	E

6.6 Answer Explanations: Data Sufficiency

The following discussion of Data Insights is intended to familiarize you with the most efficient and effective approaches to the kinds of problems common to Data Insights. The particular questions in this chapter are generally representative of the kinds of Data Insights questions you will encounter on the GMAT exam. Remember that it is the problem-solving strategy that is important, not the specific details of a particular question.

Questions 1 to 38 — Difficulty: **Easy**

1. Each car at a certain dealership is either blue or white. What is the average (arithmetic mean) sticker price of all the cars at the dealership?

    (1) Of all the cars at the dealership, $\frac{1}{3}$ are blue and have an average sticker price of $21,000.

    (2) Of all the cars at the dealership, $\frac{2}{3}$ are white and have an average sticker price of $24,000.

    Algebra Statistics

    Let Σ_b and Σ_w be the sum of the sticker prices, respectively and in dollars, of the blue cars and the white cars at the dealership, and let n be the number of cars at the dealership. Determine the value of $\frac{\Sigma_b + \Sigma_w}{n}$.

    (1) Given that there are $\frac{1}{3}n$ blue cars having an average sticker price of $21,000, it follows that $\Sigma_b = \left(\frac{1}{3}n\right)21{,}000 = 7{,}000n$. Therefore,

    $$\frac{\Sigma_b + \Sigma_w}{n} = \frac{7{,}000n + \Sigma_w}{n} = 7{,}000 + \frac{\Sigma_w}{n},$$

    which can have more than one possible value by suitably varying Σ_w and n; NOT sufficient.

    (2) Given that there are $\frac{2}{3}n$ white cars having an average sticker price of $24,000, it follows that $\Sigma_w = \left(\frac{2}{3}n\right)24{,}000 = 16{,}000n$. Therefore, $\frac{\Sigma_b + \Sigma_w}{n} = \frac{\Sigma_b + 16{,}000n}{n} = \frac{\Sigma_b}{n} + 16{,}000$, which can have more than one possible value by suitably varying Σ_b and n; NOT sufficient.

    Taking (1) and (2) together, $\frac{\Sigma_b + \Sigma_w}{n} = \frac{7{,}000n + 16{,}000n}{n} = \frac{23{,}000n}{n} = 23{,}000.$

    The correct answer is C; both statements together are sufficient.

2. A box contains only white balls and black balls. What is the probability that a ball selected at random from the box is white?

    (1) There are 100 balls in the box.

    (2) There are 40 black balls in the box.

    Arithmetic Probability

    Determine the probability of selecting a white ball from a box that contains only white and black balls.

    (1) Given that there are 100 balls in the box, it is impossible to determine the probability of selecting a white ball because there is no information on the white/black split of the 100 balls in the box; NOT sufficient.

    (2) Given that there are 40 black balls in the box, it is impossible to determine the probability of selecting a white ball because there is no indication of either the total number of balls in the box or the number of white balls; NOT sufficient.

    Taking (1) and (2) together, there are 100 balls in the box, 40 of which are black. It follows that the number of white balls is $100 - 40 = 60$ and the probability of selecting a white ball is $\frac{60}{100} = \frac{3}{5}$.

    The correct answer is C; both statements together are sufficient.

3. Rita's monthly salary is $\frac{2}{3}$ Juanita's monthly salary. What is their combined monthly salary?

   (1) Rita's monthly salary is $4,000.
   (2) Either Rita's monthly salary or Juanita's monthly salary is $6,000.

Arithmetic Applied Problems

Let R and J be Rita's and Juanita's monthly salaries, respectively, in dollars. It is given that $R = \frac{2}{3} J$. Determine the value of their combined salary, which can be expressed as $R + J = \frac{2}{3} J + J = \frac{5}{3} J$.

   (1) Given that $R = 4,000$, it follows that $4,000 = \frac{2}{3} J$, or $J = \frac{3}{2} (4,000) = 6,000$.

   Therefore, $\frac{5}{3} J = \frac{5}{3} (6,000) = 10,000$; SUFFICIENT.

   (2) Given that $R = 6,000$ or $J = 6,000$, then $J = \frac{3}{2} (6,000) = 9,000$ or $J = 6,000$. Thus, $\frac{5}{3} J = \frac{5}{3} (9,000) = 15,000$ or $\frac{5}{3} J = \frac{5}{3} (6,000) = 10,000$, and so it is not possible to determine the value of $\frac{5}{3} J$; NOT sufficient.

   The correct answer is A; statement 1 alone is sufficient.

4. Each of the 120 students in a certain dormitory is either a junior or a senior. How many of the juniors have credit cards?

   (1) $\frac{2}{3}$ of the 120 juniors and seniors have credit cards.
   (2) The number of seniors who have credit cards is 20 more than the number of juniors who have credit cards.

Algebra First-Degree Equations

Determine the number of juniors who have credit cards among the 120 students in a certain junior/senior dormitory.

   (1) Given that $\frac{2}{3}$ of the 120 students have credit cards, it follows that 80 students have credit

cards. There is no information regarding the number of juniors in this group of 80; NOT sufficient.

   (2) Given that the number of seniors with credit cards is 20 more than the number of juniors with credit cards, it is impossible to determine how many juniors have credit cards because no information is given about the junior/senior split nor about the have/do not have credit cards split of the 120 students; NOT sufficient.

Taking (1) and (2) together, 80 students have credit cards from (1) and the number of seniors with credit cards is 20 more than the number of juniors with credit cards from (2). Thus, $J + S = 80$ or $J + (J + 20) = 80$, which can be solved for a unique value of J.

The correct answer is C; both statements together are sufficient.

5. If the average (arithmetic mean) cost per sweater for 3 pullover sweaters and 1 cardigan sweater was $65, what was the cost of the cardigan sweater?

   (1) The average cost per sweater for the 3 pullover sweaters was $55.
   (2) The most expensive of the 3 pullover sweaters cost $30 more than the least expensive.

Algebra Statistics

Letting P represent the average cost, in dollars, of 1 pullover sweater and C, the cost, in dollars, of the cardigan, it is given that $\frac{3P + C}{4} = 65$ or $3P + C = 260$. Determine the value of C.

   (1) It is given that $P = 55$. Therefore, $3P = 3(55) = 165$ and $C = 260 - 165 = 95$; SUFFICIENT.

   (2) Given that the most expensive pullover sweater cost $30 more than the least expensive, it is impossible to determine the value of C. For example, if the price of the most expensive pullover sweater was $60, the price of the least expensive was $30, and the price of the other pullover sweater was $40, then the value of $C = 260 - 60 - 30 - 40 = 130$. But if the price of the most expensive pullover sweater

was $60, the price of the least expensive was $30, and the price of the other pullover sweater was $50, then the value of $C = 260 - 60 - 30 - 50 = 120$; NOT sufficient.

The correct answer is A; statement 1 alone is sufficient.

6. In each quarter of 1998, Company M earned more money than in the previous quarter. What was the range of Company M's quarterly earnings in 1998?

    (1) In the 2nd and 3rd quarters of 1998, Company M earned $4.0 million and $4.6 million, respectively.

    (2) In the 1st and 4th quarters of 1998, Company M earned $3.8 million and $4.9 million, respectively.

Arithmetic Statistics

We know that for each of the quarters in 1998, Company M earned more money than in the previous quarter. Is it possible to determine the range of the company's quarterly earnings in 1998?

    (1) Although we are told the value of the earnings for the 2nd and 3rd quarters, Company M's 4th quarter earnings could, consistent with statement 1, be any amount that is greater than the 3rd-quarter earnings. Likewise, the company's 1st-quarter earnings could be any positive amount that is less than the company's 2nd-quarter earnings. The difference between these two values would be the range, and we see that it cannot be determined; NOT sufficient.

    (2) We are given the earnings for the 1st and 4th quarters, and we already know that, from quarter to quarter, the earnings in 1998 have always increased. We can thus infer that Company M's earnings for the 2nd and 3rd quarters are less than the 4th-quarter earnings but greater than the 1st-quarter earnings. The difference between the greatest quarterly earnings and the least quarterly earnings for 1998 is thus the difference between the 4th-quarter earnings and the 1st-quarter earnings—the values $4.9 million and $3.8 million, respectively, that we have been given; SUFFICIENT.

The correct answer is B; statement 2 alone is sufficient.

7. The range of the heights of a group of high school juniors and seniors is 20 centimeters. What is the average (arithmetic mean) of the height of the tallest senior in the group and the height of the shortest junior in the group?

    (1) The average of the heights of the juniors in the group is 165 centimeters.

    (2) The average of the heights of the seniors in the group is 179 centimeters.

Arithmetic Statistics

Determine the average of the height of the tallest senior and the height of the shortest junior.

    (1) Given that the average of the heights of the juniors is 165 cm, it is not possible to determine the average of the height of the tallest senior and the height of the shortest junior. For example, the heights of the juniors could all be 165 cm and there could be three seniors with heights 176 cm, 176 cm, and 185 cm. In this case the range of all the heights is $185 - 165 = 20$ cm, the average of the heights of the juniors is 165 cm, and the average of the height of the tallest senior and the height of the shortest junior is $\frac{185 + 165}{2} = 175$. Or the heights of the seniors could all be 179 cm and there could be three juniors with heights 159 cm, 168 cm, and 168 cm. In this case the range of all the heights is $179 - 159 = 20$ cm, the average of the heights of the juniors is 165 cm, and the average of the height of the tallest senior and the height of the shortest junior is $\frac{179 + 159}{2} = 169$; NOT sufficient.

    (2) Given that the average of the heights of the seniors is 179 cm, it is not possible to determine the average of the height of the tallest senior and the height of the shortest junior because, for each of the examples used in (1) above, the average of the heights of the seniors is 179 cm; NOT sufficient.

Taking (1) and (2) together, it is not possible to determine the average of the height of the tallest senior and the height of the shortest junior because each of the examples used in (1) above satisfies both (1) and (2).

The correct answer is E;
both statements together are still not sufficient.

8. In a certain factory, hours worked by each employee in excess of 40 hours per week are overtime hours and are paid for at $1\frac{1}{2}$ times the employee's regular hourly pay rate. If an employee worked a total of 42 hours last week, how much was the employee's gross pay for the hours worked last week?

   (1) The employee's gross pay for overtime hours worked last week was $30.

   (2) The employee's gross pay for all hours worked last week was $30 more than for the previous week.

Arithmetic Applied Problems

If an employee's regular hourly rate was R and the employee worked 42 hours last week, then the employee's gross pay for hours worked last week was $40R + 2(1.5R)$. Determine the value of $40R + 2(1.5R) = 43R$, or equivalently, the value of R.

   (1) Given that the employee's gross pay for overtime hours worked last week was $30, it follows that $2(1.5R) = 30$ and $R = 10$; SUFFICIENT.

   (2) Given that the employee's gross pay for all hours worked last week was $30 more than for the previous week, the value of R cannot be determined because nothing specific is known about the value of the employee's pay for all hours worked the previous week; NOT sufficient.

The correct answer is A;
statement 1 alone is sufficient.

9. Did Insurance Company K have more than $300 million in total net profits last year?

   (1) Last year Company K paid out $0.95 in claims for every dollar of premiums collected.

   (2) Last year Company K earned a total of $150 million in profits from the investment of accumulated surplus premiums from previous years.

Arithmetic Applied Problems

Letting R and E, respectively, represent the company's total revenue and total expenses last year, determine if $R - E > \$300$ million.

   (1) This indicates that, for $\$x$ in premiums collected, the company paid $\$0.95x$ in claims, but gives no information about other sources of revenue or other types of expenses; NOT sufficient.

   (2) This indicates that the company's profits from the investment of accumulated surplus premiums was $150 million last year, but gives no information about other sources of revenue or other types of expenses; NOT sufficient.

Taking (1) and (2) together gives information on profit resulting from collecting premiums and paying claims as well as profit resulting from investments from accumulated surplus premiums but gives no indication whether there were other sources of revenue or other types of expenses.

The correct answer is E;
both statements together are still not sufficient.

10. How many hours would it take Pump A and Pump B working together, each at its own constant rate, to empty a tank that was initially full?

   (1) Working alone at its constant rate, Pump A would empty the full tank in 4 hours 20 minutes.

   (2) Working alone, Pump B would empty the full tank at its constant rate of 72 liters per minute.

Arithmetic Applied Problems

Determine how long it would take Pumps A and B working together, each at its own constant rate, to empty a full tank.

   (1) This indicates how long it would take Pump A to empty the tank but gives no information about Pump B's constant rate; NOT sufficient.

   (2) This indicates the rate at which Pump B can empty the tank, but without information about the capacity of the tank or Pump A's rate, it is not possible to determine how long both pumps working together would take to empty the tank; NOT sufficient.

Taking (1) and (2) together gives the amount of time it would take Pump A to empty the tank and the rate at which Pump B can empty the tank, but without knowing the capacity of the tank, it is not possible to determine how long the pumps working together would take to empty the tank.

The correct answer is E; both statements together are still not sufficient.

11. Maria left home $\frac{1}{4}$ hour after her husband and drove over the same route as he had in order to overtake him. From the time she left, how many hours did it take Maria to overtake her husband?

    (1) Maria drove 60 miles before overtaking her husband.

    (2) While overtaking her husband, Maria drove at an average rate of 60 miles per hour, which was 12 miles per hour faster than her husband's average rate.

Arithmetic Rate Problems

(1) Given that Maria drove 60 miles before overtaking her husband, it is not possible to determine how many hours she spent driving this distance. For example, she could have been driving this distance at a rate of 30 miles per hour and thus spent 2 hours driving this distance. However, she could also have been driving this distance at a rate of 60 miles per hour and thus spent 1 hour driving this distance; NOT sufficient.

(2) Given that Maria drove at an average of 60 miles per hour and her husband drove at an average of $60 - 12 = 48$ miles per hour, and letting t be the number of hours it took for Maria to overtake her husband, it follows that $60t = 48(t + \frac{1}{4})$ since the distance Maria drove, $60t$ miles, is the same as the distance her husband drove, $48(t + \frac{1}{4})$ miles. Therefore, $60t = 48t + 12$, or $t = 1$, and hence it took 1 hour for Maria to overtake her husband; SUFFICIENT.

The correct answer is B; statement 2 alone is sufficient.

12. In a school that had a total of 600 students enrolled in the junior and senior classes, the students contributed to a certain fund. If all of the juniors but only half of the seniors contributed, was the total amount contributed more than $740?

    (1) Each junior contributed $1 and each senior who contributed gave $3.

    (2) There were more juniors than seniors enrolled in the school.

Arithmetic Applied Problems

The task in this question is to determine whether the respective statements are sufficient for answering the question of whether the total amount contributed was more than $740. In making this determination, it is important to remember that we are to use only the information that has been given. For example, it may seem plausible to assume that the number of seniors at the school is roughly equal to the number of juniors. However, because no such information has been provided, we cannot assume that this assumption holds. With this in mind, consider statements 1 and 2.

(1) If it were the case that half of the 600 students were seniors, then, given that half of the 300 seniors would have contributed $3, there would have been $150 \times \$3 = \$450$ in contributions from the seniors and $300 \times \$1 = \$300$ in contributions from the juniors, for a total of $750—more than the figure of $740 with which the question is concerned. However, as noted, we cannot make such an assumption. To test the conditions that we actually have been given, we can consider extreme cases, which are often relatively simple. For example, given the information provided, it is possible that only two of the students are seniors and the other 598 students are juniors. If this were the case, then the contributions from the juniors would be $598 ($1 per student) and the contributions from the seniors would be $3 ($3 for the one senior who contributes, given that only half of the 2 seniors contribute). The total contributions would then be $598 + $3 = $601; NOT sufficient.

(2)   Merely with this statement—and not statement 1—we have no information as to how much the students contributed. We therefore cannot determine the total amount contributed; NOT sufficient.

We still need to consider whether statements 1 and 2 are sufficient *together* for determining whether a minimum of $740 has been contributed. However, note that the reasoning in connection with statement 1 applies here as well. We considered there the possibility that the 600 students included only two seniors, with the other 598 students being juniors. Because this scenario also satisfies statement 2, we see that statements 1 and 2 taken together are not sufficient.

The correct answer is E; both statements together are still not sufficient.

13.   How much did credit-card fraud cost United States banks in year X to the nearest $10 million?

(1)   In year X, counterfeit cards and telephone and mail-order fraud accounted for 39 percent of the total amount that card fraud cost the banks.

(2)   In year X, stolen cards accounted for $158.4 million, or 16 percent, of the total amount that credit-card fraud cost the banks.

Arithmetic Percents

(1)   It is given that certain parts of the total fraud cost have a total that is 39% of the total fraud cost, but since no actual dollar amounts are specified, it is not possible to estimate the total fraud cost to the nearest $10 million; NOT sufficient.

(2)   Given that $158.4 million represents 16% of the total fraud cost, it follows that the total fraud cost equals $158.4 million divided by 0.16; SUFFICIENT.

The correct answer is B; statement 2 alone is sufficient.

14.   Company X's profits this year increased by 25% over last year's profits. Was the dollar amount of Company X's profits this year greater than the dollar amount of Company Y's?

(1)   Last year, the ratio of Company Y's profits to Company X's profits was 5:2.

(2)   Company Y experienced a 40% drop in profits from last year to this year.

Algebra Applied Problems

Let P_X and P'_X, respectively, be the profits of Company X last year and this year, and let P_Y and P'_Y, respectively, be the profits of Company Y last year and this year. Then $P'_X = 1.25 P_X$. Is $P'_X > P'_Y$?

(1)   Given that $\dfrac{P_Y}{P_X} = \dfrac{5}{2}$, it is not possible to determine whether $P'_X > P'_Y$ because nothing is known about the value of P'_Y other than P'_Y is positive; NOT sufficient.

(2)   Given that $P'_Y = 0.6 P_Y$, it is not possible to determine whether $P'_X > P'_Y$ because nothing is known that relates the profits of Company X for either year to the profits of Company Y for either year; NOT sufficient.

Taking (1) and (2) together, it is given that $P'_X = 1.25 P_X$ and from (1) it follows that $\dfrac{P_Y}{P_X} = \dfrac{5}{2}$, or $P_X = \dfrac{2}{5} P_Y$, and thus $P'_X = (1.25)\left(\dfrac{2}{5} P_Y\right)$. From (2) it follows that $P'_Y = 0.6 P_Y$, or $P_Y = \dfrac{1}{0.6} P'_Y$, and thus $P'_X = (1.25)\left(\dfrac{2}{5}\right)\left(\dfrac{1}{0.6} P'_Y\right)$. Since the last equation expresses P'_X as a specific number times P'_Y, it follows that it can be determined whether or not $P'_X > P'_Y$. Note that $(1.25)\left(\dfrac{2}{5}\right)\left(\dfrac{1}{0.6}\right) = \left(\dfrac{5}{4}\right)\left(\dfrac{2}{5}\right)\left(\dfrac{5}{3}\right) = \dfrac{5}{6}$, and so the answer to the question "Is $P'_X > P'_Y$" is no.

The correct answer is C; both statements together are sufficient.

15.   A certain company consists of three divisions, A, B, and C. Of the employees in the three divisions, the employees in Division C have the greatest average (arithmetic mean) annual salary. Is the average annual salary of the employees in the three divisions combined less than $55,000?

(1)   The average annual salary of the employees in Divisions A and B combined is $45,000.

(2)   The average annual salary of the employees in Division C is $55,000.

Algebra Statistics

(1) Given that the average annual salary of the employees in Divisions A and B combined is \$45,000, each of the divisions could have exactly two employees such that the annual salaries in Division A are \$45,000 and \$45,000, the annual salaries in Division B are \$45,000 and \$45,000, and the annual salaries in Division C are \$50,000 and \$50,000, in which case Division C has the greatest average annual salary and the average annual salary in Divisions A, B, and C combined is less than \$55,000. On the other hand, each of the divisions could have exactly two employees such that the annual salaries in Division A are \$45,000 and \$45,000, the annual salaries in Division B are \$45,000 and \$45,000, and the annual salaries in Division C are \$1 million and \$1 million, in which case Division C has the greatest average annual salary and the average annual salary in Divisions A, B, and C combined is greater than \$55,000; NOT sufficient.

(2) Given that the average annual salary in Division C is \$55,000, we have

$$\frac{\Sigma_C}{N_C} = 55,000,$$ where Σ_C is the sum of the annual salaries, in dollars, of the employees in Division C and N_C is the number of employees in Division C. Moreover, letting Σ_A and Σ_B be the sums of the annual salaries, respectively and in dollars, of the employees in Divisions A and B, and letting N_A and N_B be the numbers of employees, respectively, in Divisions A and B, then we have

$$\frac{\Sigma_A}{N_A} < 55,000 \text{ and } \frac{\Sigma_B}{N_B} < 55,000,$$ since the employees in Division C have the greatest average annual salary. Note that these two inequalities and this equation can be rewritten as $\Sigma_A < 55,000N_A$, $\Sigma_B < 55,000N_B$, and $\Sigma_C = 55,000N_C$. Therefore, the average annual salary of the employees in the three divisions combined is $$\frac{\Sigma_A + \Sigma_B + \Sigma_C}{N_A + N_B + N_C} =$$

$$\frac{\Sigma_A + \Sigma_B + 55,000N_C}{N_A + N_B + N_C},$$ which is less than

$$\frac{55,000N_A + 55,000N_B + 55,000N_C}{N_A + N_B + N_C} =$$

$$\frac{55,000(N_A + N_B + N_C)}{N_A + N_B + N_C} = 55,000;$$
SUFFICIENT.

The correct answer is B; statement 2 alone is sufficient.

16. A candle company determines that, for a certain specialty candle, the supply function is $p = m_1 x + b_1$ and the demand function is $p = m_2 x + b_2$, where p is the price of each candle, x is the number of candles supplied or demanded, and m_1, m_2, b_1, and b_2 are constants. At what value of x do the graphs of the supply function and demand function intersect?

    (1) $m_1 = -m_2 = 0.005$
    (2) $b_2 - b_1 = 6$

Algebra First-Degree Equations

The graphs will intersect at the value of x such that $m_1 x + b_1 = m_2 x + b_2$ or $(m_1 - m_2)x = b_2 - b_1$.

(1) This indicates that $m_1 = -m_2 = 0.005$. It follows that $m_1 - m_2 = 0.01$, and so $0.01x = b_2 - b_1$ or $x = 100(b_2 - b_1)$, which can vary as the values of b_2 and b_1 vary; NOT sufficient.

(2) This indicates that $b_2 - b_1 = 6$. It follows that $(m_1 - m_2)x = 6$. This implies that $m_1 \neq m_2$, and so $x = \dfrac{b_2 - b_1}{m_1 - m_2} = \dfrac{6}{m_1 - m_2}$, which can vary as the values of m_1 and m_2 vary; NOT sufficient.

Taking (1) and (2) together, $m_1 - m_2 = 0.01$ and $b_2 - b_1 = 6$ and so the value of x is $\dfrac{6}{0.01} = 600$.

The correct answer is C; both statements together are sufficient.

17. A certain ski shop sold 125 pairs of skis and 100 pairs of ski boots for a total of \$75,000. What was the average (arithmetic mean) selling price of a pair of the ski boots?

    (1) The average selling price of a pair of skis was \$300.
    (2) The selling price of a pair of ski boots varied from \$150 to \$900.

Arithmetic Statistics

Let Σ_{skis} be the sum of the selling prices, in dollars, of all 125 pairs of skis and let Σ_{boots} be the sum of the selling prices, in dollars, of all 100 pairs of ski boots. We are given that $\Sigma_{skis} + \Sigma_{boots} = 75,000$. Determine the value of $\dfrac{\Sigma_{boots}}{100}$, or equivalently, determine the value of Σ_{boots}.

(1) Given that $\dfrac{\Sigma_{skis}}{125} = 300$, or $\Sigma_{skis} = 300(125) = 37,500$, it follows from $\Sigma_{skis} + \Sigma_{boots} = 75,000$ that $\Sigma_{boots} = 75,000 - \Sigma_{skis} = 75,000 - 37,500 = 37,500$; SUFFICIENT.

(2) Given that the selling price of a pair of ski boots varied from $150 to $900, it is possible that there were 40 pairs of ski boots each with a selling price of $150, 60 pairs of ski boots each with a selling price of $900, and 125 pairs of skis each with a selling price of $120 for a total selling price of $40(\$150) + 60(\$900) + 125(\$120) = \$75,000$, and thus it is possible that $\Sigma_{boots} = 40(150) + 60(900) = 6,000 + 54,000 = 60,000$. However, it is also possible that there were 60 pairs of ski boots each with a selling price of $150, 40 pairs of ski boots each with a selling price of $900, and 125 pairs of skis each with a selling price of $240 for a total selling price of $60(\$150) + 40(\$900) + 125(\$240) = \$75,000$, and thus it is also possible that $\Sigma_{boots} = 60(150) + 40(900) = 9,000 + 36,000 = 45,000$; NOT sufficient.

**The correct answer is A;
statement 1 alone is sufficient.**

18. Last year Publisher X published 1,100 books, consisting of first editions, revised editions, and reprints. How many first editions did Publisher X publish last year?

    (1) The number of first editions published was 50 more than twice the number of reprints published.

    (2) The number of revised editions published was half the number of reprints published.

Algebra Simultaneous Equations

Let A be the number of first editions, B be the number of revised editions, and C be the number of reprints. Then $A + B + C = 1,100$. Determine the value of A.

(1) Given that $A = 50 + 2C$, it is not possible to determine the value of A. This is because by choosing different values of C, different values of A can be obtained by using the equation $A = 50 + 2C$, and then the equation $A + B + C = 1,100$ can be used to determine whether acceptable values of B (nonnegative integers) exist for these values of A and C. For example, choosing $C = 100$ leads to $A = 250$ and $B = 750$, and choosing $C = 200$ leads to $A = 450$ and $B = 450$; NOT sufficient.

(2) Given that $B = \dfrac{1}{2}C$, or $C = 2B$, it is not possible to determine the value of A. This is because by choosing different values of B, different values of C can be obtained by using the equation $C = 2B$, and then the equation $A + B + C = 1,100$ can be used to determine different values of A. For example, choosing $B = 100$ leads to $C = 200$ and $A = 800$, and choosing $B = 200$ leads to $C = 400$ and $A = 500$; NOT sufficient.

Taking $A = 50 + 2C$ from (1) and $C = 2B$ from (2) together gives $A = 50 + 4B$. Thus, in the equation $A + B + C = 1,100$, A can be replaced with $50 + 4B$ and C can be replaced with $2B$ to give $(50 + 4B) + B + 2B = 1,100$. Solving for B gives $B = 150$, and hence $C = 2B = 300$ and $A = 50 + 2C = 650$.

**The correct answer is C;
both statements together are sufficient.**

19. How old is Jane?

    (1) Ten years ago she was one-third as old as she is now.

    (2) In 15 years, she will be twice as old as she is now.

Algebra First-Degree Equations

Determine the value of J, where J represents Jane's current age.

(1) In symbols, $J - 10$ represents Jane's age ten years ago and $\frac{1}{3}J$ represents one-third her current age. These expressions are equal by (1), so $J - 10 = \frac{1}{3}J$. This is a first-degree equation in the variable J and has a unique solution; SUFFICIENT.

(2) In symbols, $J + 15$ represents Jane's age 15 years from now and $2J$ represents twice her current age. These expressions are equal by (2), so $J + 15 = 2J$. This is a first-degree equation in the variable J and has a unique solution; SUFFICIENT.

The correct answer is D;
each statement alone is sufficient.

20. What was the population of City X in 2002?

  (1) X's population in 2002 increased by 2 percent, or 20,000 people, over 2001.

  (2) In 2001, X's population was 1,000,000.

Algebra Percents

Letting P_1 and P_2 represent City X's population in 2001 and 2002, respectively, the percent increase in population from 2001 to 2002 is given as a decimal by $\frac{P_2 - P_1}{P_1}$.

  (1) By (1) the percent increase was 2 percent, so $\frac{P_2 - P_1}{P_1} = 0.02$ or $P_2 - P_1 = 0.02P_1$. Also, by (1), $P_2 - P_1 = 20{,}000$, so $20{,}000 = 0.02P_1$ from which the value of P_1 can be uniquely determined. Then $P_1 + 20{,}000 = P_2$, which is the population of City X in 2002; SUFFICIENT.

  (2) Even though (2) gives $P_1 = 1{,}000{,}000$, it gives no information about the population of City X in 2002 either by itself or in relation to the population in 2001; NOT sufficient.

The correct answer is A;
statement 1 alone is sufficient.

21. Yesterday Bookstore B sold twice as many softcover books as hardcover books. Was Bookstore B's revenue from the sale of softcover books yesterday greater than its revenue from the sale of hardcover books yesterday?

  (1) The average (arithmetic mean) price of the hardcover books sold at the store yesterday was $10 more than the average price of the softcover books sold at the store yesterday.

  (2) The average price of the softcover and hardcover books sold at the store yesterday was greater than $14.

Arithmetic Statistics

Letting s represent the number of softcover books sold; h, the number of hardcover books sold; S, the average price of the softcover books sold; and H, the average price of the hardcover books sold, determine whether the revenue from the sale of softcover books is greater than the revenue from the sale of hardcover books or if $sS > hH$, where $s = 2h$.

  (1) Given that $H = S + 10$, if $S = 10$, $H = 20$, $s = 10$, and $h = 5$, then $sS = 100$ and $hH = 100$, so $sS = hH$. On the other hand, if $S = 40$, $H = 50$, $s = 8$, and $h = 4$, then $sS = 320$ and $hH = 200$, so $sS > hH$; NOT sufficient.

  (2) Given that $\frac{sS + hH}{s + h} > 14$, if $s = 6$, $S = 10$, $h = 3$, and $H = 30$, $\frac{6(10) + 3(30)}{6 + 3} = \frac{150}{9} > 14$ and $6(10) < 3(30)$. On the other hand, if $s = 10$, $S = 15$, $h = 5$, and $H = 20$, $\frac{10(15) + 5(20)}{10 + 5} = \frac{250}{15} > 14$ and $10(15) > 5(20)$; NOT sufficient.

Taking (1) and (2) together,

$\dfrac{sS + hH}{s + h}$	$>$	14	from (2)
$\dfrac{2h(H - 10) + hH}{2h + h}$	$>$	14	$s = 2h$ (given) and $H = S + 10$ from (1)
$\dfrac{3H - 20}{3}$	$>$	14	cancel h and simplify
$3H - 20$	$>$	42	multiply both sides by 3
H	$>$	$\dfrac{62}{3}$	solve for H

To show that this leads to $sS > hH$, start with $sS > hH$ and then reverse the steps.

sS	$>$	hH	
$2h(H-10)$	$>$	hH	$s = 2h$ and $S = H - 10$
$2hH - 20h$	$>$	hH	distributive property
$2hH$	$>$	$hH + 20h$	add $20h$ to both sides
hH	$>$	$20h$	subtract hH from both sides
H	$>$	20	divide both sides by $h > 0$

Now reverse the steps.

H	$>$	$\dfrac{62}{3}$	derived earlier
H	$>$	20	$\dfrac{62}{3} > 20$
hH	$>$	$20h$	multiply both sides by $h > 0$
$2hH$	$>$	$hH + 20h$	add hH to both sides
$2hH - 20h$	$>$	hH	subtract $20h$ from both sides
$2h(H-10)$	$>$	hH	factor
sS	$>$	hH	$s = 2h$ and $S = H - 10$

Thus, the revenue from the sale of softcover books was greater than the revenue from the sale of hardcover books.

The correct answer is C; both statements together are sufficient.

22. A customer purchased 6 shirts priced at $10.99 each, excluding sales tax. How much sales tax did he pay on this purchase?

    (1) The customer paid a 5 percent sales tax on the total price of the shirts.

    (2) The customer paid a total of $11.54 for each shirt, including sales tax.

Arithmetic Percents

Determine the sales tax paid by a customer who bought six shirts for $10.99 each, excluding sales tax.

(1) Given that the sales tax was 5%, the customer paid sales tax totaling $3.30, which is 6(0.05)($10.99), rounded to the nearest cent; SUFFICIENT.

(2) Given that each shirt cost $11.54 including sales tax, the customer paid a total of 6($11.54 − $10.99) = $3.30 in sales tax; SUFFICIENT.

The correct answer is D; each statement alone is sufficient.

23. The sum of the lengths of two pieces of rope is 65 feet. How long is the shorter piece?

    (1) The lengths of the pieces of rope are in the ratio 8:5.

    (2) One piece of rope is 15 feet longer than the other piece.

Algebra Ratio and Proportion; First-Degree Equations

The sum of the lengths of two pieces of rope is 65 feet. Determine the length of the shorter piece of rope.

(1) Given that the lengths of the pieces of rope are in the ratio 8:5, it follows that $8x + 5x = 65$, for some value of x. Hence, $13x = 65$ and $x = 5$. The length of the shorter piece is $5(5) = 25$; SUFFICIENT.

(2) Given that one piece is 15 feet longer than the other piece, if s represents the length of the shorter piece, it follows that $s + (s + 15) = 65$, $2s + 15 = 65$, $2s = 50$, and $s = 25$; SUFFICIENT.

The correct answer is D; each statement alone is sufficient.

24. An initial investment of $10,000 was deposited in a bank account one year ago, and additional deposits were made during the year. If no withdrawals were made, what was the total amount of interest earned on this account during the year?

    (1) The additional deposits during the year totaled $5,000.

    (2) The account earned interest at the annual rate of 6 percent compounded quarterly.

Arithmetic Applied Problems

Determine the interest earned in one year by an initial investment of $10,000 with additional deposits, but no withdrawals, during the year.

(1) Given that the additional deposits total $5,000, it is not possible to determine the interest earned by both the initial investment and the additional deposits together without information about the interest rate and when during the year the additional deposits were made; NOT sufficient.

(2) Given that the annual interest rate is 6% compounded quarterly, it is not possible to determine the interest earned by both the initial investment and the additional deposits together without information about the amount of the additional deposits and when during the year the additional deposits were made; NOT sufficient.

Taking (1) and (2) together, it is not possible to determine the interest earned by both the initial investment and the additional deposits together without information about when during the year the additional deposits were made. For example, if one deposit of $5,000 were made after 6 months, then the interest for the year would be more than it would have been had the $5,000 been deposited after 9 months.

**The correct answer is E;
both statements together are still not sufficient.**

25. A poplar tree was 3 feet high when it was planted on January 1, 1970. During what year did it pass the height of 20 feet?

    (1) On January 1, 1973, it was 24 feet high.
    (2) It doubled its height during each year.

Arithmetic Series and Sequences

(1) Given that the tree was 24 feet high at the beginning of 1973, it is not possible to determine during which year the tree passed the height of 20 feet.

year	beginning height (ft)	ending height (ft)	feet grown (ft)
1970	3	15	12
1971	15	21	6
1972	21	24	3
1973	24	30	6

year	beginning height (ft)	ending height (ft)	feet grown (ft)
1970	3	6	3
1971	6	12	6
1972	12	24	12
1973	24	30	6

The first table shows that the tree could have passed the height of 20 feet during 1971 and the second table shows that the tree could have passed the height of 20 feet during 1972; NOT sufficient.

(2) Given that the tree doubled its height during each year, the tree would have been 6 feet high at the beginning of 1971, 12 feet high at the beginning of 1972, and 24 feet high at the beginning of 1973. Therefore, the tree would have passed the height of 20 feet during 1972; SUFFICIENT.

**The correct answer is B;
statement 2 alone is sufficient.**

26. Which weighs more, a cubic unit of water or a cubic unit of liquid X?

    (1) A cubic unit of water weighs more than $\frac{1}{3}$ cubic unit of liquid X.

    (2) A cubic unit of liquid X weighs less than 3 cubic units of water.

Algebra Inequalities

Determine which is greater: the weight of a cubic unit of water, represented by W, or a cubic unit of Liquid X, represented by X.

(1) Given that $W > \frac{1}{3}X$, it is not possible to determine which of W and X is greater. For example, if $W = 4$ and $X = 9$, then $W > \frac{1}{3}X$ and X is greater than W, but if $W = 10$ and $X = 9$, then $W > \frac{1}{3}X$ and W is greater than X; NOT sufficient.

(2) Given that $X < 3W$, it is not possible to determine which of W and X is greater. For example, if $X = 9$ and $W = 4$, then $X < 3W$ and X is greater than W, but if $X = 9$ and $W = 10$, then $X < 3W$ and W is greater than X; NOT sufficient.

Taking (1) and (2) together gives no more information than (1) or (2) alone since the same examples used to show that (1) is not sufficient also show that (2) is not sufficient.

The correct answer is E; both statements together are still not sufficient.

27. What were the individual prices of the vases that an antique dealer bought at store X?

    (1) The antique dealer bought exactly 3 vases at store X.
    (2) The antique dealer's total bill at store X was $225.

Arithmetic Applied Problems

Determine the individual prices of the vases.

(1) Given that there are 3 vases, it is not possible to determine the individual prices because no information about prices is known or can be determined; NOT sufficient.

(2) Given that the total bill was $225, it is not possible to determine the individual prices because neither the number of vases nor whether the vases are identically or otherwise priced is known or can be determined; NOT sufficient.

Taking (1) and (2) together, it is still not possible to determine the individual prices of the vases. For example, the prices of the 3 vases could be $200, $20, and $5 for a total bill of $225. However, the prices of the 3 vases could also be $100, $100, and $25 for a total bill of $225.

The correct answer is E; both statements together are still not sufficient.

28. Was the average (arithmetic mean) sale price of a new home in region R last month at least $100,000?

    (1) Last month the median sale price of a new home in region R was at least $100,000.
    (2) Last month the sale prices of new homes in region R ranged from $75,000 to $150,000.

Arithmetic Statistics

(1) Given that the median price was at least $100,000, the following two examples show that it cannot be determined whether the average price was at least $100,000.

Example 1: Average price is greater than $100,000

$75,000	**$100,000**	$150,000
$100,000		$150,000
$100,000		$150,000

The median of these 7 prices is $100,000 and the average of these prices is greater than $100,000, since the sum of these 7 prices is 7($100,000) + (−$25,000 + $50,000 + $50,000 + $50,000), which is greater than 7($100,000).

Example 2: Average price is less than $100,000

$75,000	**$100,000**	$150,000
$100,000		$150,000
$100,000		$150,000

The median of these 7 prices is $100,000 and the average of these prices is less than $100,000, since the sum of these 7 prices is 7($100,000) + (−$25,000 − $25,000 − $25,000 + $50,000), which is less than 7($100,000); NOT sufficient.

(2) Given that the prices ranged from $75,000 to $150,000, the same examples above show that it cannot be determined whether the average price was at least $100,000; NOT sufficient.

Taking (1) and (2) together, it cannot be determined whether the average price was at least $100,000 because the two examples above each satisfy both (1) and (2).

The correct answer is E; both statements together are still not sufficient.

29. If the capacity of tank X is less than the capacity of tank Y and both tanks begin to fill at the same time, which tank will be filled first?

    (1) Tank X is filled at a constant rate of 1.5 liters per minute.

    (2) Tank Y is filled at a constant rate of 120 liters per hour.

Arithmetic Applied Problems

Determine which tank, X or Y, will be filled first if X has less capacity than Y and they start filling at the same time.

(1) Given that X fills at a rate of 1.5 liters per minute, which is equivalent to 90 liters per hour, it is not possible to determine which tank will be filled first because no information is given about the rate at which Y fills or about how much larger in capacity Y is than X; NOT sufficient.

(2) Given that Y fills at a rate of 120 liters per hour, it is not possible to determine which tank will be filled first because no information is given about the rate at which X fills or about how much larger in capacity Y is than X; NOT sufficient.

Taking (1) and (2) together, if the capacity of X is 90 liters and the capacity of Y is 200 liters, then X will be filled in 1 hour but Y will be only 60% filled in 1 hour. Therefore, X will be filled first. However, if the capacity of X is 90 liters and the capacity of Y is 100 liters, then Y will be filled in $\frac{5}{6}$ hours while X will take a full hour to be filled. Thus, Y will be filled first.

The correct answer is E; both statements together are still not sufficient.

30. At a certain company, 30 percent of the employees live in City R. If 25 percent of the company's employees live in apartments in City R, what is the number of the employees who live in apartments in City R?

    (1) Of the employees who live in City R, 6 do not live in apartments.

    (2) Of the employees, 84 do not live in City R.

Arithmetic Percents

Determine how many employees of a certain company live in apartments in City R, where 30% of the employees live in City R and 25% of the employees live in apartments in City R. Let T represent the total number of employees at the company.

(1) Given that 6 of the employees who live in City R do not live in apartments, it follows that $6 = (0.30 - 0.25)T$. Thus $0.05T = 6$, $T = 120$, and the number of employees who live in apartments in City R can be determined; SUFFICIENT.

(2) Given that 84 employees do not live in City R, it follows that $(1 - 0.3)T = 84$, from which it follows that $T = 120$ and the number of employees who live in apartments in City R can be determined; SUFFICIENT.

The correct answer is D; each statement alone is sufficient.

31. What was Mary's average (arithmetic mean) score on 4 tests?

    (1) Her average (arithmetic mean) score on 3 of the tests was 97.

    (2) Her score on one of the tests was 96.

Arithmetic Statistics

Since the average of the 4 scores is equal to the sum of the 4 scores divided by 4, it follows that the average of the 4 scores can be determined if and only if the sum of the 4 scores can be determined.

(1) Given that the sum of 3 of the scores was 3(97), it is not possible to determine the sum of the 4 scores, since different values for the remaining score are possible and those different values correspond to different values for the sum of the 4 scores; NOT sufficient.

(2) Given that one of the scores was 96, it is not possible to determine the sum of the 4 scores, since different values for the sum of the remaining 3 scores are possible and those different values correspond to different values for the sum of the 4 scores; NOT sufficient.

Taking (1) and (2) together, it is still not possible to determine the sum of the 4 scores. For example, the scores could be 96, 97, 98, 10 (the first 3 listed scores have an average of 97 and one of the scores is 96), which have an average that is less than 96, and the scores could be 96, 97, 98, 99 (the first 3 listed scores have an average of 97 and one of the scores is 96), which have an average that is greater than 96.

The correct answer is E;
both statements together are still not sufficient.

32. Is there a causal relationship between smoking and lung cancer?

    (1) Research consistently shows a strong correlation between smoking and the development of lung cancer.

    (2) Some medical researchers support a proposed mechanism by which smoking could cause lung cancer.

Inference

(1) Research-based evidence has consistently shown a high positive correlation between smoking and lung cancer. A strong positive correlation between two factors P and Q indicates that there is a similar pattern of variation in data for P and data for Q (the degree of similarity can vary). For example, long-term data might show that as smoking increases in a population, the data regarding the incidence of lung cancer increases in tandem. Over several years, if the data regarding smoking in a population decreases, the data for lung cancer might also decrease. In both cases, a positive correlation occurs. But such a statistical pattern, by itself, can, at best, *suggest* some *association* or *dependency*, direct or indirect, between the two factors smoking and lung cancer. But correlation evidence, by itself, provides no proof of a causal relationship; NOT sufficient.

(2) The information provided is insufficiently specific to sustain a claim that smoking is causally related to lung cancer. What (2) indicates is a *hypothesis* proposed by some researchers, but no information is provided to indicate confirmation of that hypothesis; NOT sufficient.

The correct answer is E;
both statements together are still not sufficient.

33. A research project has a successful outcome if its research is reported in a blind peer-reviewed academic publication. Can interdisciplinary collaborations on research projects at least sometimes produce a successful outcome?

    (1) Some interdisciplinary research groups experience conflict and rivalry.

    (2) A peer-reviewed and well-regarded interdisciplinary review of published papers on urban greening trends found that there was little if any evidence that planting more trees in an urban area significantly improved air quality there.

Inference

(1) The information regarding the sometimes dysfunctional social dynamics of research groups is not sufficient to show that research groups with such experiences always fail to produce successful research outcomes. So the information given here is not sufficient alone to indicate a yes or a no answer to the question posed; NOT sufficient.

(2) The information gives us an example of one interdisciplinary collaboration on research that reported in a blind peer-reviewed publication its review of research studies on urban greening. The review found that there was insufficient evidence to show that planting trees in urban areas had a significant impact on air quality in such areas. Even though the result of its review was negative, its review of scientific publications on the issue was approved in a blind peer review and published. Therefore (2), in combination with the stimulus information, is sufficient to provide at least one example of a successful outcome of an interdisciplinary research project. This, in turn, is sufficient to show that interdisciplinary research groups *can* produce a successful outcome.; SUFFICIENT

The correct answer is B;
statement 2 alone is sufficient.

34. It has been proposed that teenagers aged 10 to 15 years be restricted to less than 2 hours per day engaging with social media. Would a significant number of teens aged 10 to 15 years get an overall developmental or health benefit from such a restriction?

    (1) A peer-reviewed study indicates a 23% increase in the incidence of chronic anxiety or depression among teenagers aged 10 to 15 years who average 2 or more hours per day engaging with social media.

    (2) Certain kinds of engagement with social media averaging 2 or more hours per day by teenagers aged 10 to 15 years lead, in about 28% of cases, to meaningful friendships and social and emotional learning, both of which are valuable for development at those ages.

Inference

(1) This statement cites a study that found an association between social-media use by teenagers 10 to 15 years and an increase in the incidence of chronic anxiety or depression among 23% of the minors observed in the study. A key word here is *association*: It should be noted that this does not prove a cause-effect relationship, even if the study could motivate further investigation to see whether a causal mechanism could be identified. Even if a causal mechanism were identified, it could turn out that the use of social media was at least in part an *effect* of chronic anxiety or depression: Some teenagers might resort to social media use as a kind of escape mechanism. We should conclude that the information provided (even if the validity of the study is assumed) does not provide sufficient information to show definitively that the proposed restriction would result in developmental or health benefits for minors aged 10 to 15 years. The conclusion is that (1) is not sufficient alone; NOT sufficient.

(2) This statement indicates that use of social media by teens aged 10 to 15 years results in significant developmental benefits for 28% of teens in that age group. In other words, it indicates that social-media use by these teens *causally contributes* to a developmentally valuable effect. This implies that restriction of their social media use risks depriving a significant number of teens of the benefits resulting from their social-media use. So we can conclude that (2) is sufficient alone to provide a negative answer to the question posed; SUFFICIENT.

The correct answer is B; statement 2 alone is sufficient.

35. A milk vendor mixes water with milk and sells the mixture at the same price per liter as if it were undiluted milk. The selling price per liter of the mixture is the vendor's cost per liter of the milk plus a markup of x%. The water costs the vendor nothing. If the vendor gets a 50% profit on the sale of the mixture, what is the value of x?

    (1) If the vendor mixes half the intended quantity of water and sells every liter of the mixture at the cost price per liter of the undiluted milk, the vendor will get a 10% profit.

    (2) The concentration of milk in the mixture after adding water is 5/6.

Evaluate

The task is to ascertain whether enough information has been provided to determine the value of x.

(1) In this hypothetical scenario, we are asked to imagine that the amount of zero-cost water added to the milk is only half as much as was actually used, based on the information given in the stimulus. The profit in this hypothetical scenario is 10%, resulting from selling the mixture at the vendor's **cost price** per liter of milk (i.e., without any profit markup). Therefore, the 10% profit per liter in this hypothetical scenario consists, in effect, of selling zero-cost water at the cost price of milk. We can infer from this that the ratio of water to milk in the mixture was 1:10. When 20% **zero-cost water** is added, it can be inferred from (1) that the ratio of water to milk in the mixture is 2:10. This would result in a 20% profit if every liter of the mixture is sold at the cost price per liter of milk. But suppose that for retail sale, there is a markup of x% over cost on every liter of the mixture. We are told in the preliminary information

that a total profit of 50% accrues. The 30% difference between the 20% profit and the 50% profit results from the markup of x%. It is 30% of the cost price of milk. Note that the question concerns the value of x, not the **% profit** resulting from the markup of x%. The information in (1) and the preliminary information is sufficient to determine that $x = 25$. In other words, the markup on the vendor's cost for the milk is 25%. Some simple algebra will show that the x% markup contributes 30% to the 50% profit; SUFFICIENT.

(2) This information indicates that the water in each liter of the mixture is 1/5 of the amount of milk. So, pricing the zero-cost water as if it were milk accounts for 20% out of the 50% profit. The markup of x% on the whole mixture accounts for the remaining 30%. Therefore, the information in (2) is sufficient by itself to determine the value of x; SUFFICIENT.

The correct answer is D; each statement alone is sufficient.

36. Does it benefit a company overall to invest in employee training?

   (1) Companies that invest in comprehensive employee training programs often observe improved job performance among their workforce.

   (2) Well-trained employees are likely to excel in their roles and take the company forward.

Inference

(1) Even if companies that invest in comprehensive employee training programs **often** observe improved job performance among their workforce, many such companies might not observe any improved job performance. And even for those that do, the improvements might be too minimal to make it beneficial overall for the company to pay the costs for the training programs. Furthermore, even if investing specifically in a comprehensive employee training program did benefit a company overall, investing in most other types of employee training might not be. Thus, whether it benefits an

unspecified company overall to invest in an unspecified type of employee training cannot be determined from (1) alone; NOT sufficient.

(2) A company's investment in employee training may fail to produce any well-trained employees. And even if well-trained employees are **likely** to excel in their roles and take the company forward, many well-trained employees may not do so. Furthermore, the hazy benefits of some employees "excelling" and taking the company "forward" might not be adequate to justify the costs of employee training. Thus, whether it benefits a company overall to invest in employee training cannot be determined from (2) alone; NOT sufficient.

Even if (1) and (2) are both true, we still can't determine whether the benefits of improved job performance and of more employees excelling and moving a particular company forward would make the training benefit the company overall, considering the costs of the training. Nor can we even determine whether a specific employee training program would yield any such benefits at all.

The correct answer is E; both statements together are still not sufficient.

37. Can regular exercise reduce the risk of chronic diseases?

   (1) Regular exercise is often associated with better physical health.

   (2) Engaging in regular physical activity contributes to overall well-being.

Inference

(1) For all we know from (1), regular exercise may often be associated with better physical health simply because people in better physical health are often more inclined to exercise. And even if regular exercise promotes better physical health in some respects, it might not reduce the risk of chronic diseases specifically. Thus, whether regular exercise can reduce the risk of chronic diseases cannot be determined from (1) alone; NOT sufficient.

(2) Even if engaging in regular physical activity contributes to overall well-being, it may not reduce the risk of chronic diseases specifically. Thus, whether regular exercise can reduce the risk of chronic diseases cannot be determined from (2) alone; NOT sufficient.

Taking (1) and (2) together, even if regular exercise is both associated with better physical health and contributes to overall well-being, it may not reduce the risk of chronic diseases specifically.

The correct answer is E; both statements together are still not sufficient.

38. Does effective advertising require a higher budget expense than ineffective advertising?

   (1) Companies that allocate higher budgets to advertising tend to experience increased sales revenue.

   (2) Effective advertising can drive higher consumer demand.

Inference

   (1) Even if companies that allocate higher budgets to advertising tend to also have increased sales revenue, that might mean only that their increased sales revenue has given them more money to spend on their ineffective advertising. Furthermore, even those companies allocating high budgets to **effective** advertising might be doing so inefficiently; they might be able to cut their advertising expenses drastically without reducing their advertising effectiveness. Thus, whether effective advertising **requires** a higher budget expense than ineffective advertising cannot be determined from (1) alone; NOT sufficient.

   (2) Even if effective advertising can drive higher consumer demand, it might not need to cost much. Thus, whether effective advertising requires a higher budget expense than ineffective advertising cannot be determined from (2) alone; NOT sufficient.

Taking (1) and (2) together, even if companies that allocate higher budgets to advertising also tend to have increased sales revenue, and even if

effective advertising can drive higher consumer demand, many companies with higher budgets and increased sales revenue may nonetheless be advertising inefficiently; they might be able to cut their advertising expenses drastically without reducing advertising effectiveness. If so, effective advertising may not require a higher budget expense than ineffective advertising.

The correct answer is E; both statements together are still not sufficient.

Questions 39 to 74 — Difficulty: **Medium**

39. The table shows the number of people who responded "yes" or "no" or "don't know" when asked whether their city council should implement environmental programs X and Y. If a total of 1,000 people responded to the question about both programs, what was the number of people who did not respond "yes" to implementing either of the two programs?

   (1) The number of people who responded "yes" to implementing only Program X was 300.

   (2) The number of people who responded "no" to implementing Program X and "no" to implementing Program Y was 100.

Arithmetic Interpretation of Tables; Sets (Venn Diagrams)

   (1) Given that 300 people responded "yes" to implementing only Program X, and because 400 people altogether responded "yes" to implementing Program X, it follows that 400 − 300 = 100 people responded "yes" to implementing both Program X and Program Y. Therefore, because 300 people altogether responded "yes" to implementing Program Y, 300 − 100 = 200 people responded "yes" to implementing only Program Y. These results are shown in the Venn diagram below.

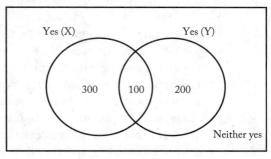

Since the Venn diagram above represents a total of 1,000 people, it follows that the number of people who did not respond "yes" to implementing either Program X or Program Y is $1,000 - (300 + 100 + 200) = 400$; SUFFICIENT.

(2) Given that 100 people responded "no" both to implementing Program X and to implementing Program Y, the table below shows a possibility whereby the number of people who did not respond "yes" to implementing either Program X or Program Y could be 400. Note that for each of the column headings "Yes," "No," and "Don't Know," the numbers under that column heading satisfy (X answered) + (Y answered) − (both answered) + (neither answered) = 1,000. Indeed, for each of these three columns a Venn diagram can be given that represents the numbers in that column.

	Yes	No	Don't Know
X	400	200	400
Y	300	350	350
Both	100	100	0
Neither	**400**	550	250
Total	1,000	1,000	1,000

However, the next table shows a possibility whereby the number of people who did not respond "yes" to implementing either Program X or Program Y could be 500.

	Yes	No	Don't Know
X	400	200	400
Y	300	350	350
Both	200	100	0
Neither	**500**	550	250
Total	1,000	1,000	1,000

Therefore, among other possibilities, the number of people who did not respond "yes" to implementing either Program X or Program Y could be 400, and this number could also be 500; NOT sufficient.

The correct answer is A; statement 1 alone is sufficient.

40. An estimate of an actual data value has an error of p percent if $p = \dfrac{100|e - a|}{a}$, where e is the estimated value and a is the actual value. Emma's estimate for her total income last year had an error of less than 20 percent. Emma's estimate of her income from tutoring last year also had an error of less than 20 percent. Was Emma's actual income from tutoring last year at most 45 percent of her actual total income last year?

(1) Emma's estimated income last year from tutoring was 30 percent of her estimated total income last year.

(2) Emma's estimated total income last year was $40,000.

Arithmetic Estimation

Given that Emma's estimates for both her total income and her income from tutoring last year, E_I and E_T, respectively, were within 20 percent of her actual total income and her actual income from tutoring, A_I and A_T, respectively, it follows that $0.8E_I < A_I < 1.2E_I$ and $0.8E_T < A_T < 1.2E_T$.

Determine whether Emma's actual income from tutoring was at most 45 percent of her actual total income or if $\dfrac{A_T}{A_I} \leq 0.45$.

(1) Given that $E_T = 0.3E_I$, it follows from $0.8E_T < A_T < 1.2E_T$ that $0.24E_I < A_T < 0.36E_I$. Then, since $0.8E_I < A_I < 1.2E_I$, it follows that

$$\frac{1}{1.2E_I} < \frac{1}{A_I} < \frac{1}{0.8E_I}.$$ Multiplying the

inequalities gives $\dfrac{0.24E_I}{1.2E_I} < \dfrac{A_T}{A_I} < \dfrac{0.36E_I}{0.8E_I}$

or $0.2 < \dfrac{A_T}{A_I} < 0.45$; SUFFICIENT.

(2) Given that Emma's estimated total income last year was $40,000, it is impossible to determine whether her actual income from tutoring was at most 45 percent of her actual total income because no information is given about her actual income from tutoring other than it was within 20 percent of her estimated income from tutoring. And there is no information from which her estimated income from tutoring can be determined; NOT sufficient.

The correct answer is A; statement 1 alone is sufficient.

41. Was Store K's profit last month at least 10 percent greater than its profit the previous month?

    (1) Store K's expenses last month were 5 percent greater than its expenses the previous month.

    (2) Store K's revenues last month were 10 percent greater than its revenues the previous month.

Algebra Applied Problems

Let P_{last}, E_{last}, and R_{last} be, respectively, the profit, expenses, and revenues for last month. Also, let $P_{previous}$, $E_{previous}$, and $R_{previous}$ be, respectively, the profit, expenses, and revenues for the previous month. Then we have $P_{last} = R_{last} - E_{last}$ and $P_{previous} = R_{previous} - E_{previous}$. Determine whether $P_{last} \geq 1.1P_{previous}$ is true, or equivalently, determine whether $R_{last} - E_{last} \geq 1.1R_{previous} - 1.1E_{previous}$ is true.

    (1) Given that $E_{last} = 1.05E_{previous}$, it follows that the inequality $R_{last} - E_{last} \geq 1.1R_{previous} - 1.1E_{previous}$ is equivalent to $R_{last} - 1.1R_{previous} \geq -0.05E_{previous}$. It is clear that, for suitable values of R_{last}, $R_{previous}$, and $E_{previous}$, this last inequality could be true and this last inequality could be false; NOT sufficient.

    (2) Given that $R_{last} = 1.1R_{previous}$, it follows that the inequality $R_{last} - E_{last} \geq 1.1R_{previous} - 1.1E_{previous}$ is equivalent to $E_{last} \leq 1.1E_{previous}$. It is clear that, for suitable values of E_{last} and $E_{previous}$, this last inequality could be true and this last inequality could be false; NOT sufficient.

Taking (1) and (2) together, the following shows that $P_{last} \geq 1.1P_{previous}$ is true.

$$\begin{aligned} P_{last} &= R_{last} - E_{last} \\ &= 1.1R_{previous} - 1.05E_{previous} \\ &\geq 1.1R_{previous} - 1.1E_{previous} \end{aligned}$$

Therefore, $P_{last} \geq 1.1(R_{previous} - E_{previous})$, and hence $P_{last} \geq 1.1P_{previous}$ is true. (The reason for using $\geq$ above instead of $>$ is to allow for the possibility that $E_{previous} = 0$.)

The correct answer is C; both statements together are sufficient.

42. Gross profit is equal to selling price minus cost. A car dealer's gross profit on the sale of a certain car was what percent of the cost of the car?

    (1) The selling price of the car was $\dfrac{11}{10}$ of the cost of the car.

    (2) The cost of the car was $14,500.

Arithmetic Applied Problems

Determine the gross profit, P, on the sale of a car as a percent of the cost, C, of the car.

    (1) Given that the selling price of the car was $\dfrac{11}{10}C$, $P = \dfrac{11}{10}C - C = \dfrac{1}{10}C$. Thus, the profit was 10% of the cost of the car; SUFFICIENT.

    (2) Given that the cost of the car was $14,500, it is impossible to determine the profit because the selling price is not known nor is there enough information to determine it; NOT sufficient.

The correct answer is A; statement 1 alone is sufficient.

43. When the wind speed is 9 miles per hour, the wind-chill factor w is given by

$$w = -17.366 + 1.19t,$$

where t is the temperature in degrees Fahrenheit. If at noon yesterday the wind speed was 9 miles per hour, was the wind-chill factor greater than 0?

    (1) The temperature at noon yesterday was greater than 10 degrees Fahrenheit.

    (2) The temperature at noon yesterday was less than 20 degrees Fahrenheit.

Algebra Applied Problems

Determine whether $-17.366 + 1.19t$ is greater than 0.

    (1) Given that $t > 10$, it follows that $-17.366 + 1.19t > -17.366 + 1.19(10)$, or $-17.366 + 1.19t > -5.466$. However, it is not possible to determine whether $-17.366 + 1.19t$ is greater than 0. For example, if $t = 19$, then $-17.366 + 1.19t = 5.244$ is greater than 0. However, if $t = 11$, then $-17.366 + 1.19t = -4.276$, which is not greater than 0; NOT sufficient.

(2) Given that $t < 20$, the same examples used in (1) show that it is not possible to determine whether $-17.366 + 1.19t$ is greater than 0; NOT sufficient.

Taking (1) and (2) together is of no more help than either (1) or (2) taken separately because the same examples were used in both (1) and (2).

The correct answer is E; both statements together are still not sufficient.

44. How many members of a certain legislature voted against the measure to raise their salaries?

    (1) $\frac{1}{4}$ of the members of the legislature did not vote on the measure.

    (2) If 5 additional members of the legislature had voted against the measure, then the fraction of members of the legislature voting against the measure would have been $\frac{1}{3}$.

Arithmetic Ratio and Proportion

The task in this question is to determine whether, on the basis of statements 1 and 2, it is possible to calculate the number of members of the legislature who voted against a certain measure.

(1) This statement, that $\frac{1}{4}$ of the members of the legislature did not vote on the measure, is compatible with any number of members of the legislature voting against the measure. After all, any number among the $\frac{3}{4}$ of the remaining members could have voted against the measure. Furthermore, based on statement 1, we do not know the number of members of the legislature (although we do know, based on this statement, that the number of members of the legislature is divisible by 4); NOT sufficient.

(2) This statement describes a scenario, in which 5 additional members of the legislature vote against the measure and stipulates that $\frac{1}{3}$ of the members of the legislature would have voted against the measure in the scenario. Given this condition, we know that the number of members of the legislature was divisible by 3 and that the legislature had at least 15 members (to

allow for the "5 additional members of the legislature" that could have voted against the measure, for a total of $\frac{1}{3}$ of the members voting against it). However, beyond this we know essentially nothing from statement 2. In particular, depending on the number of members of the legislature (which we have not been given), any number of members could have voted against the measure. For example, exactly one member could have voted against the measure, in which case the legislature would have had $(1 + 5) \times 3 = 18$ members. Exactly two members could have voted against the measure, in which case the legislature would have had $(2 + 5) \times 3 = 21$ members, and so on for 3 members voting against, 4 members voting against, and so on; NOT sufficient.

Considering the statements 1 and 2 together, the reasoning is similar to the reasoning for statement 2, but with the further condition that the total number of members of the legislature is divisible by 12 (so as to allow that both exactly $\frac{1}{4}$ of the members did not vote on the measure while exactly $\frac{1}{3}$ could have voted against the measure). For example, it could have been the case that the legislature had 24 members. In this case, $\frac{1}{3}$ of the members would have been 8 members, and, consistent with statements 1 and 2, 3 of the members $(8 - 5)$ could have voted against the measure. Or the legislature could have had 36 members, in which case, consistent with statements 1 and 2, $\frac{1}{3}(36) - 5 = 12 - 5 = 7$ members could have voted against the measure.

The correct answer is E; both statements together are still not sufficient.

45. During a certain bicycle ride, was Sherry's average speed faster than 24 kilometers per hour? (1 kilometer = 1,000 meters)

    (1) Sherry's average speed during the bicycle ride was faster than 7 meters per second.

    (2) Sherry's average speed during the bicycle ride was slower than 8 meters per second.

Arithmetic Applied Problems

This problem can be solved by converting 24 kilometers per hour into meters per second. First, 24 kilometers is equivalent to 24,000 meters and 1 hour is equivalent to 3,600 seconds. Then, traveling 24 kilometers in 1 hour is equivalent to traveling 24,000 meters in 3,600 seconds, or $\frac{24,000}{3,600} = 6\frac{2}{3}$ meters per second.

(1) This indicates that Sherry's average speed was faster than 7 meters per second, which is faster than $6\frac{2}{3}$ meters per second and, therefore, faster than 24 kilometers per hour; SUFFICIENT.

(2) This indicates that Sherry's average speed was slower than 8 meters per second. Her average speed could have been 7 meters per second (since $7 < 8$), in which case her average speed was faster than $6\frac{2}{3}$ meters per second and, therefore, faster than 24 kilometers per hour. Or her average speed could have been 5 meters per second (since $5 < 8$), in which case her average speed was not faster than $6\frac{2}{3}$ meters per second and, therefore, not faster than 24 kilometers per hour; NOT sufficient.

The correct answer is A; statement 1 alone is sufficient.

46. Working together, Rafael and Salvador can tabulate a certain set of data in 2 hours. In how many hours can Rafael tabulate the data working alone?

(1) Working alone, Rafael can tabulate the data in 3 hours less time than Salvador, working alone, can tabulate the data.

(2) Working alone, Rafael can tabulate the data in $\frac{1}{2}$ the time that Salvador, working alone, can tabulate the data.

Algebra Simultaneous Equations

We are given that Rafael and Salvador, working together, can tabulate the set of data in two hours. That is, if Rafael tabulates data at the rate of R units of data per hour and Salvador tabulates the data at the rate of S units per hour, then, if the set

of data is made up of D units, then $2R + 2S = D$. Can we determine how much time, in hours, it takes Rafael to tabulate the data if working alone?

(1) First of all, note that the choice of units used to measure the amounts of data doesn't matter. In particular, we can define one unit of data to be D. Thus, $2R + 2S = 1$. With this in mind, consider the condition that Rafael, when working alone, can tabulate the data in 3 hours less time than Salvador can when working alone. Given that Rafael tabulates R units of data per unit time, he takes $\frac{1}{R}$ units of time to tabulate one unit of data. Similarly, Salvador takes $\frac{1}{S}$ units of time to tabulate one unit of data. This unit, as defined, is simply the entire set of data. Our given condition thus becomes $\frac{1}{R} = \frac{1}{S} - 3$, and we have the set of simultaneous equations made up of this equation and the equation $2R + 2S = 1$.

One way to determine the number of hours it would take Rafael to tabulate the data is to solve one of these equations for S and then substitute this solution into the other equation. Considering the first of these equations, we multiply both sides by RS and then manipulate the result as follows.

$$S = R - 3RS$$
$$S + 3RS = R$$
$$S(1 + 3R) = R$$
$$S = \frac{R}{1 + 3R}$$

Substituting into the equation $2R + 2S = 1$,

$$2R + \frac{2R}{1 + 3R} = 1$$

Multiplying both sides by $1 + 3R$ to eliminate the fraction,

$$2R(1 + 3R) + 2R = 1 + 3R$$
$$2R + 6R^2 = 1 + R$$
$$6R^2 + R - 1 = 0$$
$$(3R - 1)(2R + 1) = 0$$

This equation has two solutions, $-\frac{1}{2}$ and $\frac{1}{3}$. However, because the rate R cannot be negative, we find that Rafael tabulates $\frac{1}{3}$ of a unit of data every hour. Since one unit is the entire set, it takes Rafael 3 hours to tabulate the entire set; SUFFICIENT.

(2) We are given that Rafael, working alone, can tabulate the data in $\frac{1}{2}$ the amount of time it takes Salvador, working alone, to tabulate the data. As in the discussion of statement 1, we have that Rafael tabulates R units of data every hour, and takes $\frac{1}{R}$ hours to tabulate one unit of data. Similarly, it takes Salvador $\frac{1}{S}$ hours to tabulate one unit of data. One unit of data has been defined to be the size of the entire set to be tabulated, so statement 2 becomes the expression

$$\frac{1}{R} = \frac{1}{2} \times \frac{1}{S} = \frac{1}{2S}$$

We thus have $2S = R$. Substituting this value for $2S$ in the equation $2R + 2S = 1$, we have $R + 2R = 1$, and $3R = 1$. Solving for R we get $\frac{1}{3}$; SUFFICIENT.

Note that, for both statements 1 and 2, it would have been possible to stop calculating once we had determined whether it was possible to find a unique value for R. The ability to make such judgments accurately is part of what the test has been designed to measure.

The correct answer is D; each statement alone is sufficient.

47. Yesterday between 9:00 a.m. and 6:00 p.m. at Airport X, all flights to Atlanta departed at equally spaced times and all flights to New York City departed at equally spaced times. A flight to Atlanta and a flight to New York City both departed from Airport X at 1:00 p.m. yesterday. Between 1:00 p.m. and 3:00 p.m. yesterday, did another pair of flights to these 2 cities depart from Airport X at the same time?

(1) Yesterday at Airport X, a flight to Atlanta and a flight to New York City both departed at 10:00 a.m.

(2) Yesterday at Airport X, flights to New York City departed every 15 minutes between 9:00 a.m. and 6:00 p.m.

Arithmetic Applied Problems

It is useful to note that although the departures discussed all lie between 9:00 a.m. and 6:00 p.m., there is no information concerning when the first departures took place during this time other than what is necessary for the information to be consistent. For example, since departures to both Atlanta and New York City took place at 1:00 p.m., the first departure to either of these cities could not have occurred after 1:00 p.m.

(1) Given that departures to both Atlanta and New York City took place at 10:00 a.m., it is not possible to determine whether simultaneous departures to these cities occurred between 1:00 p.m. and 3:00 p.m. For example, it is possible that departures to both Atlanta and New York City took place every 15 minutes beginning at 9:15 a.m., and thus it is possible that simultaneous departures to both these cities occurred between 1:00 p.m. and 3:00 p.m. However, it is also possible that departures to Atlanta took place every 3 hours beginning at 10:00 a.m. and departures to New York City took place every 15 minutes beginning at 9:15 a.m., and thus it is possible that no simultaneous departures to these cities occurred between 1:00 p.m. and 3:00 p.m.; NOT sufficient.

(2) Given that departures to New York City took place every 15 minutes, the same examples used in (1) can be used to show that it is not possible to determine whether simultaneous departures to these cities occurred between 1:00 p.m. and 3:00 p.m.; NOT sufficient.

Taking (1) and (2) together, it is still not possible to determine whether simultaneous departures to these cities occurred between 1:00 p.m. and 3:00 p.m. because both (1) and (2) are true for the examples above.

The correct answer is E; both statements together are still not sufficient.

48. Of the total number of copies of Magazine X sold last week, 40 percent were sold at full price. What was the total number of copies of the magazine sold last week?

    (1) Last week, full price for a copy of Magazine X was $1.50 and the total revenue from full-price sales was $112,500.

    (2) The total number of copies of Magazine X sold last week at full price was 75,000.

Algebra Applied Problems

For the copies of Magazine X sold last week, let n be the total number of copies sold and let $\$p$ be the full price of each copy. Then for Magazine X last week, a total of $0.4n$ copies were each sold at price $\$p$. What is the value of n?

    (1) Given that $\$p = 1.50$ and $(0.4n)(\$p) = \$112,500$, it follows that $(0.4n)(1.5) = 112,500$, or $0.6n = 112,500$, or $n = \dfrac{112,500}{0.6}$; SUFFICIENT.

    (2) Given that $0.4n = 75,000$, it follows that $n = \dfrac{75,000}{0.4}$; SUFFICIENT.

The correct answer is D; each statement alone is sufficient.

49. What is the average (arithmetic mean) annual salary of the 6 employees of a toy company?

    (1) If the 6 annual salaries were ordered from least to greatest, each annual salary would be $6,300 greater than the preceding annual salary.

    (2) The range of the 6 annual salaries is $31,500.

Arithmetic Statistics

Can we determine the arithmetic mean of the annual salaries of the 6 employees?

    (1) Given only that the 6 annual salaries can be put into a sequence from least to greatest, with a difference of $6,300 between adjacent members of the sequence, we can infer certain things about the mean of the salaries. For example, because none of the salaries would be negative, we know from statement 1 that the mean of the salaries is greater than or equal to

$$\frac{0 + \$6,300 + \$12,600 + \$18,900 + \$25,200 + \$31,500}{6}.$$

(It is not necessary to perform this calculation.) However, depending on what the least of the salaries is—that is, the value at which the sequence of salaries begins—the average of the salaries could, consistent with condition 1, take on any value greater than this quotient; NOT sufficient.

    (2) Given the statement that the range of the salaries is $31,500, reasoning similar to the reasoning for statement 1 applies. A difference between least salary and greatest salary of $31,500 is consistent with any value for the least salary, so long as the greatest salary is $31,500 greater than the least salary. Furthermore, even if we knew what the least and the greatest salaries are, it would be impossible to determine the mean merely from the range; NOT sufficient.

As reflected in the numerator of the quotient in the discussion of statement 1, we can see that statement 1 implies statement 2. In the sequence of 6 salaries with a difference of $6,300 between adjacent members of the sequence, the difference between the least salary and the greatest salary is $5 \times \$6,300 = \$31,500$. Therefore, because statement 1 is insufficient for determining the mean of the salaries, the combination of statement 1 and statement 2 is also insufficient for determining the mean of the salaries.

The correct answer is E; both statements together are not sufficient.

50. In a certain order, the pretax price of each regular pencil was $0.03, the pretax price of each deluxe pencil was $0.05, and there were 50% more deluxe pencils than regular pencils. All taxes on the order are a fixed percent of the pretax prices. The sum of the total pretax price of the order and the tax on the order was $44.10. What was the amount, in dollars, of the tax on the order?

    (1) The tax on the order was 5% of the total pretax price of the order.

    (2) The order contained exactly 400 regular pencils.

Arithmetic Percents

Let n be the number of regular pencils in the order and let $r\%$ be the tax rate on the order as a percent of the pretax

6

price. Then the order contains $1.5n$ deluxe pencils, the total pretax price of the order is $(\$0.03)n + (\$0.05)(1.5n) = \$0.105n$, and the sum of the total pretax price of the order and the tax on the order is $\left(1+\dfrac{r}{100}\right)(\$0.105n)$. Given that $\left(1+\dfrac{r}{100}\right)(\$0.105n) = \$44.10$, what is the value of $\left(\dfrac{r}{100}\right)(\$0.105n)$?

(1) Given that $r = 5$, then $\left(1+\dfrac{r}{100}\right)(\$0.105n)$ $= \$44.10$ becomes $(1.05)(0.105n) = 44.10$, which is a first-degree equation that can be solved for n. Since the value of r is known and the value of n can be determined, it follows that the value of $\left(\dfrac{r}{100}\right)(\$0.105n)$ can be determined; SUFFICIENT.

(2) Given that $n = 400$, then $\left(1+\dfrac{r}{100}\right)(\$0.105n) = \$44.10$ becomes $\left(1+\dfrac{r}{100}\right)(0.105)(400) = 44.10$, which is a first-degree equation that can be solved for r. Since the value of r can be determined and the value of n is known, it follows that the value of $\left(\dfrac{r}{100}\right)(\$0.105n)$ can be determined; SUFFICIENT.

**The correct answer is D;
each statement alone is sufficient.**

51. A total of 20 amounts are entered on a spreadsheet that has 5 rows and 4 columns; each of the 20 positions in the spreadsheet contains one amount. The average (arithmetic mean) of the amounts in row i is R_i ($1 \le i \le 5$). The average of the amounts in column j is C_j ($1 \le j \le 4$). What is the average of all 20 amounts on the spreadsheet?

(1) $R_1 + R_2 + R_3 + R_4 + R_5 = 550$
(2) $C_1 + C_2 + C_3 + C_4 = 440$

Arithmetic Statistics

It is given that R_i represents the average of the amounts in row i. Since there are four amounts in

each row, $4R_i$ represents the total of the amounts in row i. Likewise, it is given that C_j represents the average of the amounts in column j. Since there are five amounts in each column, $5C_j$ represents the total of the amounts in column j.

(1) It is given that $R_1 + R_2 + R_3 + R_4 + R_5 = 550$, and so $4(R_1 + R_2 + R_3 + R_4 + R_5) = 4R_1 + 4R_2 + 4R_3 + 4R_4 + 4R_5 = 4(550) = 2,200$. Therefore, 2,200 is the sum of all 20 amounts (4 amounts in each of 5 rows), and the average of all 20 amounts is $\dfrac{2,200}{20} = 110$; SUFFICIENT.

(2) It is given that $C_1 + C_2 + C_3 + C_4 = 440$, and so $5(C_1 + C_2 + C_3 + C_4) = 5C_1 + 5C_2 + 5C_3 + 5C_4 = 5(440) = 2,200$. Therefore, 2,200 is the sum of all 20 amounts (5 amounts in each of 4 columns), and the average of all 20 amounts is $\dfrac{2,200}{20} = 110$; SUFFICIENT.

**The correct answer is D;
each statement alone is sufficient.**

52. Was the range of the amounts of money that Company Y budgeted for its projects last year equal to the range of the amounts of money that it budgeted for its projects this year?

(1) Both last year and this year, Company Y budgeted money for 12 projects and the least amount of money that it budgeted for a project was $400.

(2) Both last year and this year, the average (arithmetic mean) amount of money that Company Y budgeted per project was $2,000.

Arithmetic Statistics

Let G_1 and L_1 represent the greatest and least amounts, respectively, of money that Company Y budgeted for its projects last year, and let G_2 and L_2 represent the greatest and least amounts, respectively, of money that Company Y budgeted for its projects this year. Determine if the range of the amounts of money Company Y budgeted for its projects last year is equal to the range of amounts budgeted for its projects this year; that is, determine if $G_1 - L_1 = G_2 - L_2$.

(1) This indicates that $L_1 = L_2 = \$400$, but does not give any information about G_1 or G_2; NOT sufficient.

(2) This indicates that the average amount Company Y budgeted for its projects both last year and this year was \$2,000 per project but does not give any information about the least and greatest amounts that it budgeted for its projects either year; NOT sufficient.

Taking (1) and (2) together, it is known that $L_1 = L_2 = \$400$ and that the average amount Company Y budgeted for its projects both last year and this year was \$2,000 per project, but there is no information about G_1 or G_2. For example, if, for each year, Company Y budgeted \$400 for each of 2 projects and \$2,320 for each of the 10 others, then (1) and (2) are true and the range for each year was \$2,320 − \$400 = \$1,920. However, if, last year, Company Y budgeted \$400 for each of 2 projects and \$2,320 for each of the 10 others, and, this year, budgeted \$400 for each of 11 projects and \$19,600 for 1 project, then (1) and (2) are true, but the range for last year was \$1,920 and the range for this year was \$19,600 − \$400 = \$19,200.

The correct answer is E; both statements together are still not sufficient.

53. What is the probability that Lee will make exactly 5 errors on a certain typing test?

(1) The probability that Lee will make 5 or more errors on the test is 0.27.

(2) The probability that Lee will make 5 or fewer errors on the test is 0.85.

Arithmetic Probability

(1) Given that 0.27 is the probability that Lee will make 5 or more errors on the test, it is clearly not possible to determine the probability that Lee will make exactly 5 errors on the test; NOT sufficient.

(2) Given that 0.85 is the probability that Lee will make 5 or fewer errors on the test, it is clearly not possible to determine the probability that Lee will make exactly 5 errors on the test; NOT sufficient.

Taking (1) and (2) together, let E be the event that Lee will make 5 or more errors on the test and let F be the event that Lee will make 5 or fewer errors on the test. Then $P(E \text{ or } F) = 1$, since it will always be the case that, when taking the test, Lee will make at least 5 errors or at most 5 errors. Also, (1) and (2) can be expressed as $P(E) = 0.27$ and $P(F) = 0.85$, and the question asks for the value of $P(E \text{ and } F)$. Using the identity $P(E \text{ or } F) = P(E) + P(F) - P(E \text{ and } F)$, it follows that $1 = 0.27 + 0.85 - P(E \text{ and } F)$, or $P(E \text{ and } F) = 0.27 + 0.85 - 1 = 0.12$. Therefore, the probability that Lee will make exactly 5 errors on the test is 0.12.

The correct answer is C; both statements together are sufficient.

54. A small factory that produces only upholstered chairs and sofas uses 1 cushion for each chair and 4 cushions for each sofa. If the factory used a total of 300 cushions on the furniture it produced last week, how many sofas did it produce last week?

(1) Last week the factory produced more chairs than sofas.

(2) Last week the factory produced a total of 150 chairs and sofas.

Algebra Simultaneous Equations

Let c and s be the numbers, respectively, of chairs and sofas produced last week. From the information given about the cushions used last week, we have $c + 4s = 300$. Can we determine the value of s?

(1) Given that $c > s$, it is not possible to determine the value of s. For example, it is possible that $c = 200$ and $s = 25$ (for these values, $c > s$ and $c + 4s = 200 + 4(25) = 300$) and it is possible that $c = 100$ and $s = 50$ (for these values, $c > s$ and $c + 4s = 100 + 4(50) = 300$); NOT sufficient.

(2) Given that $c + s = 150$, by subtracting this equation from $c + 4s = 300$ we get $(c + 4s) - (c + s) = 300 - 150$, or $3s = 150$. Therefore, $s = 50$; SUFFICIENT.

The correct answer is B; statement 2 alone is sufficient.

DISTRIBUTION OF SALESPERSONS
BY GENDER IN THREE SECTORS, YEAR X

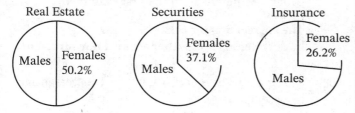

55. In year X were there more female salespersons in the securities sector than in the insurance sector?

(1) There were more male salespersons in the insurance sector than in the securities sector.

(2) The total number of salespersons was greater in the securities sector than in the insurance sector.

Arithmetic Percents

From the graphs, 37.1% of the salespersons in securities are females and $(100 - 37.1)\% = 62.9\%$ are males; 26.2% of the salespersons in insurance are females and $(100 - 26.2)\% = 73.8\%$ are males. Let S and I represent the number of salespersons in securities and insurance, respectively. Let F_S, M_S, F_I, and M_I, represent the numbers of female and male salespersons, respectively, in securities and insurance, respectively. Determine if the inequality $F_S > F_I$ is true.

(1) Given that $M_I > M_S$, it is not possible to determine if $F_S > F_I$ is true. For example, if $S = 10{,}000$ and $I = 9{,}000$, then $M_S = 0.629(10{,}000) = 6{,}290$, $M_I = 0.738(9{,}000) = 6{,}642$, $F_S = 0.371(10{,}000) = 3{,}710$, and $F_I = 0.262(9{,}000) = 2{,}358$. These numbers are summarized in the table below, from which it is easy to see that $M_I > M_S$ and $F_S > F_I$.

Sector	Number of employees	Males	Females
Securities	10,000	6,290	3,710
Insurance	9,000	6,642	2,358

However, if $S = 10{,}000$ and $I = 20{,}000$, then $M_S = 0.629(10{,}000) = 6{,}290$, $M_I = 0.738(20{,}000) = 14{,}760$,

$F_S = 0.371(10{,}000) = 3{,}710$ and $F_I = 0.262(20{,}000) = 5{,}240$. These numbers are summarized in the table below, from which it is easy to see that $M_I > M_S$ and $F_S < F_I$; NOT sufficient.

Sector	Number of employees	Males	Females
Securities	10,000	6,290	3,710
Insurance	20,000	14,760	5,240

(1) Given that $S > I$, it follows that $0.371S > 0.371I$ and $0.371I > 0.262I$, so $0.371S > 0.262I$ and $F_S > F_I$; SUFFICIENT.

The correct answer is B; statement 2 alone is sufficient.

56. If a club made a gross profit of $0.25 for each candy bar it sold, how many candy bars did the club sell?

(1) The total revenue from the sale of the candy bars was $300.

(2) If the club had sold 80 more candy bars, its gross profits would have increased by 20 percent.

Algebra First-Degree Equations

Let n be the number of candy bars sold. The gross profit from selling the n candy bars was $0.25n$. What is the value of n, or equivalently, what is the value of $0.25n$?

(1) Given that the total revenue was $300, it is not possible to determine how many candy bars the club sold because nothing is known about the total cost, which is the value of $300 - 0.25n$; NOT sufficient.

(2) Given that the gross profit from selling $(n + 80)$ candy bars is equal to $(1.2)(0.25n)$, it follows that $(0.25)(n + 80) = (1.2)(0.25n)$. Therefore, $0.25n + 20 = (1.2)(0.25n)$, or $20 = (0.2)(0.25n)$, and hence $0.25n = 100$; SUFFICIENT.

The correct answer is B; statement 2 alone is sufficient.

57. In one year 2,100 malpractice claims were filed with insurance company X and of these $\frac{1}{4}$ resulted in a financial settlement. Of those resulting in a financial settlement of less than $400,000, what was the average payment per claim?

    (1) Company X paid a total of 24.5 million dollars to the claimants.

    (2) Only 5 claims resulted in payments of $400,000 or more.

Arithmetic Statistics

A total of $\frac{1}{4}(2,100)$ = 525 claims were paid. What was the average payment per claim of those claims having a payment less than $400,000?

(1) Given that the total payment for the 525 paid claims was $24.5 million, it is not possible to determine the average payment per claim. This is because almost nothing is known about the total payment for those claims less than $400,000 or the number of those claims less than $400,000 (we only know they cannot exceed $24.5 million and 525 paid claims), and thus, more than one value is possible for the average payment per claim for those claims less than $400,000; NOT sufficient.

(2) Given that a total of 5 paid claims had payments of $400,000 or greater, it is not possible to determine the average payment per claim. This is because nothing is known about the total payment for those claims less than $400,000, and thus, more than one value is possible for this total payment divided by 520 (i.e., the average payment per claim for those claims less than $400,000); NOT sufficient.

Taking (1) and (2) together, it is still not possible to determine the average payment per claim. For example, if each of the 5 paid claims of over $400,000 was equal to $500,000, then the average payment per claim for those claims less than $400,000 would be $\dfrac{\$24.5 \text{ million} - \$2.5 \text{ million}}{520} =$ $\dfrac{\$22 \text{ million}}{520}$. However, if each of the 5 paid claims of over $400,000 was equal to $4 million, then the average payment per claim for those claims less than $400,000 would

be $\dfrac{\$24.5 \text{ million} - \$20 \text{ million}}{520} = \dfrac{\$4.5 \text{ million}}{520}$, which is different from the first example.

The correct answer is E; both statements together are still not sufficient.

58. If there are 13 boys in club X, what is the average age of these boys?

    (1) The oldest boy is 13 years old and the youngest boy is 9 years old.

    (2) Eleven of the boys are either 10 years old or 11 years old.

Arithmetic Statistics

What is the average age of the 13 boys, or equivalently, what is the sum of the ages of the 13 boys?

(1) Given that the oldest boy is 13 and the youngest boy is 9, it is not possible to determine the sum of their ages. For example, if their ages were such that one is 9, eleven are 10, and one is 13, then the sum of their ages would be less than if their ages were such that one is 9, eleven are 11, and one is 13; NOT sufficient.

(2) Given that eleven of the boys are either 10 or 11, it is not possible to determine the sum of their ages, because the same examples used above are such that eleven of the boys are either 10 or 11; NOT sufficient.

Taking (1) and (2) together, it is not possible to determine the sum of their ages because the examples above satisfy both (1) and (2).

The correct answer is E; both statements together are still not sufficient.

59. If all the employees of a company fall into one and only one of 3 groups, X, Y, or Z, with 250, 100, and 20 members in each group, respectively, what is the average (arithmetic mean) weekly salary of all the employees of this company, if all employees are paid every week of the year?

    (1) The average (arithmetic mean) annual salary of the employees in Group X is $10,000, in Group Y $15,000 and in Group Z $20,000.

    (2) The total annual payroll is $4,400,000.

Arithmetic Statistics

The average of the weekly salaries is the average of the annual salaries divided by 52, and thus the average of the weekly salaries can be determined if and only if the average of the annual salaries can be determined. What is the average of the annual salaries, or equivalently, what is the sum of the annual salaries?

(1) Given that the average of the annual salaries of employees in Groups X, Y, and Z is $10,000, $15,000, and $20,000, respectively, it follows that the sum of the annual salaries of employees in Groups X, Y, and Z is 250($10,000), 100($15,000), and 20($20,000), respectively. Therefore, the sum of the annual salaries is the sum of these three amounts; SUFFICIENT.

(2) We are given that the sum of the annual salaries is $4,400,000; SUFFICIENT.

The correct answer is D; each statement alone is sufficient.

DISTRIBUTION OF SALES INCOME
FOR STORE *S* LAST WEEK

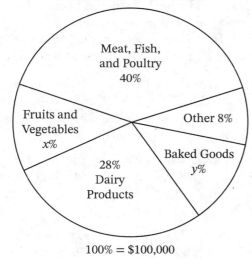

100% = $100,000

60. According to the graph above, the sale of fruits and vegetables in Store *S* last week accounted for what percent of the total sales income for the week?

(1) Last week the total income from the sale of fruits and vegetables in Store S was $16,000.

(2) $x = 2y$

Algebra Percents

According to the graph, sales of fruits and vegetables accounted for x% of the total sales,

baked goods accounted for y%, and all other categories combined accounted for 76%. It follows that $x + y = 100 - 76 = 24$. Determine the value of x.

(1) Given that sales of fruits and vegetables accounted for x% of the total sales of $100,000 and this amounted to $16,000, it follows that $\frac{x}{100}(100,000) = 16,000$. Thus, $x = 16$; SUFFICIENT.

(2) Given that $x = 2y$, it follows that $x + y = 3y = 24$, $y = 8$, and $x = 16$; SUFFICIENT.

The correct answer is D; each statement alone is sufficient.

61. Larry saves x dollars per month. Will Larry's total savings one year from now exceed his present savings by at least $500? (Assume that there is no interest.)

(1) In 6 months Larry's total savings will be $900.

(2) In 3 months Larry's total savings will exceed his present savings by $150.

Algebra Applied Problems

Let $\$p$ be Larry's present savings. Larry saves $\$x$ per month. One year from now (i.e., 12 months from now), Larry will have saved an additional $\$12x$. Determine if $(p + 12x) - p > 500$ or, equivalently, determine if $12x > 500$.

(1) Given that in 6 months Larry will have saved a total of $900, it follows that $p + 6x = 900$, but since the value of p is unknown, it cannot be determined if $12x > 500$; NOT sufficient.

(2) Given that $(p + 3x) - p = \$150$, it follows that $x = 50$, $12x = 600$, and $12x > 500$; SUFFICIENT.

The correct answer is B; statement 2 alone is sufficient.

62. If Randy has twice as many coins as Alice, and if Maria has 7 times as many coins as Alice, what is the combined number of coins that all three of them have?

(1) Alice has 4 fewer coins than Randy.

(2) Maria has 20 more coins than Randy.

Algebra Simultaneous Equations

Determine the total number of coins that Randy, Alice, and Maria have, given that Randy has twice as many coins as Alice and Maria has 7 times as many coins as Alice. In other words, determine the value of $R + A + M$, where $R, A,$ and M represent the number of coins, respectively, that Randy, Alice, and Maria have, given that $R = 2A$ and $M = 7A$.

(1) Given that Alice has 4 fewer coins than Randy, it follows that $A = R - 4$. Since $R = 2A$, it follows that $A = 2A - 4$, from which the value of A can be determined. From the value of A, values for R and M can be determined and $R + A + M$ can also be determined; SUFFICIENT.

(2) Given that Maria has 20 more coins than Randy, it follows that $M = R + 20$. Since $M = 7A$ and $R = 2A$, it follows that $7A = 2A + 20$, from which the value of A can be determined. From the value of A, values for R and M can be determined and $R + A + M$ can also be determined; SUFFICIENT.

**The correct answer is D;
each statement alone is sufficient.**

63. A line of people waiting to enter a theater consists of seven separate and successive groups. The first person in each group purchases one ticket for each person in the group and for no one else. If n is the total number of tickets sold for the first six groups, is n an even number?

    (1) There are no more than 4 people in each group.
    (2) The 19th person in line purchases the tickets for the seventh group.

Arithmetic Applied Problems

Determine whether the total number of people in the first six groups is an even number.

(1) Given that each group contains at most 4 people, it is not possible to determine whether the total number of people in the first six groups is an even number. For example, if the numbers of people in the first six groups were 2, 2, 2, 2, 2, and 2, then the total number of people in the first

six groups would be 12, which is an even number. However, if the numbers of people in the first six groups were 2, 2, 2, 2, 2, and 3, then the total number of people in the first six groups would be 13, which is not an even number; NOT sufficient.

(2) Given that the 19th person in line purchased the tickets for the seventh group, it follows that the total number of people in the first six groups was 18, which is an even number; SUFFICIENT.

**The correct answer is B;
statement 2 alone is sufficient.**

64. If John has exactly 10 coins each of which was minted in 1910 or 1920 or 1930, how many of his coins were minted in 1920?

    (1) Exactly 6 of his coins were minted in 1910 or 1920.
    (2) Exactly 7 of his coins were minted in 1920 or 1930.

Algebra Simultaneous Equations

Let $x, y,$ and z be the numbers of coins John has that were minted in, respectively, 1910, 1920, and 1930. Then $x, y,$ and z are nonnegative integers and $x + y + z = 10$. What is the value of y?

(1) Given that $x + y = 6$, it is possible that $y = 2$ (e.g., $x = 4, y = 2,$ and $z = 4$) and it is possible that $y = 4$ (e.g., $x = 2, y = 4,$ and $z = 4$); NOT sufficient.

(2) Given that $y + z = 7$, it is possible that $y = 3$ (e.g., $x = 3, y = 3,$ and $z = 4$) and it is possible that $y = 4$ (e.g., $x = 3, y = 4,$ and $z = 3$); NOT sufficient.

Taking (1) and (2) together, from $x + y + z = 10$ and (1) it follows that $6 + z = 10$, or $z = 4$. Substituting $z = 4$ into $y + z = 7$ gives $y + 4 = 7$, or $y = 3$.

**The correct answer is C;
both statements together are sufficient.**

65. The total profit of corporation K was $3,400,000 in year X. What was the total profit in year Y?

    (1) Income in year Y was 30 percent more than in year X.

(2) Costs in year Y were 40 percent more than in year X.

Algebra Applied Problems

Let $\$C_X$ be costs in year X, $\$I_X$ be income in year X, $\$C_Y$ be costs in year Y, and $\$I_Y$ be income in year Y. Given that $I_X - C_X = 3,400,000$, determine the value of $I_Y - C_Y$.

(1) Given that $I_Y = 1.3I_X$, some information about income in year Y is known, but since nothing is known about costs in year Y, the profit in year Y cannot be determined; NOT sufficient.

(2) Given that $C_Y = 1.4C_X$, some information about costs in year Y is known, but since nothing is known about income in year Y, the profit in year Y cannot be determined; NOT sufficient.

Taking (1) and (2) together, $I_Y - C_Y = 1.3I_X - 1.4C_X = 1.3(I_X - C_X) - 0.1C_X = 1.3(3,400,000) - 0.1C_X$, which can have more than one possible value. The table below gives two specific examples that illustrate this.

C_X	1,000,000	2,000,000
I_X	4,400,000	5,400,000
$I_X - C_X$	3,400,000	3,400,000
$C_Y = 1.4C_X$	1,400,000	2,800,000
$I_Y = 1.3I_X$	5,720,000	7,020,000
$I_Y - C_Y$	4,320,000	4,220,000

The correct answer is E; both statements together are still not sufficient.

66. Zelma scored 90, 88, and 92 on 3 of the 6 mathematics tests that she took. What was her average (arithmetic mean) score on the 6 tests?

(1) Her average (arithmetic mean) score on 5 of the tests was 90.

(2) Her score on one of the tests was 91.

Arithmetic Statistics

Determine the average (arithmetic mean) of Zelma's 6 test scores, given that 3 of the scores are 90, 88, and 92.

(1) Given that the average score on 5 of the 6 tests was 90, it is not possible to determine the average of all 6 test scores. For example, the 6 test scores could be 89, 91, 90, 88, 92, and 100 for an average score of $91\frac{2}{3}$ or the 6 test scores could be 89, 91, 90, 88, 92, and 50 for an average score of $83\frac{1}{3}$; NOT sufficient.

(2) Given that one of the scores was 91, it is not possible to determine the average of all 6 test scores. For example, the 6 test scores could be 89, 91, 90, 88, 92, and 100 for an average score of $91\frac{2}{3}$ or the 6 test scores could be 89, 91, 90, 88, 92, and 50 for an average score of $88\frac{1}{3}$; NOT sufficient.

Taking (1) and (2) together and noting that the examples that were used to show that (2) is not sufficient were the same examples that were used to show that (1) is not sufficient, the average of Zelma's 6 test scores cannot be determined.

The correct answer is E; both statements together are still not sufficient.

67. Will a company lose sales if its strategy focuses on consumer well-being rather than exploiting consumer fears?

(1) The company's current marketing strategy exploits its consumers' fears to drive sales, resulting in increased profits.

(2) From an ethical standpoint, the company should prioritize consumer well-being over short-term profits and refrain from exploiting their fears.

Inference

(1) Even if the company's current fear-based marketing strategy has increased sales and profits, a new strategy focused on consumer well-being might work even better. Thus, whether the company will lose sales if its strategy focuses on consumer well-being rather than exploiting consumer feats cannot be determined from (1) alone; NOT sufficient.

(2) What the company should do from an ethical standpoint is irrelevant to whether any marketing strategy will make the company lose sales. Thus, whether the company will lose sales if its strategy focuses on consumer well-being rather than exploiting consumer feats cannot be determined from (2) alone; NOT sufficient.

Since (1) alone is insufficient to answer the question, and (2) is completely irrelevant to answering it, both (1) and (2) together are insufficient to answer it. Whether or not the company's current fear-based marketing strategy has been profitable, and whether or not that strategy is ethical, a new strategy focused on consumer well-being might or might not make the company lose sales.

The correct answer is E; both statements together are still not sufficient.

68. Should a holistic approach be used to measure academic success?

    (1) Traditional education policies focus on standardized testing as the primary measure of academic success.
    (2) To foster holistic learning, education policies should prioritize a well-rounded curriculum that includes critical thinking, creativity, and practical skills.

Inference

(1) The observation that traditional education policies focus on standardized testing to measure academic success tells us nothing about whether or not this traditional approach is better than, worse than, or even distinct from a "holistic" approach. Thus, whether a holistic approach should be used to measure academic success cannot be determined from (1) alone; NOT sufficient.

(2) Even if education policies should prioritize a well-rounded curriculum to foster holistic learning, a holistic approach might not be the best way to measure academic success. Thus, whether a holistic approach should be used to measure academic success cannot be determined from (2) alone; NOT sufficient.

Now suppose traditional education policies measure academic success with standardized testing as (1) says, while education policies should prioritize a well-rounded curriculum to foster holistic learning as (2) says. In that case, a holistic approach to measuring academic success might or might not be better than, worse than, or even distinct from the traditional approach.

The correct answer is E; both statements together are still not sufficient.

69. Can financial budgeting help individuals avoid debt?

    (1) Many individuals struggle with mounting debt due to excessive spending resulting from a lack of financial planning.
    (2) To avoid taking out loans, individuals should practice responsible budgeting, enabling them to save for emergencies and achieve financial stability.

Inference

(1) The claim that many individuals struggle with mounting debt due to excessive spending resulting from lack of financial planning implies that they might not struggle with mounting debt if they *did* use financial planning to avoid excessive spending; that is, if they practiced financial budgeting. In other words, (1) implies that financial budgeting could help these individuals avoid the mounting debt that they struggle with. Thus, (1) alone entails that financial budgeting can help in avoiding debt; SUFFICIENT.

(2) The claim that individuals should practice responsible budgeting in order to avoid taking out loans implies that responsible budgeting can help them avoid taking out loans. Assuming that in at least some of these cases, avoiding taking out a loan can allow one to avoid the debt from that loan, this means that responsible financial budgeting can help in avoiding debt. Thus, (2) alone entails that financial budgeting can help in avoiding debt; SUFFICIENT.

The correct answer is D; each statement alone is sufficient.

70. What kind of behavior is usually displayed by conflicting factions?

    (1) In conflicts, some factions resort to aggression and hostility, which escalates the situation.

    (2) To promote peaceful resolutions, factions should engage in open communication, empathy, and compromise to find mutually beneficial solutions.

Inference

(1) Even if some factions in conflicts resort to hostility and aggression, conflicting factions might not usually display such behavior. Thus, what kind of behavior conflicting factions usually display cannot be determined from (1) alone; NOT sufficient.

(2) A claim about what conflicting factions should do in order to promote peaceful resolutions doesn't clearly indicate what they usually do in reality. Thus, what kind of behavior conflicting factions usually display cannot be determined from (2) alone; NOT sufficient.

(1)'s observation that some conflicting factions resort to hostility and aggression, even together with (2)'s claim that such factions should behave differently to promote peaceful resolutions, still doesn't tell us how conflicting factions usually behave.

The correct answer is E; both statements together are still not sufficient.

71. What is the probability of landing on tails at least once in a sequence of 100 tosses of a specific coin?

    (1) When tossing the coin, there are only two possible outcomes, heads or tails, and both have an equal chance of occurring.

    (2) In a series of 100 tosses of the coin, we can expect almost 50 heads.

Evaluate

(1) Since (1) tells us that there are only two possible outcomes to tossing the coin, that each of those outcomes has a 50% chance of occurring, and that one of them is tails, we can calculate the chance of landing on tails at least once in a series of 100 tosses of the coin as $1 - (0.5)^{100}$. Thus, (1) alone lets us determine this probability; SUFFICIENT.

(2) The vague thought that "we can expect almost 50 heads" in a series of 100 tosses of the coin doesn't tell us the probability of the coin landing on tails with each toss, so it doesn't give us enough information to calculate the probability of landing on tails at least once in a series of 100 tosses. Thus, (2) alone doesn't let us determine this probability. NOT SUFFICIENT.

The correct answer is A; statement 1 alone is sufficient.

72. What are some possible signs of impending rainfall in Exville today?

    (1) The weather forecast correctly predicts a 90% chance of rain in Exville today based on heavy cloud cover and low-pressure systems moving into the region.

    (2) Given the darkening sky, the sudden drop in temperature, and strong winds, it is highly likely that a rainstorm is imminent in Exville today.

Inference

(1) If a weather forecast is correct in predicting a 90% chance of rain in a town because of heavy cloud cover and low-pressure systems moving into the region, then heavy cloud cover and low-pressure systems must be two of the possible signs of impending rainfall in that town. Thus, (1) alone provides examples of some possible signs of impending rainfall in Exville today; SUFFICIENT.

(2) If a darkening sky, a sudden drop in temperature, and strong winds are reasons why it is highly likely that a rainstorm is imminent in Exville today, then those factors must be three of the possible signs of impending rainfall in Exville today. Thus, (2) alone provides examples of some possible signs of impending rainfall in Exville today; SUFFICIENT.

The correct answer is D; each statement alone is sufficient.

73. A patient experiencing cold-like symptoms goes to a doctor. Is the patient suffering from a viral infection?

   (1) Based on their symptoms and medical history, the patient thinks they are suffering from a viral infection.

   (2) Due to their knowledge of common illnesses in the local area, the doctor thinks it is more likely that seasonal allergies are the cause of the patient's symptoms.

Inference

(1) Even if the patient's symptoms and medical history give the patient reason to believe that a viral infection is causing the symptoms, that belief may be mistaken. Thus, whether the patient is suffering from a viral infection cannot be determined from (1) alone; NOT sufficient.

(2) Even if the doctor reasonably believes that seasonal allergies are more likely than a viral infection to be causing the patient's symptoms, a viral infection might still be the cause. Thus, whether the patient is suffering from a viral infection cannot be determined from (2) alone; NOT sufficient.

If (1) and (2) are both true, the patient and the doctor have opposing beliefs about the likelihood that the patient has a viral infection. These opposing beliefs don't settle the question of whether the patient has such an infection or not.

**The correct answer is E;
both statements together are still not sufficient.**

74. What should generally be expected if you venture into areas surrounding a road closure?

   (1) With a major G20 event happening at the Jawahar Lal Nehru Stadium tonight and reports of road closures in the area, there's a strong likelihood of congestion.

   (2) Given the large number of attendees expected at an event at the Jawahar Lal Nehru Stadium tonight, shuttle buses will be provided between the stadium and the International Media Centre.

Inference

(1) Observations about specific conditions around a stadium on a specific night can't support any broad generalization about what to expect around areas surrounding road closures. Thus, what should generally be expected if you venture into areas surrounding a road closure cannot be determined from (1) alone; NOT sufficient.

(2) Observations about specific conditions around a stadium on a specific night can't support any broad generalization about what to expect around areas surrounding road closures. Thus, what should generally be expected if you venture into areas surrounding a road closure cannot be determined from (2) alone; NOT sufficient.

(1) and (2) both describe conditions around the same stadium on a specific night. Thus, even both statements together can't support any broad generalization about what to expect around areas surrounding road closures.

**The correct answer is E;
both statements together are still not sufficient.**

Questions 75 to 110 — Difficulty: Hard

75. What percent of the students at University X are enrolled in a science course but are not enrolled in a biology course?

   (1) 28 percent of the students at University X are enrolled in a biology course.

   (2) 70 percent of the students at University X who are enrolled in a science course are enrolled in a biology course.

Algebra Percents

Under the assumption that a biology course is a type of science course, determine the percent of University X students who are enrolled in a science course, but not in a biology course.

   (1) Given that 28% of the students at University X are enrolled in a biology course, if 100% of the students are enrolled in a science course, then $(100 - 28)\% = 72\%$ are enrolled in a science course, but not in

a biology course. On the other hand if 50% of the students at University X are enrolled in a science course, then $(50 − 28)\% = 22\%$ are enrolled in a science course, but not in a biology course; NOT sufficient.

(2) Given that 70% of the students at University X who are enrolled in a science course are enrolled in a biology course, if 100% of the students at University X are enrolled in a science course, then $(100 − 70)\% = 30\%$ are enrolled in a science course, but not in a biology course. On the other hand if 50% of the students at University X are enrolled in a science course, then 70% of 50% = 35% are enrolled in a biology course, $(50 − 35)\% = 15\%$ are enrolled in a science course, but not in a biology course; NOT sufficient.

Taking (1) and (2) together, $0.28 = 0.7x$ where x is the percent of the students at University X who are enrolled in a science course. It follows that $x = 0.4$ or 40%. Thus, $(40 − 28)\% = 12\%$ of the students at University X are enrolled in a science course, but not in a biology course.

The correct answer is C; both statements together are sufficient.

76. Each Type A machine fills 400 cans per minute, each Type B machine fills 600 cans per minute, and each Type C machine installs 2,400 lids per minute. A lid is installed on each can that is filled and on no can that is not filled. For a particular minute, what is the total number of machines working?

(1) A total of 4,800 cans are filled that minute.

(2) For that minute, there are 2 Type B machines working for every Type C machine working.

Algebra Simultaneous Equations

(1) Given that 4,800 cans were filled that minute, it is possible that 12 Type A machines, no Type B machines, and 2 Type C machines were working, for a total of 14 machines, since $(12)(400) + (0)(600) = 4,800$ and $(2)(2,400) = 4,800$. However, it is also possible that no Type A machines, 8 Type B machines, and 2 Type C machines were working, for a total of 10 machines,

since $(0)(400) + (8)(600) = 4,800$ and $(2)(2,400) = 4,800$; NOT sufficient.

(2) Given that there are 2 Type B machines working for every Type C machine working, it is possible that there are 6 machines working—3 Type A machines, 2 Type B machines, and 1 Type C machine. This gives $3(400) + 2(600) = 2,400$ cans and $1(2,400) = 2,400$ lids. It is also possible that there are 12 machines working—6 Type A machines, 4 Type B machines, and 2 Type C machines. This gives $6(400) + 4(600) = 4,800$ cans and $2(2,400) = 4,800$ lids; NOT sufficient.

Taking (1) and (2) together, since there were 4,800 cans filled that minute, there were 4,800 lids installed that minute. It follows that 2 Type C machines were working that minute, since $(2)(2,400) = 4,800$. Since there were twice this number of Type B machines working that minute, it follows that 4 Type B machines were working that minute. These 4 Type B machines filled $(4)(600) = 2,400$ cans that minute, leaving $4,800 − 2,400 = 2,400$ cans to be filled by Type A machines. Therefore, the number of Type A machines working that minute was $\frac{2,400}{400} = 6$, and it follows that the total number of machines working that minute was $2 + 4 + 6 = 12$.

The correct answer is C; both statements together are sufficient.

77. In a two-month survey of shoppers, each shopper bought one of two brands of detergent, X or Y, in the first month and again bought one of these brands in the second month. In the survey, 90 percent of the shoppers who bought Brand X in the first month bought Brand X again in the second month, while 60 percent of the shoppers who bought Brand Y in the first month bought Brand Y again in the second month. What percent of the shoppers bought Brand Y in the second month?

(1) In the first month, 50 percent of the shoppers bought Brand X.

(2) The total number of shoppers surveyed was 5,000.

Arithmetic Percents

This problem can be solved by using the following contingency table where A and B represent, respectively, the number of shoppers who bought Brand X and the number of shoppers who bought Brand Y in the first month; C and D represent, respectively, the number of shoppers who bought Brand X and the number of shoppers who bought Brand Y in the second month; and T represents the total number of shoppers in the survey. Also in the table, $0.9A$ represents the 90% of the shoppers who bought Brand X in the first month and also bought it in the second month, and $0.1A$ represents the $(100 - 90)\% = 10\%$ of the shoppers who bought Brand X in the first month and Brand Y in the second month. Similarly, $0.6B$ represents the 60% of the shoppers who bought Brand Y in the first month and also bought it in the second month, and $0.4B$ represents the $(100 - 60)\% = 40\%$ of the shoppers who bought Brand Y in the first month and Brand X in the second month.

		Second Month		
		X	Y	Total
First Month	X	$0.9A$	$0.1A$	A
	Y	$0.4B$	$0.6B$	B
	Total	C	D	T

Determine the value of $\dfrac{D}{T}$ as a percentage.

(1) This indicates that 50% of the shoppers bought Brand X in the first month, so $A = 0.5T$. It follows that the other 50% of the shoppers bought Brand Y in the first month, so $B = 0.5T$. Then, $D = 0.1A + 0.6B = 0.1(0.5T) + 0.6(0.5T) = 0.05T + 0.30T = 0.35T$. It follows that $\dfrac{D}{T} = \dfrac{0.35T}{T} = 0.35$, which is 35%; SUFFICIENT.

(2) This indicates that $T = 5,000$, as shown in the following table:

		Second Month		
		X	Y	Total
First Month	X	$0.9A$	$0.1A$	A
	Y	$0.4B$	$0.6B$	B
	Total	C	D	5,000

But not enough information is given to be able to determine D or D as a percentage of 5,000; NOT sufficient.

The correct answer is A; statement 1 alone is sufficient.

78. If the total price of n equally priced shares of a certain stock was $12,000, what was the price per share of the stock?

(1) If the price per share of the stock had been $1 more, the total price of the n shares would have been $300 more.

(2) If the price per share of the stock had been $2 less, the total price of the n shares would have been 5 percent less.

Arithmetic Arithmetic Operations; Percents

Since the price per share of the stock can be expressed as $\dfrac{\$12,000}{n}$, determining the value of n is sufficient to answer this question.

(1) A per-share increase of $1 and a total increase of $300 for n shares of stock mean together that $n(\$1) = \$300$. It follows that $n = 300$; SUFFICIENT.

(2) If the price of each of the n shares had been reduced by $2, the total reduction in price would have been 5 percent less or $0.05(\$12,000)$. The equation $2n = 0.05(\$12,000)$ expresses this relationship. The value of n can be determined to be 300 from this equation; SUFFICIENT.

The correct answer is D; each statement alone is sufficient.

79. In Year X, 8.7 percent of the men in the labor force were unemployed in June compared with 8.4 percent in May. If the number of men in the labor force was the same for both months, how many men were unemployed in June of that year?

(1) In May of Year X, the number of unemployed men in the labor force was 3.36 million.

(2) In Year X, 120,000 more men in the labor force were unemployed in June than in May.

Arithmetic Percents

Since 8.7 percent of the men in the labor force were unemployed in June, the number of unemployed men could be calculated if the total number of men in the labor force was known. Let t represent the total number of men in the labor force.

(1) This implies that for May $(8.4\%)t = 3,360,000$, from which the value of t can be determined; SUFFICIENT.

(2) This implies that $(8.7\% - 8.4\%)t = 120,000$ or $(0.3\%)t = 120,000$. This equation can be solved for t; SUFFICIENT.

The correct answer is D; each statement alone is sufficient.

80. On Monday morning a certain machine ran continuously at a uniform rate to fill a production order. At what time did it completely fill the order that morning?

(1) The machine began filling the order at 9:30 a.m.

(2) The machine had filled $\frac{1}{2}$ of the order by 10:30 a.m. and $\frac{5}{6}$ of the order by 11:10 a.m.

Arithmetic Arithmetic Operations

(1) This merely states what time the machine began filling the order; NOT sufficient.

(2) In the 40 minutes between 10:30 a.m. and 11:10 a.m., $\frac{5}{6} - \frac{1}{2} = \frac{1}{3}$ of the order was filled. Therefore, the entire order was completely filled in $3 \times 40 = 120$ minutes, or 2 hours. Since half the order took 1 hour and was filled by 10:30 a.m., the second half of the order, and thus the entire order, was filled by 11:30 a.m.; SUFFICIENT.

The correct answer is B; statement 2 alone is sufficient.

81. After winning 50 percent of the first 20 games it played, Team A won all of the remaining games it played. What was the total number of games that Team A won?

(1) Team A played 25 games altogether.

(2) Team A won 60 percent of all the games it played.

Arithmetic Percents

Let r be the number of the remaining games played, all of which the team won. Since the team won $(50\%)(20) = 10$ of the first 20 games and the r remaining games, the total number of games the team won is $10 + r$. Also, the total number of games the team played is $20 + r$. Determine the value of r.

(1) Given that the total number of games played is 25, it follows that $20 + r = 25$, or $r = 5$; SUFFICIENT.

(2) It is given that the total number of games won is $(60\%)(20 + r)$, which can be expanded as $12 + 0.6r$. Since it is also known that the number of games won is $10 + r$, it follows that $12 + 0.6r = 10 + r$. Solving this equation gives $12 - 10 = r - 0.6r$, or $2 = 0.4r$, or $r = 5$; SUFFICIENT.

The correct answer is D; each statement alone is sufficient.

82. Michael arranged all his books in a bookcase with 10 books on each shelf and no books left over. After Michael acquired 10 additional books, he arranged all his books in a new bookcase with 12 books on each shelf and no books left over. How many books did Michael have before he acquired the 10 additional books?

(1) Before Michael acquired the 10 additional books, he had fewer than 96 books.

(2) Before Michael acquired the 10 additional books, he had more than 24 books.

Arithmetic Properties of Numbers

If x is the number of books Michael had before he acquired the 10 additional books, then x is a multiple of 10. After Michael acquired the 10 additional books, he had $x + 10$ books and $x + 10$ is a multiple of 12.

(1) If $x < 96$, where x is a multiple of 10, then $x = 10, 20, 30, 40, 50, 60, 70, 80,$ or 90 and $x + 10 = 20, 30, 40, 50, 60, 70, 80, 90,$ or 100. Since $x + 10$ is a multiple of 12, then $x + 10 = 60$ and $x = 50$; SUFFICIENT.

(2) If $x > 24$, where x is a multiple of 10, then x must be one of the numbers 30, 40, 50, 60, 70, 80, 90, 100, 110, …, and $x + 10$ must be one of the numbers 40, 50, 60, 70, 80, 90, 100, 110, 120, …. Since there is more than

one multiple of 12 among these numbers (for example, 60 and 120), the value of $x + 10$, and therefore the value of x, cannot be determined; NOT sufficient.

**The correct answer is A;
statement 1 alone is sufficient.**

83. Last year in a group of 30 businesses, 21 reported a net profit and 15 had investments in foreign markets. How many of the businesses did not report a net profit nor invest in foreign markets last year?

    (1) Last year 12 of the 30 businesses reported a net profit and had investments in foreign markets.

    (2) Last year 24 of the 30 businesses reported a net profit or invested in foreign markets, or both.

Arithmetic Concepts of Sets

Consider the Venn diagram below in which x represents the number of businesses that reported a net profit and had investments in foreign markets. Since 21 businesses reported a net profit, $21 - x$ businesses reported a net profit only. Since 15 businesses had investments in foreign markets, $15 - x$ businesses had investments in foreign markets only. Finally, since there is a total of 30 businesses, the number of businesses that did not report a net profit and did not invest in foreign markets is $30 - (21 - x + x + 15 - x) = x - 6$.

Determine the value of $x - 6$, or equivalently, the value of x.

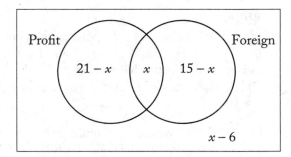

(1) It is given that $12 = x$; SUFFICIENT.

(2) It is given that $24 = (21 - x) + x + (15 - x)$. Therefore, $24 = 36 - x$, or $x = 12$.

Alternatively, the information given is exactly the number of businesses that are not among those to be counted in answering the question posed in the problem, and

therefore the number of businesses that are to be counted is $30 - 24 = 6$; SUFFICIENT.

**The correct answer is D;
each statement alone is sufficient.**

84. For each landscaping job that takes more than 4 hours, a certain contractor charges a total of r dollars for the first 4 hours plus $0.2r$ dollars for each additional hour or fraction of an hour, where $r > 100$. Did a particular landscaping job take more than 10 hours?

    (1) The contractor charged a total of $288 for the job.

    (2) The contractor charged a total of $2.4r$ dollars for the job.

Algebra Applied Problems

If y represents the total number of hours the particular landscaping job took, determine if $y > 10$.

(1) This indicates that the total charge for the job was $288, which means that $r + 0.2r(y - 4) = 288$. From this it cannot be determined if $y > 10$. For example, if $r = 120$ and $y = 11$, then $120 + 0.2(120)(7) = 288$, and the job took more than 10 hours. However, if $r = 160$ and $y = 8$, then $160 + 0.2(160)(4) = 288$, and the job took less than 10 hours; NOT sufficient.

(2) This indicates that $r + 0.2r(y - 4) = 2.4r$, from which it follows that

$$r + 0.2ry - 0.8r = 2.4r \quad \text{use distributive property}$$
$$0.2ry = 2.2r \quad \text{subtract } (r - 0.8r) \text{ from both sides}$$
$$y = 11 \quad \text{divide both sides by } 0.2r$$

Therefore, the job took more than 10 hours; SUFFICIENT.

**The correct answer is B;
statement 2 alone is sufficient.**

85. If 75 percent of the guests at a certain banquet ordered dessert, what percent of the guests ordered coffee?

    (1) 60 percent of the guests who ordered dessert also ordered coffee.

    (2) 90 percent of the guests who ordered coffee also ordered dessert.

Arithmetic Concepts of Sets; Percents

Consider the Venn diagram below that displays the various percentages of 4 groups of the guests. Thus, x percent of the guests ordered both dessert and coffee and y percent of the guests ordered coffee only. Since 75 percent of the guests ordered dessert, $(75 - x)\%$ of the guests ordered dessert only. Also, because the 4 percentages represented in the Venn diagram have a total sum of 100 percent, the percentage of guests who did not order either dessert or coffee is $100 - [(75 - x) + x + y] = 25 - y$. Determine the percentage of guests who ordered coffee, or equivalently, the value of $x + y$.

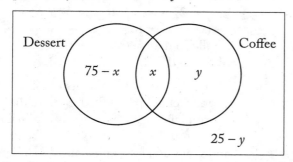

    (1) Given that x is equal to 60 percent of 75, or 45, the value of $x + y$ cannot be determined; NOT sufficient.

    (2) Given that 90 percent of $x + y$ is equal to x, it follows that $0.9(x + y) = x$, or $9(x + y) = 10x$. Therefore, $9x + 9y = 10x$, or $9y = x$. From this the value of $x + y$ cannot be determined. For example, if $x = 9$ and $y = 1$, then all 4 percentages in the Venn diagram are between 0 and 100, $9y = x$, and $x + y = 10$. However, if $x = 18$ and $y = 2$, then all 4 percentages in the Venn diagram are between 0 and 100, $9y = x$, and $x + y = 20$; NOT sufficient.

Given both (1) and (2), it follows that $x = 45$ and $9y = x$. Therefore, $9y = 45$, or $y = 5$, and hence $x + y = 45 + 5 = 50$.

The correct answer is C; both statements together are sufficient.

86. A tank containing water started to leak. Did the tank contain more than 30 gallons of water when it started to leak? (Note: 1 gallon = 128 ounces)

    (1) The water leaked from the tank at a constant rate of 6.4 ounces per minute.

    (2) The tank became empty less than 12 hours after it started to leak.

Arithmetic Rate Problems

    (1) Given that the water leaked from the tank at a constant rate of 6.4 ounces per minute, it is not possible to determine if the tank leaked more than 30 gallons of water. In fact, any nonzero amount of water leaking from the tank is consistent with a leakage rate of 6.4 ounces per minute, since nothing can be determined about the amount of time the water was leaking from the tank; NOT sufficient.

    (2) Given that the tank became empty in less than 12 hours, it is not possible to determine if the tank leaked more than 30 gallons of water because the rate at which water leaked from the tank is unknown. For example, the tank could have originally contained 1 gallon of water that emptied in exactly 10 hours or the tank could have originally contained 31 gallons of water that emptied in exactly 10 hours; NOT sufficient.

Given (1) and (2) together, the tank emptied at a constant rate of

$$\left(6.4 \frac{\text{oz}}{\text{min}}\right)\left(60 \frac{\text{min}}{\text{hr}}\right)\left(\frac{1}{128} \frac{\text{gal}}{\text{oz}}\right) = \frac{(64)(6)}{128} \frac{\text{gal}}{\text{hr}} =$$

$$\frac{(64)(6)}{(64)(2)} \frac{\text{gal}}{\text{hr}} = 3 \frac{\text{gal}}{\text{hr}} \text{ for less than 12 hours.}$$

If t is the total number of hours the water leaked from the tank, then the total amount of water emptied from the tank, in gallons, is $3t$, which is therefore less than $(3)(12) = 36$. From this it is not possible to determine if the tank originally contained more than 30 gallons of water. For example, if the tank leaked water for a total of 11 hours, then the tank originally contained $(3)(11)$ gallons of water, which is more than 30 gallons of water. However, if the tank leaked water for a total of 2 hours, then the tank originally contained (3)(2) gallons of water, which is not more than 30 gallons of water.

**The correct answer is E;
both statements together are still not sufficient.**

87. Each of the 45 books on a shelf is written either in English or in Spanish, and each of the books is either a hardcover book or a paperback. If a book is to be selected at random from the books on the shelf, is the probability less than $\frac{1}{2}$ that the book selected will be a paperback written in Spanish?

    (1) Of the books on the shelf, 30 are paperbacks.
    (2) Of the books on the shelf, 15 are written in Spanish.

Arithmetic Probability

(1) This indicates that 30 of the 45 books are paperbacks. Of the 30 paperbacks, 25 could be written in Spanish. In this case, the probability of randomly selecting a paperback book written in Spanish is $\frac{25}{45} > \frac{1}{2}$. On the other hand, it is possible that only 5 of the paperback books are written in Spanish. In this case, the probability of randomly selecting a paperback book written in Spanish is $\frac{5}{45} < \frac{1}{2}$; NOT sufficient.

(2) This indicates that 15 of the books are written in Spanish. Then, at most 15 of the 45 books on the shelf are paperbacks written in Spanish, and the probability of randomly selecting a paperback book written in Spanish is at most $\frac{15}{45} < \frac{1}{2}$; SUFFICIENT.

**The correct answer is B;
statement 2 alone is sufficient.**

88. A small school has three foreign language classes, one in French, one in Spanish, and one in German. How many of the 34 students enrolled in the Spanish class are also enrolled in the French class?

    (1) There are 27 students enrolled in the French class, and 49 students enrolled in either the French class, the Spanish class, or both of these classes.

(2) One-half of the students enrolled in the Spanish class are enrolled in more than one foreign language class.

Arithmetic Sets

Given that 34 students are enrolled in the Spanish class, how many students are enrolled in both the Spanish and French classes? In other words, given that $x + y = 34$ in the diagram below, what is the value of y?

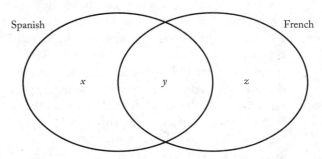

(1) It is given that $y + z = 27$ and $x + y + z = 49$. Adding the equations $x + y = 34$ and $y + z = 27$ gives $x + 2y + z = 34 + 27 = 61$, or $y + (x + y + z) = 61$. Since $x + y + z = 49$, it follows that $y + 49 = 61$, or $y = 12$; SUFFICIENT.

(2) Given that half the students enrolled in the Spanish class are enrolled in more than one foreign language class, then it is possible that no students are enrolled in the French and German classes only and 17 students are enrolled in both the Spanish and French classes. On the other hand, it is also possible that there are 17 students enrolled in the French and German classes only and no students enrolled in both the Spanish and French classes; NOT sufficient.

**The correct answer is A;
statement 1 alone is sufficient.**

89. Last year $\frac{3}{5}$ of the members of a certain club were males. This year the members of the club include all the members from last year plus some new members. Is the fraction of the members of the club who are males greater this year than last year?

    (1) More than half of the new members are male.
    (2) The number of members of the club this year is $\frac{6}{5}$ the number of members last year.

Arithmetic Operations with Fractions

Let L represent the number of members last year; N the number of new members added this year; and x the number of members added this year who are males. It is given that $\frac{3}{5}$ of the members last year were males. It follows that the number of members who are male this year is $\frac{3}{5}L + x$. Also, the total number of members this year is $L + N$. Determine if $\frac{\frac{3}{5}L + x}{L + N} > \frac{3}{5}$, or equivalently, determine if $3L + 5x > 3L + 3N$ or simply if $x > \frac{3}{5}N$.

(1) This indicates that $x > \frac{1}{2}N$. If, for example, $N = 20$ and $x = 11$, then $11 > \frac{1}{2}(20) = 10$, but $11 \not> \frac{3}{5}(20) = 12$. On the other hand, if $N = 20$ and $x = 16$, then $16 > \frac{1}{2}(20) = 10$, and $16 > \frac{3}{5}(20) = 12$; NOT sufficient.

(2) This indicates that $L + N = \frac{6}{5}L$. It follows that $N = \frac{1}{5}L$. If, for example, $L = 100$, then $N = \frac{1}{5}(100) = 20$. If $x = 11$, then $11 \not> \frac{3}{5}(20) = 12$. On the other hand, if $x = 16$, then $16 > \frac{1}{2}(20) = 10$, and $16 > \frac{3}{5}(20) = 12$; NOT sufficient.

Taking (1) and (2) together is of no more help than (1) and (2) taken separately since the same examples were used to show that neither (1) nor (2) is sufficient.

The correct answer is E; both statements together are still not sufficient.

90. Machines K, M, and N, each working alone at its constant rate, produce 1 widget in x, y, and 2 minutes, respectively. If Machines K, M, and N work simultaneously at their respective constant rates, does it take them less than 1 hour to produce a total of 50 widgets?

(1) $x < 1.5$
(2) $y < 1.2$

Algebra Work Problems

Because Machine N produces 1 widget every 2 minutes, Machine N produces $\frac{60}{2} = 30$ widgets in 1 hour = 60 minutes.

(1) Given that $x < 1.5$, it follows that Machine K, which produces $\frac{60}{x} =$ widgets in 60 minutes, produces more than $\frac{60}{1.5} = 40$ widgets in 1 hour = 60 minutes.

Thus, regardless of the number of widgets produced by Machine M, when all three machines are working simultaneously at their respective constant rates, more than $30 + 40 = 70$ widgets will be produced in 1 hour. Therefore, the three machines will together have produced 50 widgets in less than 1 hour; SUFFICIENT.

(2) Given that $y < 1.2$, it follows that Machine M, which produces $\frac{60}{y} =$ widgets in 60 minutes, produces more than $\frac{60}{1.2} = 50$ widgets in 1 hour = 60 minutes.

Thus, regardless of the number of widgets produced by Machine K, when all three machines are working simultaneously at their respective constant rates, more than $30 + 50 = 80$ widgets will be produced in 1 hour. Therefore, the three machines will together have produced 50 widgets in less than 1 hour; SUFFICIENT.

The correct answer is D; each statement alone is sufficient.

91. Stations X and Y are connected by two separate, straight, parallel rail lines that are 250 miles long. Train P and train Q simultaneously left Station X and Station Y, respectively, and each train traveled to the other's point of departure. The two trains passed each other after traveling for 2 hours. When the two trains passed, which train was nearer to its destination?

(1) At the time when the two trains passed, train P had averaged a speed of 70 miles per hour.

(2) Train Q averaged a speed of 55 miles per hour for the entire trip.

Arithmetic Applied Problems; Rates

(1) This indicates that Train P had traveled $2(70) = 140$ miles when it passed Train Q. It follows that Train P was $250 − 140 = 110$ miles from its destination and Train Q was 140 miles from its destination, which means that Train P was nearer to its destination when the trains passed each other; SUFFICIENT.

(2) This indicates that Train Q averaged a speed of 55 miles per hour for the entire trip, but no information is given about the speed of Train P. If Train Q traveled for 2 hours at an average speed of 55 miles per hour and Train P traveled for 2 hours at an average speed of 70 miles per hour, then Train P was nearer to its destination when the trains passed. However, if Train Q traveled for 2 hours at an average speed of 65 miles per hour and Train P traveled for 2 hours at an average speed of 60 miles per hour, then Train Q was nearer to its destination when the trains passed. Note that if Train Q traveled at $\frac{(120)(55)}{140} = 47\frac{1}{7}$ miles per hour for the remainder of the trip, then its average speed for the whole trip was 55 miles per hour; NOT sufficient.

The correct answer is A; statement 1 alone is sufficient.

92. In a two-story apartment complex, each apartment on the upper floor rents for 75 percent as much as each apartment on the lower floor. If the total monthly rent is \$15,300 when rent is collected on all of the apartments, what is the monthly rent on each apartment on the lower floor?

    (1) An apartment on the lower floor rents for \$150 more per month than an apartment on the upper floor.
    (2) There are 6 more apartments on the upper floor than on the lower floor.

Algebra Simultaneous Equations

Let x be the number of apartments on the lower floor, y be the number of apartments on the upper floor, and \$$R$ be the monthly rent on each apartment on the lower floor. Then the monthly

rent on each apartment on the upper floor is $0.75R$ and $Rx + 0.75Ry = 15,300$. Determine the value of R.

(1) Given that $R = 150 + 0.75R$, it follows that $0.25R = 150$, or $R = 600$; SUFFICIENT.

(2) Given that $y = x + 6$ thus, $Rx + 0.75R(x + 6) = 15,300$, or $1.75Rx + 4.5R = 15,300$, which can be true for more than one value of R and a corresponding positive integer value of x. For example, it is possible that $R = 600$ and $x = 12$, and it is possible that $R = 425$ and $x = 18$; NOT sufficient.

The correct answer is A; statement 1 alone is sufficient.

93. A motorboat, which is set to travel at k kilometers per hour in still water, travels directly up and down the center of a straight river so that the change in the boat's speed relative to the shore depends only on the speed and direction of the current. What is the value of k?

    (1) It takes the same amount of time for the boat to travel 4 kilometers directly downstream as it takes for it to travel 3 kilometers directly upstream.
    (2) The current flows directly downstream at a constant rate of 2.5 kilometers per hour.

Algebra Applied Problems

Letting c represent the speed of the current, the boat travels $(k + c)$ kilometers per hour (kph) when traveling in the same direction as the current (downstream) and $(k − c)$ kph when traveling in the opposite direction as the current. Determine the value of k.

(1) Given that it takes the same amount of time to travel 4 kilometers (km) downstream as it takes to travel 3 km upstream, it follows that $\frac{4}{k + c} = \frac{3}{k + c}$, or $k = 7c$, which shows that the value of k depends on the value of c; NOT sufficient.

(2) Given that $c = 2.5$ kph, it is not possible to determine the value of k since no information is given about the value of k or its relationship with c; NOT sufficient.

Taking (1) and (2) together, $k = 7c = 7(2.5) = 17.5$.

The correct answer is C; both statements together are sufficient.

94. If the book value of a certain piece of equipment was $5,000 exactly 5 years ago, what is its present book value?

    (1) From the time the piece of equipment was purchased, its book value decreased by 10 percent of its purchase price each year of its life.

    (2) The present book value of another piece of equipment is $2,000.

Algebra Applied Problems

Determine the present book value of a piece of equipment, of which the book value exactly 5 years ago was $5,000.

(1) Given that the book value decreased 10% of the purchase price each year, it is not possible to determine the present book value because the purchase price is unknown as is the number of years ago the equipment was purchased. Consider the following chart, where P represents the purchase price.

Years after purchase	Depreciation	Book value
0	0	P
1	$0.1P$	$0.9P$
2	$0.1P$	$0.8P$
3	$0.1P$	$0.7P$
4	$0.1P$	$0.6P$
5	$0.1P$	$0.5P$
6	$0.1P$	$0.4P$
7	$0.1P$	$0.3P$
8	$0.1P$	$0.2P$
9	$0.1P$	$0.1P$
10	$0.1P$	0
11	0	0
12	0	0
13	0	0

For example, if "5 years ago" was 6 years after purchase and the book value was

$5,000, then $5,000 = 0.4P$ and $P = \$12,500$. In this case, the present book value (i.e., 5 years hence) is $0. On the other hand, if "5 years ago" was 2 years after purchase and the book value was $5,000, then $5,000 = 0.8P$ and $P = \$6,250$. In this case, the present book value (i.e., 5 years hence) is $0.3(\$6,250) = \$1,875$; NOT sufficient.

(2) Given that the present book value of another piece of equipment is $2,000 gives no information about the certain piece of equipment under consideration; NOT sufficient.

Taking (1) and (2) together gives no more information than (1) alone since (2) gives information about another piece of equipment, not the piece under consideration.

The correct answer is E; both statements together are not sufficient.

95. The total cost to charter a bus was shared equally by the people who went on a certain trip. If the total cost to charter the bus was $360, how many people went on the trip?

    (1) Each person who went on the trip paid $9 to charter the bus.

    (2) If 4 fewer people had gone on the trip, each person's share of the total cost to charter the bus would have increased by $1.

Algebra First-Degree Equations

Let n be the number of people who went on the trip and $\$p$ be the amount that each person paid. Then $np = 360$. What is the value of n?

(1) Given that $p = 9$, then $9n = 360$, or $n = 40$; SUFFICIENT.

(2) Given that $(n - 4)(p + 1) = 360$, or $np + n - 4p - 4 = 360$, it follows from $np = 360$ that $n - 4p - 4 = 0$. Multiplying both sides of this last equation by n gives $n^2 - 4np - 4n = 0$, or $n^2 - 4(360) - 4n = 0$, or $n^2 - 4n - 1,440 = 0$. Factoring gives $(n - 40)(n + 36) = 0$, and hence $n = 40$ since n is a positive integer; SUFFICIENT.

The correct answer is D; each statement alone is sufficient.

96. If each of the stamps Carla bought cost 20, 25, or 30 cents and she bought at least one of each denomination, what is the number of 25-cent stamps that she bought?

    (1) She spent a total of $1.45 for stamps.
    (2) She bought exactly 6 stamps.

Arithmetic Applied Problems

Let x, y, and z be the number of 20, 25, and 30 cent stamps, respectively, that Carla bought. What is the value of y?

(1) Given that $20x + 25y + 30z = 145$, it is not possible to determine the value of y. For example, if $x = 3$, $y = 1$, and $z = 2$, then each of x, y, and z is a positive integer and $20x + 25y + 30z = 145$. However, if $x = 2$, $y = 3$, and $z = 1$, then each of x, y, and z is a positive integer and $20x + 25y + 30z = 145$; NOT sufficient.

(2) Given that $x + y + z = 6$, it is not possible to determine the value of y, because each the two examples used in (1) satisfies $x + y + z = 6$; NOT sufficient.

Taking (1) and (2) together, it is not possible to determine the value of y because the two examples above each satisfy both (1) and (2).

The correct answer is E; both statements together are still not sufficient.

97. A car traveled a distance of d miles in t minutes at an average rate of r miles per minute. What is the ratio of d to r?

    (1) $t = 30$
    (2) $d = 25$

Algebra Applied Problems

Determine the ratio of d to r for a car that traveled d miles in t minutes at an average rate of r miles per minute. Note that since $d = rt$ and $\frac{d}{r} = t$, determining the ratio of d to r amounts to determining t.

(1) Given that $t = 30$, it follows that $\frac{d}{r} = 30$; SUFFICIENT.

(2) Given that $d = 25$, it is not possible to determine the ratio of d to r since no information is given about the value of r nor

is information given from which to obtain the value of r; NOT sufficient.

The correct answer is A; statement 1 alone is sufficient.

98. Pat is reading a book that has a total of 15 chapters. Has Pat read at least $\frac{1}{3}$ of the pages in the book?

    (1) Pat has just finished reading the first 5 chapters.
    (2) Each of the first 3 chapters has more pages than each of the other 12 chapters in the book.

Arithmetic Applied Problems

Determine if Pat has read at least $\frac{1}{3}$ of the pages in a 15-chapter book.

(1) Given that Pat has just finished reading the first 5 chapters in the book, she may or may not have read $\frac{1}{3}$ of the pages in the book. If the first 5 chapters were very short and she has read no other pages in the book, it is possible that she has read less than $\frac{1}{3}$ of the pages in the book. If the first 5 chapters were very long and/or she has read other pages in the book, it is possible that she has read at least $\frac{1}{3}$ of the pages in the book; NOT sufficient.

(2) Given that each of the first 3 chapters has more pages than each of the other 12 chapters, it is impossible to determine whether Pat has read at least $\frac{1}{3}$ of the pages in the book because information is not given about how many chapters or which chapters of the book Pat has read; NOT sufficient.

Taking (1) and (2) together, if Pat has read just the first 5 chapters and each of the first 3 chapters has 10 pages, each of chapters 4 and 5 has 1 page, and each of the other 10 chapters has 9 pages, then Pat has read 32 pages of the book, which has $32 + 90 = 122$ pages and $\frac{32}{122} < \frac{1}{3}$. On the other hand, if Pat has read at least the first 5 chapters, each of the first 3 chapters has 10 pages and each of the other 12 chapters has 9 pages, then Pat has read at least 48 pages of the book, which has $48 + 90 = 138$ pages and $\frac{48}{138} > \frac{1}{3}$.

The correct answer is E; both statements together are still not sufficient.

99. Should the choices made by 100 participants in a survey about Product X be said to proportionately represent the preferences of the entire population?

    (1) In the survey of 100 participants, 70% said they preferred Product X.

    (2) While the survey provided valuable insights into Product X, the small sample may not be representative of the entire population's preferences.

Inference

(1) Whatever specific percentage of the survey participants said they preferred Product X, the percentage of individuals with that preference in a much larger population might be exactly the same or much different. Thus, whether the survey participants' choices should be said to proportionately represent the entire population's preferences cannot be determined from (1) alone; NOT sufficient.

(2) The statement that a small sample may not be representative of a population's preferences suggests that the sample also may be representative of that population's preferences. Thus, whether the survey participants' choices should be said to proportionately represent the entire population's preferences cannot be determined from (2) alone; NOT sufficient.

If (1) and (2) are both true, it is possible that 70% of the broader population prefers Product X, just as 70% of the survey respondents claimed to prefer it, but it's also possible that some much different percentage of the broader population prefers Product X. Thus, whether the survey participants' choices should be said to proportionately represent the entire population's preferences cannot be determined even from both statements together.

The correct answer is E; both statements together are still not sufficient.

100. What is a limiting factor when it comes to us using the most effective solution?

    (1) We have identified several potential solutions, but a lack of funding hinders their implementation.

    (2) As the most effective solution requires extensive resources, we must opt for a more affordable option given our budget.

Inference

(1) Even if a lack of funding hinders the implementation of several potential solutions we have identified, maybe none of those potential solutions is the most effective solution. Perhaps the most effective solution is well within our budget, but we haven't identified it. Thus, an example of a limiting factor when it comes to us using the most effective solution cannot be determined from (1) alone; NOT sufficient.

(2) If the extensive resources required by the most effective solution require us to opt for a more affordable option given our budget, then cost must be one limiting factor when it comes to us using the most effective solution. Thus, (2) alone provides an example of a limiting factor when it comes to us using the most effective solution; SUFFICIENT.

The correct answer is B; statement 2 alone is sufficient.

101. What are all the important considerations for making accurate projections?

    (1) Based on the available data, we believe that the market demand for our product will increase by 20% in the next quarter.

    (2) Without comprehensive market research, our projection may not account for external factors that could influence fluctuations in demand.

Inference

(1) An observation about how "we" believe market demand for a product will change in the next quarter provides no information about important considerations for making accurate projections. Thus, what considerations are important for making accurate projections cannot be determined from (1) alone; NOT sufficient.

(2) (2)'s claim that our projection may not account for external factors without comprehensive market research doesn't tell us what considerations are generally important for making accurate projections. (2) leaves open the possibility that our projection may account for external factors without comprehensive market research. It also leaves open the possibility that

the projection may be accurate even if it doesn't account for external factors, or that it may be inaccurate even if it does account for such factors. Furthermore, even if comprehensive market research were one important consideration for making our projection, that wouldn't tell us what the other important considerations for making the projection are. And finally, even if we knew all the important considerations for making this particular projection, that wouldn't tell us what considerations are important for making accurate projections in general. Thus, what considerations are important for making accurate projections cannot be determined from (2) alone; NOT sufficient.

Since (1) is completely irrelevant to determining the considerations important for making accurate projections, while (2) is inadequate for determining them, even both statements together can't tell us what considerations are important for making accurate projections.

**The correct answer is E;
both statements together are still not sufficient.**

102. Does Company X strive to maintain a low defect rate in order to ensure product quality?

    (1) Company X's manufacturing process has a defect rate of 2% according to quality control data.

    (2) Monitoring the defect rate in a manufacturing process is essential to ensure product quality, and a low percentage indicates a well-maintained production process.

Inference

(1) Knowing that quality control data says the defect rate for Company's X's manufacturing process is 2% tells us nothing about whether Company X strives to maintain a low defect rate. First, the quality control data may be inaccurate or fraudulent. Second, without further context, we can't tell whether a 2% defect rate is low or high. And finally, even if a 2% defect rate is low, we don't know whether Company X is striving to keep it low to ensure product

quality. Thus, whether Company X strives to maintain a low defect rate in order to ensure product quality cannot be determined from (1) alone; NOT sufficient.

(2) Even if monitoring the defect rate in a manufacturing process is essential to ensure product quality, Company X may not monitor it. And even if a low defect rate indicates a well-maintained production process, Company X's defect rate may be high. Thus, whether Company X strives to maintain a low defect rate in order to ensure product quality cannot be determined from (2) alone; NOT sufficient.

Even if (1) is true, the real defect rate for Company X's manufacturing process might be higher than the quality control data suggests. And even if the defect rate is really 2%, that might be quite a high rate for Company X's product and manufacturing process. If the defect rate is high, then (2) does not imply that Company X is striving to maintain a low defect rate. Thus, (1) and (2) together don't tell us whether Company X strives to maintain a low defect rate.

**The correct answer is E;
both statements together are still not sufficient.**

103. How might career advancement be described as potentially linked to both growth and decline?

    (1) Working long hours and overtime may lead to higher productivity and career advancement but is likely to cause a decline in physical and mental well-being.

    (2) Maintaining a work-life balance is important to reduce the negative effect that working too much has on a person's quality of life.

Inference

(1) (1) describes how working long hours and overtime is potentially linked to a type of growth (in productivity) and also to a type of decline (in well-being) as well as to career advancement. That is, (1) directly describes a way that career advancement is potentially linked to both growth and decline, via working long hours and overtime. Since (1) itself is an answer to the question, it is sufficient to answer it; SUFFICIENT.

(2)   (2) says nothing about growth or career advancement. Thus, (2) alone doesn't tell us how career advancement might be described as potentially linked to both growth and decline. NOT sufficient.

The correct answer is A; statement 1 alone is sufficient.

104. What is an example of how investment in healthcare resources might sometimes create a challenge?

    (1)   Investment in both advanced medical technology and specialized treatments can improve patient outcomes for certain conditions. Nevertheless, it may put a strain on healthcare budgets.

    (2)   When it comes to allocating resources in the healthcare sector, directing money toward the purchase of advanced medical equipment could potentially limit access to other essential services and treatments.

Inference

    (1)   (1) gives an example of how investment in certain healthcare resources (advanced medical technology and specialized treatments) might create a challenge (by straining healthcare budgets). Thus, (1) alone directly answers the question; SUFFICIENT.

    (2)   (2) gives an example of how investment in certain healthcare resources (advanced medical equipment) might create a challenge (by limiting access to other essential services and treatments). Thus, (2) alone directly answers the question; SUFFICIENT.

The correct answer is D; each statement alone is sufficient.

105. A person bought x number of apples, y number of oranges, and z number of mangoes from a shop. What is the total price of this transaction if each apple costs $2, each orange costs $2.50, and each mango costs $3?

    (1)   The number of apples bought is 12 more than the number of oranges bought. The number of mangoes bought is half the number of apples bought.

    (2)   The average number of fruits purchased from the three varieties is greater than 29 and less than 33.

Applied Problems

    (1)   (1) tells us that $x = y + 12 = 2z$. But this doesn't tell us exactly how much fruit was purchased. For example, it could be that x is 14, y is 2, and z is 7. Or it could be that x is 16, y is 4, and z is 8. The total price would be greater in the latter case, because more fruit of each type would have been purchased. Thus, the total price of the transaction cannot be determined from (1) alone; NOT sufficient.

    (2)   (2) tells us only a range of values for the average number of fruits purchased of the three varieties. Even if we knew more precisely that the average was exactly 30, we still couldn't tell the total price of the transaction, because the different types of fruit differ in price. For example, this average would be 30 if the transaction included 10 apples, 30 oranges, and 50 mangoes. But the average would also be 30 if the transaction included exactly 30 apples, 30 oranges, and 30 mangoes. The total price would be higher in the former case than in the latter, because the mangoes cost more apiece than the apples. Thus, the total price of the transaction cannot be determined from (2) alone; NOT sufficient.

If (1) and (2) are both true, then we know from (1) that $x = y + 12 = 2z$. And we know from (2) that the average number of fruits of the three varieties is greater than 29 and less than 33; that is, $3(29) = 87 < x + y + z < 3(33) = 99$. But this still doesn't tell us exactly how much fruit was purchased. Notice that the average need not be a whole number. It could be a fraction. For example, it's possible that x is 40, y is 28, and z is 20. That gives us $x + y + z = 88$, yielding an average of 88/3 = 29 1/3—which is greater than 29 and less than 33. Or it could be that x is 42, y is 30, and z is 21, which gives us $x + y + z = 93$, yielding an average of 93/3 = 31—which is also greater than 29 and less than 33. The total price would be greater in the latter case, because more fruit of each type would have been purchased. Thus, the total price of the transaction cannot be determined even from the two statements together.

The correct answer is E; both statements together are still not sufficient.

106. Adam received a certain monetary amount in bills having only three denominations: $1, $5, and $10. What is the total monetary amount in bills that he received?

    (1) The numbers of $1, $5, and $10 bills Adam received, respectively, are in the ratio 3:5:8.

    (2) The ratio of the monetary amount Adam received in $1 bills to the monetary amount he received in $10 bills is 3:80.

Applied Problems

    (1) More than one total monetary amount in bills is possible that satisfies the given information and (1). For example, the numbers of $1, $5, and $10 bills, respectively, could be 3, 5, and 8 for a total monetary amount of $108. Or the numbers of $1, $5, and $10 bills, respectively, could be 6, 10, and 16 for a total monetary amount of $216; NOT sufficient.

    (2) Since no information is given about the number of $5 bills, the total monetary amount in bills cannot be determined; NOT sufficient.

Letting k be the proportionality constant in (1), it follows that the numbers of $1, $5, and $10 bills, respectively, are $3k$, $5k$, and $8k$. Hence, the total monetary amount Adam received in $1 bills is $3k(\$1) = \$3k$, and the total monetary amount he received in $10 bills is $8k(\$10) = \$80k$. Thus, (1) implies that the ratio of the monetary amount Adam received in $1 bills to the monetary amount he received in $10 bills is $3k:80k$, or 3:80. Since this result is identical to the information provided by (2), it follows that taking (1) and (2) together provides no more information than (1) alone, which is not sufficient. Therefore, (1) and (2) together are not sufficient.

**The correct answer is E;
both statements together are still not sufficient.**

107. Exactly 3 investors—A, B, and C—invested in a certain business, each for a certain number of months. For these investments, what is the ratio of the profit earned by A to the profit earned by B to the profit earned by C? (Note: Profit earned is proportional to the product of investment amount and investment duration.)

    (1) A invested twice as much as B, and C invested half as much as A and B together.

    (2) All 3 investments were for the same number of months.

Applied Problems

Let x, y, and z be the numbers of months, respectively, that A, B, and C invested. Let $\$a$, $\$b$, and $\$c$ be the amounts, respectively, that A, B, and C invested. Then, if k is the constant of proportionality associated with these investments, the profits earned by A, B, and C, respectively, are $\$kax$, $\$kby$, and $\$kcz$. We are to determine the ratio $kax:kby:kcz$. Equivalently, we are to determine the ratio $ax:by:cz$.

    (1) We are given that $a = 2b$ and $c = \frac{1}{2}(a + b)$. Since we are given no information about x, y, or z, it is not possible to determine the ratio $ax:by:cz$; NOT sufficient.

    (2) We are given that $x = y = z$. Since we are given no information about a, b, or c, it is not possible to determine the ratio $ax:by:cz$; NOT sufficient.

From (2) we have $ax:by:cz = ax:bx:cx = a:b:c$. From (1) we have $a = 2b$ and $c = \frac{1}{2}a + \frac{1}{2}b$, and hence $c = \frac{1}{2}(2b) + \frac{1}{2}b$, $= b$. Therefore, $a:b:c = 2b:b:\frac{1}{2}b = 2:1:\frac{1}{2}$, or 4:2:3.

**The correct answer is C;
both statements together are sufficient.**

108. The ratio of A's current age to B's current age is 5:8. What will be the sum of their ages 10 years from now? (Note: Assume that neither A nor B dies in the next 10 years.)

    (1) If A had been born 2 years later and B had been born 2 years earlier, then the ratio of A's current age to B's current age would be 14:25.

    (2) A's age 5 years ago was half the age that B will be 2 years from now.

Applied Problems

Let k be the constant of proportionality for the 5:8 ratio of A's current age to B's current age. Then A's current age is $5k$ and B's current age is $8k$. We are to determine the value of $(5k + 10) + (8k + 10) = 13k + 20$, or equivalently, we are to determine the value of k.

(1) If A had been born 2 years later, then A's current age would be $5k - 2$, and if B had been born 2 years earlier, then B's current age would be $8k + 2$. We are told that the ratio $(5k - 2):(8k + 2)$ is equal to 14:25. Thus, $\frac{(5k - 2)}{(8k + 2)} = \frac{14}{25}$. Cross multiplying gives a first-degree equation that can be solved for a unique value of k. Although it is not necessary to find the value of k, solving this equation gives $k = 6$; SUFFICIENT.

(2) We are given that $5k - 5 = \frac{1}{2}(8k + 2)$, which can be solved for a unique value of k. Although it is not necessary to find the value of k, solving this equation gives $k = 6$; SUFFICIENT.

**The correct answer is D;
each statement alone is sufficient.**

109. A's father is 6 years older than her mother. The ratio of A's age to her mother's age is 1:4. What is the age of A's father?

(1) A's father is 30 years older than A.
(2) The ratio of A's age to her father's age is 4:19.

Applied Problems

Let a, f, and m be, respectively, the ages of A, A's father, and A's mother. We are given that $f = m + 6$ and $\frac{a}{m} = \frac{1}{4}$. Thus, $m = f - 6$, and hence we get $\frac{a}{(f - 6)} = \frac{1}{4}$, or $4a = f - 6$. We are to determine the value of $f = 4a + 6$.

(1) We are given that $f = 30 + a$. Since we also know that $f = 4a + 6$, it follows that $30 + a = 4a + 6$. This is a first-degree equation that can be solved for a unique value of a, which can then be used to determine a unique value of $f = 4a + 6$. Although it is not necessary to find these values, solving gives $a = 8$ and $f = 38$; SUFFICIENT.

(2) We are given that $\frac{a}{f} = \frac{4}{19}$. Since we also know that $f = 4a + 6$, it follows that $\frac{a}{(4a + 6)} = \frac{4}{19}$. Cross multiplying gives a first-degree equation that can be solved for a unique value of a, which can then be used to determine a unique value of f. Although it is not necessary to find these values, solving gives $a = 8$ and $f = 38$; SUFFICIENT.

**The correct answer is D;
each statement alone is sufficient.**

110. The salary of A is what percentage of the combined salaries of B and C?

(1) Twice the salary of A is equal to three times the salary of B.
(2) 150% of B's salary is $160 more than 120% of C's salary.

Applied Problems

Let $\$a$, $\$b$, and $\$c$ be the salaries, respectively, of A, B, and C. We are to determine a as a percent of $b + c$, or equivalently, we are to determine the value of $\frac{a}{b + c}$.

(1) We are given that $2a = 3b$, or $a = \frac{3}{2}b$. Since we are given no information about the value of the positive number c, it follows that the value of $\frac{a}{b + c}$ cannot be determined; NOT sufficient.

(2) We are given that $1.5b = 160 + 1.2c$. Since we are given no information about the value of the positive number a, it follows that the value of $\frac{a}{b + c}$ cannot be determined; NOT sufficient.

From (1) we have $\frac{a}{b + c} = \frac{\frac{3}{2}b}{b + c}$. From (2) we have $15b = 1,600 + 12c$, or $12c = 15b - 1,600$. To avoid additional complications with fractions when incorporating $12c = 15b - 1,600$ into $\frac{\frac{3}{2}b}{b + c}$, multiply the numerator and denominator of this last fraction by 12 to get $\frac{18b}{12b + 12c}$. Now replace $12c$ in this fraction with $15b - 1,600$ to get $\dfrac{18b}{12b + 15b - 1,600} = \dfrac{18b}{27b - 1,600}$. This last fraction is equal to the value of $\dfrac{a}{b + c}$, and it is clear that the value of this last fraction can vary. For example, if b is very large, then $\dfrac{18b}{27b - 1,600} \approx \dfrac{18b}{27b} = \dfrac{2}{3}$; and if $27b$ is only a little larger than $1,600$, then $\dfrac{18b}{27b - 1,600} = \dfrac{18b}{\text{small positive number}}$

will be much larger than $\dfrac{2}{3}$ (e.g., if $b = 60$, then the value of this fraction is 54). Therefore, (1) and (2) together are NOT sufficient.

The correct answer is E;
both statements together are still not sufficient.

6.7 Practice Questions: Two-Part Analysis

Each Two-Part Analysis Question tells you everything you need to know to pick the right answers. Rely on the information provided to answer the question. Pick one answer in the first column and one answer in the second column.

Questions 111 to 118 — Difficulty: Easy

111. Two employees of Company X, Winnie and Ali, have been informed that they will each receive bonuses this year, and that, for these bonuses, they will share a total amount of 560,000 KES (Kenyan shillings). Winnie makes a base salary of 4,600,000 KES per annum, and Ali makes a base salary of 3,400,000 KES per annum.

    Assuming that the two employees receive the same percentage of their respective per annum base salaries as bonuses, indicate below the bonus amount that Winnie will receive and the bonus amount that Ali will receive. Make only two selections, one in each column.

Winnie	Ali	
		216,000
		238,000
		256,000
		304,000
		322,000

112. After a 16-member team at Company A saw a certain software demonstration, each of the team members gave the software exactly one of the ratings 1, 2, 3, 4, or 5, where greater numbers indicate higher ratings. The team's manager intended to record the 16 ratings but accidentally recorded one team member's rating twice. The ratings she recorded show two ratings of 1, two ratings of 2, two ratings of 3, two ratings of 4, and nine ratings of 5, for a total of 17 ratings.

    The manager determined that the extra rating was ____P____, and after this extra rating was removed, the average (arithmetic mean) of the remaining 16 ratings was exactly ____Q____.

    Select for *P* and for *Q* the options that create a statement that is consistent with the information provided. Make only two selections, one in each column.

P	Q	
		1
		2
		3
		4
		5

113. Natural gas, when burned as fuel for heat, produces about 1,000 BTU of heat per cubic foot of gas when fully burned. Propane, another gas used as fuel, produces about 2,500 BTU per cubic foot of gas when fully burned.

    Furnaces burning either fuel burn at various efficiencies, according to the proportion of heat energy available from the fuel that actually contributes to the heating of the building to be heated (as opposed, e.g., to escaping up a chimney in the form of dissipated heat or unburned fuel).

    Kgomotso is shopping for a furnace that will produce about 50,000 BTU per hour of usable heat. None of the available furnaces burns both propane and natural gas. Also, no two of them operate at the same efficiency. In the table, identify, if possible, a price per cubic foot of *Propane* and a price per cubic foot of *Natural gas*, such that the fuel-cost per BTU of usable heat is the same using either fuel. If this determination is impossible with the given information, then choose "Undeterminable" in each column. Make only two selections, one in each column.

Propane	Natural gas	Price per cubic foot
		$0.0035
		$0.0070
		$0.0110
		$0.0175
		$0.0350
		Undeterminable

114. At Company X, a new firm which is at present devoted entirely to the design of software applications, all employees are required to agree to the following policy:

Any idea or invention conceived of by employees that is related to Company X's past, present, or future business is owned exclusively by Company X, not the individual employee.

Thus, if a Company X employee has conceived of an idea or invention during his/her employment with Company X related in any manner to Company X's business, that invention is owned by Company X. The employee may not use or exploit that idea or invention for his or her personal benefit.

An employee of Company X has recently sold a children's novel to a publisher. Company X has claimed ownership of the novel on the basis of the stated policy, and the employee intends to dispute the company's claim.

If ___1___, then a successful defense of the company's claimed ownership rights would likely include a statement that ___2___.

Select for 1 and for 2 the options whereby the statement is most clearly supported. Make only two selections, one in each column.

1	2	
		mere use of Company X's resources in an activity is sufficient grounds for regarding that activity as related to Company X's business
		mere use of Company X's resources in an activity is not sufficient grounds for regarding that activity as related to Company X's business
		the employee wrote the novel on a computer owned by the company
		the employee has received a significant amount of money from the sale
		the company has plans to expand into publishing

115. A village's ordinances require residents to exercise reasonable care to avoid disturbing their neighbors with noise. The village council may impose fines for noise violations in response to formal complaints. But unless there have been formal complaints from multiple residents, the council will not consider a complaint if the complaining individual has not attempted to resolve the issue directly with the alleged violator or with the violator's landlord if the violator is a renter. The council's first action in response to any formal verbal or written complaint that they are considering will be to offer to mediate the dispute.

Select for 1 and for 2 two different events such that the guidelines most clearly indicate that if the event selected for 1 occurs, then the event selected for 2 either will occur or has already occurred. Make only two selections, one in each column.

1	2	
		The council imposes a fine for noise violation.
		The council considers a formal written noise complaint.
		The complaining individual attempts to resolve the issue with the alleged violator.
		The council offers to mediate a dispute about noise.
		The complaining individual contacts the alleged violator's landlord.

116. Manager S: Our company provides a small annual monetary benefit for each employee who submits documentation to the company proving that the employee had a comprehensive medical exam in a given year. The policy has been successful in increasing the number of employees who get the exam annually precisely because the benefit requires this specific form of documentation, and this success has resulted in improved employee health. **[Insert Sentence 1.]**

Manager T: I agree that the overall policy has improved employee health, and it is good to improve employee health. However, the required documentation resulted in our company having access to an employee's private medical data. The benefit to employee health is not worth compromising employee privacy. **[Insert Sentence 2.]**

Select for Sentence 1 the sentence that best completes Manager S's argument, and select for Sentence 2 the sentence that best completes Manager T's argument. Make only two selections, one in each column.

Sentence 1	Sentence 2	
		Requiring the documentation has no effect on employees.
		Our company should continue requiring the specific documentation that it does.
		Our company should not require that form of documentation.
		Promoting employee health with financial incentives is counterproductive.
		Promoting employee health with financial incentives is worthwhile.

117. Ethics board member: All actions that are permissible under the code of ethics are also legal in all of the jurisdictions in which our company operates. Furthermore, regardless of whether it has been determined if an action is legal, it is always permissible to ask the ethics board to review the action for conformity to the code of ethics.

Statements: Without exception, an action is permissible under the code of ethics _____1_____ it is legal in all of the jurisdictions in which the company operates. Furthermore, one is permitted to ask the ethics board to review an action for conformity to the code of ethics _____2_____ the legality of the action has been established.

Select for *1* and for *2* the two different options that complete the statements so that they most accurately paraphrase the ethics board member's assertions. Make only two selections, one in each column.

1	2	
		if
		only if
		unless
		whether or not
		or

118. A corporation uses a model of diminishing returns to make predictions about the expected returns on research investment. For this model, in order to produce an $x\%$ increase in annual profits in subsequent years, the corporation must invest $y\%$ of annual profits into research, where $y = 2x^2$.

Select two different numbers that are jointly compatible with the information provided and could be the values for x and for y. Make only two selections, one in each column.

x	y	
		1
		3
		5
		20
		50
		80

Questions 119 to 136 — Difficulty: **Medium**

119. A small business has just invested in a new piece of equipment. The business's accountant estimates that the value of the equipment will decrease over time at a constant rate. Based on this assumption, the accountant properly estimates the value of the equipment 3 years afterward to be $X, 6 years afterward to be $Y, and 8 years afterward to be, for the first time, $0.

Select values for X and for Y that are jointly consistent with the given information. Make only two selections, one in each column.

X	Y	
		200
		300
		400
		500
		600

120. Pavel made a list of 31 chores he needed to complete over the next 7 days. On the first 5 days, he completed 3, 5, 7, 2, and 6 of the listed chores, respectively. On the next 2 days, he completed the remaining 8 chores.

Select for *Least possible median* and for *Greatest possible median* values that are consistent with the information provided and give the least and greatest possible values, respectively, for the median of the numbers of the listed chores Pavel completed on each of the 7 days. Make only two selections, one in each column.

Least possible median	Greatest possible median	
		2
		3
		4
		5
		6

121. Literary critic: When a reader feels an emotion that is focused on the events and characters in a work of fiction, the reader is psychologically somewhat detached from that emotion. Lacking the immediacy of emotions about events in the reader's own life, emotions evoked by fiction are enjoyed as pure sensations independent of ___1___. Consequently, the reader can find pleasure even in sadness when it is focused on the events and characters in fictional works, because the work's beauty consists partly in its ability to evoke such ___2___.

Select options to fill in the two blanks above to complete the literary critic's statements most coherently. Make only two selections, one in each column.

1	2	
		beauty
		psychological detachment
		typically unpleasant emotions
		fictional events
		real events

122. The equation $6 \times 5 - 4 \div 2 - 3 + 7)^0 - 1)^2 = 6$ is missing two opening parentheses. It can be made true if opening parentheses are placed immediately before each of two of the numbers.

Assume that standard order-of-operations principles are followed, whereby multiplication and division are performed before addition and subtraction, unless parentheses indicate otherwise. Select in the table a number before which the first opening parenthesis could be placed and a number before which the second opening parenthesis could be placed, such that the equation would express a true statement. Make only two selections, one in each column.

First parenthesis immediately before	Second parenthesis immediately before	
		2
		3
		4
		5
		6

123. Historian: New York City became an influential art center in the twentieth century, as seen, for example, in the influential 1913 Armory Show and the growth of museums. This was due primarily to a combination of New York's large and varied population, its basic resources, and its access to European art trends. The city could never have become an influential art center without the era's increased local wealth, which allowed more people to buy art. However, the changes were driven principally by the diversity of the city's population, including intellectuals and artists from Europe, and a culture that prized energy and creativity, which stimulated the artistic endeavors of many people.

Select for *Precondition* the statement that the passage most strongly suggests describes a precondition for New York becoming an influential art center. And select for *Strengthener* the statement that would, if true, most clearly strengthen the support for the historian's explanation of why the city became an influential art center. Make only two selections, one in each column.

Precondition	Strengthener	
		New York showed significant economic development leading up to the early twentieth century.
		New York afforded easy access to major art museums in other cities in the United States.
		Members of the Hudson River School of painters helped promote art in New York.
		The Armory Show and other influential New York shows like it featured many prominent European artists.
		The composition of European groups immigrating to New York changed in the early 1900s.

124. A farmer wants to allocate her expenditures to maximize her profits during the coming year. Let C be her spending on cropland, F her spending on fertilizer, L her spending on labor, M her spending on machinery, and S her spending on seed. She has estimated that, if she allocates at least 100 euros to each of these categories, then her profit during the coming year will be $(C - 97)(L - 92)(S - 95)(M - 87)(F - 90)$ euros. She wishes to calculate the benefits of expenditure greater than 100 euros in one of these categories, if she were to spend exactly 100 euros in each of the others.

Select for *Greatest returns* the resource for which, according to the desired calculation from the model, each euro of spending beyond 100 euros is predicted to make the greatest contribution to profits (or least contribution to losses). And select for *Least returns* the resource for which, according to the desired calculation, each euro of spending beyond the minimum necessary amount is predicted to make the least contribution to profits (or greatest contribution to losses). Make only two selections, one in each column.

Greatest returns	Least returns	
		Cropland
		Fertilizer
		Labor
		Machinery
		Seed

125. At a certain factory, 4 processes—A, B, C, and D—are carried out 24 hours per day, 7 days per week. Process A operates on a 60-hour cycle; that is, Process A takes 60 hours to complete and immediately begins again when it is completed. Likewise, Process B operates on a 24-hour cycle, Process C operates on a 27-hour cycle, and Process D operates on a 9-hour cycle. On Monday, all 4 processes began together at 10:00 in the morning.

On the basis of the information provided, select for *Processes A, B, and D* the day of the week on which Processes A, B, and D will next begin together at 10:00 in the morning. Also select for *All 4 processes* the day of the week on which Processes A–D will next begin together at 10:00 in the morning. Make only two selections, one in each column.

Processes A, B, and D	All 4 processes	
		Monday
		Tuesday
		Wednesday
		Thursday
		Friday

126. An amateur athletic team has the following requirement: "Each athlete who fails to return to his or her designated room prior to a designated time will be suspended for the next athletic event." The requirement was violated by the team's best athlete on the night before a prominent athletic event.

Assistant Coach A: The only reason to not suspend the athlete is if the athlete broke the requirement because of factors outside the athlete's control. Since that was not the reason, no exception should be made for this athlete.

Assistant Coach B: I know that we would normally punish the athlete with a suspension, but doing so in this case would harm the team. I think we should punish the athlete in another way that would not harm the team.

Select for *Supports Assistant Coach A* the principle that most strongly supports the reasoning expressed by Assistant Coach A, and select for *Supports Assistant Coach B* the principle that most strongly supports the reasoning expressed by Assistant Coach B. Make only two selections, one in each column.

Supports Assistant Coach A	Supports Assistant Coach B	
		Amateur athletic teams should not punish elite team members who break team requirements.
		The punishment of a team member for breaking a team requirement should be based on the likely outcomes for the team rather than the punishment specified for breaking the requirement.
		The punishment specified for breaking a team requirement should always be administered in order to ensure that all team members are treated equally.
		If an athlete is reasonably able to fulfill a team requirement, then the punishment specified for breaking the requirement should be administered.
		If a punishment of a team member specified by a team requirement would harm the team, then the team member should not be punished.

127. Rashika is beginning a new job in human resources and expects to be assigned to several of the many human resources work groups. She has been told that there is a probability of 12 that she will be assigned to the Recruitment Work Group and that there is a probability of 34 that she will be assigned to the New Technology Work Group. She has no other information about the probabilities of the various possible assignments, or whether her assignment to one of these groups affects her chances of assignment to the other.

Select for *Greatest probability for both assignments* the greatest probability, compatible with the given probabilities, that Rashika will be assigned to both the Recruitment Work Group and the New Technology Work Group. And select for *Least probability for both assignments* the least probability, compatible with the given probabilities, that Rashika will be assigned to both of these groups. Make only two selections, one in each column.

Greatest probability for both assignments	Least probability for both assignments	
		0
		$\frac{1}{4}$
		$\frac{1}{2}$
		$\frac{3}{4}$
		1

128. In a study conducted over several years, seabird and domesticated cat populations on a geographically isolated island changed from year to year. Researchers found that over the course of the study, the relationship (R) between seabirds and domesticated cats was such that the island's seabird population was three times as likely to decrease from the previous year if the island's domesticated cat population increased (even if slightly) during the same year. The researchers are about to begin a second, follow-up study with the same duration as the first study. Based on recent trends, the researchers made the following projections: R will hold and the island's domesticated cat population will decrease during more years of the second study than it did in their first study.

Assuming that the information above is true, select for *Can be inferred as true* the statement that can be most reasonably inferred as true from the information provided, and select for *Can be inferred as false* the statement that can be most reasonably inferred as false from the information provided. Make only two selections, one in each column.

Can be inferred as true	Can be inferred as false	
		If the researchers' projections are accurate, the island's seabird population is likely to increase during more years of the second study than it did in the first.
		During the first study, most years had an increase in the island's domesticated cat population.
		If the researchers' projections are accurate, the island's seabird population is likely to increase during most of the years of the second study.
		During the first study, the island's seabird population decreased only when the island's domesticated cat population increased.
		During the first study, most years during which the island's seabird population decreased were years during which the island's domesticated cat population increased.

129. According to a prominent investment adviser, Company X has a 50% chance of posting a profit in the coming year, whereas Company Y has a 60% chance of posting a profit in the coming year.

Select for *Least probability for both* the least probability, compatible with the probabilities provided by the investment adviser, that both Company X and Company Y will post a profit in the coming year. And select for *Greatest probability for both* the greatest probability, compatible with the probabilities provided by the investment adviser, that both Company X and Company Y will post a profit in the coming year. Make only two selections, one in each column.

Least probability for both	Greatest probability for both	
		5%
		10%
		25%
		50%
		60%
		80%

130. Lee is planning a trip and estimates that, rounded to the nearest 5 kilometers (km), the length of the trip will be 560 km and that, rounded to the nearest 14 hours, the driving time for the trip will be 7 hours. If these estimates are correct, then Lee's average driving speed during the trip will be between ____x____ kilometers per hour and ____y____ kilometers per hour, where $x < y$.

From the values given in the table, select for x and for y the values that complete the statement in such a way that the interval between the selected values includes all possible average speeds for Lee's trip and $y - x$ is minimal. Make only two selections, one in each column.

x	y	
		73
		76
		79
		82
		85

131. A certain theater has 500 seats. Some are on the main floor and sell for $50 each; some are in the first balcony and sell for $45 each; and the rest are in the second balcony and sell for $35 each. When all of the seats are sold for a performance, the gross revenue for that performance is $20,900. Of the three seating areas, the second balcony has the most seats.

Select for *First balcony* a number of seats in this theater's first balcony, and select for *Second balcony* a number of seats in this theater's second balcony such that the selections are jointly consistent with the information provided. Make only two selections, one in each column.

First balcony	Second balcony	
		100
		150
		190
		210
		250
		300

132. A company purchased at least 10 units of a certain product from each of Suppliers X and Y. Supplier X charged a $100 fixed cost, $20 per unit for each of the first 10 units, and $5 per unit for each unit purchased in excess of 10 units. Supplier Y charged a $150 fixed cost, $15 per unit for each of the first 10 units, and $10 per unit for each unit purchased in excess of 10 units. Including the fixed costs, the combined average cost for the units was $20 per unit.

Select a *number of units purchased from Supplier X* and a *number of units purchased from Supplier Y* that are jointly consistent with the given information. Make only two selections, one in each column.

Number of units purchased from Supplier X	Number of units purchased from Supplier Y	
		15
		20
		22
		25
		27
		30

133. A financial adviser was showing a client the value, rounded to the nearest cent, of an initial investment of $100.00 after 5, 10, 15, 20, 25, and 30 years, under the assumption that the value increases by r% per year for some positive constant r. The adviser correctly gave $130.01 for the value after 5 years. However,

the adviser inadvertently made two transcription errors, and as a result, two of the remaining values shown to the client were incorrect.

Assuming the options provided are the remaining five amounts shown to the client, select for *First error* the lesser of the two incorrectly transcribed values, and select for *Second error* the greater of the two incorrectly transcribed values. Make only two selections, one in each column.

First error	Second error	
		$160.02
		$219.75
		$285.70
		$317.43
		$482.90

134. A clothing retailer used to sell only "fast-fashion" pieces, which were low priced and had a profit markup of 50 percent of the per-item cost (including, e.g., the costs of wholesale purchase and marketing). On average, each customer spent $850 annually on around 65 such pieces from the retailer. Now the retailer wishes to double its total profits by selling only "classic" pieces. It plans to double its percentage profit markup per item and generate more revenue per customer while leaving unchanged the company's total costs. The plan assumes that for each classic piece, on average, customers will pay five times what they paid for each fast-fashion piece and that the total number of customers for the retailer's clothing products will remain the same.

Statements: Customers paid an average of ____1____ dollars (rounded to the nearest dollar) for each of the retailer's fast-fashion pieces. The retailer will need to sell an average minimum of ____2____ classic pieces per person (rounded to the nearest whole number) to achieve its profit goals for classic pieces.

Select values for *1* and for *2* that create the statements that are most strongly supported by the information provided and in accordance with the retailer's plan. Make only two selections, one in each column.

1	2	
		10
		13
		15
		17
		21
		25

135. A certain mail-order company sells T-shirts, buttons, stickers, and current and past issues of its magazine. Each order placed to the company consists of one or more items, and, for each order, the company packages all of the items in the order together. Any employee who packages an order packages the entirety of that order. Among the orders placed to the company today:

None includes both a T-shirt and a magazine.

All of those that include a past issue of the magazine also include the current issue of the magazine.

Most of those that include a magazine also include a sticker.

None of those that include a button also include a sticker.

Statement: For the orders placed to the company today, if one employee were to package all of the orders that include a ____1____, that employee would also package all of the orders that include a ____2____.

Select for *1* and for *2* the two different options that complete the statement so that it is most accurate based on the information provided. Make only two selections, one in each column.

1	2	
		button
		current issue of the magazine
		past issue of the magazine
		sticker
		T-shirt

136. A group of paleobotanists collected samples of sediments containing pollen and spores from various plant species. Each sample was analyzed to determine the number of spores in the sample, the number of pollen grains in the sample, and the species to which those spores and pollen grains belong. Samples S1 and S2 were collected and analyzed in this way. For these two samples:

S1 had the greater total number of spores, and it contained pollen grains from Species P as well as spores from Species Q.

S2 had the greater total number of species represented, and all of the spores it contained were from Species Q.

Statement: Among these two samples, S1 had the greater ratio of total number of ____1____ to total number of ____2____.

Select for *1* and for *2* the options that complete the statement so that it is accurate based on the information provided. Make only two selections, one in each column.

1	2	
		pollen grains
		pollen grains from Species P
		species represented
		spores
		spores from Species Q

Questions 137 to 165 — Difficulty: **Hard**

137. Biologist: Conservation biologists working to prevent species extinction have long acknowledged that popular species such as lions, eagles, and pandas receive disproportionately large amounts of funding and public attention as compared to less-popular species such as invertebrates and amphibians. Indeed, many of these less-popular species are more in danger of extinction than the more-popular species. Although many conservation biologists have accepted this pattern of disproportionate funding, I believe it needs to stop. For, despite the substantial and continuing expenditure of resources on the more-popular species,

very few of these species have any chance of escaping extinction.

The biologist's reasoning is subject to the criticism that the claim that ___A___, which is used to justify the main point, undermines the support for the point that ___B___.

Select for *A* and for *B* the options such that criticism of the zoologist's reasoning is strongest. Make only two selections, one in each column.

A	B	
		popular species receive a disproportionate amount of the money and public attention devoted to the preservation of endangered species
		funding and public attention should not be wasted on the preservation of endangered species
		certain popular species are more endangered than many believe
		many species that are not popular are likely to escape extinction
		very few of the more-popular species have any chance of escaping extinction

138. Historian: In the collection of the Science Museum, London, there is a small bottle that is purported to contain the entire original batch of artificial mauve dye created by Sir William Perkin in his laboratory in 1856. Indeed, in his experiments that preceded his commercial production of mauve dyes, he made only a few grams of the substance, but this batch would likely have been completely used up when he tested it as a dye. Also, the early version of mauve dye that Perkin produced commercially consisted of an impure paste rather than the pure crystalline form of the substance contained in the bottle.

Statement: The historian's statements imply that the bottle does not contain ___1___ at least in part because the substance in the bottle is ___2___.

Select for *1* and for *2* the options that create the statement that is most strongly supported by the information above. Make only two selections, one in each column.

1	2	
		any of Perkin's original batch of mauve dye
		a dye produced in Perkin's laboratory
		a dye created in 1856
		a commercially produced dye

139. When a user conducts a search of a certain library database, the database returns the results as a list of items (books, magazines, etc.) that match the search criteria. The user can select from two settings to establish a maximum number of items—either 12 or 24—to be displayed at a time. If the list contains more items than the established maximum, the list will be displayed on multiple pages, with each page (with the possible exception of the last page) containing the established maximum number of items and with each item in the list appearing on exactly one of the pages. The maximum established by the user does not affect the total number of items listed.

For the list of *n* items returned by a particular search of the database, the number of items, *X*, displayed on the last page when the established maximum is 12 is different from the number of items, *Y*, displayed on the last page when the established maximum is 24.

Select for *X* and for *Y* values that are jointly consistent with the information provided. Make only two selections, one in each column.

X	Y	
		1
		5
		7
		12
		17

140. In a group of 100 tourists visiting Scandinavia, 10% visited Norway, Sweden, and Denmark; 48% visited only two of these countries; 42% visited only one of these countries; and 100% visited at least one of these countries. Twenty-three tourists in the group visited at least Norway and Sweden, and 28 tourists in the group visited both Norway and Denmark. Furthermore, 3 tourists in the group visited only Denmark, and 32 tourists in the group visited only Sweden.

In the table, select the number of tourists in the group who *visited at least Norway*, and select the number of tourists in the group who *visited at least Sweden*. Make only two selections, one in each column.

Visited at least Norway	Visited at least Sweden	
		40
		48
		54
		62
		68
		72

141. A city council member standing for reelection has been asked to rate how much she agrees or disagrees that various cultural establishments should receive more city funding. Expressing her overall views regarding budgeting priorities, she answers "Absolutely agree" for the art museum, "Somewhat agree" for the children's theater, "Neither agree nor disagree" for the historical society, "Somewhat disagree" for the symphony orchestra, and "Absolutely disagree" for the metropolitan ballet.

Suppose that the city council member's responses reflect genuine opinions that are logically consistent with her other opinions, and suppose that she believes that funding for any one of the institutions does not affect funding for any of the others. In the first column of the table, rate how much she most clearly agrees that *At least two* of the five institutions should receive more funding. In the second column, rate how much she most clearly agrees that *At most four* of the five institutions should receive more funding. Make only two selections, one in each column.

At least two	At most four	
		Absolutely agrees
		Somewhat agrees
		Neither agrees nor disagrees
		Somewhat disagrees
		Absolutely disagrees

142. There are exactly three steps—Steps 1, 2, and 3, in that order—used to assemble light bulbs at a particular factory. Some of the bulbs fail to make it through every step in the assembly process; if a bulb fails a given step, it will not proceed to the next step. For the most recent month, the factory manager knows the number of bulbs that were started as well as each of the following:

A = the number of bulbs making it through Step 1 only;

B = the number of bulbs making it through at least Step 2;

C = the number of bulbs making it through all three steps.

The manager wishes to know the fraction of the bulbs that made it through Step 1 that also made it through all three steps. In the table, choose for *Numerator* and *Denominator* the expressions that will give the factory owner the fraction desired. Make only two selections, one in each column.

Numerator	Denominator	
		A
		B
		C
		A + B
		A − C
		B + C

143. Legal advocate: The Métis people of Canada are of First Nations and European ancestry. The government grants certain special rights to Métis individuals. To receive these rights, an individual must self-identify as Métis and must not have self-identified only recently in order to receive these rights. The individual must also have Métis ancestry and be accepted as Métis by a modern Métis community. Acceptance by a modern Métis community is shown only by long-standing participation in the community's cultural or political activities.

In the table, select characteristics *H* and *N*, such that an individual having *H* and NOT having *N* would most clearly satisfy the legal advocate's stated criterion for receiving the rights associated with Métis membership. Make only two selections, one in each column.

H	N	
		Self-identifies as Métis due to long-standing Métis ancestry
		Self-identifies as Métis due to long-standing participation in Métis political activities
		Has recent ancestry that is Métis and participates in Métis political activities
		Has recent ancestry that is not Métis
		Has never participated in Métis political activities

144. Tickets for next month's production of *The Sea Gull* at the local community theater went on sale yesterday. The ticket price for a person older than 12 is $*A*, and the ticket price for a person 12 or under is $*C*, where *A* > *C*. Yesterday, the sale of 33 tickets generated a total revenue of $323, and today the sale of 44 tickets generated a total revenue of $424.

In the table, select a value for *A* and a value for *C* that are jointly consistent with the given information. Make only two selections, one in each column.

A	C	
		6
		8
		10
		11
		12

145. Companies A and B are part of the same industry and are located in the same city. For Company A, the average (arithmetic mean) salary of its employees, in United Arab Emirates dirhams (AED), is 10,000 AED higher than that for Company B. However, more than half of the employees at Company A have salaries below the average for Company B.

Statement: If the average salary at Company B is __1__, then the median salary at Company A is __2__.

Select for *1* and for *2* the options that complete the statement so that it most accurately reflects the information provided. Make only two selections, one in each column.

1	2	
		greater than 100,000 AED
		less than 100,000 AED
		equal to 110,000 AED
		between 100,000 and 110,000 AED
		greater than 110,000 AED

146. In comparing the results of a recent annual spring census to those of the previous year, biologists observed dramatic changes in the numbers of frogs of two species—Species X and Species Y—and an overall decrease in the combined number of frogs of these species. The biologists hypothesized that this decrease was caused by the unusually cold weather between the two censuses.

Select for *A* and for *B* the statements such that the biologists' hypothesis would have the most support if A is true and B is false. Make only two selections, one in each column.

A	B	
		Species X is susceptible to unusually cold weather, whereas Species Y is not.
		Species X has a later mating season than does Species Y.
		Both Species X and Species Y are susceptible to similar contaminants.
		The number of Species X frogs decreased from the previous spring census.

147. A certain company defines its *annual labor turnover rate* as the number of employees who left the company during the year divided by the average of the number of employees on the first day of the year and the number of employees on the last day of that year. Last year, the company had a labor turnover rate of exactly 25%.

Assuming that the information above is true, select for *Statement 1* and for *Statement 2* the statements such that if Statement 1 is true, then Statement 2 must be true, but it could be the case that Statement 2 is true and Statement 1 is false. Make only two selections, one in each column.

Statement 1	Statement 2	
		Last year, more people left the company than began work at the company.
		Exactly 25% of the employees working at the company on the first day of last year left the company last year.
		More than 25% of the employees working at the company on the first day of last year left the company last year.
		All and only those who were employees at the company on the first day of last year were employees on the last day of last year.
		Last year, the number of employees on the first day of the year was equal to the number of employees on the last day of the year.

148. Newspaper editor: Published photojournalism must always present the events covered without distorting those events. Sometimes an image distorts the events a photojournalist attempts to capture, such as when the photojournalist has an equipment failure. In such cases, photojournalists are permitted to make minimal changes to an image, but only to the extent that (1) they are certain about what they observed, and (2) those changes reduce the distortion. Photojournalists' photos are often compelling works of art as well as documents of newsworthy events. However, for publication as journalism, a photo's aesthetic features are allowed to be considered only after the photo is shown to accurately portray relevant features of the event it depicts. In accordance with these criteria, in our journalistic coverage of Event E, we elected to publish photograph P1 rather than photograph P2.

Statement: Assuming the editor's statements are true, if ____1____, then it must be the case that ____2____.

Select for *1* and for *2* the two different options that create the statement that is most strongly supported by the information provided. Make only two selections, one in each column.

1	2	
		P1 was altered
		P2 was altered
		P1 and P2 were taken with malfunctioning equipment
		P1 was chosen over P2 at least in part for its aesthetic features
		both P1 and P2 accurately portray the relevant features of Event E

149. A stock trader working for a hedge fund has estimated that the stock of a certain company has probability 0.4 of increasing in price by at least 5 dollars during a certain trading day and probability 0.1 of increasing in price by at least 10 dollars during the trading day.

Based on the trader's estimates, select for X and for Y the options such that the following statement is most accurate. Make only two selections, one in each column.

If the trader multiplies ___X___ by the reciprocal of ___Y___, then the result is the probability that the price of the stock will increase by at least 10 dollars during the trading day, given that the price increases by at least 5 dollars during the trading day.

X	Y	
		0.1
		0.4
		0.1 divided by 0.4
		the reciprocal of 0.1
		the product of 0.1 and 0.4

150. Throughout a certain decade in a European city, the mean monthly rents for studio apartments varied yearly, from a low of €804 to a high of €1,173. Those for one-bedroom apartments also varied yearly, from a low of €1,060 to a high of €1,497. But some individual studio apartments rented for as little as €420 in some years, and some one-bedroom apartments rented for up to €2,262. To visually assess how the ratio of mean monthly rents for studio apartments to those for one-bedroom apartments varied yearly over the decade, Maria requires a graph with the following characteristics. The graph will have two axes of equal length, with mean rents for one-bedroom apartments shown on the horizontal axis and mean rents for studio apartments shown on the vertical axis, and with the same scale on both axes. For each year, mean rents will be plotted as a point.

From the following options, select for *Horizontal axis* a range for the points on the horizontal axis and select for *Vertical axis* a range for the points on the vertical axis that together would satisfy Maria's requirements for the graph. Make only two selections, one in each column.

Horizontal axis	Vertical axis	
		€0 to €1,500
		€400 to €1,100
		€800 to €1,200
		€1,000 to €2,300
		€1,100 to €1,500

151. A statistician reached the following conclusions about games between university soccer teams: Overall, a team playing on its home field has a 45% chance of a win, a 25% chance of a loss, and a 30% chance of a draw (a tied outcome). In the games where one or more goals are scored, the team that scores the first goal has a 55% chance of scoring it in the game's first half and a 45% chance of scoring it later in the game. When that team is the home team (i.e., a team playing on its home field), there is a 40% chance that the other team will score no goals at all, and therefore a 60% chance that it will score one or more goals.

Select for X and for Y two different outcomes such that the information provided explicitly includes the statistician's estimates of the probability that if X occurs, so will Y. Make only two selections, one in each column.

X	Y	
		The home team scores at least two goals in the game.
		The home team scores the first goal.
		A goal is scored in the first half of the game.
		A goal is scored in the second half of the game.
		The team opposing the home team scores at least one goal.

152. To ensure computer security, a firm has rules about access of managerial and nonmanagerial employees to various networked computer drives. In accordance with the rules, some but not all nonmanagerial employees are allowed access to both Drive B and Drive D. Some are required to have such access. Every nonmanagerial employee must have access to at least one of Drive B and Drive D. No nonmanagerial

employee is allowed to have access to both Drive B and Drive E. The rules do not restrict the access of managerial employees to any of the drives mentioned.

From the following statements about computer security practices in relation to the firm's employees, select for *Required* the statement that, based on the information provided, describes a practice that is required by the rules, and select for *Permitted* the statement that describes a practice that is permitted, but NOT required, by the rules. Make only two selections, one in each column.

Required	Permitted	
		At least one nonmanagerial employee is currently not allowed access to any of the three drives B, D, and E.
		Managerial employees, and only those, are currently allowed access to Drive E.
		The nonmanagerial employees who are currently allowed access to Drive D are also allowed access to Drive E.
		The managerial and nonmanagerial employees who are currently allowed access to Drive B are also allowed access to Drive E.
		Any nonmanagerial employees currently allowed access to Drive E are also allowed access to Drive D.

153. Giulia is planning to sell her car, which is fueled by gasoline (petrol) and averages 20 miles per gallon (mpg), and purchase a diesel-fueled car that averages 30 mpg. She estimates that her future cost per gallon of diesel fuel will be 5% higher than her present cost per gallon of gasoline. She wishes to estimate (1) the annual cost of fuel for her new car if she maintains her present annual total miles driven and (2) the annual total miles she can drive her new car if she maintains her present annual expenditure on fuel.

Let x represent Giulia's present annual cost per gallon of gasoline in US dollars, and let y equal her present annual total of miles driven. Select for *Cost* an appropriate expression for Giulia's estimate of (1)

above, and select for *Miles* an appropriate expression for her estimate of (2) above. Make only two selections, one in each column.

Cost	Miles	
		$\frac{2}{3}(1.05x)$
		$\frac{3}{2}\left(\frac{y}{1.05}\right)$
		$\frac{3}{2}(1.05y)$
		$\frac{1.05xy}{30}$
		$\frac{1.05xy}{20}$
		$\frac{20xy}{1.05}$

154. Each of three botanists made a hypothesis regarding specimens of a particular plant species:

Botanist 1: Any individual specimen possessing the gene for curly stems has either the gene for long roots or the gene for purple flowers, or both.

Botanist 2: Any individual specimen possessing the gene for long roots has either the gene for flat leaves or the gene for round seeds, or both.

Botanist 3: No individual specimen that possesses either the gene for curly stems or the gene for flat leaves or both has the gene for purple flowers.

The discovery of an individual specimen of the plant species in question having the gene for ___1___ but NOT the gene for ___2___ would show that at least one of the three hypotheses described is incorrect.

Select for *1* and for *2* the characteristics that would most accurately complete the statement, based on the information given. Make only two selections, one in each column.

1	2	
		curly stems
		flat leaves
		long roots
		purple flowers
		round seeds

155. An inventory of a neighborhood's trees found that 32 percent were conifers and most of the rest were deciduous. Among the conifers were 258 spruces and 112 pines, along with some cedars and other species. Most of the deciduous trees were oaks, but one in eight was a maple. Of the oaks, 65 percent were red oaks and 25 percent were white oaks. Of the maples, 20 percent were Japanese maples.

Select for *A* and for *B* two types of trees such that the ratio of the number of trees of the type selected for *A* to the number of trees of the type selected for *B* can be determined and is less than 1. Make only two selections, one in each column.

A	B	
		cedars
		conifers
		deciduous trees
		Japanese maples
		red oaks
		spruces

156. A manufacturing company plans to begin automating production and reducing its workforce by installing industrial robots at the start of each year over five years. Each robot will result in annual labor-cost savings of €150,000 beginning with the year of its installation and will have an up-front cost of €400,000. For robot installation in Year 1 of the program, the company will budget €600,000, plus the total amount of labor costs that will be saved by robotic production in that year. The robot-installation budget for each subsequent year will consist of the total amount of labor costs that will be saved by robotic production in that year plus any money left over from the previous year's robot-installation budget.

Statement: Within budget constraints, the maximum number of robots that can be installed in Year 1 of the program is ___X___, and the maximum number of robots that can be in service in Year 3 is ___Y___.

Select values for *X* and for *Y* that create the statement that follows logically from the information provided. Make only two selections, one in each column.

X	Y	
		2
		3
		4
		5
		6
		7

157. While designing a game involving chance, Desmond noticed that the probability a fair coin lands face up exactly 2 times when the coin is tossed 3 times is equal to the probability that a fair coin lands face up exactly *m* times when the coin is tossed *n* times, where $n > 3$.

Select for *m* and for *n* values consistent with the given information. Make only two selections, one in each column.

m	n	
		1
		2
		3
		4
		5
		6

158. Linguist: Plosives and fricatives are two classes of consonants. A "voicing contrast" is a distinction between two consonants that are identical except that one is voiced and the other is unvoiced. In language family X, languages with voicing contrasts in their fricatives always have voicing contrasts in their plosives. This means that in that family, any given language has a voicing contrast in its fricatives _____ it has a voicing contrast in its plosives. In other words, a given language in that family lacks any voicing contrasts in its plosives _____ it lacks any such contrasts in its fricatives.

Select for *First blank* the word or phrase that most logically completes the statement with the first blank. And select for *Second blank* the word or phrase that most logically completes the statement with the second blank. Make only two selections, one in each column.

First blank	Second blank	
		and
		if
		only if
		or
		unless

159. At a certain university, there is a strong positive correlation between the time of day at which university classes are offered and the classes' average (arithmetic mean) grades, with earlier times associated with lower grades. However, for the classes offered at the earliest time but not for any other classes, there was a strong negative correlation between the grades of students in those classes and the number of scheduled classes they missed. In fact, when the grades of students who missed at least 5 scheduled classes were excluded, classes offered at the earliest time more often than not had significantly higher average grades than classes offered at any other time.

Consider the following statement:

At the university in question, classes offered at earlier times ___1___ lower average grades than classes offered later in the day, but when the grades of students who missed at least 5 scheduled classes were excluded, classes offered at the earliest time ___2___ higher average grades than classes offered later in the day.

Select for 1 and for 2 the options that complete the sentence so that it most accurately summarizes the information provided. Make only two selections, one in each column.

1	2	
		tended to have
		tended not to have
		almost always had
		seldom, if ever, had
		possibly had

160. Each Monday through Friday (a *workweek*), Avinash will bring either exactly one apple or exactly one banana with him to his workplace for an afternoon snack. To avoid having to decide which to bring, each morning Avinash will toss a coin with a face on exactly one side that is equally likely to land face up or face down. If the coin lands face up, then he will bring an apple, and if the coin lands face down, then he will bring a banana. Avinash correctly determined the probability that, for a given workweek, either he would bring an apple on at least 4 consecutive days or he would bring a banana on at least 4 consecutive days. This probability was m divided by n.

Select for m and for n values jointly consistent with the given information. Make only two selections, one in each column.

m	n	
		4
		6
		8
		12
		20
		32

161. Philosophy student: Some objects that are considered beautiful by everyone who has observed them may not be, in fact, truly beautiful. To see that this is so, consider this: No one doubts that some objects that are appreciated by many people have aesthetic flaws that are discernible only to sophisticated observers. But even these sophisticated observers are limited by their finite intellects and experiences. Thus, an object that appears beautiful to the most sophisticated actual observers may nonetheless have subtle but severe aesthetic shortcomings that would make it appear hideous to hypothetical observers of even greater sophistication. Such an object would be ugly, regardless of any actual person's opinion.

In general, if an object ___1___, then that object ___2___.

Select for 1 and for 2 the two different options that complete the sentence in such a way that it expresses a principle on which the philosophy student's argument relies. Make only two selections, one in each column.

1	2	
		is considered beautiful by everyone
		is thought by most observers to have some aesthetic flaws
		would appear hideous to hypothetical observers of even greater sophistication than the most sophisticated actual observers
		is not truly beautiful
		is not widely appreciated by unsophisticated observers

162. The following statements describe certain characteristics of a certain pool of candidates for a position. Any candidate who did not meet the minimum qualifications for the position was immediately excluded from consideration. The two candidates who met the minimum qualifications for the position and met all of the desired qualifications also had multiple recommendations. All candidates who received a telephone interview also had extensive experience. All candidates who had extensive experience and impressed the hiring committee during the telephone interview were invited to interview on-site. At least one candidate declined an invitation for an on-site interview, and exactly one candidate was interviewed on-site without receiving a telephone interview.

Consider the following incomplete sentence:

If any candidate ____1____, then that candidate ____2____.

Select for *1* and for *2* two different options that best complete the sentence such that it can be logically inferred from the information provided. Make only two selections, one in each column.

1	2	
		did not meet the minimum qualifications
		had multiple recommendations
		had extensive experience
		impressed the hiring committee during the telephone interview
		interviewed on-site

163. On a 12-hour analog clock, the hour hand moves at a constant rate of 1 revolution every 12 hours, and the minute hand moves at a constant rate of 1 revolution every hour. The hands are perpendicular at 3:00 in the morning. To the nearest second, the next time they are superimposed (i.e., both pointing at the same point on the outer rim of the clock face) is M minutes and S seconds after 3:00 in the morning.

Select for M and for S values that are consistent with the information provided. Make only two selections, one in each column.

M	S	
		15
		16
		17
		20
		22
		34

164. The following argument is logically flawed. The author's goal was to craft the argument so that the conclusion follows logically from Premises 1 and 2 and so that both premises are necessary to draw the conclusion.

Premise 1: Every respondent to our survey who **reported feeling satisfied** also reported being in a good mood.

Premise 2: Every respondent to our survey who **reported having a central goal** also **reported being in a good mood**.

Conclusion: Therefore, assuming all of the reports were accurate and complete, every respondent to our survey who **felt satisfied** also **had a central goal**.

Select for *Boldface A* and for *Boldface B* two of the boldfaced phrases in the argument such that Boldface A occurs earlier in the argument than Boldface B, and exchanging the positions of those two phrases in the argument would make it so the argument fulfills the author's goal. Make only two selections, one in each column.

Boldface A	Boldface B	
		reported feeling satisfied
		reported having a central goal
		reported being in a good mood
		felt satisfied
		had a central goal

165. In Country C, some but not all eligible voters are required to vote. The particulars of the country's laws governing voting are as follows:

Every citizen who is eligible must vote on election day.

A person is eligible if (and only if) he or she meets the age requirement and either is a citizen or meets the residency requirement for noncitizens.

The age requirement is that every voter must be at least 19 years old on election day.

The residency requirement for noncitizens is that the voter must have been a resident of Country C for at least 5 years on election day.

Consider the following individuals:

Abigail: a citizen who is currently 19 years old

Barbara: a 7-year resident noncitizen who is currently 19 years old

Charles: a 7-year resident noncitizen who is currently 18 years old

For an election held today, select the individual or individuals who must vote, based on the information provided, and select the individual or individuals who must not vote, based on the information provided. Make only two selections, one in each column.

Must vote	Must not vote	
		Abigail only
		Barbara only
		Charles only
		Abigail and Barbara only
		Abigail and Charles only
		Barbara and Charles only

6.8 Answer Key: Two-Part Analysis

	Response 1	Response 2
111.	322,000	238,000
112.	1	4
113.	Undeterminable	Undeterminable
114.	the employee wrote the novel on a computer owned by the company	mere use of Company X's resources in an activity is sufficient grounds for regarding that activity as related to Company X's business
115.	The council considers a formal written noise complaint.	The council offers to mediate a dispute about noise.
116.	Our company should continue requiring the specific documentation that it does.	Our company should not require that form of documentation.
117.	only if	whether or not
118.	5	50
119.	500	200
120.	4	5
121.	real events	typically unpleasant emotion
122.	5	3
123.	New York showed significant economic development leading up to the early twentieth century.	The Armory Show and other influential New York shows like it featured many prominent European artists.
124.	Cropland	Machinery
125.	Tuesday	Thursday
126.	If an athlete is reasonably able to fulfill a team requirement, then the punishment specified for breaking the requirement should be administered.	The punishment of a team member for breaking a team requirement should be based on the likely outcomes for the team rather than the punishment specified for breaking the requirement.

	Response 1	Response 2
127.	$\frac{1}{2}$	$\frac{1}{4}$
128.	If the researcher's projections are accurate, the island's seabird population is likely to increase during more years of the second study than it did in the first.	During the first study, the island's seabird population decreased only when the island's cat population increased.
129.	10%	50%
130.	76	82
131.	190	210
132.	20	15
133.	$160.02	$317.43
134.	13	17
135.	current issue of the magazine	past issue of the magazine
136.	spores	species represented
137.	very few of the more-popular species have any chance of escaping extinction	popular species receive a disproportionate amount of the money and public attention devoted to the preservation of endangered species
138.	any of Perkin's original batch of mauve dye	a crystalline form of the dye
139.	5	17
140.	48	72
141.	Somewhat agrees	Absolutely agrees
142.	C	A + B
143.	Self-identifies as Métis due to long-standing participation in Métis political activities	Has recent ancestry that is not Métis
144.	11	6
145.	less than 100,000 AED	less than 100,000 AED

	Response 1	**Response 2**
146.	Species X is susceptible to unusually cold weather, whereas Species Y is not.	The number of Species Y frogs decreased from the previous spring census.
147.	All and only those who were employees at the company on the first day of last year were employees on the last day of last year.	Last year, the number of employees on the first day was equal to the number of employees on the last day of the year.
148.	P1 was chosen over P2 at least in part for its aesthetic features	both P1 and P2 accurately portray the relevant features of Event E
149.	0.1	0.4
150.	€0 to €1,500	€0 to €1,500
151.	The home team scores the first goal.	The team opposing the home team scores at least one goal.
152.	Any nonmanagerial employees currently allowed access to Drive E are also allowed access to Drive D.	Managerial employees, and only those, are currently allowed access to Drive E.
153.	$\dfrac{(1.05xy)}{(30)}$	$\left(\dfrac{3}{2}\right)\left(\dfrac{y}{1.05}\right)$

	Response 1	**Response 2**
154.	curly stems	long roots
155.	Japanese	deciduous
156.	2	5
157.	2	4
158.	only if	only if
159.	tended to have	tended to have
160.	6	32
161.	would appear hideous to hypothetical observers of even greater sophistication than the most sophisticated actual observers	not truly beautiful
162.	impressed the hiring committee during the telephone interview	had extensive experience
163.	16	22
164.	reported having a central goal	reported being in a good mood
165.	Abigail only	Charles only

6.9 Answer Explanations: Two-Part Analysis

The following discussion of Data Insights is intended to familiarize you with the most efficient and effective approaches to the kinds of problems common to Data Insights. The particular questions in this chapter are generally representative of the kinds of Data Insights questions you will encounter on the GMAT exam. Remember that it is the problem-solving strategy that is important, not the specific details of a particular question.

Questions 111 to 118 — Difficulty: Easy

111. Two employees of Company X, Winnie and Ali, have been informed that they will each receive bonuses this year, and that, for these bonuses, they will share a total amount of 560,000 KES (Kenyan shillings). Winnie makes a base salary of 4,600,000 KES per annum, and Ali makes a base salary of 3,400,000 KES per annum.

Assuming that the two employees receive the same percentage of their respective per annum base salaries as bonuses, indicate below the bonus amount that Winnie will receive and the bonus amount that Ali will receive. Make only two selections, one in each column.

Winnie	Ali	
		216,000
		238,000
		256,000
		304,000
		322,000

Answer Explanation:

Infer

Winnie:

Winnie and Ali will each get the same percentage of their per annum base salaries as bonuses. That means that Winnie's bonus must be the same percentage of her and Ali's combined total bonus amount of 560,000 KES that her per annum base salary is of their combined total per annum base salaries of 4,600,000 KES + 3,400,000 KES = 8,000,000 KES. Thus, Winnie will get a bonus of W KES such that $= \dfrac{W}{560,000} = \dfrac{4,600,000}{8,000,000} = 0.575$.

Therefore, Winnie's bonus is
$W = 0.575 \times 560,000 = 322,000$.

The correct answer is *322,000*.

Ali:

We saw above that Winnie will get 322,000 KES of the total 560,000 KES bonus she's splitting with Ali. Thus, Ali's share of the bonus will be 560,000 KES – 322,000 KES = 238,000 KES.

The correct answer is *238,000*.

112. After a 16-member team at Company A saw a certain software demonstration, each of the team members gave the software exactly one of the ratings 1, 2, 3, 4, or 5, where greater numbers indicate higher ratings. The team's manager intended to record the 16 ratings but accidentally recorded one team member's rating twice. The ratings she recorded show two ratings of 1, two ratings of 2, two ratings of 3, two ratings of 4, and nine ratings of 5, for a total of 17 ratings.

The manager determined that the extra rating was ____P____, and after this extra rating was removed, the average (arithmetic mean) of the remaining 16 ratings was exactly ____Q____.

Select for P and for Q the options that create a statement that is consistent with the information provided. Make only two selections, one in each column.

P	Q	
		1
		2
		3
		4
		5

Answer Explanation:

Infer

P:

All the response options are whole numbers. One of them must equal Q, the arithmetic mean of the 16 ratings other than P (i.e., the extra rating). Since Q is a whole number, the sum of those 16 ratings must be divisible by 16. That is, the sum of all 17 ratings minus P is divisible by 16. The 17 ratings sum to $2 \times (1 + 2 + 3 + 4) + 9 \times 5 = 65$. And $65 - 1 = 64 = 4 \times 16$. Since the sum of the 17 ratings minus 1 is divisible by 16, $P = 1$.

The correct answer is *1*.

Q:

The mean of the 16 ratings other than P is the sum of those ratings divided by 16. We saw above that the sum of those 16 ratings is 64, so their mean is $64/16 = 4$.

The correct answer is *4*.

113. Natural gas, when burned as fuel for heat, produces about 1,000 BTU of heat per cubic foot of gas when fully burned. Propane, another gas used as fuel, produces about 2,500 BTU per cubic foot of gas when fully burned.

    Furnaces burning either fuel burn at various efficiencies, according to the proportion of heat energy available from the fuel that actually contributes to the heating of the building to be heated (as opposed, e.g., to escaping up a chimney in the form of dissipated heat or unburned fuel).

    Kgomotso is shopping for a furnace that will produce about 50,000 BTU per hour of usable heat. None of the available furnaces burns both propane and natural gas. Also, no two of them operate at the same efficiency. In the table, identify, if possible, a price per cubic foot of *Propane* and a price per cubic foot of *Natural gas*, such that the fuel-cost per BTU of usable heat is the same using either fuel. If this determination is impossible with the given information, then choose "Undeterminable" in each column. Make only two selections, one in each column.

Propane	Natural gas	Price per cubic foot
		$0.0035
		$0.0070
		$0.0110
		$0.0175
		$0.0350
		Undeterminable

Answer Explanation:

Infer

Let $p\%$ and $n\%$ be the percent of heat energy available to heat a building (i.e., usable heat) for a furnace that burns propane and a furnace that burns natural gas, respectively. If P and N represent the price per cubic foot of propane and natural gas, respectively, then $\left(\dfrac{p}{100}\right)(2{,}500)(P)$ represents the price per BTU of usable heat using propane and $\left(\dfrac{n}{100}\right) - (1{,}000)(N)$ represents the price per BTU of usable heat using natural gas. The task is to determine, if possible, P and N such that $\left(\dfrac{p}{100}\right)(2{,}500)(P) = \left(\dfrac{n}{100}\right)(1{,}000)(N)$ or equivalently, $5pP = 2nN$.

Propane:

Since p and n vary from furnace to furnace and values are not included in the given information, it is impossible to determine P, the price per cubic foot of propane for which the fuel-cost per BTU of usable heat will be the same as that for natural gas.

The correct answer is *Undeterminable*.

Natural Gas:

Since p and n vary from furnace to furnace and values are not included in the given information, it is impossible to determine N, the price per cubic foot of natural gas for which the fuel-cost per BTU of usable heat will be the same as that for propane.

The correct answer is *Undeterminable*.

114. At Company X, a new firm which is at present devoted entirely to the design of software applications, all employees are required to agree to the following policy:

Any idea or invention conceived of by employees that is related to Company X's past, present, or future business is owned exclusively by Company X, not the individual employee.

Thus, if a Company X employee has conceived of an idea or invention during his/her employment with Company X related in any manner to Company X's business, that invention is owned by Company X. The employee may not use or exploit that idea or invention for his or her personal benefit.

An employee of Company X has recently sold a children's novel to a publisher. Company X has claimed ownership of the novel on the basis of the stated policy, and the employee intends to dispute the company's claim.

If ____1____, then a successful defense of the company's claimed ownership rights would likely include a statement that ____2____.

Select for *1* and for *2* the options whereby the statement is most clearly supported. Make only two selections, one in each column.

1	2	
		mere use of Company X's resources in an activity is sufficient grounds for regarding that activity as related to Company X's business
		mere use of Company X's resources in an activity is not sufficient grounds for regarding that activity as related to Company X's business
		the employee wrote the novel on a computer owned by the company
		the employee has received a significant amount of money from the sale
		the company has plans to expand into publishing

Answer Explanation:

Strategize

Note that because the two blanks are part of the same conditional sentence, you must consider both responses together.

1 and *2*:

All employees are required to agree to a policy stating that any idea or invention conceived by employees that is related to the business of Company X belongs to that company. On the basis of this policy, the company claims ownership of the children's novel that a Company X employee has sold. A successful defense of the company's ownership rights would link the novel as an idea or invention in some way to the company's business. Suppose it is the case that the employee used a computer owned by Company X. Then a successful defense of the claimed ownership right would likely appeal to a claim that the mere use of Company X's resources (such as a computer) in an activity is sufficient grounds for regarding that activity as related to Company X's business.

The correct answer to 1 is *the employee wrote the novel on a computer owned by the company.*

The correct answer to 2 is *mere use of Company X's resources in an activity is sufficient grounds for regarding that activity as related to Company X's business.*

115. A village's ordinances require residents to exercise reasonable care to avoid disturbing their neighbors with noise. The village council may impose fines for noise violations in response to formal complaints. But unless there have been formal complaints from multiple residents, the council will not consider a complaint if the complaining individual has not attempted to resolve the issue directly with the alleged violator or with the violator's landlord if the violator is a renter. The council's first action in response to any formal verbal or written complaint that they are considering will be to offer to mediate the dispute.

Select for *1* and for *2* two different events such that the guidelines most clearly indicate that if the event selected for *1* occurs, then the event selected for *2* either will occur or has already occurred. Make only two selections, one in each column.

1	2	
		The council imposes a fine for noise violation.
		The council considers a formal written noise complaint.
		The complaining individual attempts to resolve the issue with the alleged violator.
		The council offers to mediate a dispute about noise.
		The complaining individual contacts the alleged violator's landlord.

Answer Explanation:

Recognize

The final sentence implies that, in response to any formal verbal or written complaint made to the council, the council will offer to mediate the dispute. Therefore, if the council is considering a formal written noise complaint, then the council will offer to mediate the dispute about noise.

1:

The correct answer is *The council considers a formal written noise complaint.*

2:

The correct answer is *The council offers to mediate a dispute about noise.*

116. Manager S: Our company provides a small annual monetary benefit for each employee who submits documentation to the company proving that the employee had a comprehensive medical exam in a given year. The policy has been successful in increasing the number of employees who get the exam annually precisely because the benefit requires this specific form of documentation, and this success has resulted in improved employee health. **[Insert Sentence 1.]**

Manager T: I agree that the overall policy has improved employee health, and it is good to improve employee health. However, the required documentation resulted in our company having access to an employee's private medical data. The benefit to employee health is not worth compromising employee privacy. **[Insert Sentence 2.]**

Select for *Sentence 1* the sentence that best completes Manager S's argument, and select for *Sentence 2* the sentence that best completes Manager T's argument. Make only two selections, one in each column.

Sentence 1	Sentence 2	
		Requiring the documentation has no effect on employees.
		Our company should continue requiring the specific documentation that it does.
		Our company should not require that form of documentation.
		Promoting employee health with financial incentives is counterproductive.
		Promoting employee health with financial incentives is worthwhile.

Answer Explanation:

Evaluate

Sentence 1:

Each of the first, third, and fourth answer choices at least somewhat conflicts with Manager S's views. Also, although the fifth answer choice is in agreement with Manager S's views, it does not mention documentation, which is an important aspect of Manager S's argument. Therefore, only the second answer choice could support Manager S's argument. Moreover, since Manager S argues that the specific form of documentation now used is desirable, a concluding sentence (such as the second answer choice) that the company should continue requiring the specific documentation that it does would complete Manager S's argument.

The correct answer is *Our company should continue requiring the specific documentation that it does.*

Sentence 2:

Each of the first, second, and fourth answer choices at least somewhat conflicts with Manager T's views. Also, although the fifth answer choice is in agreement with Manager T's views, it does not mention employee privacy concerns, which is an important aspect of Manager T's argument. Therefore, only the third answer choice could support Manager T's argument. Moreover, since Manager T argues that the documentation could compromise employee privacy, which Manager T feels is very important, a concluding sentence (such as the third answer choice) that the company should not require the specific documentation that it does would complete Manager T's argument.

The correct answer is *Our company should not require that form of documentation.*

117. Ethics board member: All actions that are permissible under the code of ethics are also legal in all of the jurisdictions in which our company operates. Furthermore, regardless of whether it has been determined if an action is legal, it is always permissible to ask the ethics board to review the action for conformity to the code of ethics.

Statements: Without exception, an action is permissible under the code of ethics ___1___ it is legal in all of the jurisdictions in which the company operates. Furthermore, one is permitted to ask the ethics board to review an action for conformity to the code of ethics ___2___ the legality of the action has been established.

Select for *1* and for *2* the two different options that complete the statements so that they most accurately paraphrase the ethics board member's assertions. Make only two selections, one in each column.

1	2	
		if
		only if
		unless
		whether or not
		or

Answer Explanation:

Recognize

1:

The ethics board member's first sentence states that for all actions, if that action is permissible under the code of ethics, then it is legal in all of the jurisdictions in which the company operates. Since "for all actions" means without exception (when applied to actions), and a statement of the form "if P, then Q" is logically equivalent to "P only if Q," it follows that the ethics board member's first sentence is logically equivalent to saying that without exception, an action is permissible under the code of ethics **only if** it is legal in all of the jurisdictions in which the company operates.

To see that each of the other options gives a less accurate paraphrase, let P and Q represent the assertions as suggested above. Thus, the ethics board member's first sentence is logically equivalent to "for all actions, if P, then Q." The selection **if** gives a statement logically equivalent to "for all actions, if Q, then P" (not a paraphrase), the selection **unless** gives a statement logically equivalent to "for all actions, if not-Q, then P" (not a paraphrase), the selection **whether or not** gives a statement logically equivalent to "for all actions, P if and only if Q" (not a paraphrase), and the selection **or** gives a statement logically equivalent to "for all actions, P or Q" (not a paraphrase).

The correct answer is *only if.*

2:

Since "whether it has been determined" means the same as "whether or not it has been determined," the ethics board member's second sentence is logically equivalent to "whether or not R, then S," where R represents "it has been determined if an action is legal" and S represents "it is permissible to ask the ethics board to review the action for conformity to the code of ethics." This is logically equivalent to "S whether or not R," which corresponds to the selection **whether or not**.

To see that each of the other options gives a less accurate paraphrase, let R and S represent the assertions as suggested above. Thus, the ethics board member's second sentence is logically equivalent to "if R or not-R, then S," which is logically equivalent to "if R, then S, and if not-R, then S." The selection **if** gives a statement logically equivalent to "if R, then S" (doesn't include the provision that we have S when not-R holds), the selection **only if** gives a statement logically equivalent to "if S, then R" (doesn't allow S to be concluded), the selection **unless** gives a statement logically equivalent to "if not-R, then S" (doesn't include the provision that we have S when R holds), and the selection **or** gives a statement logically equivalent to "S or R" (doesn't include the provision that we have S when R holds).

The correct answer is *whether or not*.

118. A corporation uses a model of diminishing returns to make predictions about the expected returns on research investment. For this model, in order to produce an x% increase in annual profits in subsequent years, the corporation must invest y% of annual profits into research, where $y = 2x^2$.

Select two different numbers that are jointly compatible with the information provided and could be the values for x and for y. Make only two selections, one in each column.

x	y	
		1
		3
		5
		20
		50
		80

Answer Explanation:

Infer

The following table shows the value of $2x^2$ for each possible selection for x.

x	$2x^2$
1	2
3	18
5	**50**
20	800
50	5,000
80	12,800

The table shows that among the possible selections for x, only $x = 5$ gives a value of $2x^2$ that is equal to one of the possible selections for $2x^2$. Therefore, $x = 5$ and $y = 50$.

x:

The correct answer is *5*.

y:

The correct answer is *50*.

Questions 119 to 136 — Difficulty: **Medium**

119. A small business has just invested in a new piece of equipment. The business's accountant estimates that the value of the equipment will decrease over time at a constant rate. Based on this assumption, the accountant properly estimates the value of the equipment 3 years afterward to be $X, 6 years afterward to be $Y, and 8 years afterward to be, for the first time, $0.

Select values for X and for Y that are jointly consistent with the given information. Make only two selections, one in each column.

X	Y	
		200
		300
		400
		500
		600

Answer Explanation:

Evaluate

X:

The accountant estimates that the equipment's value will decrease at a constant rate to $0 over eight years. If that's true, the decrease will be 1/8 of the equipment's current value per year for eight years. Thus, after 3 years the equipment will be worth 5/8 of its current value, and after 6 years it will be worth 2/8 of its current value. So, the value $Y after 6 years will be 2/5 of the value $X after 3 years. Among the five answer options, only $X = 500$ and $Y = 200$ are such that Y is 2/5 of X. Thus, $X = 500$ and $Y = 200$.

The correct answer is *500*.

Y:

As explained above, $Y = 200$.

The correct answer is *200*.

120. Pavel made a list of 31 chores he needed to complete over the next 7 days. On the first 5 days, he completed 3, 5, 7, 2, and 6 of the listed chores, respectively. On the next 2 days, he completed the remaining 8 chores.

    Select for *Least possible median* and for *Greatest possible median* values that are consistent with the information provided and give the least and greatest possible values, respectively, for the median of the numbers of the listed chores Pavel completed on each of the 7 days. Make only two selections, one in each column.

Least possible median	Greatest possible median	
		2
		3
		4
		5
		6

Answer Explanation:

Evaluate

Least possible median:

Over the final 2 of the 7 days, Pavel finished 8 chores, so for some whole numbers x and y, he must have finished exactly x chores on one day and y chores on the other day such that $x + y = 8$ and $x \le y$. To find the median number of chores he finished per day over all 7 days, rank the days in order of how many chores he finished on each. The median is the number of chores he finished on the day ranked 4th out of the 7. If $x = y = 4$, then the ranking is {2, 3, 4, 4, 5, 6, 7}, so the median is 4. Otherwise, $y \ge 5$ and $x \le 3$. In that case, the four days on each of which he finished the most chores must be the days on which he finished y, 5, 6, and 7 chores, respectively. Since $y \ge 5$, the number of chores he finished on the day ranked 4th out of the 7 must then be 5, so 5 must be the median. Thus, we've shown that the median number of chores must be either 4 or 5. So 4 is the least possible value of the median.

The correct answer is *4*.

Greatest possible median:

As explained above, the median number of chores must be either 4 or 5. So 5 is the greatest possible value of the median.

The correct answer is *5*.

121. Literary critic: When a reader feels an emotion that is focused on the events and characters in a work of fiction, the reader is psychologically somewhat detached from that emotion. Lacking the immediacy of emotions about events in the reader's own life, emotions evoked by fiction are enjoyed as pure sensations independent of ___1___. Consequently, the reader can find pleasure even in sadness when it is focused on the events and characters in fictional works, because the work's beauty consists partly in its ability to evoke such ___2___.

    Select options to fill in the two blanks above to complete the literary critic's statements most coherently. Make only two selections, one in each column.

1	2	
		beauty
		psychological detachment
		typically unpleasant emotions
		fictional events
		real events

Answer Explanation:

Evaluate

1:

We need to determine the word or phrase that best fills blank 1 to complete the sentence. To correctly complete the sentence, we must determine what emotions, evoked by fiction and enjoyed as pure sensations, are independent of. At the beginning of the second sentence, we are told that emotions evoked by fiction lack "the immediacy of emotions about events in the reader's own life." It seems reasonable to say here that the emotions evoked by fiction are enjoyed as pure sensations independent of *real events*.

The correct answer is *real events*.

2:

We need to determine the word or phrase that best fills blank 2 to complete the sentence. Once the blank is appropriately filled, the sentence is supposed to support—along with the sentence completed by the answer that fills blank 1—the claim that a reader of fiction can find pleasure in sadness when the sadness is focused on events and characters in fictional works. Which of the possible responses would help create a sentence that would support that claim? Sadness is typically an unpleasant emotion. So, if a work of fiction's beauty consists in its ability to evoke typically unpleasant emotions such as sadness, but the sadness can be evoked by fiction without the unpleasantness, then a reader can find pleasure even in sadness, as long as the sadness is evoked independent of real events (i.e., as when it is focused on the events and characters in fictional works).

The correct answer is *typically unpleasant emotion*.

122. The equation $6 \times 5 - 4 \div 2 - 3 + 7)^0 - 1)^2 = 6$ is missing two opening parentheses. It can be made true if opening parentheses are placed immediately before each of two of the numbers.

Assume that standard order-of-operations principles are followed, whereby multiplication and division are performed before addition and subtraction, unless parentheses indicate otherwise. Select in the table a number before which the first opening parenthesis could be placed and a number before which the second opening parenthesis could be placed, such that the equation would express a true statement. Make only two selections, one in each column.

First parenthesis immediately before	Second parenthesis immediately before	
		2
		3
		4
		5
		6

Answer Explanation:

Apply

Try all possible placements of the two opening parentheses:

Before 5 and 4	$6 \times (5 - (4 \div 2 - 3 + 7)^0 - 1)^2$	$= 54$
Before 5 and 2	$6 \times (5 - 4 \div (2 - 3 + 7)^0 - 1)^2$	$= 0$
Before 5 and 3	$6 \times (5 - 4 \div 2 - (3 + 7)^0 - 1)^2$	$= 6$
Before 5 and 7	$6 \times (5 - 4 \div 2 - 3 + (7)^0 - 1)^2$	$= 0$
Before 5 and 1	$6 \times (5 - 4 \div 2 - 3 + 7)^0 - (1)^2$	$= 5$
Before 4 and 2	$6 \times 5 - (4 \div (2 - 3 + 7)^0 - 1)^2$	$= 21$
Before 4 and 3	$6 \times 5 - (4 \div 2 - (3 + 7)^0 - 1)^2$	$= 30$
Before 4 and 7	$6 \times 5 - (4 \div 2 - 3 + (7)^0 - 1)^2$	$= 29$
Before 4 and 1	$6 \times 5 - (4 \div 2 - 3 + 7)^0 - (1)^2$	$= 28$
Before 2 and 3	$6 \times 5 - 4 \div (2 - (3 + 7)^0 - 1)^2$	$=$ undefined division by 0
Before 2 and 7	$6 \times 5 - 4 \div (2 - 3 + (7)^0 - 1)^2$	$= 26$
Before 2 and 1	$6 \times 5 - 4 \div (2 - 3 + 7)^0 - (1)^2$	$= 25$

Before 3 and 7 $6 \times 5 - 4 \div 2 - (3 + (7)^0 - 1)^2 = 10$

Before 3 and 1 $6 \times 5 - 4 \div 2 - (3 + 7)^0 - (1)^2 = 26$

Before 7 and 1 $6 \times 5 - 4 \div 2 - 3 + (7)^0 - (1)^2 = 25$

First parenthesis immediately before:

The third row of the table shows an expression with value 6. The first opening parenthesis is before 5.

The correct answer is *5*.

Second parenthesis immediately before:

The third row of the table shows an expression with value 6. The second opening parenthesis is before 3.

The correct answer is *3*.

123. Historian: New York City became an influential art center in the twentieth century, as seen, for example, in the influential 1913 Armory Show and the growth of museums. This was due primarily to a combination of New York's large and varied population, its basic resources, and its access to European art trends. The city could never have become an influential art center without the era's increased local wealth, which allowed more people to buy art. However, the changes were driven principally by the diversity of the city's population, including intellectuals and artists from Europe, and a culture that prized energy and creativity, which stimulated the artistic endeavors of many people.

Select for *Precondition* the statement that the passage most strongly suggests describes a precondition for New York becoming an influential art center. And select for *Strengthener* the statement that would, if true, most clearly strengthen the support for the historian's explanation of why the city became an influential art center. Make only two selections, one in each column.

Precondition	Strengthener	
		New York showed significant economic development leading up to the early twentieth century.
		New York afforded easy access to major art museums in other cities in the United States.
		Members of the Hudson River School of painters helped promote art in New York.
		The Armory Show and other influential New York shows like it featured many prominent European artists.
		The composition of European groups immigrating to New York changed in the early 1900s.

Answer Explanation:

Evaluate

Precondition:

The first answer choice is strongly suggested as a precondition in the passage's third sentence: "The city could never have become an influential art center without the era's increased local wealth, which allowed more people to buy art." Also, none of the other answer choices strongly suggests such a precondition—the second and third answer choices involve issues not mentioned in the passage, the fourth answer choice is a misrepresentation of an aftereffect, and, at best, the fifth answer choice is only suggested as one of the reasons for the changes that led New York to become an influential art center.

The correct answer is *New York showed significant economic development leading up to the early 20th century.*

Strengthener:

The first and fifth answer choices are arguably included in the passage, and thus would essentially add nothing to strengthen the historian's explanation. Although the second and third answer choices might provide some strengthening of the historian's explanation, neither is particularly relevant to the issues that are actually mentioned in the passage. The fourth answer choice mentions "prominent European artists" in a way that supports the passage's linking of them to New York's economic development.

The correct answer is *The Armory Show and other influential New York shows like it featured many prominent European artists*.

124. A farmer wants to allocate her expenditures to maximize her profits during the coming year. Let *C* be her spending on cropland, *F* her spending on fertilizer, *L* her spending on labor, *M* her spending on machinery, and *S* her spending on seed. She has estimated that, if she allocates at least 100 euros to each of these categories, then her profit during the coming year will be $(C - 97)(L - 92)(S - 95)(M - 87)(F - 90)$ euros. She wishes to calculate the benefits of expenditure greater than 100 euros in one of these categories, if she were to spend exactly 100 euros in each of the others.

Select for *Greatest returns* the resource for which, according to the desired calculation from the model, each euro of spending beyond 100 euros is predicted to make the greatest contribution to profits (or least contribution to losses). And select for *Least returns* the resource for which, according to the desired calculation, each euro of spending beyond the minimum necessary amount is predicted to make the least contribution to profits (or greatest contribution to losses). Make only two selections, one in each column.

Greatest returns	Least returns	
		Cropland
		Fertilizer
		Labor
		Machinery
		Seed

Answer Explanation:

Strategize

Let $P = (C - 97)(L - 92)(S - 95)(M - 87)(F - 90)$. Let x represent the amount by which an expenditure is greater than 100 euros. The

following table summarizes the calculations for P given certain constraints. For example, if $C = 100 + x$ and $L = S = M = F = 100$, then $P = (100 + x - 97)(100 - 92)(100 - 95)(100 - 87)(100 - 90) = (3 + x)(8)(5)(13)(10) = (3 + x)(5,200) = 15,600 + 5,200x$.

C	$100 + x$	100	100	100	100
L	100	$100 + x$	100	100	100
S	100	100	$100 + x$	100	100
M	100	100	100	$100 + x$	100
F	100	100	100	100	$100 + x$
P	$15,600 + 5,200x$	$15,600 + 1,950x$	$15,600 + 3,120x$	$15,600 + 1,200x$	$15,600 + 1,560x$

From the table, for every euro spent beyond 100 euros, cropland increases profit by 5,200 euros, labor by 1,950 euros, seed by 3,120 euros, machinery by 1,200 euros, and fertilizer by 1,560 euros.

***Greatest returns*:**

The greatest of these increases in profits for every euro spent beyond 100 euros is for cropland.

The correct answer is *Cropland*.

***Least returns*:**

The least of these increases in profits for every euro spent beyond 100 euros is for machinery.

The correct answer is *Machinery*.

125. At a certain factory, 4 processes—A, B, C, and D—are carried out 24 hours per day, 7 days per week. Process A operates on a 60-hour cycle; that is, Process A takes 60 hours to complete and immediately begins again when it is completed. Likewise, Process B operates on a 24-hour cycle, Process C operates on a 27-hour cycle, and Process D operates on a 9-hour cycle. On Monday, all 4 processes began together at 10:00 in the morning.

On the basis of the information provided, select for *Processes A, B, and D* the day of the week on which Processes A, B, and D will next begin together at 10:00 in the morning. Also select for *All 4 processes* the day of the week on which Processes A–D will next begin together at 10:00 in the morning. Make only two selections, one in each column.

Processes A, B, and D	All 4 processes	
		Monday
		Tuesday
		Wednesday
		Thursday
		Friday

Answer Explanation:

Apply

Processes A, B, and D:

Processes A, B, and D will all end at 10:00 a.m. on the same day and therefore will begin together at 10:00 a.m. the next time when the time elapsed since they started together is the least common multiple of 60, 24, and 9. This can be found by analyzing the prime factorizations of 60, 24, and 9, which are $2^2 \times 3 \times 5$, $2^3 \times 3$, and 3^2, respectively. The least common multiple is the product of the greatest power of each of the prime factors in the three numbers, so the least common multiple of 60, 24, and 9 is $2^3 \times 3^2 \times 5$ = 360. Thus, the three processes will begin at the same time 360 hours, which is $\frac{360}{24}$ = 15 days, after they began together; 15 days (or 2 weeks and 1 day) after Monday is Tuesday.

The correct answer is *Tuesday*.

All 4 processes:

Processes A, B, C, and D will all end at 10:00 a.m. on the same day and therefore will begin together at 10:00 a.m. the next time when the time elapsed since they started together is the least common multiple of 60, 24, 27, and 9. It has already been determined that the least common multiple of 60, 24, and 9 is $2^3 \times 3^2 \times 5$ = 360. The prime factorization of 27 is 3^3, so any multiple of 27 must have 3 factors of 3. Thus, the least common multiple of 60, 24, 27, and 9 is $2^3 \times 3^3 \times 5$ = 1,080,

which is $\frac{1,080}{24}$ = 45 days; 45 days (or 6 weeks and 3 days) after Monday is Thursday.

The correct answer is *Thursday*.

126. An amateur athletic team has the following requirement: "Each athlete who fails to return to his or her designated room prior to a designated time will be suspended for the next athletic event." The requirement was violated by the team's best athlete on the night before a prominent athletic event.

Assistant Coach A: The only reason to not suspend the athlete is if the athlete broke the requirement because of factors outside the athlete's control. Since that was not the reason, no exception should be made for this athlete.

Assistant Coach B: I know that we would normally punish the athlete with a suspension, but doing so in this case would harm the team. I think we should punish the athlete in another way that would not harm the team.

Select for *Supports Assistant Coach A* the principle that most strongly supports the reasoning expressed by Assistant Coach A, and select for *Supports Assistant Coach B* the principle that most strongly supports the reasoning expressed by Assistant Coach B. Make only two selections, one in each column.

Supports Assistant Coach A	Supports Assistant Coach B	
		Amateur athletic teams should not punish elite team members who break team requirements.
		The punishment of a team member for breaking a team requirement should be based on the likely outcomes for the team rather than the punishment specified for breaking the requirement.
		The punishment specified for breaking a team requirement should always be administered in order to ensure that all team members are treated equally.

		If an athlete is reasonably able to fulfill a team requirement, then the punishment specified for breaking the requirement should be administered.
		If a punishment of a team member specified by a team requirement would harm the team, then the team member should not be punished.

Answer Explanation:

Evaluate

Supports Assistant Coach A:

Assistant Coach A claims that it was not because of anything outside the control of the athlete in question that the athlete broke the requirement, and, as a result, there should be no exception made for the athlete. What would help support this thinking? Suppose that the following principle is true: If an athlete is reasonably able to fulfill any particular team requirement, then the punishment specified for breaking the requirement should be administered. Assistant Coach A claims that it was not because of anything outside the athlete's control that the athlete broke the requirement. It follows, then, that the athlete should have been able to fulfill that team requirement, and yet the athlete didn't. This principle, then, would support Assistant Coach A's conclusion that there should be no exception made for the athlete.

The correct answer is *If an athlete is reasonably able to fulfill a team requirement, then the punishment specified for breaking the requirement should be administered.*

Supports Assistant Coach B:

Assistant Coach B states that punishing the athlete in question with a suspension would harm the team, so the athlete should be punished in another way that would not harm the team. Suppose that the following principle is true: The punishment of a team member for breaking a team requirement should be based on the likely outcomes for the team rather than the punishment specified for breaking the

requirement. Assistant Coach B claims that the punishment specified by the requirement would harm the team. Therefore, assuming the stated principle is true, and the reasonable assumption that the team should not be harmed just because one member of the team violated a requirement, Assistant Coach B is correct that the athlete should be punished in some other way that would not harm the team.

The correct answer is *The punishment of a team member for breaking a team requirement should be based on the likely outcomes for the team rather than the punishment specified for breaking the requirement.*

127. Rashika is beginning a new job in human resources and expects to be assigned to several of the many human resources work groups. She has been told that there is a probability of 12 that she will be assigned to the Recruitment Work Group and that there is a probability of 34 that she will be assigned to the New Technology Work Group. She has no other information about the probabilities of the various possible assignments, or whether her assignment to one of these groups affects her chances of assignment to the other.

Select for *Greatest probability for both assignments* the greatest probability, compatible with the given probabilities, that Rashika will be assigned to both the Recruitment Work Group and the New Technology Work Group. And select for *Least probability for both assignments* the least probability, compatible with the given probabilities, that Rashika will be assigned to both of these groups. Make only two selections, one in each column.

Greatest probability for both assignments	Least probability for both assignments	
		0
		$\frac{1}{4}$
		$\frac{1}{2}$
		$\frac{3}{4}$
		1

Answer Explanation:

Infer

Greatest probability for both assignments:

In terms of the probability x that Rashika will be assigned to both groups, consider the probabilities involved. For example, the probability that Rashika will be assigned to the Recruitment Work Group and not be assigned to the New Technology Work Group is $\left(\frac{1}{2} - x\right)$, and the probability that Rashika will be assigned to the Recruitment Work Group is $\left(\frac{1}{2} - x\right) + x = \frac{1}{2}$. The two constraints that follow give all restrictions on the values that can appear in the regions in this graph: (1) Each value is between 0 and 1, inclusive. (2) The sum of the three values is between 0 and 1, inclusive. In particular, from (1) we have $\frac{1}{2} - x \geq 0$, or $x \leq \frac{1}{2}$. Moreover, since $x = \frac{1}{2}$ satisfies both (1) and (2), it follows that the greatest possible value of x is $\frac{1}{2}$.

The correct answer is $\frac{1}{2}$.

Least probability for both assignments:

In the explanation above, from (2) we have $\left(\frac{1}{2} - x\right) + x + \left(\frac{3}{4} - x\right) \leq 1$, or $x \geq \frac{1}{4}$. Moreover, since $x = \frac{1}{4}$ satisfies both (1) and (2), it follows that the least possible value of x is 14.

The correct answer is $\frac{1}{4}$.

128. In a study conducted over several years, seabird and domesticated cat populations on a geographically isolated island changed from year to year. Researchers found that over the course of the study, the relationship (*R*) between seabirds and domesticated cats was such that the island's seabird population was three times as likely to decrease from the previous year if the island's domesticated cat population increased (even if slightly) during the same year. The researchers are about to begin a second, follow-up study with the same duration as the first study. Based on recent trends, the researchers made the following projections: *R* will hold and the island's domesticated cat population will decrease during more years of the second study than it did in their first study.

Assuming that the information above is true, select for *Can be inferred as true* the statement that can be most reasonably inferred as true from the information provided, and select for *Can be inferred as false* the statement that can be most reasonably inferred as false from the information provided. Make only two selections, one in each column.

Can be inferred as true	Can be inferred as false	
		If the researchers' projections are accurate, the island's seabird population is likely to increase during more years of the second study than it did in the first.
		During the first study, most years had an increase in the island's domesticated cat population.
		If the researchers' projections are accurate, the island's seabird population is likely to increase during most of the years of the second study.
		During the first study, the island's seabird population decreased only when the island's domesticated cat population increased.
		During the first study, most years during which the island's seabird population decreased were years during which the island's domesticated cat population increased.

Answer Explanation:

Evaluate

Can be inferred as true:

In each year of a study that was conducted over a period of several years, the populations of both seabirds and domesticated cats on a geographically isolated island changed—that is, the populations either increased or decreased each year from the previous year's numbers. The researchers found that a certain relationship *R* held: The island's seabird population was three times as likely to decrease from the previous year if the island's domesticated cat population increased even slightly during the same year. Because the populations of each of the two types of animals changed each year, we can infer that when the domesticated cat population decreased, the seabird population was only one-third as likely to increase as when the cat population decreased. It also follows, then, that the seabird population was more likely to increase when the cat population decreased than when it increased. So, if the researchers are correct that R will hold during the second, follow-up study that will last the same number of years as the first study, and that the domesticated cat population will decrease during more years than it did during the first study, then it can reasonably be inferred that the seabird population will increase in more years than it did in the first study.

The correct answer is *If the researcher's projections are accurate, the island's seabird population is likely to increase during more years of the second study than it did in the first.*

Can be inferred as false:

If it was determined in the first study that the island's seabird population was three times as likely to decrease in years when the island's domesticated cat population increased, then it cannot be true that the island's seabird's population *never* decreased in years when the island's domesticated cat population did not increase. To see this, consider that for R to hold, the number of years x in which the island's cat population increased and the island's seabird population decreased has to be three times as great as the number of years y in which the island's cat population did *not* increase and the island's seabird population decreased. In other words, $\frac{x}{y} = 3$. And if $\frac{x}{y} = 3$, then y cannot equal 0.

Therefore, it must NOT be the case that, during the first study, the island's seabird population decreased only when the island's cat population increased.

The correct answer is *During the first study, the island's seabird population decreased only when the island's cat population increased.*

129. According to a prominent investment adviser, Company X has a 50% chance of posting a profit in the coming year, whereas Company Y has a 60% chance of posting a profit in the coming year.

Select for *Least probability for both* the least probability, compatible with the probabilities provided by the investment adviser, that both Company X and Company Y will post a profit in the coming year. And select for *Greatest probability for both* the greatest probability, compatible with the probabilities provided by the investment adviser, that both Company X and Company Y will post a profit in the coming year. Make only two selections, one in each column.

Least probability for both	Greatest probability for both	
		5%
		10%
		25%
		50%
		60%
		80%

Answer Explanation:

Infer

Least probability for both:

To determine what the least probability is of both Company X and Company Y posting a profit in the coming year, determine what is the greatest probability of one of the companies— say Company X—posting a profit and the other company—Company Y—not posting a profit, and then subtract that result from the probability of Company X posting a profit. Because the probability of Company Y posting a profit in the coming year is 60%, then the probability of Company Y *not* posting a profit in the coming year is 40%. The greatest probability of Company X posting a profit and Company Y *not* posting a profit in the coming year cannot exceed the lesser of the probability of Company X posting a profit in the coming year—which is 50%—and the probability of Company Y *not* posting a profit in the coming year—which is 40%. Therefore, at most, the probability of both Company X posting a profit but Company Y *not* posting a profit in the coming year is 40%. Subtracting the 40% probability of Company X posting a profit from the probability of Company Y *not* posting a profit from the 50% probability of Company X posting a profit gives us the least probability of both Company X and Company Y posting a profit in the coming year, namely 10%.

The correct answer is *10%*.

Greatest probability for both:

The greatest probability of both Company X and Company Y posting a profit in the coming year cannot exceed the lesser of the probability of Company X posting a profit in the coming year—which is 50%—and the probability of Company Y posting a profit in the coming year—which is 60%. Therefore, the greatest probability of both Company X and Company Y posting a profit in the coming year is 50%.

The correct answer is *50%*.

130. Lee is planning a trip and estimates that, rounded to the nearest 5 kilometers (km), the length of the trip will be 560 km and that, rounded to the nearest 14 hours, the driving time for the trip will be 7 hours. If these estimates are correct, then Lee's average driving speed during the trip will be between ____*x*____ kilometers per hour and ____*y*____ kilometers per hour, where $x < y$.

From the values given in the table, select for *x* and for *y* the values that complete the statement in such a way that the interval between the selected values includes all possible average speeds for Lee's trip and $y - x$ is minimal. Make only two selections, one in each column.

x	y	
		73
		76
		79
		82
		85

Answer Explanation:

Infer

The least distance that rounds to 560 kilometers (km) when rounding to the nearest 5 km is 557.5 km and the greatest is 562.5 km. The least length of time that rounds to 7 hours when rounding to the nearest $\frac{1}{4}$ hour is $6\frac{7}{8} = $ 6.875 hours and the greatest is $7\frac{1}{8} = $ 7.125 hours.

x:

The least possible average speed is $\frac{557.5}{7.125} \approx 78.25$.

Since the value of *x* must be less than 78.25, it follows that 73 and 76 are the only possible values. Because $y - x$ must be minimal, $x = 76$.

The correct answer is *76*.

y:

The greatest possible average speed is $\frac{562.5}{6.875} \approx$ 81.82. Since the value of *y* must be greater than 81.82, it follows that 82 and 85 are the only possible values. Because $y - x$ must be minimal, $y = 82$.

The correct answer is *82*.

131. A certain theater has 500 seats. Some are on the main floor and sell for $50 each; some are in the first balcony and sell for $45 each; and the rest are in the second balcony and sell for $35 each. When all of the seats are sold for a performance, the gross revenue for that performance is $20,900. Of the three seating areas, the second balcony has the most seats.

Select for *First balcony* a number of seats in this theater's first balcony, and select for *Second balcony* a number of seats in this theater's second balcony such that the selections are jointly consistent with the information provided. Make only two selections, one in each column.

First balcony	Second balcony	
		100
		150
		190
		210
		250
		300

Answer Explanation:

Infer

If x represents the number of seats in the first balcony and y represents the number of seats in the second balcony, then $500 - (x + y) = 500 - x - y$ represents the number of seats on the main floor. The following equation represents the given information.

$$50(500 - x - y) + 45x + 35y = 20{,}900$$
$$25{,}000 - 50x - 50y + 45x + 35y = 20{,}900$$
$$-5x - 15y = -4{,}100$$
$$x + 3y = 820$$

Since the second balcony has the most seats, it follows that $y = 210$ or $y = 250$ or $y = 300$. If $y = 210$, then $x = 190$. If $y = 250$, then $x = 70$, which is not among the answer choices. If $y = 300$, then $x = -80$, which is not a valid value for x. Therefore, the first balcony has 190 seats, and the second balcony has 210 seats.

First balcony:

The correct answer is *190*.

Second balcony:

The correct answer is *210*.

132. A company purchased at least 10 units of a certain product from each of Suppliers X and Y. Supplier X charged a $100 fixed cost, $20 per unit for each of the first 10 units, and $5 per unit for each unit purchased in excess of 10 units. Supplier Y charged a $150 fixed cost, $15 per unit for each of the first 10 units, and $10 per unit for each unit purchased

in excess of 10 units. Including the fixed costs, the combined average cost for the units was $20 per unit.

Select a *number of units purchased from Supplier X* and a *number of units purchased from Supplier Y* that are jointly consistent with the given information. Make only two selections, one in each column.

Number of units purchased from Supplier X	Number of units purchased from Supplier Y	
		15
		20
		22
		25
		27
		30

Answer Explanation:

Strategize

If x represents the number of units purchased from Supplier X and y represents the number of units purchased from Supplier Y, then from the given information,

$$\frac{(100 + 20(10) + 5(x - 10) + 150 + 15(10) + 10(y - 10))}{(x + y)} = 20$$
$$450 + 5x + 10y = 20x + 20y$$
$$450 = 15x + 10y$$
$$90 = 3x + 2y$$

The value of x must be even because if x is odd, then $3x + 2y$ cannot equal an even number. Therefore, $x = 20$ or $x = 22$ or $x = 30$. If $x = 20$, then $2y = 30$ and $y = 15$.

If $x = 22$, then $2y = 24$ and $y = 12$. If $x = 30$, then $2y = 0$ and $y = 0$. Of these three possible values for y, only 15 is among the answer choices.

Number of units purchased from Supplier X:

As shown above, the company purchased 20 units of the product from Supplier X.

The correct answer is *20*.

Number of units purchased from Supplier Y:

As shown above, the company purchased 15 units of the product from Supplier Y.

The correct answer is *15*.

133. A financial adviser was showing a client the value, rounded to the nearest cent, of an initial investment of $100.00 after 5, 10, 15, 20, 25, and 30 years, under the assumption that the value increases by r% per year for some positive constant r. The adviser correctly gave $130.01 for the value after 5 years. However, the adviser inadvertently made two transcription errors, and as a result, two of the remaining values shown to the client were incorrect.

Assuming the options provided are the remaining five amounts shown to the client, select for *First error* the lesser of the two incorrectly transcribed values, and select for *Second error* the greater of the two incorrectly transcribed values. Make only two selections, one in each column.

First error	Second error	
		$160.02
		$219.75
		$285.70
		$317.43
		$482.90

Answer Explanation:

Strategize

It is given that after 5 years, the value of the investment was $130.01. It follows that 100 $\left(1 + \frac{r}{100}\right)^5 = 130.01$, so $\left(1 + \frac{r}{100}\right)^5 = 1.3001$.

After 10 years, the value of the investment is 100 $\left(1 + \frac{r}{100}\right)^{10} = 100\left(\left(1 + \frac{r}{100}\right)^5\right)^2 = 100(1.3001)^2$ $= 130.01(1.3001) = 169.02$.

After 15 years, the value of the investment is 100 $\left(1 + \frac{r}{100}\right)^{15} = 100\left(\left(1 + \frac{r}{100}\right)^5\right)^3 = 100(1.3001)^3$ $= 169.02(1.3001) = 219.75$.

After 20 years, the value of the investment is 100 $\left(1 + \frac{r}{100}\right)^{20} = 100\left(\left(1 + \frac{r}{100}\right)^5\right)^4 = 100(1.3001)^4$ $= 219.75(1.3001) = 285.70$.

After 25 years, the value of the investment is 100 $\left(1 + \frac{r}{100}\right)^{25} = 100\left(\left(1 + \frac{r}{100}\right)^5\right)^5 = 100(1.3001)^5$ $= 285.70(1.3001) = 371.44$.

After 30 years, the value of the investment is 100 $\left(1 + \frac{r}{100}\right)^{30} = 100\left(\left(1 + \frac{r}{100}\right)^5\right)^6 = 100(1.3001)^6$ $= 371.44(1.3001) = 482.90$.

First error:

The value of the investment after 10 years was $169.02, but the financial adviser gave $160.02. This was the financial adviser's first error.

The correct answer is *$160.02*.

Second error:

The value of the investment after 25 years was $371.43, but the financial adviser gave $317.43. This was the financial adviser's second error.

The correct answer is *$317.43*.

134. A clothing retailer used to sell only "fast-fashion" pieces, which were low priced and had a profit markup of 50 percent of the per-item cost (including, e.g., the costs of wholesale purchase and marketing). On average, each customer spent $850 annually on around 65 such pieces from the retailer. Now the retailer wishes to double its total profits by selling only "classic" pieces. It plans to double its percentage profit markup per item and generate more revenue per customer while leaving unchanged the company's total costs. The plan assumes that for each classic piece, on average, customers will pay five times what they paid for each fast-fashion piece, and that the total number of customers for the retailer's clothing products will remain the same.

Statements: Customers paid an average of ___1___ dollars (rounded to the nearest dollar) for each of the retailer's fast-fashion pieces. The retailer will need to sell an average minimum of ___2___ classic pieces per person (rounded to the nearest whole number) to achieve its profit goals for classic pieces.

Select values for *1* and for *2* that create the statements that are most strongly supported by the information provided and in accordance with the retailer's plan. Make only two selections, one in each column.

1	2	
		10
		13
		15
		17
		21
		25

Answer Explanation:

Strategize

1:

Customers paid an average of $\frac{\$850}{65} \approx \$13.07$ or $13 rounded to the nearest dollar.

The correct answer is *13*.

2:

For fast-fashion items, let $C represent the cost per item. For these items, there is a 50% markup on the per-item cost. The customer pays an average of $\frac{\$850}{65}$ per item, so $\frac{\$850}{65} = 1.5(\$C) = \frac{3}{2}(\$C)$. It follows that the retailer's per-item cost $C is $\frac{2}{3}\left(\frac{\$850}{65}\right)$. The retailer's profit per item is $\frac{\$850}{65} - \frac{2}{3}\left(\frac{\$850}{65}\right) = \frac{1}{3}\left(\frac{\$850}{65}\right)$. The retailer's total profit per customer is $65\left(\frac{1}{3}\left(\frac{\$850}{65}\right)\right) = \frac{\$850}{3}$.

For classic items, let $c be the per-item cost. The retailer plans to double the percentage profit markup of the cost to generate revenue of 2($c) per item. However, the customer is willing to pay $5\left(\frac{\$850}{65}\right)$, so the retailer's cost per item, $c, is $\frac{5}{2}\left(\frac{\$850}{65}\right)$. It follows that the retailer's per-item

profit is $5\left(\frac{\$850}{65}\right) - \frac{5}{2}\left(\frac{\$850}{65}\right) = \frac{5}{2}\left(\frac{\$850}{65}\right)$. The retailer also plans to double the per-customer profit to $\frac{2(\$850)}{3}$, and to do this, the retailer will need to sell an average minimum of n items per customer. It follows that $n\left(\frac{5}{2}\left(\frac{\$850}{65}\right)\right) = \frac{2(\$850)}{3}$ and $n = \frac{2(\$850)}{3} \cdot \frac{2(65)}{5(\$850)} = \frac{52}{3} \approx 17.33$ or 17 rounded to the nearest whole number.

The correct answer is *17*.

Note that the retailer's total cost for fast-fashion items is $\frac{2}{3}\left(\frac{\$850}{65}\right)(65) \approx \$566.67$, and for classic items it is $\frac{5}{2}\left(\frac{\$850}{65}\right)\left(\frac{52}{3}\right) \approx \$566.67$, so the retailer's total costs are left unchanged in the switch from selling fast-fashion items to selling classic items.

135. A certain mail-order company sells T-shirts, buttons, stickers, and current and past issues of its magazine. Each order placed to the company consists of one or more items, and, for each order, the company packages all of the items in the order together. Any employee who packages an order packages the entirety of that order. Among the orders placed to the company today:

None includes both a T-shirt and a magazine.

All of those that include a past issue of the magazine also include the current issue of the magazine.

Most of those that include a magazine also include a sticker.

None of those that include a button also include a sticker.

Statement: For the orders placed to the company today, if one employee were to package all of the orders that include a ____1____, that employee would also package all of the orders that include a ____2____.

Select for *1* and for *2* the two different options that complete the statement so that it is most accurate based on the information provided. Make only two selections, one in each column.

1	2	
		button
		current issue of the magazine
		past issue of the magazine
		sticker
		T-shirt

Answer Explanation:

Infer

The second statement about the orders placed today implies that all orders containing a past issue of the magazine are among the orders containing a current issue of the magazine. Therefore, if an employee were to package all the orders containing a current issue of the magazine, then the employee would also package all the orders containing a past issue of the magazine.

1:

The correct answer is *current issue of the magazine*.

2:

The correct answer is *past issue of the magazine*.

136. A group of paleobotanists collected samples of sediments containing pollen and spores from various plant species. Each sample was analyzed to determine the number of spores in the sample, the number of pollen grains in the sample, and the species to which those spores and pollen grains belong. Samples S1 and S2 were collected and analyzed in this way. For these two samples:

S1 had the greater total number of spores, and it contained pollen grains from Species P as well as spores from Species Q.

S2 had the greater total number of species represented, and all of the spores it contained were from Species Q.

Statement: Among these two samples, S1 had the greater ratio of total number of ___1___ to total number of ___2___.

Select for *1* and for *2* the options that complete the statement so that it is accurate based on the information provided. Make only two selections, one in each column.

1	2	
		pollen grains
		pollen grains from Species P
		species represented
		spores
		spores from Species Q

Answer Explanation:

Infer

Let (# spores 1), (# spores 2), (# species 1), and (# species 2) be the respective total number of spores in Sample S1, the total number of spores in Sample 2, the total number of species represented in Sample 1, and the total number of species represented in Sample 2.

(# spores 1) > (# spores 2)	given in first bullet assertion
(# species 1) < (# species 2)	given in second bullet assertion
$\dfrac{1}{(species\ 1)} > \dfrac{1}{(species\ 2)}$	take reciprocal of both sides of previous inequality
$\dfrac{(spores\ 1)}{(species\ 1)} > \dfrac{(spores\ 2)}{(species\ 2)}$	multiply corresponding left- and right-hand sides of first inequality and previous inequality

The last inequality above states that the ratio of total number of spores to total number of species represented was greater in Sample S1 than in Sample S2.

1:

The correct answer is *spores*.

2:

The correct answer is *species represented*.

Questions 137 to 165 — Difficulty: **Hard**

137. Biologist: Conservation biologists working to prevent species extinction have long acknowledged that popular species such as lions, eagles, and pandas receive disproportionately large amounts of funding and public attention as compared to less-popular species such as invertebrates and amphibians. Indeed, many of these less-popular species are more in danger of extinction than the more-popular species. Although many conservation biologists have accepted this pattern of disproportionate funding, I believe it needs to stop. For, despite the substantial and continuing expenditure of resources on the more-popular species, very few of these species have any chance of escaping extinction.

The biologist's reasoning is subject to the criticism that the claim that ____A____, which is used to justify the main point, undermines the support for the point that ____B____.

Select for A and for B the options such that criticism of the zoologist's reasoning is strongest. Make only two selections, one in each column.

A	B	
		popular species receive a disproportionate amount of the money and public attention devoted to the preservation of endangered species
		funding and public attention should not be wasted on the preservation of endangered species
		certain popular species are more endangered than many believe
		many species that are not popular are likely to escape extinction
		very few of the more-popular species have any chance of escaping extinction

Answer Explanation:

Evaluate

A:

The biologist's reasoning starts with the claim that popular species receive disproportionate

amounts of funding and public attention compared to less-popular species. The second sentence supports this point by noting that many of the less-popular species are at greater risk of extinction than the more-popular species. The third sentence includes the biologist's main conclusion, that the disproportionate funding of the more-popular species should stop. And the final sentence supports that main conclusion by asserting that very few of the more-popular species have any chance of escaping extinction. But clearly if almost all of the more-popular species have *no chance* of escaping extinction, as the final sentence claims, then the claim in the second sentence that many of the less-popular species are at even *greater* risk of extinction must be false. Thus, the claim in the final sentence, which is used to justify the main point, undermines the claim in the second sentence, which is used to support the point in the first sentence. That is, the claim that very few of the more-popular species have any chance of escaping extinction undermines the claim used to support the point that popular species receive a disproportionate amount of the money and funding devoted to preservation of species.

The correct answer is *very few of the more-popular species have any chance of escaping extinction*.

B:

As explained above, the claim that very few of the more-popular species have any chance of escaping extinction undermines the claim used to support the point that popular species receive a disproportionate amount of the money and funding devoted to preservation of species.

The correct answer is *popular species receive a disproportionate amount of the money and public attention devoted to the preservation of endangered species*.

138. Historian: In the collection of the Science Museum, London, there is a small bottle that is purported to contain the entire original batch of artificial mauve dye created by Sir William Perkin in his laboratory in 1856. Indeed, in his experiments that preceded his commercial production of mauve dyes, he made only a few grams of the substance, but this batch would likely have been completely used up when he tested it as a dye. Also, the early version of mauve dye that Perkin produced commercially consisted of an impure paste rather than the pure crystalline form of the substance contained in the bottle.

Statement: The historian's statements imply that the bottle does not contain ____1____ at least in part because the substance in the bottle is ___2___.

Select for *1* and for *2* the options that create the statement that is most strongly supported by the information above. Make only two selections, one in each column.

1	2	
		any of Perkin's original batch of mauve dye
		a dye produced in Perkin's laboratory
		a dye created in 1856
		a commercially produced dye
		a crystalline form of the dye

Answer Explanation:

Infer

1:

The historian gives two reasons to conclude that the bottle doesn't contain any of Perkin's original batch of mauve dye: first, that the original batch would likely have been completely used up in testing; and second, that the dye in the bottle is crystalline, unlike the earliest version of Perkin's mauve dye produced commercially.

The correct answer is *any of Perkin's original batch of mauve dye*.

2:

One of the two reasons the historian gives to doubt that the bottle contains any of Perkin's original batch of mauve dye is that the dye in the bottle is crystalline, unlike the earliest version of Perkin's mauve dye produced commercially.

The correct answer is *a crystalline form of the dye*.

139. When a user conducts a search of a certain library database, the database returns the results as a list of items (books, magazines, etc.) that match the search criteria. The user can select from two settings to establish a maximum number of items—either 12 or 24—to be displayed at a time. If the list contains more items than the established maximum, the list will be displayed on multiple pages, with each page (with the possible exception of the last page) containing the established maximum number of items and with each item in the list appearing on exactly one of the pages. The maximum established by the user does not affect the total number of items listed.

For the list of n items returned by a particular search of the database, the number of items, X, displayed on the last page when the established maximum is 12 is different from the number of items, Y, displayed on the last page when the established maximum is 24.

Select for X and for Y values that are jointly consistent with the information provided. Make only two selections, one in each column.

X	Y	
		1
		5
		7
		12
		17

Answer Explanation:

Infer

X:

Since X is the number of the n items left to be displayed on the last page when each previous page displayed exactly 12 items, X must be either 12 or the remainder of $n/12$. Similarly, Y must be either 24 or the remainder of $n/24$. Because 24 is 2×12, if $Y \neq X$, then $Y = X + 12$. We are told that $Y \neq X$. Thus, $Y = X + 12$. Among the five response options, only $X = 5$ and $Y = 17$ are such that $Y = X + 12$. That means $X = 5$, so 5 of the n items must be displayed on the last page when the established maximum is 12.

The correct answer is *5*.

Y:

As explained above, $Y = 17$. That is, 17 of the n items must be displayed on the last page when the established maximum is 24.

The correct answer is *17*.

140. In a group of 100 tourists visiting Scandinavia, 10% visited Norway, Sweden, and Denmark; 48% visited only two of these countries; 42% visited only one of these countries; and 100% visited at least one of these countries. Twenty-three tourists in the group visited at least Norway and Sweden, and 28 tourists in the group visited both Norway and Denmark. Furthermore, 3 tourists in the group visited only Denmark, and 32 tourists in the group visited only Sweden.

    In the table, select the number of tourists in the group who *visited at least Norway,* and select the number of tourists in the group who *visited at least Sweden.* Make only two selections, one in each column.

Visited at least Norway	Visited at least Sweden	
		40
		48
		54
		62
		68
		72

Answer Explanation:

Infer

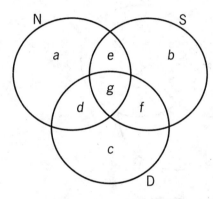

Consider the Venn diagram above with labels N, S, and D for Norway, Sweden, and Denmark, respectively, and variables a through g representing numbers of the 100 tourists visiting these countries.

Since 10% of the tourists visited Norway, Sweden, and Denmark, it follows that $g = 0.10(100) = 10$.

Also, 28 tourists in the group visited both Norway and Denmark, so $d + g = d + 10 = 28$, from which $d = 18$.

Furthermore, 23 tourists in the group visited at least Norway and Sweden, so $e + g = e + 10 = 23$, from which $e = 13$.

Since 32 tourists in the group visited only Sweden, $b = 32$.

It is given that 48% of the tourists or 0.48(100) = 48 visited only two of the countries, from which it follows that $d + e + f = 48$, so $18 + 13 + f = 48$, from which $f = 17$.

Given that 3 tourists in the group visited only Denmark, $c = 3$.

Given that 42% of the 100 tourists visited only one of these countries, $a + b + c = 0.42(100) = 42$, from which it follows that $a + 32 + 3 = 42$ and $a = 7$.

The Venn diagram below shows the values of a through g.

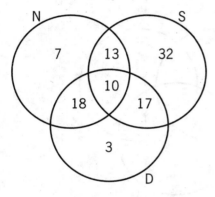

Visited at least Norway:

The number of the 100 tourists who visited at least Norway is $7 + 13 + 10 + 18 = 48$.

The correct answer is _48_.

Visited at least Sweden:

The number of the 100 tourists who visited at least Sweden is $13 + 32 + 17 + 10 = 72$.

The correct answer is _72_.

141. A city council member standing for reelection has been asked to rate how much she agrees or disagrees that various cultural establishments should receive more city funding. Expressing her overall views regarding budgeting priorities, she answers "Absolutely agree" for the art museum, "Somewhat agree" for the children's theater, "Neither agree nor disagree" for the historical society, "Somewhat disagree" for the symphony orchestra, and "Absolutely disagree" for the metropolitan ballet.

Suppose that the city council member's responses reflect genuine opinions that are logically consistent with her other opinions, and suppose that she believes that funding for any one of the institutions does not affect funding for any of the others. In the first column of the table, rate how much she most clearly agrees that *At least two* of the five institutions should receive more funding. In the second column, rate how much she most clearly agrees that *At most four* of the five institutions should receive more funding. Make only two selections, one in each column.

At least two	At most four	
		Absolutely agrees
		Somewhat agrees
		Neither agrees nor disagrees
		Somewhat disagrees
		Absolutely disagrees

Answer Explanation:

Infer

At least two:

The city council member gave a response of "Absolutely agree" for increased funding for the art museum and "Somewhat agree" for increased funding for the children's theater. Therefore, given the assumptions about her responses, opinions, and beliefs, the city council member clearly somewhat agrees that at least two of the five institutions should receive more funding. That is, there are at least two of the five institutions that it would be false to say that she disagrees or neither agrees nor disagrees with a claim that the institutions should receive increased funding. And, because there is only one institution that she absolutely agrees should receive increased funding, it would be unjustified to conclude that she absolutely agrees that there are two institutions that should receive more funding.

The correct answer is _Somewhat agrees_.

At most four:

Of the five institutions, there is only one that the city council member gave a response of "Absolutely disagree" for increased funding for, namely the metropolitan ballet. The other four she at most just somewhat disagrees with the idea of increasing funding for. Therefore, given the assumptions about her responses, opinions, and beliefs, the city council member clearly absolutely agrees that at most four of the five institutions should receive more funding. That is, she absolutely does not want all five to have increased funding because she absolutely does not want the metropolitan ballet to receive increased funding.

The correct answer is *Absolutely agrees*.

142. There are exactly three steps—Steps 1, 2, and 3, in that order—used to assemble light bulbs at a particular factory. Some of the bulbs fail to make it through every step in the assembly process; if a bulb fails a given step, it will not proceed to the next step. For the most recent month, the factory manager knows the number of bulbs that were started as well as each of the following:

A = the number of bulbs making it through Step 1 only;

B = the number of bulbs making it through at least Step 2;

C = the number of bulbs making it through all three steps.

The manager wishes to know the fraction of the bulbs that made it through Step 1 that also made it through all three steps. In the table, choose for *Numerator* and *Denominator* the expressions that will give the factory owner the fraction desired. Make only two selections, one in each column.

Numerator	Denominator	
		A
		B
		C
		A + B
		A − C
		B + C

Answer Explanation:

Infer

The fraction of the bulbs that made it through Step 1 (# through Step 1) that also made it through all three steps (# through Steps 1 – 3) is

$$\frac{(\#\text{through Step 1}-3)}{(\#\text{through Step 1})} = \frac{(\#\text{through Step 1}-3)}{(\#\text{ through Step 1 then failed}) + (\#\text{ through Step 1 and didn't fail})} =$$

$$\frac{(\#\text{through Step 1}-3)}{(\#\text{ through Step 1 then failed}) + (\#\text{ through at least Step 2})} = \frac{C}{(A+B)}$$

Numerator:

In the fraction above, the numerator is C.

The correct answer is *C*.

Denominator:

In the fraction above, the denominator is A + B.

The correct answer is *A + B*.

143. Legal advocate: The Métis people of Canada are of First Nations and European ancestry. The government grants certain special rights to Métis individuals. To receive these rights, an individual must self-identify as Métis and must not have self-identified only recently in order to receive these rights. The individual must also have Métis ancestry and be accepted as Métis by a modern Métis community. Acceptance by a modern Métis community is shown only by long-standing participation in the community's cultural or political activities.

In the table, select characteristics H and N, such that an individual having H and NOT having N would most clearly satisfy the legal advocate's stated criterion for receiving the rights associated with Métis membership. Make only two selections, one in each column.

H	N	
		Self-identifies as Métis due to long-standing Métis ancestry
		Self-identifies as Métis due to long-standing participation in Métis political activities
		Has recent ancestry that is Métis and participates in Métis political activities
		Has recent ancestry that is not Métis
		Has never participated in Métis political activities

Answer Explanation:

Apply

As a preliminary observation, note that the following three conditions must apply to obtain the special rights:

Self-identify as Métis (not recently)

Have Métis ancestry

Long-standing participation in Métis cultural or political activities

***H*:**

In what follows, possible pairings for H and N will be denoted as

(*Self-identifies as Métis due to long-standing participation in Métis political activities*, not *Has never participated in Métis political activities*),

(*Has recent ancestry that is not Métis*, not *Self-identifies as Métis due to long-standing Métis ancestry*), etc. where, for example, (*Self-identifies as Métis due to long-standing Métis ancestry*, not *Has never participated in Métis political activities*) means the selection of characteristic *Self-identifies as Métis due to long-standing Métis ancestry* for H and characteristic *Has never participated in Métis political activities* for N.

Only characteristics *Has recent ancestry that is not Métis* and *Has never participated in Métis political activities* are such that not having the characteristic could contribute toward receiving the rights, and therefore only characteristics *Has recent ancestry that is not Métis* and *Has never participated in Métis political activities* need to be considered as possibilities for N. Thus, only

(*Self-identifies as Métis due to long-standing Métis ancestry*, not *Has recent ancestry that is not Métis*),

(*Self-identifies as Métis due to long-standing participation in Métis political activities*, not *Has recent ancestry that is not Métis*),

(*Has recent ancestry that is Métis and participates in Métis political activities*, not *Has recent ancestry that is not Métis*),

(*Self-identifies as Métis due to long-standing Métis ancestry*, not *Has never participated in Métis political activities*),

(*Self-identifies as Métis due to long-standing participation in Métis political activities*, not *Has never participated in Métis political activities*), and

(*Has recent ancestry that is Métis and participates in Métis political activities*, not *Has never participated in Métis political activities*) need to be considered.

(Note: Below, weakly-(3) means participation in Métis cultural or political activities, but it is not known whether the participation is long-standing.)

(*Self-identifies as Métis due to long-standing Métis ancestry*, not *Has recent ancestry that is not Métis*) — the individual satisfies conditions (1) and (2).

(***Self-identifies as Métis due to long-standing participation in Métis political activities***, not *Has recent ancestry that is not Métis*) — **the individual satisfies conditions (1), (2), and (3).**

(*Has recent ancestry that is Métis and participates in Métis political activities*, not *Has recent ancestry that is not Métis*) — the individual satisfies conditions (2) and weakly-(3).

(*Self-identifies as Métis due to long-standing Métis ancestry*, not *Has never participated in Métis political activities*) — the individual satisfies conditions (1), (2), and weakly-(3).

(*Self-identifies as Métis due to long-standing participation in Métis political activities*, not *Has never participated in Métis political activities*) — the individual satisfies conditions (1) and (3).

(*Has recent ancestry that is Métis and participates in Métis political activities*, not *Has never participated in Métis political activities*) — the individual satisfies conditions (2) and weakly-(3).

From the above, it follows that the selection of characteristic *Self-identifies as Métis due to long-standing participation in Métis political activities* for *H* and characteristic *Has recent ancestry that is not Métis* for *N* most clearly satisfies the legal advocate's criterion.

The correct answer is *Self-identifies as Métis due to long-standing participation in Métis political activities*.

N:

The explanation above shows that the correct selection for *N* is characteristic *Has recent ancestry that is not Métis*.

The correct answer is *Has recent ancestry that is not Métis*.

144. Tickets for next month's production of *The Sea Gull* at the local community theater went on sale yesterday. The ticket price for a person older than 12 is $*A*, and the ticket price for a person 12 or under is $*C*, where *A* > *C*. Yesterday, the sale of 33 tickets

generated a total revenue of $323, and today the sale of 44 tickets generated a total revenue of $424.

In the table, select a value for *A* and a value for *C* that are jointly consistent with the given information. Make only two selections, one in each column.

A	C	
		6
		8
		10
		11
		12

Answer Explanation:

Infer

Note that 44 − 33 = 11 more tickets were sold today than yesterday and $424 − $323 = $101 more revenue was generated today than yesterday. If *a* represents the number of these 11 tickets that were adult tickets (i.e., tickets for those older than 12), then 11 − *a* represents the number of these 11 tickets that were child tickets (i.e., tickets for those 12 or under) and $aA + (11 − a)C = 101$ represents the revenue, in dollars, generated by the sale of these 11 tickets.

Note that at least one of *A* or *C* must be odd, because if both are even, then $aA + (11 − a)C$ is even and cannot be 101. Of the possible values of *A* and *C* in the answer choices, 11 is the only odd number. Therefore, *A* = 11 or *C* = 11. If *A* = 11, then the possible choices for *C* are 6, 8, and 10. Note that *C* ≠ 12 because *A* > *C*. If *C* = 11, then *A* = 12 because *A* > *C*.

If *A* = 11 and *C* = 6,

$aA + (11 − a)C = 101$	given
$11a + 6(11 − a) = 101$	substitution
$11a + 66 − 6a = 101$	distributive property
$5a + 66 = 101$	combine like terms
$5a = 35$	subtract 66 from both sides
$a = 7$	divide both sides by 5

This is a valid value for *a*.

If $A = 11$, and $C = 8$, then

$aA + (11 - a)C = 101$ given
$11a + 8(11 - a) = 101$ substitution
$11a + 88 - 8a = 101$ distributive property
$3a + 88 = 101$ combine like terms
$3a = 13$ subtract 88 from both sides
$a = 133$ divide both sides by 3

Since *a* must be a nonnegative integer, 133 is not a valid value for *a*.

If $A = 11$ and $C = 10$, then

$aA + (11 - a)C = 101$ given
$11a + 10(11 - a) = 101$ substitution
$11a + 110 - 10a = 101$ distributive property
$a + 110 = 101$ combine like terms
$a = -9$ subtract 110 from both sides

Since *a* must be a nonnegative integer, −9 is not a valid value for *a*.

If $A = 12$ and $C = 11$, then

$aA + (11 - a)C = 101$ given
$12a + 11(11 - a) = 101$ substitution
$12a + 121 - 11a = 101$ distributive property
$a + 121 = 101$ combine like terms
$a = -20$ subtract 121 from both sides

Since *a* must be a nonnegative integer, −20 is not a valid value for *a*.

A:

From the work above, letting $A = 11$ and $C = 6$ gives the only valid value for *a*.

The correct answer is *11*.

C:

From the work above, letting $A = 11$ and $C = 6$ gives the only valid value for *a*.

The correct answer is *6*.

Note that $A = 11$ and $C = 6$ are consistent with the given information. First, since $11 > 6$, $A > C$. Also, there exist numbers of adult and child tickets sold yesterday, namely 25 and 8, respectively, such that 33 tickets ($25 + 8 = 33$) were sold yesterday and they generated revenue of $(25)(11) + (8)(6) = 275 + 48 = 323$ dollars. Furthermore, there exist numbers of adult and child tickets sold today, namely 32 and 12, respectively, such that 44 tickets ($32 + 12 = 44$) were sold yesterday and they generated revenue of $(32)(11) + (12)(6) = 352 + 72 = 424$ dollars.

145. Companies A and B are part of the same industry and are located in the same city. For Company A, the average (arithmetic mean) salary of its employees, in United Arab Emirates dirhams (AED), is 10,000 AED higher than that for Company B. However, more than half of the employees at Company A have salaries below the average for Company B.

Statement: If the average salary at Company B is $\frac{1}{2}$, then the median salary at Company A is $\underline{\quad 2 \quad}$.

Select for *1* and for *2* the options that complete the statement so that it most accurately reflects the information provided. Make only two selections, one in each column.

1	2	
		greater than 100,000 AED
		less than 100,000 AED
		equal to 110,000 AED
		between 100,000 and 110,000 AED
		greater than 110,000 AED

Answer Explanation:

Infer

The statement that more than half of the employees at Company A have salaries below the average salary at Company B is equivalent to the median salary at Company A is less than the average salary at Company B.

Therefore, the information provided can be summarized as

(i) $a = 10,000 + b$ and

(ii) $m < b$,

where

a = average salary at Company A
b = average salary at Company B
m = median salary at Company A

1:

The statement asserts that if b satisfies a certain numerical condition, then m satisfies a certain (possibly different) numerical condition. Because this statement involves only b and m, it is reasonable to begin by considering (ii), which asserts that b is the larger of the two numbers b and m. Since knowing that the larger of two numbers is less than some given value implies that the smaller of the two numbers is also less than that given value, it follows that if b is less than 100,000, then m is less than 100,000. Moreover, if one is so inclined, it is not difficult to check that no other choice of options for *1* and *2* is necessarily true. Note that (i) is essentially irrelevant in selecting the options that complete the statement.

The correct answer is *less than 100,000 AED*.

2:

As shown above, the statement most accurately reflects the information provided for a certain choice of options in which the option for the second selection is the same as the option for the first selection.

The correct answer is *less than 100,000 AED*.

146. In comparing the results of a recent annual spring census to those of the previous year, biologists observed dramatic changes in the numbers of frogs of two species—Species X and Species Y—and an overall decrease in the combined number of frogs of these species. The biologists hypothesized that this decrease was caused by the unusually cold weather between the two censuses.

Select for *A* and for *B* the statements such that the biologists' hypothesis would have the most support if

A is true and B is false. Make only two selections, one in each column.

A	B	
		Species X is susceptible to unusually cold weather, whereas Species Y is not.
		Species X has a later mating season than does Species Y.
		Both Species X and Species Y are susceptible to similar contaminants.
		The number of Species X frogs decreased from the previous spring census.
		The number of Species Y frogs decreased from the previous spring census.

Answer Explanation:

Evaluate

Because the stem asks us to consider the likelihood of something occurring when A is true but B is false, we must consider both selections together.

A and B:

The biologists hypothesized that the decrease in the size between two censuses of the combined population of Species X and Species Y was caused by unusually cold weather between the two censuses. What would support this hypothesis? One possibility would be evidence that both Species X and Species Y are susceptible to unusually cold weather. Notice, however, that this is not one of the options to choose from. The closest option to this is the one stating "Species X is susceptible to unusually cold weather, whereas Species Y is not." This would support the hypothesis if, but only if, it is not the case that Species Y decreased between the two censuses and did so for some reason other than unusually cold weather. If that were the case, it could be that this other reason is what caused the combined population to decline between the two censuses and not unusually cold weather. Thus, the hypothesis would be supported if it were true that Species X is susceptible to unusually cold weather but Species Y is not while it is false that the number of Species Y frogs decreased from the previous spring census (in other words, the number of Species Y frogs either did not change or increased).

The correct answer for A is *Species X is susceptible to unusually cold weather, whereas Species Y is not.*

The correct answer for B is *The number of Species Y frogs decreased from the previous spring census.*

147. A certain company defines its *annual labor turnover rate* as the number of employees who left the company during the year divided by the average of the number of employees on the first day of the year and the number of employees on the last day of that year. Last year, the company had a labor turnover rate of exactly 25%.

Assuming that the information above is true, select for *Statement 1* and for *Statement 2* the statements such that if Statement 1 is true, then Statement 2 must be true, but it could be the case that Statement 2 is true and Statement 1 is false. Make only two selections, one in each column.

Statement 1	Statement 2	
		Last year, more people left the company than began work at the company.
		Exactly 25% of the employees working at the company on the first day of last year left the company last year.
		More than 25% of the employees working at the company on the first day of last year left the company last year.
		All and only those who were employees at the company on the first day of last year were employees on the last day of last year.
		Last year, the number of employees on the first day of the year was equal to the number of employees on the last day of the year.

Answer Explanation:

Evaluate

Note that because Statement 1 and Statement 2 must be chosen by determining whether a certain relationship between them holds—namely, that if Statement 1 is true, then Statement 2 must be true, but if Statement 2 is true, Statement 1 can be false—the two answer selections must be chosen together.

***Statement 1* and *Statement 2*:**

We are told that a certain company "defines its *annual labor turnover rate* as the number of employees who left the company during the year divided by the average of the number of employees on the first day of the year and the number of employees on the last day of that year." We are also told that the labor turnover rate last year was 25%. To answer this question correctly, you must find two statements such that if one of them (Statement 1) is true, then the other (Statement 2) must be true, but the reverse may not hold (i.e., if Statement 2 is true, Statement 1 can be false). Consider the fourth answer choice, "All and only those who were employees at the company on the first day of last year were employees on the last day of last year." If that is true, that means that last year, the number of employees on the first day of the year was equal to the number of employees on the last day of the year. Notice that that is what the fifth answer choice says. So, the fourth and fifth answer choices are likely candidates for the answer. (Note that it may seem odd that the company would have exactly the same employees on the first and last day of the year, given that the company had a 25% annual turnover rate. But that turnover rate might occur if, for instance, the company hired some workers during the year for a short-term project, and all those workers who were hired at some point after the first day were no longer employed there on the last day.) So, we've seen that if the fourth answer choice is true, the fifth answer choice must also be true. But does the fourth have to be true if the fifth is? No, because some people who were employees on the first of the year could have left during the year, and an equal number of employees were hired to replace them, all of whom remained employees on the last day of the year. That would result in the first and last days of the year having an equal number of employees, though not all the employees on the first day were employees on the last day.

The correct answer for Statement 1 is *All and only those who were employees at the company on the first day of last year were employees on the last day of last year*.

The correct answer for Statement 2 is *Last year, the number of employees on the first day was equal to the number of employees on the last day of the year*.

148. Newspaper editor: Published photojournalism must always present the events covered without distorting those events. Sometimes an image distorts the events a photojournalist attempts to capture, such as when the photojournalist has an equipment failure. In such cases, photojournalists are permitted to make minimal changes to an image, but only to the extent that (1) they are certain about what they observed, and (2) those changes reduce the distortion. Photojournalists' photos are often compelling works of art as well as documents of newsworthy events. However, for publication as journalism, a photo's aesthetic features are allowed to be considered only after the photo is shown to accurately portray relevant features of the event it depicts. In accordance with these criteria, in our journalistic coverage of Event E, we elected to publish photograph P1 rather than photograph P2.

Statement: Assuming the editor's statements are true, if _____1_____, then it must be the case that _____2_____.

Select for *1* and for *2* the two different options that create the statement that is most strongly supported by the information provided. Make only two selections, one in each column.

1	2	
		P1 was altered
		P2 was altered
		P1 and P2 were taken with malfunctioning equipment
		P1 was chosen over P2 at least in part for its aesthetic features
		both P1 and P2 accurately portray the relevant features of Event E

Answer Explanation:

Apply

Note that because the two responses are related to each other (they are both parts of a single conditional statement), the correct selections must be chosen together.

1 **and** *2*:

The newspaper editor's statements discuss a condition that must be met for photojournalism to be published—namely, the photos must accurately present the events without distorting the events—and when photojournalists are allowed to make changes to a photo—namely, when the photojournalists are certain about what they observed and the changes reduce the distortion. Some of the possible answer choices for this question might seem promising in light of these conditions expressed by the editor, but in each case, there isn't another appropriate answer choice to pair with it when based on those statements from the editor. For instance, the first answer choice, "P1 was altered," could be the answer for *1* if another answer choice was "The alteration of P1 reduced the distortion," but that is not an available answer choice. Instead, the correct answer choices to this question are based on another condition expressed by the editor, namely that a photo's aesthetic features can be considered only after determining that the photo accurately portrays the relevant features of the event it captures. This suggests that the fourth and fifth answer choices are good candidates as answers for *1* and *2*. If P1 was chosen for publication over P2, and that choice was based at least in part on P1's aesthetic features, then it must be that both P1 and P2 accurately portray the relevant features of Event E because to be published at all, P1 must accurately portray those features, and if P2 didn't accurately portray them as well, then the aesthetic features of P1 wouldn't have been relevant in choosing between P1 and P2 because P2 simply could not be published.

The correct answer for 1 is *P1 was chosen over P2 at least in part for its aesthetic features*.

The correct answer for 2 is *both P1 and P2 accurately portray the relevant features of Event E*.

149. A stock trader working for a hedge fund has estimated that the stock of a certain company has probability 0.4 of increasing in price by at least 5 dollars during a certain trading day and probability 0.1 of increasing in price by at least 10 dollars during the trading day.

    Based on the trader's estimates, select for *X* and for *Y* the options such that the following statement is most accurate. Make only two selections, one in each column.

    If the trader multiplies ____X____ by the reciprocal of ____Y____, then the result is the probability that the price of the stock will increase by at least 10 dollars during the trading day, given that the price increases by at least 5 dollars during the trading day.

X	Y	
		0.1
		0.4
		0.1 divided by 0.4
		the reciprocal of 0.1
		the product of 0.1 and 0.4

Answer Explanation:

Strategize

Let Event *A* be "the stock increases in price by at least 5 dollars on a certain day," and let Event *B* be "the stock increases in price by at least 10 dollars on that day." The probability of *B* given

A is $\dfrac{\text{(the probability of A and B.)}}{\text{(the probability of A)}}$.

The probability of *A* is given as 0.4. The probability of *A* and *B* is the same as the probability of *B* because Event *A* is contained in Event B (i.e., if the stock increased in price by at least $10, then the price certainly increased by at least $5). Therefore, the probability of *A* and *B* is the same as the probability of *B*, which is 0.1.

X:

The correct answer is *0.1*.

Y:

Because dividing by a number is equivalent to multiplying by the reciprocal of that number, the probability of *A* and *B* divided by the probability of *A* is equivalent to the probability of *A* and *B* multiplied by the reciprocal of the probability of *A*.

The correct answer is *0.4*.

150. Throughout a certain decade in a European city, the mean monthly rents for studio apartments varied yearly, from a low of €804 to a high of €1,173. Those for one-bedroom apartments also varied yearly, from a low of €1,060 to a high of €1,497. But some individual studio apartments rented for as little as €420 in some years, and some one-bedroom apartments rented for up to €2,262. To visually assess how the ratio of mean monthly rents for studio apartments to those for one-bedroom apartments varied yearly over the decade, Maria requires a graph with the following characteristics. The graph will have two axes of equal length, with mean rents for one-bedroom apartments shown on the horizontal axis and mean rents for studio apartments shown on the vertical axis, and with the same scale on both axes. For each year, mean rents will be plotted as a point.

    From the following options, select for *Horizontal axis* a range for the points on the horizontal axis and select for *Vertical axis* a range for the points on the vertical axis that together would satisfy Maria's requirements for the graph. Make only two selections, one in each column.

Horizontal axis	Vertical axis	
		€0 to €1,500
		€400 to €1,100
		€800 to €1,200
		€1,000 to €2,300
		€1,100 to €1,500

Answer Explanation:

Strategize

Because both axes must be the same length and have the same scale, the range for both axes must start low enough to accommodate €804 and go high enough to accommodate €1,497. The range €0 to €1,500 accommodates both the low of €804 and the high of €1,497. Neither of the ranges

€400 to €1,100 and €800 to €1,200 goes high enough to accommodate €1,497, and neither of the ranges €1,000 to €2,300 and €1,100 to €1,500 goes low enough to accommodate €804.

Horizontal axis:

The correct answer is *€0 to €1,500*.

Vertical axis:

The correct answer is *€0 to €1,500*.

151. A statistician reached the following conclusions about games between university soccer teams: Overall, a team playing on its home field has a 45% chance of a win, a 25% chance of a loss, and a 30% chance of a draw (a tied outcome). In the games where one or more goals are scored, the team that scores the first goal has a 55% chance of scoring it in the game's first half and a 45% chance of scoring it later in the game. When that team is the home team (i.e., a team playing on its home field), there is a 40% chance that the other team will score no goals at all, and therefore a 60% chance that it will score one or more goals.

Select for *X* and for *Y* two different outcomes such that the information provided explicitly includes the statistician's estimates of the probability that if X occurs, so will Y. Make only two selections, one in each column.

X	Y	
		The home team scores at least two goals in the game.
		The home team scores the first goal.
		A goal is scored in the first half of the game.
		A goal is scored in the second half of the game.
		The team opposing the home team scores at least one goal.

Answer Explanation:

Recognize

The key information for determining outcomes X and Y such that if X occurs, then so does Y is "When that team (where 'that team' refers to the team that scores the first goal) is the home team

..., there is ... a 60% chance that it (where 'it' refers to the other team) will score one or more goals." Therefore, from the given information, if the home team scores the first goal, the statistician's estimate of the probability that the team opposing the home team scores at least one goal is 0.6.

X:

The correct answer is *The home team scores the first goal*.

Y:

The correct answer is *The team opposing the home team scores at least one goal*.

152. To ensure computer security, a firm has rules about access of managerial and nonmanagerial employees to various networked computer drives. In accordance with the rules, some but not all nonmanagerial employees are allowed access to both Drive B and Drive D. Some are required to have such access. Every nonmanagerial employee must have access to at least one of Drive B and Drive D. No nonmanagerial employee is allowed to have access to both Drive B and Drive E. The rules do not restrict the access of managerial employees to any of the drives mentioned.

From the following statements about computer security practices in relation to the firm's employees, select for *Required* the statement that, based on the information provided, describes a practice that is required by the rules, and select for *Permitted* the statement that describes a practice that is permitted, but NOT required, by the rules. Make only two selections, one in each column.

Required	Permitted	
		At least one nonmanagerial employee is currently not allowed access to any of the three drives B, D, and E.
		Managerial employees, and only those, are currently allowed access to Drive E.
		The nonmanagerial employees who are currently allowed access to Drive D are also allowed access to Drive E.

		The managerial and nonmanagerial employees who are currently allowed access to Drive B are also allowed access to Drive E.
		Any nonmanagerial employees currently allowed access to Drive E are also allowed access to Drive D.

Answer Explanation:

Infer

Required:

Since each nonmanagerial employee is allowed access to Drive B or Drive D, regardless of whether the employee is allowed access to Drive E, it follows that each nonmanagerial employee who is allowed access to Drive E is allowed access to Drive B or Drive D. Because no nonmanagerial employee is allowed access to both Drive B and Drive E, it follows that each nonmanagerial employee who is allowed access to Drive E is also allowed access to Drive D.

The correct answer is *Any nonmanagerial employees currently allowed access to Drive E are also allowed access to Drive D.*

Permitted:

The rules do not restrict access to Drive E by managerial employees, so managerial employees are allowed access to Drive E. While the rules include a provision regarding access to Drive E by nonmanagerial employees, none of the rules requires that there exists a nonmanagerial employee who is allowed access to Drive E.

The correct answer is *Managerial employees, and only those, are currently allowed access to Drive E.*

153. Giulia is planning to sell her car, which is fueled by gasoline (petrol) and averages 20 miles per gallon (mpg), and purchase a diesel-fueled car that averages 30 mpg. She estimates that her future cost per gallon of diesel fuel will be 5% higher than her present cost per gallon of gasoline. She wishes to estimate (1) the annual cost of fuel for her new car if she maintains her present annual total miles driven and (2) the annual total miles she can drive her new car if she maintains her present annual expenditure on fuel.

Let x represent Giulia's present annual cost per gallon of gasoline in US dollars, and let y equal her present annual total of miles driven. Select for *Cost* an appropriate expression for Giulia's estimate of (1) above, and select for *Miles* an appropriate expression for her estimate of (2) above. Make only two selections, one in each column.

Cost	Miles	
		$\frac{2}{3}(1.05x)$
		$\frac{3}{2}\left(\frac{y}{1.05}\right)$
		$\frac{3}{2}(1.05y)$
		$\frac{1.05xy}{30}$
		$\frac{1.05xy}{20}$
		$\frac{20xy}{1.05}$

Answer Explanation:

Strategize

Cost:

The annual cost of fuel for her new car is (price per gallon)(number of gallons per year).

For her new car, the price of fuel per gallon will be 5% greater than the price of fuel per gallon for her present car. Given that x represents the price of fuel per gallon for her present car, the price of fuel per gallon for her new car is represented by $1.05x$.

If her new car averages 30 miles per gallon of fuel and she drives y miles annually, she will use $\frac{y}{30}$ gallons of fuel per year. Thus, the annual cost of fuel for her new car is represented by $1.05x\left(\frac{y}{30}\right)$.

The correct answer is $\frac{1.05xy}{30}$.

Miles:

Her present annual expenditure on fuel is $x\dfrac{y}{20} = \dfrac{xy}{20}$. If T represents the total miles she can drive her new car while maintaining her present annual expenditure on fuel, then $(1.05x)\left(\dfrac{T}{30}\right) = \dfrac{xy}{20}$, from which it follows that $T = \left(\dfrac{30}{1.05x}\right)\left(\dfrac{xy}{20}\right) = \dfrac{3}{2}\left(\dfrac{y}{1.05}\right)$.

The correct answer is $\dfrac{3}{2}\left(\dfrac{y}{1.05}\right)$.

154. Each of three botanists made a hypothesis regarding specimens of a particular plant species:

     Botanist 1: Any individual specimen possessing the gene for curly stems has either the gene for long roots or the gene for purple flowers, or both.

     Botanist 2: Any individual specimen possessing the gene for long roots has either the gene for flat leaves or the gene for round seeds, or both.

     Botanist 3: No individual specimen that possesses either the gene for curly stems or the gene for flat leaves or both has the gene for purple flowers.

     The discovery of an individual specimen of the plant species in question having the gene for ___1___ but NOT the gene for ___2___ would show that at least one of the three hypotheses described is incorrect.

     Select for 1 and for 2 the characteristics that would most accurately complete the statement, based on the information given. Make only two selections, one in each column.

1	2	
		curly stems
		flat leaves
		long roots
		purple flowers
		round seeds

Answer Explanation:

Apply

1:

If an individual specimen had the gene for curly stems and not the gene for long roots, then the hypothesis of Botanist 1 implies that the specimen would have the gene for purple flowers, and hence, by the hypothesis of Botanist 3, the specimen would not have the gene for curly stems (and also would not have the gene for flat leaves), which contradicts the fact that the specimen has the gene for curly stems. Therefore, such a specimen would show that at least one of the three hypotheses is incorrect. More precisely, such a specimen would show that at least one of the hypotheses of Botanist 1 and Botanist 3 is incorrect.

The correct answer is *curly stems*.

2:

As shown in the explanation above, the specimen having the gene for curly stems and not having the gene for long roots would show that at least one of the three hypotheses is incorrect.

The correct answer is *long roots*.

155. An inventory of a neighborhood's trees found that 32 percent were conifers and most of the rest were deciduous. Among the conifers were 258 spruces and 112 pines, along with some cedars and other species. Most of the deciduous trees were oaks, but one in eight was a maple. Of the oaks, 65 percent were red oaks and 25 percent were white oaks. Of the maples, 20 percent were Japanese maples.

     Select for A and for B two types of trees such that the ratio of the number of trees of the type selected for A to the number of trees of the type selected for B can be determined and is less than 1. Make only two selections, one in each column.

A	B	
		cedars
		conifers
		deciduous trees
		Japanese maples
		red oaks
		spruces

Answer Explanation:

Apply

Let T, C, D, O, M, and J be, respectively, the total number of trees in the neighborhood, the number of conifers, the number of deciduous trees, the number of oak trees, the number of maple trees, and the number of Japanese maple trees. It is given that $C = 0.32T$, $D > 0.50(1 - 0.32T)$ since "most of the rest were deciduous," and $O > 0.50D$ since "most of the deciduous trees were oaks." Also, it is given that $M = \frac{1}{8}D$ and $J = 0.20M$. It follows that $J = 0.20\left(\frac{1}{8}D\right) = \frac{1}{40}D$. Therefore, $JD = \frac{1}{40}$ and $\frac{1}{40} < 1$.

A:

From the explanation above, the ratio $\dfrac{\text{Japanese}}{\text{deciduous}}$ can be determined and is less than 1.

The correct answer is *Japanese*.

B:

From the explanation above, the ratio $\dfrac{\text{Japanese}}{\text{deciduous}}$ can be determined and is less than 1.

The correct answer is *deciduous*.

Alternatively, using the answer choices, cedars can be eliminated since "some cedars" doesn't give any precise amount to determine a ratio with any of the other answer choices. Although conifers make up 32 percent of all the trees in the neighborhood and there are 258 spruces, this information is not specific enough to determine a ratio with conifers and spruces. Since there is no information to determine a ratio between spruces and any of the other answer choices, spruces can

be eliminated from further consideration. There is also no information to pair deciduous trees, which include Japanese maples and red oaks, with conifers. Thus, conifers can be eliminated from further consideration. Of the three answer choices remaining—deciduous trees, Japanese maples, and red oaks—there is insufficient information to determine a ratio between red oaks and deciduous trees because, even though red oaks comprise 65 percent of all oaks, there is no information as to how many oaks or how many deciduous trees are in the neighborhood. This leaves Japanese maples, which comprise 20 percent of the maples, and deciduous trees, one out of eight of which is a maple. Thus, Japanese maples = 0.2(maples) = $0.2\left(\frac{1}{8}\text{ deciduous}\right) = \frac{1}{40}$ deciduous. It follows that $\dfrac{\text{Japanese maples}}{\text{deciduous trees}} = \frac{1}{40}$ and $\frac{1}{40} < 1$.

156. A manufacturing company plans to begin automating production and reducing its workforce by installing industrial robots at the start of each year over five years. Each robot will result in annual labor-cost savings of €150,000 beginning with the year of its installation and will have an up-front cost of €400,000. For robot installation in Year 1 of the program, the company will budget €600,000, plus the total amount of labor costs that will be saved by robotic production in that year. The robot-installation budget for each subsequent year will consist of the total amount of labor costs that will be saved by robotic production in that year plus any money left over from the previous year's robot-installation budget.

Statement: Within budget constraints, the maximum number of robots that can be installed in Year 1 of the program is ___X___, and the maximum number of robots that can be in service in Year 3 is ___Y___.

Select values for *X* and for *Y* that create the statement that follows logically from the information provided. Make only two selections, one in each column.

X	Y	
		2
		3
		4
		5
		6
		7

Answer Explanation:

Apply

Let x be the number of robots that can be installed in Year 1. Then

$$600,000 + 150,000x \geq 400,000x$$
$$600,000 \geq 250,000x$$
$$\frac{600,000}{250,000} \geq x$$
$$2.4 \geq x$$

The maximum number of robots that can be installed in Year 1 is 2. The budget remaining to be carried over to Year 2 is $600,000 + 2(150,000) - 2(400,000) = 100,000$.

Assuming that at the beginning of Year 2 there are 2 robots working, let t be the number of robots that can be installed in Year 2. Then

$$100,000 + 2(150,000) + 150,000t \geq 400,000t$$
$$400,000 \geq 250,000t$$
$$\frac{400,000}{250,000} \geq t$$
$$1.6 \geq t$$

The maximum number of robots that can be installed in Year 2 is 1. The budget remaining to be carried over to Year 3 is $100,000 + 3(150,000) - 400,000 = 150,000$.

Assuming that at the beginning of Year 3 there are $2 + 1 = 3$ robots working, let y be the number of robots that can be installed in Year 3. Then

$$150,000 + 3(150,000) + 150,000y \geq 400,000y$$
$$600,000 \geq 250,000y$$
$$\frac{600,000}{250,000} \geq y$$
$$2.4 \geq y$$

The maximum number of robots that can be installed in Year 3 is 2.

X:

From the explanation above, the maximum number of robots that can be installed in Year 1 is 2.

The correct answer is 2.

Y:

From the explanation above, the maximum numbers of robots that can be installed in Years 1, 2, and 3, respectively, are 2, 1, and 2. The maximum number of robots that can be in service in Year 3 is $2 + 1 + 2 = 5$.

The correct answer is 5.

157. While designing a game involving chance, Desmond noticed that the probability a fair coin lands face up exactly 2 times when the coin is tossed 3 times is equal to the probability that a fair coin lands face up exactly m times when the coin is tossed n times, where $n > 3$.

Select for m and for n values consistent with the given information. Make only two selections, one in each column.

m	n	
		1
		2
		3
		4
		5
		6

Answer Explanation:

Infer

m:

If a coin is tossed 3 times and each toss can land only one of face up (U) or face down (D), then there are 3 possible outcomes where the coin lands face up exactly 2 times: UUD, UDU, and DUU. Here the notation is such that UDU, for example, means the coin landed face up, face down, and face up for the first, second, and third tosses, respectively. Since the coin is fair, for each toss, the probability of landing face up is $\frac{1}{2}$ and the probability of landing face down is $\frac{1}{2}$. Therefore, the probability of each of the possibilities UUD, UDU, and DUU is $\left(\frac{1}{2}\right)\left(\frac{1}{2}\right)\left(\frac{1}{2}\right) = \left(\frac{1}{2}\right)^3$, and the probability that one of these three possibilities occurs is $3 \cdot \left(\frac{1}{2}\right)^3 = 38$.

If the coin is tossed 4 times (i.e., $n = 4$), then the probability of each of the possibilities UUUU, UUUD, UUDU,…, UDDU, and so on is $\left(\frac{1}{2}\right)\left(\frac{1}{2}\right)\left(\frac{1}{2}\right)\left(\frac{1}{2}\right) = \left(\frac{1}{2}\right)^4$, and the probability that the coin lands face up exactly m times for $m = 0, 1, 2, 3,$ and 4 is given in the following table.

m = number of times face up	possible outcomes	number of possible outcomes	probability
0	DDDD	1	$1 \cdot \left(\frac{1}{2}\right)^4$
1	DDDU, DDUD, DUDD, UDDD	4	$4 \cdot \left(\frac{1}{2}\right)^4$
2	DDUU, DUDU, DUUD, UUDD, UDUD, UDDU	6	$6 \cdot \left(\frac{1}{2}\right)^4$
3	UUUD, UUDU, UDUU, DUUU	4	$4 \cdot \left(\frac{1}{2}\right)^4$
4	UUUU	1	$1 \cdot (12)4$

Since $6 \cdot \left(\frac{1}{2}\right)^4 = \frac{3}{8}$, the correct selection of values is $m = 2$ and $n = 4$.

The correct answer is *2*.

n:

The explanation above shows that $n = 4$ for the correct selection of values of m and n.

The correct answer is *4*.

158. Linguist: Plosives and fricatives are two classes of consonants. A "voicing contrast" is a distinction between two consonants that are identical except that one is voiced and the other is unvoiced. In language family X, languages with voicing contrasts in their fricatives always have voicing contrasts in their plosives. This means that in that family, any given language has a voicing contrast in its fricatives _____ it has a voicing contrast in its plosives. In other words, a given language in that family lacks any voicing contrasts in its plosives _____ it lacks any such contrasts in its fricatives.

Select for *First blank* the word or phrase that most logically completes the statement with the first blank. And select for *Second blank* the word or phrase that most logically completes the statement with the second blank. Make only two selections, one in each column.

First blank	Second blank	
		and
		if
		only if
		or
		unless

Answer Explanation:

Recognize

First blank:

Letting P denote "has a voicing contrast in its fricatives" and Q denote "has a voicing contrast in its plosives," then the first identified sentence states that given P, we have Q, or "if P, then Q," which is logically equivalent to "P only if Q."

The correct answer is *only if*.

Second blank:

Letting P and Q be as above, we are to put the second identified sentence into the form "not-Q _____ not-P." Since the contrapositive of the first identified sentence is "if not-Q, then not-P," which is logically equivalent to the first identified sentence, it follows that a logically equivalent restatement of the first identified sentence is "not-Q only if not-P."

The correct answer is *only if*.

159. At a certain university, there is a strong positive correlation between the time of day at which university classes are offered and the classes' average (arithmetic mean) grades, with earlier times associated with lower grades. However, for the classes offered at the earliest time but not for any other classes, there was a strong negative correlation between the grades of students in those classes and the number of scheduled classes they missed. In fact, when the grades of students who missed at least 5 scheduled classes were excluded, classes offered at the earliest time more often than not had significantly higher average grades than classes offered at any other time.

Consider the following statement:

At the university in question, classes offered at earlier times ___1___ lower average grades than classes offered later in the day, but when the grades of students who missed at least 5 scheduled classes were excluded, classes offered at the earliest time ___2___ higher average grades than classes offered later in the day.

Select for *1* and for *2* the options that complete the sentence so that it most accurately summarizes the information provided. Make only two selections, one in each column.

1	2	
		tended to have
		tended not to have
		almost always had
		seldom, if ever, had
		possibly had

Answer Explanation:

Recognize

1:

Because there is a strong positive correlation between the time of day and class average, earlier times tend to correspond to lower class averages. Thus, it is clear that none of the second, fourth, or fifth answer choices correctly completes the sentence. Also, the following argument shows that the use of the third answer choice less accurately summarizes the information provided than the use of the first answer choice. To see that the third answer choice may not accurately convey that there is a strong positive correlation between time of day and class average, note that a strong positive correlation can exist between two equal-sized collections of data values without almost all of the data values in one collection being in the same numerical order as the corresponding data values in the other collection. This can occur, for example, when relatively few of the data values in each collection are extremes and have the same corresponding order and relatively many of the data values in each collection are nearly equal and have the opposite corresponding order.

The correct answer is *tended to have*.

2:

According to the information provided, when grades of students who missed at least 5 scheduled classes are excluded, there is a strong negative correlation between the grades for classes offered at the earliest time and grades for classes offered at later times. Therefore, with this exclusion, grades for the earliest time tend to be higher than grades for later times. Thus, it is clear that none of the second, fourth, or fifth answer choices correctly completes the sentence. Also, an argument similar to that given above shows that the use of the third answer choice less accurately summarizes the information provided than the use of the first answer choice.

The correct answer is *tended to have*.

160. Each Monday through Friday (a *workweek*), Avinash will bring either exactly one apple or exactly one banana with him to his workplace for an afternoon snack. To avoid having to decide which to bring, each morning Avinash will toss a coin with a face on exactly one side that is equally likely to land face up or face down. If the coin lands face up, then he will bring an apple, and if the coin lands face down, then he will bring a banana. Avinash correctly determined the probability that, for a given workweek, either he would bring an apple on at least 4 consecutive days or he would bring a banana on at least 4 consecutive days. This probability was *m* divided by *n*.

Select for *m* and for *n* values jointly consistent with the given information. Make only two selections, one in each column.

m	n	
		4
		6
		8
		12
		20
		32

Answer Explanation:

Infer

m:

In a given workweek, Avinash will toss the coin 5 times. There are 6 possible outcomes from tossing the coin 5 times that result in Avinash bringing an apple on at least 4 consecutive days or bringing a banana on at least 4 consecutive days: UUUUD, DUUUU, UUUUU, DDDDU, UDDDD, and DDDDD. Here the notation is such that DDDDU, for example, means the coin landed face down from Monday through Thursday and face up on Friday. Since the coin is equally likely to land face up or face down, for each of the 5 days in the workweek, the probability is $\frac{1}{2}$ that Avinash will bring an apple, and the probability is $\frac{1}{2}$ that Avinash will bring a banana. Therefore, the probability of each of these

possibilities is $\left(\frac{1}{2}\right)\left(\frac{1}{2}\right)\left(\frac{1}{2}\right)\left(\frac{1}{2}\right)\left(\frac{1}{2}\right) = \left(\frac{1}{2}\right)^5$, and the probability that one of these 6 possibilities occurs is $6 \cdot \left(\frac{1}{2}\right)^5 = \frac{6}{32}$. The correct selection of values is *m* = 6 and *n* = 32.

The correct answer is *6*.

n:

The explanation above shows that *n* = 32 for the correct selection of values of *m* and *n*.

The correct answer is *32*.

161. Philosophy student: Some objects that are considered beautiful by everyone who has observed them may not be, in fact, truly beautiful. To see that this is so, consider this: No one doubts that some objects that are appreciated by many people have aesthetic flaws that are discernible only to sophisticated observers. But even these sophisticated observers are limited by their finite intellects and experiences. Thus, an object that appears beautiful to the most sophisticated actual observers may nonetheless have subtle but severe aesthetic shortcomings that would make it appear hideous to hypothetical observers of even greater sophistication. Such an object would be ugly, regardless of any actual person's opinion.

In general, if an object ____1____, then that object ____2____.

Select for *1* and for *2* the two different options that complete the sentence in such a way that it expresses a principle on which the philosophy student's argument relies. Make only two selections, one in each column.

1	2	
		is considered beautiful by everyone
		is thought by most observers to have some aesthetic flaws
		would appear hideous to hypothetical observers of even greater sophistication than the most sophisticated actual observers
		is not truly beautiful
		is not widely appreciated by unsophisticated observers

Answer Explanation:

Evaluate

The philosophy student's argument is based on extrapolating from a claim that the student asserts everyone agrees with, namely, that there are art objects that many people appreciate but that have aesthetic flaws that only more sophisticated observers can discern. The student notes that even the most sophisticated observers have finite intellects and experiences.

The student then suggests that because of this, there may be art objects that sophisticated viewers appreciate but nonetheless have aesthetic flaws that a hypothetical even-more-sophisticated observer might discern and, as a result, would find the art object ugly. The student draws the conclusion that such an object would in fact be ugly, even if no actual person discerns the flaw.

Finally, the student infers from all this that some objects that everyone considers beautiful may not be truly beautiful. To answer this question correctly, we must construct a sentence that expresses a principle that underlies the student's argument.

Note that the student's argument moves from an assertion about hypothetic observers with greater sophistication than any actual observers who find an art object hideous to a claim about art objects that may not truly be beautiful even though all actual observers think the object is beautiful. The student must be assuming that there is a link between hypothetical sophisticated viewers finding an object hideous and the object not being truly beautiful.

Therefore, the student's argument seems to rely on the principle that, in general, if an object would appear hideous to hypothetical observers of even greater sophistication than the most sophisticated actual observers, then that object is not truly beautiful.

1:

The correct answer is *would appear hideous to hypothetical observers of even greater sophistication than the most sophisticated actual observers.*

2:

The correct answer is *not truly beautiful.*

162. The following statements describe certain characteristics of a certain pool of candidates for a position. Any candidate who did not meet the minimum qualifications for the position was immediately excluded from consideration. The two candidates who met the minimum qualifications for the position and met all of the desired qualifications also had multiple recommendations. All candidates who received a telephone interview also had extensive experience. All candidates who had extensive experience and impressed the hiring committee during the telephone interview were invited to interview on-site. At least one candidate declined an invitation for an on-site interview, and exactly one candidate was interviewed on-site without receiving a telephone interview.

Consider the following incomplete sentence:

If any candidate _____1_____, then that candidate _____2_____.

Select for *1* and for *2* two different options that best complete the sentence such that it can be logically inferred from the information provided. Make only two selections, one in each column.

1	2	
		did not meet the minimum qualifications
		had multiple recommendations
		had extensive experience
		impressed the hiring committee during the telephone interview
		interviewed on-site

Answer Explanation:

Infer

If any candidate impressed the hiring committee during the telephone interview, then it follows that the candidate had a telephone interview, and hence (directly by one of the statements) the candidate had extensive experience. Therefore, if any candidate impressed the hiring committee during the telephone interview, then that candidate had extensive experience.

1:

The correct answer is *impressed the hiring committee during the telephone interview.*

2:

The correct answer is *had extensive experience.*

163. On a 12-hour analog clock, the hour hand moves at a constant rate of 1 revolution every 12 hours, and the minute hand moves at a constant rate of 1 revolution every hour. The hands are perpendicular at 3:00 in the morning. To the nearest second, the next time they are superimposed (i.e., both pointing at the same point on the outer rim of the clock face) is *M* minutes and *S* seconds after 3:00 in the morning.

Select for *M* and for *S* values that are consistent with the information provided. Make only two selections, one in each column.

M	S	
		15
		16
		17
		20
		22
		34

Answer Explanation:

Infer

M:

For convenience, label the points on the outer rim of the clock by "rim-minutes" (rm), where, for example, the point corresponding to 1:00 is 5 rm, the point corresponding to 2:00 is 10 rm, the point corresponding to 3:00 corresponds to 15 rm, and so on. Let t denote the number of minutes of time after 3:00 when the minute hand and hour hand are next superimposed. In t minutes after 3:00, the minute hand, which was initially pointing at 0 rm and travels at a rate of 1 rm/min, will be pointing at $(t \text{ min})(1 \text{ rm/min}) + 0$ rm = t rm. Also, in t minutes after 3:00, the hour

hand, which was initially pointing at 15 rm and travels at a rate that is $\frac{1}{12}$ the rate of the minute hand (i.e., travels at a rate of 112 rm/min), will be pointing at $(t \text{ min})\left(\frac{1}{12} \text{ rm/min}\right) + 15$ rm = $\left(\frac{1}{12}t + 15\right)$ rm. Since the minute hand and the hour hand will be pointing at the same point on the rim t minutes after 3:00, it follows that $t = \frac{1}{12}t + 15$, or $t = \frac{180}{11} \approx 16.36$ min. Therefore, the desired time is 16 minutes and a certain number (less than 60) of seconds.

The correct answer is *16*.

S:

Because $\frac{180}{11} = 16 + \frac{4}{11}$, and $\frac{4}{11}$ minutes equals $60\left(\frac{4}{11}\right) \approx 21.818$ seconds, to the nearest second the desired time after 3:00 is 16 minutes and 22 seconds.

The correct answer is *22*.

164. The following argument is logically flawed. The author's goal was to craft the argument so that the conclusion follows logically from Premises 1 and 2 and so that both premises are necessary to draw the conclusion.

Premise 1: Every respondent to our survey who **reported feeling satisfied** also reported being in a good mood.

Premise 2: Every respondent to our survey who **reported having a central goal** also **reported being in a good mood**.

Conclusion: Therefore, assuming all of the reports were accurate and complete, every respondent to our survey who **felt satisfied** also **had a central goal**.

Select for *Boldface A* and for *Boldface B* two of the boldfaced phrases in the argument such that Boldface A occurs earlier in the argument than Boldface B, and exchanging the positions of those two phrases in the argument would make it so the argument fulfills the author's goal. Make only two selections, one in each column.

Boldface A	Boldface B	
		reported feeling satisfied
		reported having a central goal
		reported being in a good mood
		felt satisfied
		had a central goal

Answer Explanation:

Strategize

A simple example involving only two respondents can be used to show the original argument is logically flawed. Assume only Respondent X felt satisfied, only Respondent Y had a central goal, and only Respondents X and Y were in a good mood. In this example, the two original premises are true, but the conclusion is false because Respondent X felt satisfied and did not have a central goal.

If the positions of the second and third boldfaced phrases are exchanged, then the revised argument is the following, in which the conclusion logically follows from both premises and both premises are necessary.

Premise 1: Every respondent **feeling satisfied** was in a **good mood.**
Premise 2: Every respondent in a **good mood** has a **central goal.**
Conclusion: Every respondent **feeling satisfied** has a **central goal.**

Boldface A:

The correct answer is *reported having a central goal*.

Boldface B:

The correct answer is *reported being in a good mood*.

165. In Country C, some but not all eligible voters are required to vote. The particulars of the country's laws governing voting are as follows:

Every citizen who is eligible must vote on election day.

A person is eligible if (and only if) he or she meets the age requirement and either is a citizen or meets the residency requirement for noncitizens.

The age requirement is that every voter must be at least 19 years old on election day.

The residency requirement for noncitizens is that the voter must have been a resident of Country C for at least 5 years on election day.

Consider the following individuals:

Abigail: a citizen who is currently 19 years old

Barbara: a 7-year resident noncitizen who is currently 19 years old

Charles: a 7-year resident noncitizen who is currently 18 years old

For an election held today, select the individual or individuals who must vote, based on the information provided, and select the individual or individuals who must not vote, based on the information provided. Make only two selections, one in each column.

Must vote	Must not vote	
		Abigail only
		Barbara only
		Charles only
		Abigail and Barbara only
		Abigail and Charles only
		Barbara and Charles only

Answer Explanation:

Recognize

Must vote:

The information given states that in Country C, some eligible voters, but not all, are required to vote. Among the particulars of the laws governing voting for Country C, there is only one regarding who *must vote*, namely the first particular listed, which states that every citizen who is eligible must vote on election day. Of the three individuals under consideration—Abigail, Barbara, and Charles—only Abigail is a citizen, and Abigail is currently 19, which is the minimum age for voting. Given that every citizen who meets the age requirement is eligible and—as we've seen—every eligible citizen must vote, then for an election held today in Country C, Abigail must vote, and of the three individuals under consideration, Abigail is the only one of them who *must vote*.

The correct answer is *Abigail only*.

Must not vote:

As discussed above, Abigail *must vote*, so we can immediately rule out each of the responses that include Abigail because if she *must vote*, then it cannot be the case that she *must not vote*. What about Barbara and Charles? Barbara is currently 19 years old and is a 7-year resident noncitizen; Charles is currently 18 years old and is also a 7-year resident noncitizen. The particulars listed indicate that a voter is eligible if, and only if, he or she meets the age requirement, which is 19, and either is a citizen or meets the residency requirement for noncitizens, which is a minimum of 5 years. Both Barbara and Charles meet the residency requirement for eligibility, but only Barbara meets the age requirement. Therefore, although Barbara is eligible, Charles is not eligible, and therefore he, and only he among the three individuals under consideration, *must not vote* in any election held today in Country C.

The correct answer is *Charles only*.

7.0 GMAT™ Official Guide Data Insights Review Question Index

7.0 GMAT™ Official Guide Data Insights Review Question Index

The Data Insights Review Question Index is organized by the section, difficulty level, and then by mathematical concept. The question number, page number, and answer explanation page number are listed so that questions within the book can be quickly located.

Data Insights — Chapter 6 – Page 118

Data Sufficiency – Page 130

Difficulty	Concept	Question #	Question ID #	Page	Answer Explanation Page
Easy	Applied Problems	3	700110	130	145
Easy	Applied Problems	8	700305	131	147
Easy	Applied Problems	9	700290	131	147
Easy	Applied Problems	10	700109	131	147
Easy	Applied Problems	12	700317	131	148
Easy	Applied Problems	14	700107	131	149
Easy	Applied Problems	24	700129	132	153
Easy	Applied Problems	27	700140	133	155
Easy	Applied Problems	29	700142	133	156
Easy	Evaluate	35	700325	133	158
Easy	First-Degree Equations	4	700298	130	145
Easy	First-Degree Equations	16	700108	131	150
Easy	First-Degree Equations	19	700125	132	151
Easy	Inequalities	26	700135	132	154
Easy	Inference	32	700322	133	157
Easy	Inference	33	700323	133	157
Easy	Inference	34	700324	133	158
Easy	Inference	36	700326	134	159
Easy	Inference	37	700327	134	159
Easy	Inference	38	700328	134	160
Easy	Percents	13	700309	131	149
Easy	Percents	20	700126	132	152

(Continued)

Difficulty	Concept	Question #	Question ID #	Page	Answer Explanation Page
Easy	Percents	22	700127	132	153
Easy	Percents	30	700143	133	156
Easy	Probability	2	700299	130	144
Easy	Rate Problems	11	700295	131	148
Easy	Ratio and Proportion; First-Degree Equations	23	700128	132	153
Easy	Series and Sequences	25	700132	132	154
Easy	Simultaneous Equations	18	700124	132	151
Easy	Statistics	1	700291	130	144
Easy	Statistics	5	700293	130	145
Easy	Statistics	6	700292	130	146
Easy	Statistics	7	700288	131	146
Easy	Statistics	15	700289	131	149
Easy	Statistics	17	700286	132	150
Easy	Statistics	21	700294	132	152
Easy	Statistics	28	700141	133	155
Easy	Statistics	31	700147	133	156
Medium	Applied Problems	41	700296	134	162
Medium	Applied Problems	42	700304	134	162
Medium	Applied Problems	43	700321	134	162
Medium	Applied Problems	45	700100	135	163
Medium	Applied Problems	47	700111	135	165
Medium	Applied Problems	48	700316	135	166
Medium	Applied Problems	61	700138	137	171
Medium	Applied Problems	63	700145	137	172
Medium	Applied Problems	65	700148	137	172
Medium	Estimation	40	700287	134	161
Medium	Evaluate	71	700333	138	175
Medium	First-Degree Equations	56	700131	136	169
Medium	Inference	67	700329	137	173

Difficulty	Concept	Question #	Question ID #	Page	Answer Explanation Page
Medium	Inference	68	700330	137	174
Medium	Inference	69	700331	138	174
Medium	Inference	70	700332	138	175
Medium	Inference	72	700334	138	175
Medium	Inference	73	700335	138	176
Medium	Inference	74	700336	138	176
Medium	Interpretation of Tables; Sets (Venn Diagrams)	39	700282	134	160
Medium	Percents	50	700116	135	166
Medium	Percents	55	700130	136	169
Medium	Percents	60	700137	137	171
Medium	Probability	53	700311	136	168
Medium	Ratio and Proportion	44	700308	135	163
Medium	Simultaneous Equations	46	700106	135	164
Medium	Simultaneous Equations	54	700117	136	168
Medium	Simultaneous Equations	62	700144	137	171
Medium	Simultaneous Equations	64	700146	137	172
Medium	Statistics	49	700302	135	166
Medium	Statistics	51	700319	135	167
Medium	Statistics	52	700104	135	167
Medium	Statistics	57	700133	136	170
Medium	Statistics	58	700134	136	170
Medium	Statistics	59	700136	136	170
Medium	Statistics	66	700149	137	173
Hard	Applied Problems	84	700285	139	180
Hard	Applied Problems	93	700119	140	184
Hard	Applied Problems	94	700120	140	185
Hard	Applied Problems	96	700122	141	186
Hard	Applied Problems	97	700123	141	186
Hard	Applied Problems	98	700139	141	186

(Continued)

Difficulty	Concept	Question #	Question ID #	Page	Answer Explanation Page
Hard	Applied Problems	105	700343	141	189
Hard	Applied Problems	106	700344	142	190
Hard	Applied Problems	107	700345	142	190
Hard	Applied Problems	108	700346	142	190
Hard	Applied Problems	109	700347	142	191
Hard	Applied Problems	110	700348	142	191
Hard	Applied Problems; Rates	91	700318	140	183
Hard	Arithmetic Operations	80	700115	139	179
Hard	Arithmetic Operations; Percents	78	700113	139	178
Hard	Concepts of Sets	83	700314	139	180
Hard	Concepts of Sets; Percents	85	700284	139	181
Hard	First-Degree Equations	95	700121	140	185
Hard	Inference	99	700337	141	187
Hard	Inference	100	700338	141	187
Hard	Inference	101	700339	141	187
Hard	Inference	102	700340	141	188
Hard	Inference	103	700341	141	188
Hard	Inference	104	700342	141	189
Hard	Operations with Fractions	89	700102	140	182
Hard	Percents	75	700297	138	176
Hard	Percents	77	700303	138	177
Hard	Percents	79	700114	139	178
Hard	Percents	81	700112	139	179
Hard	Probability	87	700283	139	182
Hard	Properties of Numbers	82	700300	139	179
Hard	Rate Problems	86	700306	139	181
Hard	Sets	88	700310	140	182
Hard	Simultaneous Equations	76	700105	138	177
Hard	Simultaneous Equations	92	700118	140	184
Hard	Work Problems	90	700301	140	183

Two-Part Analysis – Page 193

Difficulty	Concept	Question #	Question ID #	Page	Answer Explanation Page
Easy	Evaluate	116	700257	194	217
Easy	Infer	111	700355	193	214
Easy	Infer	112	700356	193	214
Easy	Infer	113	700155	193	215
Easy	Infer	118	700275	195	219
Easy	Recognize	115	700240	194	216
Easy	Recognize	117	700271	195	218
Easy	Strategize	114	700197	194	216
Medium	Apply	122	700184	196	221
Medium	Apply	125	700194	197	223
Medium	Evaluate	119	700350	195	219
Medium	Evaluate	120	700354	196	220
Medium	Evaluate	121	700174	196	220
Medium	Evaluate	123	700191	196	222
Medium	Evaluate	126	700196	197	224
Medium	Evaluate	128	700201	198	226
Medium	Infer	127	700198	198	225
Medium	Infer	129	700202	199	227
Medium	Infer	130	700231	199	228
Medium	Infer	131	700232	199	228
Medium	Infer	135	700256	201	231
Medium	Infer	136	700266	201	232
Medium	Strategize	124	700192	197	223
Medium	Strategize	132	700233	200	229
Medium	Strategize	133	700234	200	230
Medium	Strategize	134	700242	200	230
Hard	Apply	143	700177	204	238
Hard	Apply	148	700215	205	243

(*Continued*)

Difficulty	Concept	Question #	Question ID #	Page	Answer Explanation Page
Hard	Apply	154	700228	207	247
Hard	Apply	155	700239	208	247
Hard	Apply	156	700241	208	248
Hard	Evaluate	137	700349	201	233
Hard	Evaluate	146	700203	204	241
Hard	Evaluate	147	700205	205	242
Hard	Evaluate	161	700264	209	252
Hard	Infer	138	700352	202	234
Hard	Infer	139	700353	202	234
Hard	Infer	140	700157	203	235
Hard	Infer	141	700170	203	236
Hard	Infer	142	700176	203	237
Hard	Infer	144	700186	204	239
Hard	Infer	145	700200	204	240
Hard	Infer	152	700226	206	245
Hard	Infer	157	700252	208	249
Hard	Infer	160	700259	209	252
Hard	Infer	162	700265	210	253
Hard	Infer	163	700268	210	254
Hard	Recognize	151	700225	206	245
Hard	Recognize	158	700253	208	250
Hard	Recognize	159	700258	209	251
Hard	Recognize	165	700280	211	255
Hard	Strategize	149	700222	206	244
Hard	Strategize	150	700224	206	244
Hard	Strategize	153	700227	207	246
Hard	Strategize	164	700278	210	254

Appendix A   Answer Sheet

Data Sufficiency Answer Sheet

1.	23.	45.	67.	89.
2.	24.	46.	68.	90.
3.	25.	47.	69.	91.
4.	26.	48.	70.	92.
5.	27.	49.	71.	93.
6.	28.	50.	72.	94.
7.	29.	51.	73.	95.
8.	30.	52.	74.	96.
9.	31.	53.	75.	97.
10.	32.	54.	76.	98.
11.	33.	55.	77.	99.
12.	34.	56.	78.	100.
13.	35.	57.	79.	101.
14.	36.	58.	80.	102.
15.	37.	59.	81.	103.
16.	38.	60.	82.	104.
17.	39.	61.	83.	105.
18.	40.	62.	84.	106.
19.	41.	63.	85.	107.
20.	42.	64.	86.	108.
21.	43.	65.	87.	109.
22.	44.	66.	88.	110.

Two-Part Analysis Answer Sheet

111.	122.	133.	144.	155.
112.	123.	134.	145.	156.
113.	124.	135.	146.	157.
114.	125.	136.	147.	158.
115.	126.	137.	148.	159.
116.	127.	138.	149.	160.
117.	128.	139.	150.	161.
118.	129.	140.	151.	162.
119.	130.	141.	152.	163.
120.	131.	142.	153.	164.
121.	132.	143.	154.	165.

Notes

Notes

Notes

Notes

Notes

GMAT™

Elevate your prep with our free resources!

(1) GMAT™ Official Starter Kit

Sample 70+ real GMAT questions, a guided review, and Official Practice Exams 1 & 2, which simulate the real exam format and test-taking experience.

scan here to get yours!